ARANSAS

ARANSAS

The Life of a Texas Coastal County

by

William Allen
and
Sue Hastings Taylor

EAKIN PRESS ★ AUSTIN, TEXAS

★ **Cover design by Thom Evans** ★

Published in the United States of America
By Eakin Press
A Division of Sunbelt Media, Inc.
P.O. Drawer 90159
Austin, TX 78709
email: EAKINPUB@sig.net

4 5 6 7 8 9

ISBN 1-57168-205-8

Library of Congress Cataloging-in-Publication Data

Allen, William.
    Aransas: The Life of a Texas Coastal County / by William Allen
and Sue Hastings Taylor.
        p. cm.
    Includes bibliographical references (p.   ) and index.
    ISBN 1-57168-166-3
    1. Aransas County (Tex.)—History.   I. Taylor, Sue Hastings.
II. Title.
F392.A6A44 1997
976.4'122—dc21   97-14504
                                                    CIP

DEDICATED TO

the People of Aransas County
—past, present and future—

and especially to our Patrons, Sponsors, and Donors

PATRONS

Mr. and Mrs. Perry R. Bass
Charles Butt
Kathryn (Mrs. Frank) Hastings

Mr. and Mrs. Edward M. Armstrong
Clayton Black and Susie Bracht Black
Cecile Hough Frost
Valerie and Glenn Guillory
The James C. and Edith Sneed Herring Family
The Norvell F. Jackson Family
Marie O'Connor Sorenson
James H. Sorenson, Jr.

SPONSORS

Aransas County Historical Society
H. T. Bailey and Holley Beckley-Bailey
Mr. and Mrs. Joe L. Johnson, Jr.
Laguna Reef
Mr. and Mrs. Robert G. Little
Sandra Spencer Musser
Rockport Art Association

DONORS

Mr. and Mrs. Robert Albin
Dr. and Mrs. Gilbert I. Anderson
Mr. and Mrs. Leon Bateman
Lola L. Bonner
Mr. and Mrs. John T. Cabaniss
Ruth Sneed and Malcolm Carroll
Mrs. Velma M. Cleveland
Urania Sorenson Collier
Alice Hynes Picton Craig
Mr. and Mrs. Bruce G. Davis
Dr. John and Margaret Patrick Eiband
Thom Evans
Patti Bailey Francisco
Colleen Smith Freeman
Griffith and Brundett Surveying
David and Nell Herring
Mr. and Mrs. Raulie L. Irwin
Nan Jackson
Mr. and Mrs. Al Johnson
Charles and Kathleen Johnson
Elizabeth F. Jones
Dr. and Mrs. Lowell Kepp
John D. and Gail B. Leslie
W. G. McCampbell, Jr., Trust
Clara McDavid

J. McDavid (Travis and Louisa Johnson)
Philip and Sue Sorenson Maxwell
Vernon and Cassandra Sneed Moore
Wesley and Jo Ann Smith Morgan
Mr. and Mrs. Stuart Nolan
Mr. and Mrs. Ray J. O'Brien
Louise S. O'Connor
Mr. and Mrs. David C. Ogle
Mary Willeen Schmidt
Mr. and Mrs. Gene A Smith
Charles R. Sneed
Joe W. and Rita F. Sneed, Jr.
Kennon and Patti Ballou Stewart
Mr. and Mrs. George K. Taggart III
Sue and Austin Taylor
Helen McCampbell Torian Trust
Almuth C. and Elaine L. Vandeveer
Hays R. and Sandra L. Warden
Heather W. Welder
John D. Wendell
Myrtle Stewart Wendell
Mr. and Mrs. Thomas White
Mr. and Mrs. Winston J. Woellert
Mr. and Mrs. Asa H. Yeamans

In Memoriam

to

All the Men and Women of

Aransas

*who gave their Lives
in all Wars from the
Texas Revolution
to this Date.*

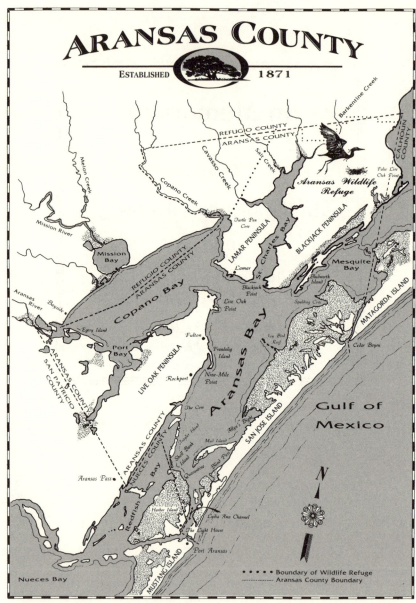

ARANSAS COUNTY

ESTABLISHED 1871

Barkentine Creek

REFUGIO COUNTY
ARANSAS COUNTY

CALHOUN COUNTY

Melon Creek

Copano Creek

Cavasso Creek

Salt Creek

False Live Oak Point

Aransas Wildlife Refuge

Mission River

Turtle Pen Cove

LAMAR PENINSULA

St Charles Bay

BLACKJACK PENINSULA

Mission Bay

Lamar

Mesquite Bay

REFUGIO COUNTY
ARANSAS COUNTY

Copano Bay

Blackjack Point

Bludworth Island

Aransas River

Bayside

Egery Island

Live Oak Point

Spalding Creek

MATAGORDA ISLAND

Port Bay

Fulton

Franholig Island

Aransas Bay

Jay Bird Reef

Cedar Bayou

ARANSAS COUNTY
SAN PATRICIO COUNTY

LIVE OAK PENINSULA

Rockport

Nine-Mile Point

The Cove

Gulf of
Mexico

Allyn's Bight

SAN JOSE ISLAND

ARANSAS COUNTY
NUECES COUNTY

Traylor Island

Mud Island

Shell Bank Island

Quarantine

Blind Pass

N

Aransas Pass

Redfish Bay

Harbor Island

Lydia Ann Channel

The Light House

Port Aransas

MUSTANG ISLAND

Nueces Bay

• • • • • Boundary of Wildlife Refuge
---------- Aransas County Boundary

ARANSAS COUNTY IS THE FIFTH SMALLEST IN THE STATE OF TEXAS. IT ENCOM-
PASSES A TOTAL AREA OF MORE THAN THREE HUNDRED AND TWENTY-SIX SQUARE MILES,
BUT MUCH OF THIS IS UNDER WATER. NO TWO AGENCIES COME UP WITH THE SAME FIGURE FOR
THE LAND AREA, PROBABLY BECAUSE OF TIDAL VARIATIONS, BUT MOST SUGGEST SOMETHING
CLOSE TO TWO HUNDRED AND FIFTY SQUARE MILES.

Aransas County, Texas, 1997. Illustration by Chris Blum.

Contents

Foreword

by Perry R. Bass

ARANSAS: The Life of a Texas Coastal County is a wonderfully researched history of an exciting part of our state, an area that I have loved since I was a little boy. Many friends have been curious about my connection both with Aransas County and my family's island, San José. Perhaps a brief recounting of the connection will make a minor addition to this magnificently written chronicle.

In the fall of 1925, my family "discovered" San José Island. We went down there duck hunting on Captain Adolphus' houseboat, which was an old wooden barge with a shack on it, pulled by a "mullet masher" which in turn was powered by a Buick engine that was kept in reverse since that was the lowest gear. There is a mullet masher in the yard of the Maritime Museum. The museum people just don't *know* what the natives called it back then.

We heard quail whistling on the island and my daddy and my Uncle Sid Richardson got Captain Adolphus to take them down to the island headquarters where fortunately the owner, Mr. Giesecke from San Antonio, was there. He was kind enough to give us permission to hunt quail on the island, and we fell in love with it that trip. Mr. Giesecke also promised my daddy and uncle that if he ever got ready to sell the island, he would contact them first.

In 1936 Mr. Giesecke called my Uncle Sid and said he was ready to talk about selling the island. My daddy had passed away three years previously. Uncle Sid managed to borrow $25,000 from the bank as a down payment and bought the island.

Uncle Sid came up to Yale where I was about to graduate, having studied engineering and geology, and said, "Bass, you are an engineer, and I want you to build me a house." My bachelor uncle had never had a home and wanted a home on the island.

I arrived in Rockport early July 1937 to build him a home. I paid $900 to have a fifty foot by twenty foot barge built to haul materials to the island. Then I had to build a harbor to land the barge. Then I built the garage where I would put a power plant so I would have electricity and could use electric tools. After that, I closed in the porch of the bunkhouse to have room for more workers and then built the servants' quarters to have still more workers' accommodations. Next, I had to build a barn to store the materials that went in the house. I started digging a foundation for the house on January 2, 1938, and my uncle moved in the day before Thanksgiving that same year. When that happened, I had built on the job 93,000 shellcrete eight inch by eight inch by sixteen inch building blocks from a mixture of cement, oyster shell, and beach sand that met American Cement Association specifications.

My office in Rockport was the pay telephone booth in Mr. Moore's Magnolia filling station. Mr. Moore was very kind to my family and told me tales of catching forty-pound redfish at Cedar Bayou on hand lines when he was a boy. I have worked long and hard to try to see those days return.

My wife Nancy Lee also has a connection with Aransas County. I have a picture of her taken as a two-year-old girl sitting on the steps of the Fulton Mansion. Her grandfather had rented the mansion for the summer and invited one-by-one his children's families to come and spend several weeks with him. Most summers he and a group of friends would spend time at the Kool Koast Kamp. In those times, it took two long, hard days to drive from Fort Worth to Rockport.

One December day Nancy Lee and Uncle Sid and I came in at lunch time from quail hunting and were told that the Japanese were bombing Pearl Harbor. We were listening to the radio when Mr. Moore sent a boat from Rockport to say that President Roosevelt was calling Mr. Richardson. The president's message in essence was, "Sid, I want you to have lunch with me next Sunday and tell me what shape we are in for petroleum. I don't trust those major company bastards." The next Sunday we were in Washington and for several days thereafter.

I had just gotten back to Texas from Jacksonville, Florida, where for the last year and a half I had been working as a naval architect at Huckins Yacht Corporation, helping design and build a prototype torpedo boat for the navy. I had studied naval architecture while at college while trying to learn how to make my sailboat go faster. While in Washington after Pearl Harbor Day, I went into the Navy Department's Bureau of Ships and saw my good friend, Lt. Bill Lehea, whom I had worked with on torpedo boat design. I told him I had come to put on a blue suit. He said, "Perry, you cannot wear a blue suit. The first thing I know some admiral would have you counting caps. Go to the Coast Guard and see the admiral and design and build him some fire boats. His naval architects have been tied up designing a tug for two years and haven't gotten it done yet."

I secured a contract from the Coast Guard and designed and built six harbor fire boats for the Coast Guard. Three other builders had been given similar orders, and the Coast Guard had a fire boat contest at New Orleans. The Bass fire boat was chosen as the best design. It was both the fastest and simplest to operate. The Coast Guard ended up building over one hundred of these craft, known as "Bass Fire Boats," which were taken to the Pacific to fight the fires caused by the Japanese bombing our island bases. I am rather proud of the contribution by the Bass Boat Works at Fulton, Texas.

My boat works were between Cecil Casterline's place and Rouquette and Wendell. I will always be grateful to Zeph Rouquette and Bunk Wendell. They would call me over to their place several times a week to give me oysters, shrimp, and fish to take home for Nancy Lee to cook. Food was not overly plentiful. The local grocery had potatoes and carrots, and that was about it in the line of vegetables. One day, on a Corpus Christi buying trip, I found a five-inch cucumber in the market which cost sixty-five cents. I proudly paid the exorbitant price and brought it home as a great treat. My boat works were destroyed in the 1945 hurricane and were never rebuilt.

Emory Spencer was considered by many to be a man to be feared. He was always exceedingly kind to me, and I would take any legal problems that I had to him. He always handled them and would never send me a bill. I will never have a better friend or one whose intelligence and integrity I admired more.

It was about that time that Nancy Lee and I developed the habit of going to San José Island any time there was a hurricane in the Gulf of Mexico. It is exciting to sit in the house I built and watch the storms. Up to now, it has been through seven hurricanes with only minor damage. After the great Hurricane Carla in 1961 that drowned cattle from the Mississippi to the Rio Grande, we sat in the living room and read the Corpus Christi paper. A reporter told the story of riding in a Coast Guard helicopter to Galveston and back. He reported that flying over San José, he found no buildings left and very few livestock. The truth of the matter was, we had a cracked window in the kitchen and lost four aged cows that probably died of heart attacks in all the excitement.

These little pieces of Aransas County history—covering the last seventy years and generally unknown—surely do not represent a typical foreword, but I am not a writer by trade. Adding my personal reminiscence to a volume of history on the scale of *ARANSAS: The Life of a Texas Coastal County* is a real pleasure. I commend this book to you, including its Notes and Sources. That section is almost a second text, as interesting to read as the main one, and as full of the stories that make Aransas so important to me and my family.

Preface

A Legacy of Giants on Texas Sand

This is the story of a little place that has played a surprisingly large role in the history of Texas. Aransas, one of the smallest counties in the state, is located in the Coastal Bend of South Texas, and includes part of the state's long barrier island chain. Its strategic maritime location accounts for much of its colorful past.

The history of Aransas, as reflected directly and by proximity to surrounding environs, presents a grand march of human exploration and settlement. Spain's Cabeza de Vaca spent years along these sandy shores. Spanish ship captain Piñeda charted the Aransas shoreline and bays, then sailed south and named Corpus Christi. Famous French explorer LaSalle, who also mapped parts of Aransas, was murdered as he traveled north from here; his 300-year-old sunken flagship *La Belle* was recently found in nearby Matagorda Bay. Béranger, another French explorer, was the first European to map the natural Aransas pass waterway, as well as to chronicle the land and its indigenous peoples. Pirate Jean Lafitte, supreme early navigator of these bays and shorelines, supposedly buried a fortune in gold here; treasure hunters still seek it today.

During Texas' battle for independence, Santa Anna's brother-in-law General Cós sailed into Aransas and Copano bays with munitions and supplies for the Battle of the Alamo. Major Burton led his cavalry into Copano Bay and captured a Mexican ship; thus, the term "Horse Marines" came into being. The Colt Brothers, who owned a fourteen-thousand-acre estate at Lamar—including most of the Lamar Peninsula and Goose Island—worked with Texas Ranger Sam Walker to perfect the Colt six-shooter. Zachary Taylor camped in Rockport with young officer Ulysses Simpson Grant before embarking on the long "Taylor Trail" to fight the Mexican

War. The first American flag to fly over Texas was raised at the southern tip of Aransas' San José Island.

Many historians have long defined the meaning or value of an area in terms of what it currently produces, how it transports its commercial products, its size and economic growth. That doubtless is why Aransas and other small, out-of-the-way places are only now beginning to have their stories told; fortunately, we are coming to realize that there is more to the human spirit, more to the value we attach to a particular place, than is offered by commerce alone. Visitors, transplants, and locals alike sense that the hard-won rich history of Aransas brings layers of depth and meaning to its present. The county still reverberates with past collisions of world empires, reflected in the features, language, and manner of a diversified culture. Its past is one of extremes, appealing to the most idealistic and primitive in human nature.

Today, Aransas is regarded as one of the nation's special sanctuaries. Here, as in scattered locales around the globe, the forces of nature have joined to create special charms that may be absent only miles away. Many such beguiling places—Taos, Big Sur, Aspen, and Key West, for example—have histories of pilgrimage and growth that have resulted in the age-old liabilities of commercial exploitation, inflation, and overpopulation. Whether such a future awaits Aransas is uncertain. Thus far, it has remained out of the mainstream of travel, yet, there is increasing growth on this third coast. Both summer and winter tourism increase yearly, partly as travelers seek alternatives to California and Florida's struggles with pollution, crime, high costs of living, and crowded conditions.

Just about all who share a love for Aransas have ready reasons for their affinity. Almost certainly, terrain—the meeting of land and sea—is a major factor, made manifest by the windswept live oaks shadowing sandy bluffs over bays and lagoons. Geologists, archaeologists, biologists, and environmentalists bring learned systems to bear. Professional and amateur ornithologists have a special vested interest in this habitat where five hundred avian species find protection, including the famous and slowly recovering whooping crane.

Aransas County is now at the dawn of a seeming destiny made up of ecotourism, vacationers, artists, descendants of founding fathers, the affluent with second homes or golden retirement. Residents dependent on a modest local economy fare less well, yet still opt for a small town lifestyle over one of urban sprawl.

To know the complete story of Aransas, from its first primordial stirrings to its modern preserved natural beauty, is to reach beyond the obvious appeal of climate and terrain. Once known, the story may become as unforgettable for winter visitors as it is for the resident descendants of strong, driven settlers who first called Aransas home. Ultimately, though, the greatest treasures in Aransas County have been created more by the laws of nature than by our ancestors. For all their effort, those human giants have left only a gentle trace on shifting sand.

— The Authors

Timeline

1000   Big Tree begins to grow at Lamar.

1519   Captain Alonso Álvarez de Piñeda, first European to sail the Gulf of Mexico's northern coast, maps and charts Aransas and Copano bays.

1528   Cabeza de Vaca is shipwrecked on San José Island, lives among the Karánkawas.

1684   LaSalle sails through Gulf in search of mouth of Mississippi to claim territory for France, subsequently mapping Aransas River and area shoreline.

1720   Jean Béranger discovers the Aransas pass, produces glossary of Karánkawa language.

1722   Spain establishes La Bahia Mission between Guadalupe and Aransas rivers.

1746   Colonel José de Escandón builds Fort Aránzazu at Live Oak Point and another fort at the south end of San José Island.

1750   El Cópano develops as port to offload supplies for missions at La Bahia, Béxar, and Santa Fé.

1754   Rosário Mission founded near Goliad as a separate institution for Karánkawas.

1775   Attwater prairie chickens estimated at one million.

1800   Napoleon regains Louisiana, then sells the territory to U.S.

1817   Pirate Jean Lafitte establishes forts at Cedar Bayou and southwest end of San José Island.

1826   James Hewetson and James Power apply for empresario grant centered on Aransas Bay.

1833   James Power sails to Ireland to recruit colonists.

1834   *Wildcat* and *Sea Lion* wreck at the Aransas pass.

1835   Power colonists sign Goliad declaration of independence. Samuel Colt patents pistol. Power sees Mexican troop ship sail into Copano Bay.

1836   Power meets with Sam Houston; revolutionary troops concentrate in area; James Fannin lands at El Cópano. The Alamo falls; battle at Refugio; massacre at Goliad; Texians victorious at San Jacinto; Santa Anna departs El Cópano, sailing home in defeat. Power and Cameron Spy Company organized; Horse Marines episode in Copano Bay.

1837   Captain James Byrne begins town on Lamar Peninsula. Aransas customs district created, customs officers seize Flour Bluff contraband.

1839   Lamar settlement becomes port of entry, rivalling Aransas City.

1840   Populations of Aransas City, Lamar, and Saint Joseph exceed that of Refugio.

1842   Aransans are captured in Mier expedition.

1845   United States flag flies on San José Island. Zachary Taylor camps on San José, then at Rocky Point, for war with Mexico.

1850s   Jane Gregory O'Connor founds Lamar Academy. Joseph Smith contests James Power's land titles.

1851   Captain Peter Johnson obtains contract to carry U.S. mail by water, erects two-story station house on bay side of San José.

1852   Refugio County remnant of Karánkawas migrates to Mexico.

1854   Stella Maris Chapel built.

1855   Construction begins on 67-foot tower of Aransas Lighthouse.

1861   Texas secedes from the Union; blockade in effect all along the coast.

1862   Marines pillage St. Joseph, shell Lamar.

1863   Captain Edwin Hobby's troops overcome Union forces on San José.

1864   Union troops raid Lamar salt works.

1865   Murdoch McRae of Lamar, as sergeant at Galveston Observatory, reads signals of Lee's surrender to Grant. First packery is established near Rockport.

1867   Doughty and Mathis build wharf on the Rocky Point; Town of Rockport founded.

1868   Meat packeries operate along Aransas shoreline. Rockport post office starts with Viktor Bracht as postmaster. Rockport citizens raise $10,000 for 600-foot dike on San José Island.

1869   Charles Bailey publishes *Transcript* newspaper in Rockport.

1870+   Ranches develop on Blackjack Peninsula.

1871   Coleman, Mathis, and Fulton form livestock company. Aransas County separates from Refugio.

1874   Morris and Cummings Cut slashes through mud flats inside the Aransas pass.

1875   Franz Josef Frandolig receives patent for bay island north of Rockport.

1877   George Fulton completes his mansion. Bracht Brothers open Rockport store.

1879   Turtle cannery operating at Fulton.

1880+   Sorenson builds chandlery on Austin Street.

1886   Fulton City Hall is built; one room school opens.

1888   San Antonio and Aransas Pass Railroad reaches Rockport; town population is 600. David Rockport Scrivener starts commercial fishing business, but finds people unfamiliar with fish as food.

1889   Moorish-design courthouse and Aransas Hotel (largest wood structure in South Texas) are built.

1890   Hoopes and Bruhl homes are built.

1890+   Bailey Pavilion is built; fishing and turtle industries flourish.

1892   First National Bank is organized.

1894   David Sinton takes control of Coleman-Fulton Pasture Company; C.P. Taft subsequently becomes manager. Whooping crane population stands at 1,000.

1895   Widow Harriet Fulton leaves mansion.

1900   La Playa Hotel built.

1900+   5,000 brown pelicans remain in Texas.

1903   Commercial hunting is banned in Texas.

1906   David Mean Picton has contract to build jetties at the Aransas pass.

1910   Gulf Coast Immigration Company announces plan to develop Aransas. Andrew Sorenson opens Port Bay Club.

1912   Two hundred whooping cranes remain worldwide.

1914   Lamar township dissolves.

1917   Heldenfels builds ships for the Great War.

1918   Fifty whooping cranes exist worldwide; Migratory Bird Treaty Act passes.

1919   Cyrus Lucas consolidates Blackjacks ranching. Major hurricane
        ravages Aransas County.

1921   Texas gives custodianship of small coastal island rookeries to
        National Audubon Society.

1922   Lucas purchases San José from Wood family. Rockport loses bid
        to become deepwater port. Thirty-five migrant whooping cranes
        remain.

1924   Leroy Denman takes over bankrupt Blackjacks ranch, imports
        exotic animals. Kool Koast Kamp is in operation.

1925   State Highway 35 and Intracoastal Canal System begin. St.
        Charles Gun Club opens.

1925+   A. M. Westergard builds pleasure boats in Rockport.

1930   Copano causeway is completed.

1930+   Rockport Harbor is constructed. Seafood operations develop in
        Fulton.

1931   Private owners deed land for Goose Island State Recreation
        Area.

1932   Mills Wharf opens.

1935   Aransas County Navigation District is established. Connie and
        Jack Hager move to Rockport. One thousand brown pelicans
        remain in Texas.

1936   Biological lab is built in Rockport. Last whooping cranes are
        seen on upper Texas coast.

1937   Blackjacks whooping crane population reduced to eighteen. Eighty-
        seven hundred Attwater prairie chicken remain; hunting them is
        forbidden. Aransas Migratory Waterfowl Refuge, precursor of
        Aransas National Wildlife Refuge, is established with 47,261 acres.

1938   Aransas County Emergency Corps forms. Civilian Conservation
        Work begins at Wildlife Refuge and Goose Island.

1939   U.S. Lighthouse Service ends.

1940   Rockport harbor breakwater is dedicated.

1940+   Shrimping industry reaches noteworthy proportions. WWII victory ship *Worthington* is torpedoed in Gulf. Rice shipyard builds PT boats.

1942   T. Noah Smith, owner of the Hoopes house and Rockport Yacht and Supply, gives private yacht to war effort.

1944   Lamar Cemetery, dating from 1854, is restored.

1945   Connie Hagar sanctuary is designated around Little Bay.

1946   Rockport Marine Lab opens. Game, Fish and Oyster Commission stops oil-transporting vessels and tankers from pumping oil into local waters.

1948   Artists Simon Michael and Estelle Stair arrive.

1950+   "Winter Texan" migration begins.

1955   Old Moorish-style courthouse is torn down and new one is erected on the site.

1956   County library is established.

1958   Carl Krueger buys Frandolig Island, planning Key Allegro canal community.

1963   Fifty brown pelicans remain.

1964   Square dancers build Paws and Taws.

1966   LBJ Causeway replaces outdated Copano span.

1967   Rockport Art Association is organized. Attwater prairie chickens, numbering just 1,000, are placed on endangered list. Aransas Refuge adds 7,568 acres.

1969   First Rockport Art Festival opens.

1972   One brown pelican is raised on entire Texas coast.

1973   Endangered Species Act is passed with brown pelicans on the list. Charles Butt purchases lighthouse, begins restoration.

1974   Seafair is instituted. Emergency Medical Service is organized.

1975   First Vietnamese family settles in Fulton.

1979   Town of Fulton incorporates.

1980   Texas Maritime Museum incorporates.

1982   Space Services Inc. of America launches rocket from Matagorda. Aransas Refuge adds Matagorda Island—19,000 acres.

1983   Fulton Mansion is restored as State Park. O'Connor gives home for Art Center. Two nesting colonies of brown pelicans thrive in San Antonio and Corpus Christi bays.

1986   Stella Maris is moved and restored.

1988   Rockport Beach Park opens. Hummer/Bird Festival begins.

1995   Connie Hagar Cottage sanctuary is dedicated as first stop on Great Texas Coastal Birding Trail.

1997   One hundred forty-five whooping cranes are counted at Aransas National Wildlife Refuge.

BOOK ONE

THE BEGINNING

"You, sitting in the stickers?" The boy could hardly believe his eyes. She was right in front of him, perched precariously in a thorn bush—the Virgin Mary!

Rodrigo de Balzátegui was a simple shepherd. On that otherwise ordinary summer day in the 1470s, he was working where he always worked—on the rugged land of north central Spain.

"You sitting in the stickers?" If Rodrigo had been Spanish, he might have used the word espinár. *It means a place of thorns and suggests a complex situation, a difficult path. This shepherd, however, was Basque; he said* aránsa. *Rodrigo stared at the Queen of Heaven and cried out in amazement:* Aránzan Zu?

The phrase stuck; Rodrigo's vision became known as the Lady of Aránsazu. Worshippers built a sanctuary where he had seen her. Later, Basque explorers would take the name of that shrine to a river and a bay on the other side of the world. Pioneers would clear land and name their towns for the bay. Ecologists would delight in the new Aransas sanctuary.

No one could imagine any of that in 1470. None could foretell arduous journeys and thorny problems on the other side of the sea. All were unaware that Arawaks lived on a string of islands, or that Incas had established an empire in Peru. European powers did not know that Tenochtitlán dominated the city-states of central Mexico, or that Mayapán, great metropolis of the Maya, lay in ruins beneath jungle vines. No European had seen Yucatán or the Gulf to its north—or the bay shores where simple people scratched out an existence.

Wild and unnoted, Texas was waiting.

LAND

The Texas shoreline forms a great semitropical arc along three hundred and seventy miles of the Gulf of Mexico. To the east, Louisiana's coast is a soft smear of bayou and swamp. Southwest, much of the Mexican coast drops abruptly from basalt mountains. Texas beaches alone rest secure behind the world's longest barrier island chain.

Each of the islands takes its name from Spanish, suggesting Texas' close link to her southern neighbor. Galveston Island lies farthest east and north, shielding oil refineries and the urban sprawl of Houston. Matagorda begins as peninsula before becoming island. San José, twenty miles long, forms the center ornament of the chain. Little Mustang blurs into great Padre, stretching one hundred and thirty miles south from Corpus Christi to the Rio Grande.

Between Matagorda and San José islands, Cedar Bayou appears as a hairline fracture in one link of the chain. It is a narrow, shallow pass, nearly hidden by its own odd angle. Below that break, the string of islands drops more directly south, and San José forms the eastern boundary of Aransas County. The turn defines the beginning of the Texas Coastal Bend, an area encompassing Corpus Christi, the King Ranch, and most of Padre Island.

The shoreline was not always this way. One hundred million years ago, there were no islands; a Cretaceous sea stopped abruptly at the escarpment now marked by San Antonio, Austin, Waco, and Dallas. A million years ago, when Ice Ages gripped the northern third of the American continent, Texas shores felt the effect. Glaciers grew and sea levels dropped; the ice retreated and sea levels rose, submerging Texas land.

One hundred and twenty thousand years ago, in the Pleistocene period, primordial rivers developed. Some were ancestors of Coastal Bend streams—Mission, Aransas, Nueces. These rivers flowed directly into the Gulf of Mexico, carrying sand and soil from the highlands. Silt fanned from the stream mouths, forming deltas.

Sea levels rose and fell throughout that epoch. Waves and currents worked the delta sediments, pushing coarse sand into a long ridge. Behind that barrier—three miles wide and as much as twenty-five feet high—marshes, lakes, and brackish bays created a rich swath of sediment.

Twenty thousand years later, glaciers built for the last time, leaving the barrier high and dry. Rivers, forcing their way through the sand and shell, raked wide valleys and gouged broad basins.

As the Ice Age neared its end, glaciers melted. The sea poured into river valleys and basins, making them bays. Streams countered the sea's incursions with a downflow of silt; stores of fresh water collected deep below the surface. Fragments of the old shell ridge remained as peninsulas.

Gulf waves continued to push loads of sand shoreward. Two to five thousand years ago, young barrier islands grew. Dunes formed. Wind shaped the dried sand, rippling it like waves in water, swirling it in shadowy mounds, reshaping the dunes again and again.

One of these fledgling islands was San José. Between it and the shell ridge peninsulas lay the lagoon now known as Aransas Bay.

LIFE

Like all lagoons, Aransas held, and holds, a rich soup. It is a hatchery where life begins. Countless organisms breed in the muck of Barkentine, Salt, and Swan lakes. They blossom in winding bayous, coves, and streams. They multiply in St. Charles, Port, Copano, and Aransas bays.

Each living thing feeds something else. "Food chain" is too simple a phrase to describe it. Aransas offers more than a sequence of organic detritus devoured by water flea, snapped up by dragonfly larva, gobbled by hatchling alligator, speared by great blue heron. At Aransas, food chains intermesh. Grasses, fish, crustaceans, mollusks, amphibians, reptiles, insects, birds, and mammals form a complex food web. It has been this way for 75,000 years.

Only a cultivated crop like sugarcane excels the ability of a salt marsh to produce plant material by photosynthesis. One marsh grass, spartina, yields three times the primary production of the best wheat lands. It follows that these tidal flats serve as the "bread basket" for many forms of coastal life.

Submerged grasses become nurseries for fingerling redfish and trout, for baby shrimp, tiny seahorses, and mollusks of every kind. The grasses decay, substratum builds; in that shallower water grow cattails, bulrushes, and reeds. Water primroses, lilies, hyacinths, and hyssop encircle the lairs of frogs, turtles, and alligators. Marsh flies and dragonflies hover above the ponds. Clouds of mosquitoes stress all mammals.

Some woody plants—mangrove, false willow, and groundsel—invade to the edge of the salt marsh. Plants like saltwort send runners along dry shores. There are beach fleas, ticks, chiggers, and ants. Spiders are the most prevalent and varied predators of all—star-bellied, humpbacked, jumping, reclusive. There are tree frogs, toads, lizards, and snakes.

On shell ridges brush takes hold; yaupon, a native holly, shares space with honey mesquite, yucca, and prickly pear. The well-drained sandy ridge soils rest upon deep reservoirs of fresh water. Only where this rare configuration occurs can wind-sculptured oaks grow down to the shore. The trees give their names to the peninsulas—Live Oak, Blackjack.

The mainland thicket seems impenetrable. It probably is, for a twenty-first century man who only wants to stroll. But trails are there, provided by the natural lay of the land, improved upon by deer and javelinas. The hiker who lives with nature, who accepts life on its own terms, can always find a trail.

Before early settlers cleared the land, fire burned through the grasses about once every three years. But as people came and brought the fires under control, brush proliferated. It choked out native plants dependent upon natural fertilizers unlocked by fire. Human disruption of natural processes had—and always has—unexpected, cascading consequences. Nature is more intricate and more delicately balanced than man expects.

On the barrier island's Gulf shore, it is relentless surf, not man, that controls the success of plants. Nothing grows at the water's edge, but on the dunes, and in the sand barrens behind them, sea oats wave over silverleaf sunflowers, croton, purslane, and sedge. Jackrabbits scamper through morning glories and evening primroses.

During the Pleistocene Age, Aransas was home to some mammals now long gone. Huge mammoths, fourteen feet to the shoulder, grazed beside stockier mastodons. Camels browsed at the edge of the prairie. Wild horses ran across the plain, looking and acting more like asses than today's Arabian steeds. Ox-sized sloths rummaged in the woods along with herbivorous bears. There were meat-eaters too—the dire wolf, the lion, the sabertooth cat.

Some scientists believe that changes in climate led to the extinction of these beasts. Others lay blame on the appearance of man.

Ancient bison lasted until the 1500s and familiar antelope until the mid-1800s. Armadillos and javelinas continue, reflecting prehistory. Coyotes, panthers, and wildcats replaced the primordial predators.

Everything at Aransas came from somewhere else. Each species has to adapt to this environment, and each new arrival has to compete with other forms already secure.

Some come only for a season. Birds form the greatest migratory group. Of approximately 750 bird species identified in the continental United States, about five hundred have been seen at Aransas.

The very size of whooping cranes advertises their arrival. Even from a great distance across the tidal flats, they are distinct, standing five feet tall, spreading their wings wider than seven feet.

Sandhill cranes fly in ragged V's to feeding grounds as far as forty miles away. Geese and ducks winter at Aransas, along with some warblers. Other songbirds arrive in early spring; so do cuckoos. In summer, wood storks fly up from Mexico.

There are transients, like swifts and swallows, heading toward points far north or south. Hummingbirds pass through each spring and fall, busy little bodies that seem to burn calories as rapidly as they consume them.

Year-round, gulls and terns soar, or rest on exposed reefs. Brown pelicans cruise fifty feet above the bay, then dive precipitously for small baitfish—mullet or menhaden. White pelicans float, seining their meals. Black skimmers plow the surface with jutting lower mandibles. Cormorants swim neck-deep, then plunge for prey.

Herons and egrets stride the shallows, stabbing fish and crabs with rapier bills. Roseate spoonbills wade the mudflats to scoop up crustaceans. Shorebirds scurry.

Wild turkeys forage the ground for insects and acorns, or flap to trees twined with wild grape. Seeds and small fruits fatten prairie chickens, doves, and quail. Raptors hunt them.

So does man.

HUMANKIND

We do not know where they came from—the first people of Aransas. Wanderers crossed the Bering land bridge 22,000 years ago. No one has found evidence that any branch of that migration came to Aransas. Those forerunners seem to have swept through the North American plains and settled there or journeyed on to Mexico, with scarcely a glance at the Gulf.

Two thousand years later, paleohunters may have wandered to the Aransas shore. Scanty bits of evidence tease us. Artifacts from other parts of Texas suggest that those hunters were canny and courageous, that they killed large numbers of bison.

A people who came 8,000 years ago seem to have vanished 3,000 years later; geology suggests a severe drought, and no evidence remains of their camps after that.

The barrier islands formed around 1000 B.C. By then, semi-permanent settlers lived in small clans along the coast. Burial mounds from Galveston to Corpus Christi bays give meager testimony that those pioneers were here. Hunter-gatherers 2,000 years ago drilled oyster shells to weight their nets. Archaeologists think they departed after a while; in any case, the tribe didn't leave much for researchers to find and learn from.

No new settlement has an easy time of it. Early humans here had to adjust, as every other creature did. Weather conditions at Aransas change rapidly, playing havoc with immune systems. A winter day may warm to the eighties just before a blue norther blows in. That sharp temperature plunge doesn't last long; within hours, the vast body of saltwater can moderate it even when chills drop temperatures to thirty-two degrees. Once every decade or so, a hard freeze immobilizes bay shore wavelets, swirls the foam like ice cream, stubbles the pier posts with icy spikes.

Summers near the Gulf carry a pervasive sense of wet. Humidity runs high, averaging eighty-nine percent at dawn, drying to sixty percent by noon. Coastal breezes comfort the afternoons and evenings, and evaporation cools damp skin. Still, the hottest days can drive oxygen from the water, suffocating fish.

Showers blow in from the Gulf, but sand layers beneath the soil suck up the moisture quickly, leaving plants and animals thirsty. Often, drought and flood come in brief, intense cycles.

Late summer and early fall bring threat of tropical storms and hurricanes. They are a part of the natural cycle, known to Caribbean indigenes variously as *uricán*, *húnrakin*, or *hurakán*.

Those fierce winds uproot plants or sear them with spray-borne salt. Many animals flee, and some die. After the storm, bay waters may be so fresh that some creatures there cannot survive. Still, life comes surging back, sometimes stronger than before. Hurricanes clean the sea, reshape the shoreline, slake the land's thirst.

Most immigrants to Aransas—plants, animals, and humans—find that the area's assets outweigh temporary discomforts of climate. By 1,000 years ago, Karánkawa clans—Caoque, Coco, Cujane, Coopite, and Cópane—lived throughout the coastal region. Cópanes favored the area around Aransas Bay.

The men, "tall, plump and shapely," generally went naked. The women—who by some reports were a little squatty—wore animal-skin skirts. Both sexes painted and tattooed their bodies, pierced their lips and nipples with slivers of cane.

Cópanes shunned the drudgery connected with agriculture, domesticated animals, sturdy homes, and great stores of edibles. They ranged according to the seasons, thoroughly understanding their home ground, collecting food when and where it was available.

On the Lamar Peninsula, a small oak flourished. Each year, when migrating Cópanes arrived, its branches spread wider, towered higher. Later, its huge size made the Big Tree an Aransas landmark.

There is good land east of that Big Tree, to the edge of St. Charles Bay. Just south of the tree, and thirty yards in from the shore, lies marsh. Between the water and the wetland, reeds and bayberry stud a strip of hard sand perfect for a Cópane camp. At low tide, oyster shells litter mud that is marked by the prints of great blue herons and small fiddler crabs. Raccoons and deer leave heavier tracks. Seaweed dries in rippled rows.

Across the narrow bay, a flock of white pelicans bides. Beyond them, blackjack oaks cover another peninsula. The world seems silent, until one listens: Wind. Bird sounds. Insect hum. Distant gull arguments. In a spot such as that, Cópanes wintered.

For shelter, they built *ba-aks*: Long willow poles were bent so that both ends stuck in the earth and the grouping of them formed a dome. The framework was covered with foliage and hides. *Ba-aks*

This current photograph of the mouth of the Aransas River depicts the timelessness of unsullied marshlands that still surround the county.
—Courtesy of Thom Evans

All that remains of the Karánkawa tribes are the occasional artifacts, such as shards and flint points, found especially after storms that erode the shorelines.
—Courtesy of Thom Evans

Arguably the largest live oak in Texas, this tree came of age with the Karánkawas, and now has outlasted them by 150 years. It remains a struggling remnant of its once magnificent form.
—Courtesy of Thom Evans

provided some respite from the incessant wind, and the Cópanes could fold them like tents when they were ready to move on.

The men fashioned six-foot-long bows from bois d'arc branches, strung them with twisted deer sinew and used cane for arrows. The arrows had fine flint points, fixed in place with natural asphalt that drifted in from deep Gulf seeps. The hunters shot with force and precision, frequently killing game from a distance of over one hundred yards—deer, peccary, ducks, geese. They strung up their prizes with strong, small ropes made from red mulberry bark.

Cópanes were excellent swimmers and canoeists. They strode the bays on long legs, following an invisible trail of sandbars, shooting *gwylayra* in bay shallows. Legends tell of Cópane men with legs sensitive as the heron's; a hunter could detect the approach of a fish through its subsurface wave. The patient indolence of hook fishing never developed, since for Cópanes a fish shot was almost always a fish dead.

Rarely did even trout or redfish swim away with Cópane arrows. Should one try, a line made of root fiber was always attached to the fish-hunting dart, making it easy for a hunter to retrieve. This economy reflected a greater one: Cópanes killed only to satisfy hunger or to protect human life.

While men poled large dugouts—*waheem*—or caught fish in cane weirs, women and children combed the beach, gathered plant foods, chased down small game. They crushed acorns to make a simple bread and cooked it over live coals.

When men caught great green turtles, *hai'tnlúkn*, sometimes three feet long, women boiled the meat in clay pots or roasted it in ashes. They dried fish for later consumption and stored it in woven baskets.

Squatting by clay banks, Cópane women created distinctive and finely crafted pottery. Skilled hands rounded the bottoms of most *ca-an* utensils, but shaped a few into cones. Both varieties sat well in soft, heaped sand.

The women decorated water jugs, pots, and bowls with notched or scalloped rims, then waterproofed the containers with *coo-ha*, the same asphalt their hunters found so useful.

One master potter smoothed the edge of her bowl and drew, half a finger's width below the rim, a single incised line encircling the bowl. She echoed the cut with a narrow line of black *coo-ha* paint. Other women shaded the *coo-ha* from black, at the base of an urn, to gray at its lip.

Artisans knew that pots of a certain clay would turn a distinctive red when fired. Other vessels they dyed purple or red, or incised, or painted with squiggly *coo-ha* lines.

The Cópanes worked whelks into hammers and clam shells into beveled-edge scrapers. Olive shells, with holes drilled at the ends, made fine, large beads. Other shells had a pearly inner layer that could be cut in one-inch squares or small rectangles; Cópanes strung the chips on fine cord fashioned from Spanish dagger leaves, creating bracelets and necklaces. Small shells, mixed with drilled coyote teeth, then strung, became tinkler beads.

Children sought yaupon bushes, marked by clusters of red berries, and picked the leaves for tea. On special evenings, Cópanes laced that tea with intoxicating buttons from mescal cactus. Perhaps, then, they lolled under the spreading branches of the Big Tree.

If the Cópanes used that tree as a council site, no evidence remains to prove it. But when resources were abundant, small bands did sometimes congregate into large groups of several hundred people. Perhaps young women, posturing beneath the Big Tree, found partners from other clans. Perhaps it was there that *conas* and *tamas* (priests and chiefs) shared information or strengthened social and ideological ties.

Meetings were important because differences between clans led to misunderstandings; small wars simmered. Though the Karánkawas were not regularly cannibalistic, they, like most American tribes, occasionally ate human flesh for magical purposes—or for revenge.

When a member of the clan died, Cópanes dug a shallow grave. They curled the body in a fetal position and set it to face east, then mounded soil over it. Rarely did the Cópanes bury possessions along with a corpse.

As winter days began to lengthen, Cópanes saw the heads of laughing gulls turn from white to black. Then they watched the mesquite bushes. When lacy green leaves obscured the thorns, no more freezing weather was likely. The mesquites put out blossoms—finger-shaped pieces of fluff—and the blossoms turned to beans.

Cópanes ate the beans and dispersed into small hunting and gathering parties; the blackberries were ripe. Throughout the summer, they found other seasonal foods; they feasted on fruits of the cactus, called *túnas*. In fall, Cópanes added pecans to their diet, then headed back to favorite campsites on the bay shore.

Inland tribes made pilgrimages to watch the sun disappear into the water. From the barrier islands they watched it, or from the peninsulas that wrapped Copano bay. The tribes knew the event was a divine favor, and they honored it, but they were not transfixed by the sight.

Cópanes were. All the Karánkawas were. In the evening, when breezes turned soft and the land hushed, hunters stood motionless for an hour or more, watching the *klos* slip out of sight. What went through the Cópanes' minds as they watched the sunset—devotion to a deity, appreciation for beauty? We will never know; the Cópanes are gone.

None of the Karánkawa tribes left behind any cities, or *stelae*, or written language. The last few of them emigrated to Mexico in the mid-1800s and disappeared forever. Most reports say that no one in Texas today can trace his lineage to the almost-forgotten tribe.

VOYAGERS

"DISCOVERY"

SPANISH EYES

When Christopher Columbus landed in the southern Bahamas, currents carried the impact all the way to Aransas. Columbus not only established a beachhead for other explorers; he was the harbinger of attitudes and behavior that would characterize future European interactions with native populations.

On that October day in 1492, "the air," Columbus wrote, "was like April in Castille." He described well-built, gentle natives with fine faces. The people were neither black nor white; Columbus described their color as like that of Canary Islanders, off the African coast. They were Taíno, but Columbus called them *indios*, since he believed he had found India.

Proudly, he wrote in his log that the natives had shouted to one another "Come see the men from heaven!" The Taínos brought gifts—parrots, spears, bundles of cotton. Those who gave gold offered it as freely as others offered gourds of water.

Columbus constructed a rough fort, staffed it with thirty-nine men, and sailed for Spain. When he returned, the fort was in ashes and the men were dead. Taínos told him some had died of disease, while others were killed battling hostile tribes. (Those may have been the ones the Spanish called *Caribales*, giving us our word "cannibal.")

A year later, Columbus returned with a flotilla of seventeen ships. Within fifty years, Spaniards and other explorers claimed many isles, spurred in part by royal greed and European wars. Forced labor and rebellion took many lives; some natives committed suicide rather than submit to European slavery. Measles, small-

13

pox, cholera and other European diseases wiped out the rest of them.

Hernán Cortés had a more direct influence on the Coastal Bend. He came to the "New World" in 1504, participated in the conquest of Cuba, then set out to take Mexico. At Vera Cruz, Cortés met, and loved, the native girl Malinché, who became his translator. Her actions as his agent led ultimately to Cortés' defeat of the Aztecs at Tenochtitlán. Then the victorious Cortés claimed vast estates in various parts of Mexico. He imported Spanish cattle to graze there.

If that made him the first *ranchero*, his patronage also led to the unique culture of *charro*, cowman hero of South Texas. Great cattle empires developed on the rough expanse of grass and brush between Aransas and the Rio Grande. Mexican frontiersmen, *patrón* and *vaquero*, branded the Coastal Bend.

In the summer of 1519, Capitán Alonso Álvarez de Piñeda sailed the Aransas shore. He had started in western Florida, then followed the north shoreline of the Gulf of Mexico, marking the major inlets and mouths of rivers with painstaking precision. Piñeda stopped, from time to time, to take formal possession of the land and to trade with its natives.

South of Aransas Bay, Piñeda anchored, as he had so many times before, then consulted his calendar: June 4—the feast of Corpus Christi. He named that bay for the feast.

When Alvar Nuñez Cabeza de Vaca landed on San José Island nine years later, he said only one word: *Malhado*. "Bad luck." The explorer had arrived under the worst of circumstances and saw little to suggest that his fortunes were improving.

For forty-five days Cabeza, Lope de Oviedo, and a few others had floated on a barge in the Gulf of Mexico, watching crew mates die. They knew nothing of the fate of men on four similar barges that had cast off from Florida with them.

Cabeza had been the treasurer and high sheriff of an expedition chartered to explore, conquer, and settle the Gulf coast. The group had intended to establish a colony in Florida, then march the coastline to the Rio Grande and rejoin the fleet. Florida, however, offered nothing but hardship and privation.

In desperation, the men had improvised five small boats, literally giving the shirts off their backs to make sails. They cropped the manes and tails of horses, then plaited the hair into ropes and rigging. The barges proved ill-suited for rough Gulf waters, and by the time they reached the mouth of the Mississippi, the sailors were starving.

Cabeza and a few others came ashore on November 6, 1528. They huddled close to a fire built for them by Cópanes and learned that another barge had landed four miles up the beach. Its survivors, including Alonso de Castillo, Andres Dorantes, and the Moor Estebánico, joined Cabeza's men the next day. Over the ensuing days, some men died. Cópanes divided the remainder of them between two clans.

The clan claiming the Castillo and Dorantes group went to the mainland to eat oysters, and Cabeza did not see his shipmates again until spring. When that clan returned to San José, the Cópanes holding Cabeza and Oviedo took them to the mainland, so the sailors remained separated.

Cabeza believed the mainland a better, richer place to be—until the next winter. Food became scarce, and the Cópanes held council. They were tired of the burden of white strangers; they could not feed so many mouths.

A towering *alanay* approached the huddled Spaniards. "You!" The gesture was clear. "You! And you!" Five times the dark man pointed. Five small citizens of Spain arose. Then the man spoke another word—"*Strie*"—and made a harsh signal of dismissal. Everyone knew the banishment was a death sentence.

The refugees wandered south, starving. According to historian Hobart Huson, Cabeza and Oviedo both reported that "the survivors of the expedition became so famished that they resorted to eating each other." The Cópanes "were horrified at the terrible aspect and would have put all the rest of the Spaniards to death, had they found this condition sooner."

On San José, a dozen Spaniards survived to greet spring. Dorantes and Castillo wanted to leave, and the Cópanes were willing to let them go. Cabeza, Lope de Oviedo, and Alanís, who were too weak to travel, watched in despair as the departing silhouettes of their countrymen grew dim on the horizon.

Cabeza remained with the Cópanes as slave, trader, and medicine man for almost six years. In 1534, when he decided to leave, Oviedo was still very ill. Cabeza carried him on his back at first, as they wandered the southwest and the great plains. Two years later— it seemed a miracle!—they met again Dorantes, Castillo, and Estebánico. Together, the five finally reached Mexico City. They told exaggerated stories of their odyssey and the Seven Gold Cities of Cíbola. Those tales brought new waves of opportunists to the Coastal Bend.

French Accents

In the fall of 1686, René Robert Cavalier, Sieur de LaSalle, toured Aransas Bay. On the map he was making, he drew a small house at a point of land between the Aransas and San Antonio rivers. He sketched another building between the Guadalupe and the Lavaca, indicating either a native village or something that he erected himself. Other maps show that LaSalle surveyed the mouths of all the large streams between the Lavaca and the Rio Grande.

It was a small part of a great plan.

LaSalle was a visionary who had spent nine years as a Jesuit novice before becoming obsessed with discovery in the New World. He had developed the fur trade around Lake Ontario and built four forts in the northwest. Then came his crowning achievement: LaSalle navigated the Mississippi River from the Ohio River valley to the Gulf of Mexico. He claimed French ownership of all territories in the river's watershed and along its tributaries. He named the land for his king, Louis XIV, and the river for French minister Jean-Baptiste Colbert. LaSalle believed that he had found a warm water port for his fur trade.

But the French king schemed to take all of New Spain from the Spanish. The first step would be to establish a colony where the Mississippi emptied into the Gulf of Mexico. Louis enlisted LaSalle for the job and equipped him with four ships.

LaSalle's flagship was the forty-five-ton *La Belle*, his personal gift from the king, beautifully appointed. *La Belle* was fifty feet long and fourteen feet wide with two masts carrying square sails. Six bronze cannons were proof that *La Belle* was a very important vessel.

Suitable colonists, however, were not easy to come by. Few Frenchmen found the New World attractive; those who sought honor preferred battles closer to home. LaSalle set sail with only a ragtag group of adventurers and cutthroats, a few "girls seeking husbands," some of his own relatives, and three priests. The thirty to forty passengers on *La Belle* might have been honored to sail on the flagship, but they were extremely crowded there.

From the start, their journey was plagued by dissension and disaster. France ended its war with Spain and lost interest in LaSalle's venture. LaSalle, shy but opinionated, seemed cold and haughty to his colonists. The expedition's naval commander, de Beaujeau, particularly resented the fact that LaSalle, his designated superior, was only a self-made man, not born to the nobility.

LaSalle lost a ketch to Spanish pirates off Hispañola. When he reached the mainland, the mouth of the Mississippi was so hidden in a maze of bayous and sand flats that he never found it. He consulted his maps and found *Rio Escondido*, the Lost River, emptying into Matagorda Bay. LaSalle believed that it might be the Mississippi, but his transport ship *Aimable* ran aground only "a cannonshot from shore."

LaSalle reflected that the Spanish had named that bay and the island. *Matagorda* means "Starvation," or, literally, "reduce fat." It was an ill omen.

Rumors circulated. Some colonists feared that LaSalle had intended to go farther, looking for the mouth of the Mississippi, until the *Aimable* was lost. Captain de Beaujeau sailed his ship, *Joly*, back to France, leaving LaSalle with only his *La Belle*.

Karánkawas crept in for a closer look. LaSalle fired his cannon to intimidate them. The Karánkawas drew back, but soon inched forward again. LaSalle gave another command and watched dark bodies fall to musket fire.

Posting a number of men to stay aboard *La Belle*, LaSalle commandeered canoes from the natives. He took his colonists inland, along Garcitas Creek, and had five or six houses built of earth and wood. He made no fortification other than a battery of eight cannons. LaSalle named the settlement Fort St. Louis, hoping to win favor with his king.

The unhappy group lived at Garcitas Creek for about a year. A canoe from the fort returned to *La Belle* for supplies from time to time. The Frenchmen ate buffalo, deer, turkey, partridge, ducks, geese, and doves. They noted "cranes and swans in large numbers." They claimed to see "lions, tigers, bears and wolves." Some of their pigs got loose and ran wild. Karánkawas called the strange animals "French dogs." But Karánkawa arrogance went further than that; the indigenes staged frequent raids in revenge for the lost canoes.

A Frenchman named Minet, who kept a journal of his adventure, watched the marshlands too: "From afar we saw something like men, but someone said that they were big birds." They may have been whooping cranes, standing over five feet tall, but such moments of wonder were rare. For the most part, all the Frenchmen were consumed by criticism and insecurity. Minet wrote of LaSalle that "this is a man who has lost his mind."

Weary of his colonists' carping, LaSalle made a series of mapping expeditions, each lasting two or three months. The crew aboard *La Belle*, too fearful of the natives to go ashore, ran out of water. Much later, the body of one of them was found in the ship's bow, curled fetal style upon a coil of rope.

Other men tried to survive on the ship's store of brandy. Emboldened by it, they decided to sail to another part of the bay. A norther hit, and the drunken captain was unable to control his ship. *La Belle* ran aground. The crew salvaged what they could from her and carried it to the colony. The goods they brought hardly made up for the bad news: the hapless adventurers were stranded.

When LaSalle returned, he saw that the situation was desperate. On January 7, 1687, he took his most able-bodied men and set off to seek help, hoping to find the Mississippi and follow it upstream to French outposts.

In the group was a Basque named Duhaut, whose elder brother had died on an earlier mapping foray. Duhaut believed that LaSalle had killed his brother, and he wanted revenge.

Duhaut was assigned to a small hunting party on March 18 and recognized that as the opportunity he had been waiting for. He outlined a plan to shoot LaSalle from ambush, and when some of the

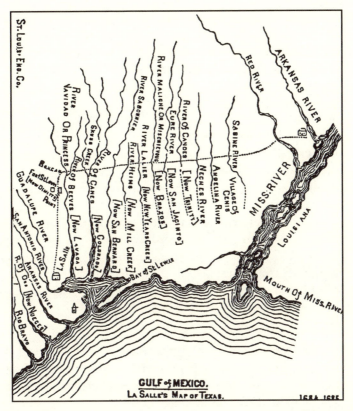

This enhanced replica of LaSalle's formative map of Texas provides the earliest known depiction of Aransas County. Note the building on the shoreline north of the Aransas River, suggesting European habitation near the present day Aransas National Wildlife Refuge.

—From journal of crew member Joutel; see Thrall

hunters refused to go along with his plot, Duhaut shot them. Then he and an accomplice hid to wait for LaSalle who, predictably, came looking.

Duhaut fired first, and accurately. A single bullet ripped through LaSalle's forehead. The man who had charted and changed a major portion of the North American continent fell dead.

Duhaut returned to the colony and coolly explained his actions to members of LaSalle's family. They could, he said, "withdraw and go wherever they wished, for he would not be able from then on to see them without pain." Apparently, the grieving relatives realized they were a minority in the midst of mutineers, for they left, intending to find LaSalle's river and head upstream toward Canada. The mutineers used the gold and trade goods from *La Belle* to buy their way home.

Throughout that long year at Garcitas Creek, various members of the LaSalle colony had returned to *La Belle* for supplies; they used the sailcloth to make clothes. Others abandoned the group to fend for themselves. Wrangling and murder continued among the two dozen who remained in the settlement after LaSalle's death. When smallpox struck them, the Karánkawas sensed advantage over the weakened colony and took final revenge.

When none was left alive in the settlement, some of the French deserters came back to bury the dead. And for years there were rumors that some of those "girls seeking husbands" became unwilling wives in Karánkawa villages. Only one of them was ever rescued. Some children of the party, raised with Indians, later returned as guides and interpreters.

Despite such adversities, France maintained a steadfast desire for presence in Texas. In 1720 Jean Béranger, ship captain and pilot, was commissioned to select the site for a new settlement of French émigrés, somewhere around Matagorda Bay.

When Béranger reached Matagorda, a strong east-southeast wind blew, and the sea was so high that he could not ride at anchor. Béranger continued southwest to 27°45' north latitude. There, he found the mouth of a pretty bay—and discovered the pass at Aransas.

When he had anchored, Béranger sent crewmen ashore to find fresh water. Almost immediately, they saw a band of Cópanes and were so frightened that they returned to the ship, leaving their water barrels on the island. Cópanes carried the casks off, and Béranger assumed it was the iron hoops they wanted.

He offered other items in trade—clothes, knives, axes, and guns. The Cópanes responded with lavish gifts, showing their appreciation for everything but the guns. Since, by this time, Cópanes had experienced what firearms could do, we can only assume they shunned the weapons as being more trouble than they were worth. Bows and arrows were more efficient.

Béranger thought the Cópanes always looked solemn, but he found them unafraid. Once, forty-five natives climbed aboard his ship, crowding the capacity of the deck in their innocent curiosity. Whenever the sailors went ashore, women rummaged boldly in the men's pockets. Other Cópanes, wounded in clan warfare, came to Béranger to have their injuries dressed.

On San José Island, Béranger found what he thought was resin. More likely, it was asphalt from Gulf seeps. Béranger discovered, as the Cópanes had before him, that the material was excellent for patching the leaks in his boats.

While his crew repaired the ships, Béranger and some officers wandered among small oak trees on Harbor Island, and Cópanes helped the men gather six casks of acorns. Béranger found a rattlesnake "coiled like a cable on some oyster shells," and killed it for the fat, which was good medicine. Almost as soon as he turned his back, however, a flock of birds carried the carcass away. When two Cópanes set out after it, they sank in mud up to their armpits and had to struggle to get out.

Béranger was ready to leave Aransas by All Saint's Day, but the wind had turned from the north. He ran up on the shoal, and three strong gusts carried waves across his ship. Béranger looked shoreward, where hundreds of Cópanes stood watching. In his frustration, Béranger imagined them, like carrion crows, waiting for him to wreck so that they could collect the spoils.

Luck was with the French, not the Cópanes. Currents lifted the boat and carried it into the Gulf. Twenty stormy days later, Béranger arrived safely in Louisiana, although most of his sails were missing, along with some poles of the bowsprit.

The next year Béranger captained a voyage to take possession of Matagorda Bay. Ensign Simars de Bellisle told him he had been on Matagorda before—as a Karánkawa captive.

Bellisle's horrifying stories of the island savages were fascinating, but they prejudiced Béranger's mood. When he arrived at Matagorda, Béranger expected the worst, and he wrote in his journal that the Karánkawas seemed very hard to please.

Nonetheless, Béranger struck a bargain with the natives, who allowed his crew to fill casks with fresh water. The sailors made two trips, but refused to go back after that. They reported that Karánkawas had shown them a heap of human bones and threatened to eat them too.

As a security during the cask-filling operation, Béranger had taken twenty Karánkawas hostage on his ship, and the expedition commander decided to take nine of them on to Louisiana. Much later, when Béranger wrote down his recollections of the voyages, he reflected on that: "I admit that I did not approve of this scheme and that it would have been more fitting to leave these peoples in the trust they had in us, since they entrusted themselves so readily."

In the long run, it was the Spanish, not the French, who marked Aransas County. Still, Béranger's reports give us a thoughtful look at the natives and the land. We struggle to imagine those natives, both innocent and helpful, and a Harbor Island covered with trees.

LAS MISIONES

French activity stirred Spain to new action along her northern perimeter. Two innovative barques, propelled by both sails and oars, set out from Vera Cruz, captained by Martín de Rivas and Antónío de Iriarte. They took careful note of every river and inlet to 30° north latitude, giving landmarks the names that are still in use along the Coastal Bend. Alonso de León, on a land mission, crossed a river near the present town of Victoria and christened it Guadalupe.

By this time, Spain had a clear understanding that the Coastal Bend offered nothing comparable to the wealth of Aztec and Inca empires. *Conquistadores* were not required. Spanish missions, with settled, agricultural Indian societies, could sufficiently stabilize the northern New World border.

The *misiones*, then, were agencies of the state as much as they were religious outposts. Missionary priests, fully subsidized by the Crown, developed Indian congregations while garrison-forts, or *presídios*, protected the communities. In time, Spain believed, the investment would pay off in taxpaying *índio* citizens capable of menial duties and military service.

The Spanish missionary priests had both an ecclesiastical function and a managerial one—without the economic risk of other *empresários*. Their job was to persuade, teach, civilize, and organize a population. They, not the militias, were ultimately responsible for Spain's failure or success in the New World.

In the spring of 1722 an expedition arrived at the site of LaSalle's old fort on Garcitas Creek. Construction began on *presídio Misión de Espíritu Santo de Zuniga de la Bahía (Loreto)*. It was the first mission ever built for Karánkawas.

Some of them, especially the Cópanes, readily adopted Catholicism. It included elements they understood, like the symbolic eating of the flesh of a great personage. What the Karánkawas could not comprehend was why their own less symbolic version of the ritual was so abhorrent to the aliens.

A priest, Padre Pena, reported that the natives were docile, willing to cultivate both "the earth and their own souls." He may have been choosing his words carefully, putting the best possible face on his experience. Enterprising friars, eager to guarantee a continuing flow of funds, often sent glowing reports.

Other Spaniards criticized the Karánkawas for preferring to "suffer hunger, nakedness and other necessities, in order to . . . idle in the woods or on the beach, giving themselves up to all kinds of vice, especially lust, theft and dancing." The Spaniards could not understand why the "savages" ate their meat "almost raw, parboiled or half roasted and dripping with blood."

Still, many reports attest that the natives of Aransas tried to meet the newcomers halfway. Where the whites were receptive, Cópanes taught them both their language and their customs. One of these customs was free access to the earth's bounty. Whites, however, fought back when Karánkawas took their livestock.

Mission outposts like La Bahía were well and good, but Spain was interested in bolder, more far-reaching action. In 1746 Don José de Escandón, a loyal subject of the Spanish crown, was commissioned to explore and settle a section of the Gulf coast from the town of Tampico north to the San Antonio River. Escandón was from Santandér, in the Basque region of Spain, and he planned from the beginning to name his territory—which included all of the Coastal Bend—*Nuevo Santandér*.

Escandón confined his exploration to the southern portion of the territory, and assigned the northern sector—from the Rio Grande to the Guadalupe—to Capt. Joaquín Oróbio y Basterra. Basterra was commandant of the La Bahía mission, by then relocated from Garcitas Creek to Mission Valley, on the Guadalupe.

As Basterra traveled southwest toward the Nueces River, he crossed six streams. Where one of them ran through yaupon and mesquite, then emptied into the bay, Basterra attempted to converse with natives. They spoke a word, possibly their name for the place, possibly *Aranama*, the name of an inland tribe. Basterra tried to understand. The word sounded Basque to him, but maybe that was only because Basterra was looking at the mesquite thorns. Nonetheless, he decided to name the river for that word, for the thorn and for the Lady of Aránsazu.

Later, when Basterra's commander, Escandón, established a fort at Live Oak Point, he called it *Aránsazu* as well. The bay between the river and the point he named *Cópano*, in honor of the natives. Escandón built another fort on the island near the Aransas pass, and at the farthest reach of Copano Bay, north of the Aransas River, a small port began to develop.

By 1749, the La Bahía mission moved again, to the site that would be Goliad. Soon the mission was receiving its supplies through the port called *El Cópano*.

In time, viceregal decree established El Cópano as the first port of Texas. It handled most of the supplies for Goliad and San Antonio, and some for Santa Fé as well. Two additional ports—Aránsazu, and Barkentine on St. Charles Bay—served as backup.

Cópanes appeared willing to convert to Catholicism, so friars founded Rosário Mission near Goliad as a separate institution for all Karánkawas. When they shunned the site, one of the priests met with Chief Great Prairie to ask why.

Great Prairie thought of the bays, and of sunsets over them. He suggested that a mission be built on the coast. There, he promised, the Christian Cópanes would gather, bringing with them "all the heathens . . . from the mouth of the Nueces to the Colorado River."

Missionary priests tried several locations—generally erecting

nothing more than a few rough wooden buildings and huts, surrounded by a stockade. Spanish soldiers gambled and flirted with
the women, expecting Karánkawa hunters to do all the work.

Perhaps it was because of that bad example, perhaps it was
something in their own nature: the Karánkawas would not settle
down. They came and went according to old migratory patterns, or
according to how well stocked the mission might be. Like every
other native tribe, the Karánkawas remained true to the culture of
their hemisphere; they were independent and free.

The Cópanes loved sites that allowed them to be surrounded
by water. They liked open bay on one side and marsh on the other,
an arrangement that provided nature's bounty at its most convenient. The Cópanes must have been pleased, indeed, when the
padres finally located their mission on the north peninsula separating Mission Bay from Copano.

In the center of the smaller bay lay Palmetto Island, long a
gathering place for Cópanes. Their Big Field burying ground lay beyond it. The Cópanes accepted the site and even set about the white
men's work of enlarging and improving a fine, natural spring of
fresh water there.

The Spanish liked the location as well as the Cópanes did. It
gave them an obvious presence on the bay to deter smugglers who
had taken the El Cópano port as their retreat, and the land was
bountiful. Swaggering snipers claimed that the area must have held
a million prairie chickens, very easy to shoot.

Then Cópanes began to die, stricken by European diseases.
Their angry survivors retreated to safety in the marshes and killed
any Spanish who sought them.

THE ANGLO-SAXON TAPESTRY

While the Spanish built missions, their northern neighbors established colonies. Each Anglo-Saxon immigrant family had its own
story, but many of their tales carry common threads—threads that
helped weave the fabric of Aransas County.

Their names were Irish like Power and O'Connor, or Scots
like Brundrett and McRae. The Dutch came to Aransas by inter-
marrying with English seafaring families like the Howlands and

Woods of Massachusetts colony. Some Aransans were French like
the Ballous and Rouquettes, or Danish like the Johnsons and Sorensons, or German like the Welders and Brachts.

Many of the earliest newcomers lived harsh and narrow lives.
They were, because they had to be, self-reliant in their struggle
against nature on the wild frontier. Although their log cabins were
rougher and less comfortable than Indian lodges, less sturdy than
Mexican adobe, the people were intelligent and literate. Their language evoked images of European cultures left behind.

As the worldwide industrial revolution generated not only tex-
tile machines and steam power, but also ideas of civil liberty and international free trade, America's seaboard colonies became prosperous and somewhat elitist. People with middle class convictions
kept heading west and south, moving frequently, restlessly pushing
the frontier. Others came directly from Europe.

When they reached Aransas, they encountered the Cópanes.
By then, all Karánkawas were accustomed to white skins. They had,
after some initial hostilities, incorporated Spanish mission life into
the pattern of their seasonal wanderings; the two cultures coexisted
peacefully. It was northern European settlers, in the 1820s and
1830s, who precipitated Karánkawa extinction.

European wars spilled over into the Americas; territories
changed hands. France ceded Louisiana to Spain, but in 1800
Napoleon Bonaparte forced Spain to return the territory by secret
treaty. Then he sold it to the United States. In 1812, the year that
Louisiana became a state, President James Madison signed a declaration of war against Great Britain.

That flourish of a pen would forever mark Aransas, although
the first battles were far away. The great southern battle did not
even take place until after a peace treaty was signed. News traveled
slowly on the American frontier.

The plot began when the British called on Frenchman Jean
Lafitte, in the bayou at Barataria. Lafitte had been a blacksmith in
New Orleans—and an agent for smugglers violating the U.S. Em-
bargo Act along the Louisiana coast. The British wanted to enlist
his aid in taking the mouth of the Mississippi from the United
States.

Lafitte, however, had other loyalties. He let the state of
Louisiana know what Britain had offered him, then joined Andrew

Jackson at the Battle of New Orleans. Since American victory there coincided with news of the peace treaty, many citizens believed the War of 1812 had ended in triumph, rather than the draw it actually was.

The United States thrilled to a new sense of nationalism that swept the Coastal Bend as well.

FREEBOOTERS

The term referred to men who lived beyond the law, who took matters into their own hands, used their own power and cunning and wits to achieve desired effects. We generally tend to think of freebooters as pirates, but the word had a broader application; not all freebooters roamed the seas. Since they rarely harassed their own kind, the highest government levels supported freebooters' activities. Governments often find that supporting mercenaries can be profitable.

When Republicans in Mexico began their battle for independence under *mestizo* priest Miguél Hidalgo, Texians stirred to the cry. August Magee resigned from the U.S. Army and met with Bernardo Gutierrez de Lara, Hidalgo's emissary to the United States. In so doing, Magee became a freebooter.

With Gutierrez, he organized an expedition to remove Spanish Royalist power in Texas—starting with Goliad, since the fortifications there would provide an advantageous base. Further, the presidio was only thirty miles from El Cópano port; reinforcements could sail from New Orleans and move quickly inland.

Magee's soldiers took Goliad by surprise. Toward the end of a four-month siege that followed, Magee died. His second in command, Samuel Kemper, went on to drive back the Spanish garrison at the Alamo.

Republican fervor went both ways: Magee's co-conspirator, Gutierrez, and other refugees from Mexico fought for the United States at the Battle of New Orleans. Jean Lafitte, the most famous freebooter of all, fought with them.

Five years later, Lafitte was in Aransas. The war had made him the darling of New Orleans society—men loved his heroics; women fancied his dashing good looks. Moving in high circles, however, had separated Lafitte from the freebooting and smuggling that provided his income. He needed to get out of Louisiana's Bayou Barataria.

Lafitte contacted a rebel regime in Venezuela and received letters of marque against Spain. With those guaranties, he could, as a private citizen, arm his ships to attack Spanish ones and seize Spanish citizens and goods.

Aransas was perfect for his purpose. Lafitte rarely boarded a ship at sea. It was more effective—and more fun—to tease a vessel into following him through a pass. Once Lafitte had his quarry in the bays, a game of cat-and-mouse began. He knew the reefs and shoals; his pursuers did not. With a series of deft moves, the freebooter could lead a tall Spanish ship to grief on a sand bar, then board her at leisure and take any treasure.

He could, when necessary, escape by sailing into a creek like Copano, Smuggler's, or Barkentine. And Lafitte alone knew how to navigate Cedar Bayou. The Spanish never understood that crooked channel. When Lafitte slipped into it from the open Gulf, they hovered helplessly outside. In utter frustration, Spanish ships watched the taunting flutter of Lafitte's topsails behind the dunes.

Lafitte established an operational base at Cedar Bayou, and another at the southwest end of San José Island, countering Spain's Fort Aránsazu on Live Oak Point. The two locations augmented a Galveston base Lafitte had taken from another privateer, Louis de Aury.

Lafitte made it clear to his men that they were to attack only Spanish vessels, leaving American ones unharmed. While they inflicted terrible damage to Spanish shipping (and others) in the Gulf of Mexico, Lafitte entertained in royal style. His guests included prestigious visitors who sought his support, as the British had, for a variety of avaricious plots.

In 1819 Spain and the United States signed a treaty ending hostilities. The U.S. officially renounced its claim to Texas, and President Madison ordered American citizens not to enter the area. Two years later, the U.S. Navy forced Lafitte to end his freebooting operations in the Gulf.

He headed for "no man's land" on Blackjack Peninsula. There, Lafitte had built a house for Madam Frank, widow of one of his captains killed in service. Her home, at the north end of the peninsula, was on the point of land separating San Antonio and Espíritu Santo bays. The spot so resembled Live Oak Point in Aransas Bay that Lafitte called it "False" Live Oak Point. Lafitte provided well for Madam Frank, making sure that she always had plenty of everything and never had to work for a living. And he could go there when, as in this instance, it became necessary.

By the time Lafitte arrived off Pass Cavallo, the entry to Matagorda Bay, five British frigates and ships of the American navy were pressing him hard. A fierce storm raged; running the bar seemed suicidal.

According to legend, Lafitte had the booty of many years loaded on his vessels. He shouted orders to his men, urging them to continue into the bay. Sailors hunched their shoulders and gritted their teeth.

His ships made the crossing, as Lafitte knew they would, but the British frigates did not. Two sank, and others went aground. Lafitte sailed into Garcitas Creek, where a dowel pin on his ship came loose. The centerboard slipped and stuck in the mud, so for some time after that, the place was known as Centerboard Reef.

Some of the freebooters moved a little south, to hideouts amid live oaks larger than any except the Big Tree of Lamar. The trees grew thickly, entwined with grape vines, and they were not so windswept as small ones closer to the bay. The land rolled a little, reminiscent of hills far inland, allowing secluded men to ignore how near the water was.

When their pursuers departed, the freebooters assembled again in Espíritu Santo Bay. For "three days and three nights," Madam Frank said, the men labored to unload treasure. Then, in a final speech, Lafitte released them from further obligation and divided the loot among them.

Lafitte's own share was, by rights, far the largest. He decided to cache it back from Madam Frank's house, there on False Live Oak Point. Madam Frank was friendly with them all. She watched each trip they made, night after night, into the thick oak motts. Lafitte, tired from the labor, told her, "There is enough treasure in those woods to ransom a nation!"

When the last cask was buried, Madam Frank said, Lafitte came out of the oaks alone; his bearers stayed forever buried with the booty.

The story has the ring of a local legend, but it may have been true. Freebooters were an amoral bunch who lived by a simple, pragmatic code. "Dead men tell no tales" was a dread slogan reflecting that expediency.

Lafitte led his flotilla to sea one last time. British and American vessels blockaded Cavallo and Aransas passes, leaving Lafitte no choice but to get to the Gulf through the shallow channel of Cedar Bayou. To lighten the draft, he ordered all excess cannon and baggage thrown into Espíritu Santo Bay. Only one ship failed to make it through.

Madam Frank heard cannonading in the direction of Cedar Bayou for days. Then all was silent. She said she never saw Jean Lafitte again.

Some stories suggest that he went to the Yucatán, or that he died on the high seas at the hands of Spain. Lafitte's own journal, now in the Sam Houston Library, has a final date of 1850, thirty years after his departure from False Live Oak Point. Some historians speculate that Lafitte circulated reports of his death as a cover, then moved to South Carolina under an assumed name. If so, he might have come back to False Live Oak Point from time to time, and made withdrawals from his deposit among the trees.

Lafitte's freebooting crews dispersed along the Texas and Louisiana coasts. According to Hobart Huson, "some became honest and successful sea captains engaged in legitimate commerce. Some . . . settled in Refugio County, some on the islands, and some on the mainland, and became substantial and highly respected citizens. The descendants of some of these old freebooters still reside in this county and make no concealment of the glamorous past of their hardy progenitors."

People in Aransas County are more reticent. Many tell tales of other times, but almost no one will talk about freebooting days.

THE *EMPRESA*

James Power and Friends

When James Power came to Aransas, he expected to fulfill a dream. It was a dream sparked in Ireland, where Power was born, and where he grew to be a man.

Throughout his boyhood, Power had chafed under English rule. It robbed the Irish of their ancestral lands, their culture, and their legal system. It denied them education and political representation. An English chancellor even stated that "no such person as an Irish Catholic is presumed to exist under English law."

By 1809, Power had endured enough. He left Ireland, sailed to America, and started a mercantile business in New Orleans. Twelve years later, he was prosperous, and the United States pulsed with nascent nationalism. But by then it was Mexico that fueled James Power's ambition.

There, a half-Indian, half-Spanish Catholic priest, Miguél Hidalgo, had led an uprising of laborers. With a flamboyant *grito*, or cry of rebellion, Hidalgo had called for a new government and a redistribution of land. When his revolution succeeded, Mexico was free of Spanish rule.

Slowly, James Power became convinced that Mexico offered Irish Catholics the good life that had filled his dreams. He closed his business in New Orleans and headed south to Saltillo.

Almost at once, Power met another Irishman, Dr. James Hewetson. This new friend was looking north, to Mexico's territory of Texas. On that wide expanse, Hewetson said, a man without

31

money could actually become rich. He had been there with Stephen Fuller Austin; he had talked with the officials.

Hewetson suggested that he and Power establish a business enterprise, an *empresa*, and become *empresários*. They could bring immigrants to a colonial area defined by an official grant. They and their settlers could work together to transplant Catholic Ireland's cultural heritage on the vast, free land called Texas. And eventually, Hewetson said, he and Power could sell portions of their own large land grants for an impressive profit.

As the Irishman explained it, each colonial family would be granted one *labór*, 177 acres, of farm land. If the family also raised stock, grazing land would be added to complete a *sítio*—4,428 acres. Families engaged only in ranching would receive the *sítio* less the *labór*.

Of course, the *empresa* would be part of Mexico. When American freebooters had tried to declare Texas independent, Mexico had drawn up a Texas constitution that proclaimed: "The State of Texas forms a part of the Mexican Republic, to which it remains inviolably joined."

Power and Hewetson saw no problem in the concept. Stephen Austin had worked amicably with local commissioners to establish his immigrant families successfully in Texas. The two Irishmen believed that they could do the same.

In 1824 Mexico passed a Republican Constitution. Its general colonization law—developed with input from Stephen Austin—stated that immigration could be by individuals or through *empresários*, and that when the population grew sufficiently, Texas could become a state separate from Coahuila.

Power discussed the colonization idea with Don Felipe Roque De La Portilla, a politically influential Mexican friend of considerable experience. In 1807 Portilla had inaugurated Texas' *empresário* system by establishing Villa de San Marcos de Nieve on the San Marcos River in south central Texas.

Although that colony had failed, beset by floods and Indian raids, Portilla encouraged Power to form an *empresa*. He even said that if Power decided to establish a colony, he would join it.

While James Power thought about the proposition, the pace of immigration quickened. Martín de León settled nearly 200 families, mostly Mexican, along the lower Guadalupe River and laid out a capital at Victoria. Green DeWitt received authorization to settle 400 families just south of Austin's colony, with a capital at Gonzales.

By the time Power was ready to act, James Hewetson had become a naturalized Mexican citizen, successful in business and influential in Coahuiltexian politics. He was still willing to join Power in a colonial application, but he would function as a silent partner. The two men made their application to the State of *Coahuila y Texas* in 1826.

Power asked for more land than he got—he included a parcel bordered by the Sabine, east of Galveston—and he pushed his luck by asking for littoral, or coastal, leagues. Mexico restricted colonization there and in the border leagues for obvious reasons of national security. But Stephen F. Austin—*Don Estev12n* to the Mexicans—spoke on Power's behalf, pointing out that he, too, had littoral leagues in Texas. And the Mexicans liked the idea that Power's Irish immigrants would all be Catholics.

Despite these assets, Power's negotiations with Mexico went on for years. Ultimately, his colony included littoral leagues between the Nueces and Guadalupe rivers—some sixty shoreline miles. Each littoral league measured ten leagues (twenty-six miles) inland along the border rivers, with a slight diversion from the Guadalupe along Coleto Creek. A straight line between the upriver points marked the area's western boundary.

In current terms, this line passed through the town of Fannin, not far from Coleto Creek, just missed Goliad and Beeville, and met the Nueces River at San Patrico. The littoral leagues referred not to bay shore, but to the Gulf, with the river boundary lines extending to include all of San José Island and parts of Matagorda and Mustang.

At the very heart of Power's *empresa* lay Copano Bay, and the *El Cópano* port where his colonists would land. Power promised to bring in 400 families of good moral character and of the Catholic religion—half native Mexicans and half natives of Ireland. He agreed to complete his colonization by 1834—just six years from the date of his grant.

Each family who came to Power's colony had its own story, although few of the tales are known today. Most often, the accounts were passed along by women. While men concentrated on hard labor in the fields, their wives recited family histories around supper tables and wrote them late by firelight. The sagas of the Fagans and Harts are only examples, but they have particular significance.

Aransas was Nicholas Fagan's last stop in a decade-long journey. In 1817, when he was thirty-two years old, Nicholas had sailed from County Cork with his wife, Kate Conally, and their two daughters, the eldest of whom was not yet three. The family landed in New York, where Nicholas' skills as a wheelwright and blacksmith were much in demand.

Soon the man felt driven to move on. He urged his family to Philadelphia, then Pittsburgh, Cincinnati, and St. Louis, where a son, John, was born. The family had moved to New Orleans before Kate Conally Fagan died in 1824.

Nicholas Fagan soon married Catharine Hanselman Balsch, who bore him two more daughters and another son before he had the urge to move again. Finally, at Aransas, Nicholas was ready to settle down. His family, and other Irishmen who clustered near them, formed a close alliance with Mexican families already on the land.

Thomas and Elizabeth Hart came after the Fagans, and their full story will be chronicled later, as it unfolds. Like many Irish families, the Harts had continued to suffer at home—until Power inspired them with visions of Texas. The Harts and their children sailed with James Power himself on the first ship carrying his colonists. Their Atlantic crossing, marked by privation and grief, exemplifies the experience of countless refugees. Their landfall represents the arrival of many who passed through Aransas.

The colonists found *El Cópano* port itself only an anchorage and a customs office; the nearest Mexican town, Refúgio, lay fifteen miles inland. Still farther from the water hunkered *Presídio La Bahía*, the Bay Fort. Its name preserved an identification with the coast, but a town beside it would later be known as Goliad.

The settlers' gateway, their portal, was the pass at Aransas. Aransas Bay led them northwest and between two peninsulas, eased them into shallow waters and close to the Copano shore. Together, the pass, the bay, the harbor, and two towns were the refuge, the new home for Fagans and Harts and others like them who would alter Aransas forever.

Fagan's Settlement

Nicholas Fagan traveled without his family on a first scouting trip to Texas. As his ship entered Copano Bay, Nicholas scanned the far shoreline. It seemed almost indistinguishable from the water, flat and featureless, but as his captain followed the dark blue trace of a natural channel, Nicholas began to notice a gentle rise on shore.

To either side the land was low, but straight ahead a bluff rose, at its highest point, to about nine feet above sea level. A crescent line of oyster reef extended from the shore like a protecting arm. Behind the Mexican Customs House, mesquite brush grew in wild tangles, running up a slight rise. In the distance, cypress trees suggested fresh water.

Nicholas stepped ashore, slipping over a broad clay bank. Ahead of him, the bluff crumbled into large grains of black dirt combined with a liberal sprinkling of small oyster shells. Nicholas scrambled up.

The Customs House was built of a material like nothing he had seen before. It was not *adobe*, he learned, like that used by Mexicans to the south; unbaked *adobe* bricks could not stand up to coastal humidity.

At Aransas, Mexicans made shellcrete. They began by burning oyster shell in shallow pits to convert it into lime, then put the solid lime in barrels. Humid air brought about a slaking process and chemical disintegration, so that the decomposed lime could be mixed with sand, oyster-shell aggregate, and water. The resulting slurry was poured into brick-shaped wooden forms to harden, and walls of the bricks were finished off with a lime and sand plaster.

Nicholas thought the shellcrete was a far cry from good Irish stone; he hoped for something better.

A more immediate concern was drinking water. When Nicholas asked about it, the Mexican customs agent showed him a shellcrete cistern beneath the office. It was thirty feet long, fifteen feet wide and ten feet deep—capable of storing over 30,000 gallons of rain water. A spring, 150 yards behind the custom house, and a creek, which fed into Mission Bay a few miles west, could provide additional water when needed.

Over ensuing days, Nicholas searched for streams, for stones, for home. When he discovered a beautiful site northwest of *El Có-pano*, on the south bank of the San Antonio River, Nicholas knew he had found what he was looking for. He went back to New Orleans for his family.

A Spanish captain agreed to take the Fagans and two other families to *El Cópano*, though he had never sailed there before. When his ship reached the dock, the captain was clearly afraid to go ashore. He said he could not imagine what had induced Nicholas and his friends to seek homes in such desolate country, with only Mexicans and Indians for neighbors. The captain wished them well, but as he sailed away he swore he would never return to that god-forsaken place.

The three immigrant families, undaunted, were eager to load their possessions on ox-carts and set off across some twenty miles of rolling prairie for their new homes. They headed out of *El Có-pano* on a bright, sunny winter morning, traveled all day, and set up camp for the night. In the twilight, no one could see a mass of steel blue cloud on the northwest horizon. Had they seen it, they would not have recognized the sign. They might even have thought it beautiful; some do. But Karánkawas and early explorers could have told the Fagans about "blue northers" that come roaring across the prairie.

That one blew in during the night, with rain and sleet. Everyone got wet and chilled to the bone, even the two babies. Frightened oxen wandered away.

The men had no choice but to go after the animals. Their women and children watched them go, then huddled alone on the cold, wet prairie. They waited, wondering if they would wait forever, wondering about Indians and wild animals, wondering all the horrors that beset those who wait, unknowing.

It was two days before the search party returned. They had found most of the missing animals, but not enough of them to pull all the supply wagons. One man volunteered to stay with the oxen-less wagons while the families went on to the homesites and set up camps there.

As slow as the toiling wagons were, they moved too fast for fifteen-year-old Annie Fagan. She begged her father to stop, then jumped down from the wagon while the others drove on. Annie's eyes absorbed the landscape, so new, so beautiful that she would remember it always. "O, it was Paradise," she wrote later, "green grass and trees in midwinter, horses running and playing over the vast prairies, deer grazing quietly or peeping curiously through the bushes, while birds were so numerous the very air seemed alive with them. . . . At peace with ourselves and all the world, what more could we ask for?"

The Fagans pitched their tents on the west bank of the San Antonio River and began to build a home. Only one other "white" settler lived in the area. He was a quiet and inoffensive man, but Mexican officials ordered him to leave because he was not Catholic. The Mexican *rancheros*, however, were friendly to the Fagans.

Their nearest neighbor, Carlos de la Garza, was happy to help the immigrants. He was related to the mother-in-law of *empresário* James Power, who would soon be bringing other settlers to the area. Carlos believed that the Irish and the Mexicans could blend their cultures successfully.

He knew the area and how it worked. Carlos had been born at Goliad, the son of a military man. He had grown up there, had married Tomasita there, built her a fine double log house and established his *rancho*. When a settlement of families developed around his home, Carlos established a store. All the while, he amassed large herds of livestock. His family lived the life of landed gentry, with servants and retainers attending them.

Carlos de la Garza gave Nicholas a few animals from his herd to get started. And he had a suggestion about Nicholas' house.

There were timbers he could use, lying on the prairie fifteen or twenty miles south. The wood was all that was left of a Spanish barkentine caught in the September hurricane of 1822. The ship, bound for *El Cópano*, had sailed up St. Charles Bay, seeking refuge in a creek; wind and high tides had carried her six or seven miles farther inland.

She had been a rich ship, loaded with gold and silver coins to pay the army at Goliad and San Antonio. When *rancheros* found her, high and dry, the crew was gone, and the gold was too. They stripped the barkentine of everything else valuable—except the wood. Nicholas could have that, Carlos said, if he was willing to do the work.

Nicholas and his sons set off for "Barkentine Creek" almost at once. Over time, they brought back not only ship's timbers, but also iron, a ship's light, door hinges and other hardware.

They supplemented the barkentine lumber with logs from the river bottom, cutting them by hand with a whipsaw. It was exhausting work. Some of the logs were so heavy that Nicholas needed six yokes of oxen to drag them to his homesite, but the result was worth his effort: a grand and sturdy two-story home, put together with wooden pegs and heavy bolts.

In visiting with Carlos de la Garza and his Mexican ranch neighbors, Nicholas learned that there was not a bushel of corn in the country. Comanches raided all the time; even if the *rancheros* got a food crop planted, the Indians wouldn't let them tend it properly.

Nicholas, eager to return favors from the Mexicans, borrowed small boats and went up the coast to Caney for a load of corn. He had brought millstones from New Orleans, and another man had a steel hand mill. Soon the whole community had corn meal and masa.

In appreciation, the Mexicans gave Nicholas Fagan a bell emblazoned with the date 1737. It was one of four bells which had hung in *Misión Nuestra Señora del Refúgio*, the last of the Spanish missions, built in 1795. The Mexican town of Refúgio had grown up around it, and when the mission was severely damaged in a storm, townspeople had taken the bells down.

The Irishman was delighted to have one of them. He had arranged the second story of his house as a chapel with altar, confessional, and priest's room. The old mission bell, hanging in his upper gallery, would once again sound the hour for services. That bell summoned Mexican families and members of a growing "Fagan Settlement"—the Wardens, McDonoughs, Sidicks, and Teals.

Although their homes were ten to twelve miles apart, women and children visited back and forth, crossing the prairies alone without fear. At the confluence of the San Antonio and Guadalupe rivers, they saw the remains of Spain's first Refugio Mission, now on Fagan land.

One day Annie Fagan and two of her girlfriends passed a

Karánkawa camp and found the Indians making beer. The natives invited the girls to join in, so they "drank from the filthy cup and so sealed their friendship with the tribe."

Everyone in Fagan's Settlement traveled to Goliad for *Diéz y Seis.* The festival's name meant more than the number sixteen; it denoted September 16, the day of Hidalgo's *grito,* and the annual celebration of the "Independence Day of the Indians."

A little Indian girl, dressed in the splendor of Indian royalty, represented the Indians of Mexico. She rode in a gaily decorated carriage pushed by officers of high rank. Twelve Spanish ladies walked on either side, holding long white ribbons that were fastened to the carriage. The ladies' elegant dresses—silks, adorned with costly laces and jewels—were rich and rare examples of beautiful Mexican handiwork.

Closer to home, the Irish learned Karánkawa rituals. They saw that tribesmen took the choicest piece of meat from their feasts and offered it first to the Great Spirit and then to the Four Winds. Finally, they buried the meat, returning it to Mother Earth, giver of all good things.

When the chief of one tribe was killed by Comanches, the Karánkawas gathered at sunset to mourn. They placed a skin on the ground in effigy of their fallen leader, then stood almost unmoving until dawn, singing a mournful dirge. At sunrise, the tribe sat around the effigy in three rows, and a leader spoke in earnest tones, pointing frequently to heaven. At the end of his speech, he went to each man, laid hands on every head and stroked from crown to nape. Then all arose. Reverently, they took up the skins and silently moved away.

The Irish settlers watched such ceremonies with awe, knowing they looked into a different world. As more Irish came to Aransas, along with Anglos, Germans, and others, that world would surely disappear, but for the moment, it was magic.

Soon the Fagans would negotiate with James Power for their land within the bounds of his *empresa.*

POWER COUNTRY

By the end of 1829, James Power and James Hewetson had

made a direct purchase from the state government: twenty-two leagues of land within their concession. For his own use, Power selected a league at Live Oak Point, adjacent to an area known by the Spanish as *Rincón de Cera*, waxy pastureland.

At the eastern tip of Power's point stood old Fort Aránsazu; across two miles of blue water, another oak-studded peninsula mirrored his own. West, beyond the wide expanse of Copano Bay, clear air revealed the shoreline of *El Cópano* Port. In short, the peninsula was a good spot for watching ships.

Power found the site especially useful since Gen. Manuél Mier y Terán had begun making his pronouncements. The Mexican, who had earned political favor as one of Hidalgo's leaders in the Mexican revolution, even renamed the old mission settlement at Presidio La Bahía. He declared that it would honor Hidalgo with an anagram of his name—Goliad. Only a silent *h* had to be dropped to make it work.

Other Terán orders were more threatening. He wanted to strengthen the fortifications at Goliad and, more significantly to Power, at Aránzasu, right on Live Oak Point. The general recommended new forts at other strategic sites—Victoria, possibly the south end of San José Island, and certainly Lipantitlán, twenty miles upriver from Nueces Bay. These forts, Terán declared, should be garrisoned with convict-soldiers.

Power was stunned. The revolution that had inspired his hope now seemed to be degenerating into military despotism. The central Mexican government put Texas under its direct control and forced citizens to trade with Mexico rather than with the United States. Fresh Mexican troops arrived at the Copano customs house to ensure that the government's orders were carried out.

There was more. Mexico would continue to recognize the colonies established by Austin, DeWitt, and Martín de León, but it suspended all other grants—including Power's. A great number of settlers, already working their land, learned that Mexican officials had denied their titles. New immigrants from the United States turned back in disappointment, and Power heard reports that Stephen Austin's colonists were planning a protest.

Power, certain that the Mexican government would change its policies once more, continued to seek colonists. The harassment just took up valuable time when he was far short of recruiting the specified number of families. As his deadline neared, Power scrambled to find settlers wherever he could—among Mexican *ranchero* families, members of Jean Lafitte's old freebooting gang, and applicants to other colonies. Some colonists immigrated directly from the United States. Others came from the Mexican interior, and from Greece, Nova Scotia, and Great Britain. But what Power really needed to do was make a trip to Ireland and seek settlers there.

Early in 1832, a second *grito*, as rebellious as Hidalgo's, echoed across Mexico. This time it issued from the throat of Antonio López de Santa Anna Pérez de Lebrón. He was no Hidalgo; Santa Anna merely understood the ritual steps for acquiring governmental power. His goal, he said, was to restore the Republican Constitution of 1824. Power and others welcomed the news; that generous document was one they could live by.

Power's *empresa* contract was again in effect, and he even had a three-year extension. With that grace period, Power felt confident that he could set a date to marry the daughter of his friend and benefactor, Don Felipe Roque De La Portilla.

By then, the Portillas were members of Power's colony, with a simple house of pickets, palm-roofed, on the bank of the Nueces River. On July 3, 1832, Dolores Portilla and James Power recited their wedding vows in nearby San Patricio, just across the river from Fort Lipantitlán.

Power wanted to provide his wife with a home on Live Oak Point, but first he built a small house in Refúgio. The thatched-roof picket house had only two rooms, but each of them boasted a large fireplace. Power used post oak rails to build a cowpen behind the home, and back of that was a stand of good trees decorated with balls of gray, mossy bromeliads. Birds twittered in the branches. Then the land dropped precipitously, flattened for some fifteen yards and sloped again, just a bit, to the Mission River. It was a brown stream, slow and narrow, but the southeast breeze, flowing across it, brought some cooling to the Powers' honeymoon home.

Right next door were the limestone walls of old Refúgio Mission. Three of its bells lay near the road, not far away. The mission was falling apart, but its red brick floor was sound, and Power set up his office in one section that still had a roof.

His attention was focused on San Felipe. Stephen Austin's colonists there had always expected to live in Texas as Americans, and they were irritated that Mexico deprived them of individual rights and privileges.

Some people had derogatory names for the Anglo-American dissidents, calling them "Austin's Roarers" or "War Dogs," but the rebellious settlers thought of themselves as patriots. For more than a decade, U.S. President Andrew Jackson had plotted with people like them, hoping to claim Mexico's land north of the Rio Grande.

In January of 1833, when Juán de Veramendi became the Cuahuiltexian governor, things began to change—but not for the better. Veramendi interpreted the Anglos' continued conferences as traditional Mexican steps toward revolution. He intended to nip the action in the bud, before Anglos raised a *grito*.

Power worried that Veramendi would cancel his colonial extension, and he faced a personal deadline as well: His wife was *enciente*, with the baby expected in April. Still, Power knew that he could no longer postpone his long-planned trip to recruit Irish colonists. He left Dolores Portilla Power to the care of her parents, booked passage for himself to New Orleans and secured transportation on a small schooner headed there.

His ship had just weighed anchor at the Aransas pass when someone saw a horseman on the beach, frantically signaling with an improvised banner. The ship's captain sent a small boat ashore, where Francisco De La Portilla, Power's brother-in-law, reported that Power was the father of a son. Dolores wanted him to return home.

Power yearned to respond, of course, but the ship captain refused to postpone his sailing unless Power paid a premium. Power couldn't afford that, and he had no idea when he might get another vessel. A long delay would jeopardize his *empresa*, so Power regretfully decided to continue his journey. More than a year would pass before he could see his son.

James Power's decision to sail on for Ireland was a wise and fateful one. While he was en route to New York, Governor Veramendi rescinded the extension to his contract, claiming it violated an article of the General Colonization Law. Power had only a year to bring in his settlers.

All along his upriver voyage from New Orleans, and during

the overland trip to Philadelphia and New York, Power stopped to spread the word about his colony in Texas. When he found people who were interested, he sent them south at once.

THE HARTS' CROSSING

James Power arrived in Ireland in late spring and set up headquarters in County Waterford, the home of his sister, Isabella O'Brien. He visited other relatives throughout south Ireland—O'Connors and Powers among them—and learned that friends and family alike were sick to death of persecution. They were eager to make a new start in a new land—but most of them had never heard of Texas. Power made handbills to cover the basic facts, and people came from all parts of Ireland to hear his detailed information.

Power promised to charter a ship at Liverpool and land the colonists at Copano. For this, he asked thirty dollars for each adult, paid in advance, and he expected the colonists to pay their own expenses en route. Power further recommended that each family bring all its household goods, farming tools, and enough provisions to last a year.

Nearly all the prospects were tenant farmers, owning little. They sold their personal property—horses, cattle, and sheep—to cover the costs of passage. Some pawned even their clothing and tools; a few sold themselves as indentured laborers to wealthier colonists.

Those who were able to liquidate their assets most promptly went to Texas in small groups, well ahead of the sailing of the main body of colonists. Indeed, some were well-equipped and had money to spare.

The *Prudence* was one of the largest ships on the Atlantic, so Thomas Hart was proud to be sailing on her with James Power. His wife, however, despaired from the moment she saw the ship. The *Prudence* was incredibly crowded with beds and provisions in every available space. There was no privacy at all, except for a sheet slung between sleeping areas. Elizabeth Hart could hardly find room to do her cooking, and she had no hope of keeping things tidy. Once, a merchant vessel followed so closely that everyone worried it held a band of pirates.

Elizabeth thought the worst was over when she saw the American coastline—then the captain announced that he was afraid to take his large ship through the Florida straits. Instead, he steered south of Cuba before heading into the Gulf of Mexico.

It was hot there. Elizabeth and her eldest daughter Rosalie could not keep five-year-old Elizabeth out of the sun. The child was a great favorite of the crew, and she insisted she had to be on deck to give orders. The captain, she said, could not do without her.

When the bubbly child became lethargic, a sailor called it sunstroke. Elizabeth bathed her namesake daughter with cool cloths and held water to her parched lips. She prayed; she implored the other children to stay out of the sun. She kept on bathing the hot, suffering body for two days, but nothing seemed to help. Young Elizabeth died in her mother's arms.

The captain mourned for Elizabeth as if she had been his own. He wanted to take her to New Orleans for interment, but his ship was becalmed. Porpoises circled the vessel in large numbers, and sailors said that if their captain did not bury the child at sea, no one would ever arrive at port. To relieve their superstitious anxieties, the captain ordered Elizabeth's body sewn in new canvas, with weights to sink her. After sailors lowered that little bundle into the Gulf, Irish immigrants stood a long time, staring at the sea.

The *Prudence* arrived in New Orleans two and a half months after she left Ireland. Like all ports, New Orleans was dirty, dangerous, and full of disease. Cholera, acutely infectious, had raged pandemic for two years, and unsanitary New Orleans—where drinking water was contaminated by human and animal waste—could not escape it.

Cholera comes on fast and ugly with profuse diarrhea and sometimes vomiting. As an afflicted person loses body fluids and salt, his muscles cramp painfully; his skin becomes wrinkled and cold. Unable to take the liquids he needs, the sufferer lapses into a coma. He may die in as little as twenty-four hours.

James Power saw that many who had gathered at the port to meet him were ill. He learned that some had died waiting for him; others were in hospitals. The rest, and the new arrivals, urged Power to get them out of New Orleans.

He moved as quickly as he could, but the immigrants felt their wait was interminable. Finally, Power arranged for two schooners to carry his people on the final leg of their voyage.

He and the Harts were among the passengers on the *Sea Lion*. John Linn, a prolific chronicler, boarded the *Wild Cat*.

According to Linn's report of his voyage, the ship arrived at the Aransas pass in stormy weather, but the captain was determined to enter the bay. The *Wild Cat* struck heavily on the bar in about five feet of water and remained fast aground. Heavy waves washed her decks; people saved themselves by clinging desperately to the ropes.

"Our staunch little craft withstood this warfare of the elements wonderfully well," Linn wrote, "but the cook announced that it would be an impossibility to get supper. We therefore contented ourselves with bread and cheese."

Through the next morning's haze, Linn saw a merchant ship, the *Cárdena*, heading straight for them. His captain tried to warn the vessel of the shallow bar; the passengers signaled furiously. The ships did not collide, but the *Cárdena* hit bottom with her broadside to the sea and wind. Linn wrote: "In about two hours she succumbed to the surf and gale and went to pieces."

Closely following the *Cárdena* was the *Sea Lion*. Her captain seemed so intent upon running aground that Colonel Power ordered him, at the point of a pistol, to change course. The captain steered too far east then and "brought up on the breakers" so that the *Sea Lion* "thumped tremendously" with unfurled sails. "Each roll of the surf would take her headlong forward, her keel grating on the bar."

A full, agonizing hour passed before the schooner fought her way past the obstacles and entered the bay. There the *Sea Lion* ran into a mud bank. Some of the passengers stayed aboard her, but others went ashore on San José Island. The *Wild Cat* eventually capsized, and all its passengers were forced onto the barren shore. Power and two other men took a small sailboat to *El Cópano* for help; crewmen tried to save the cargoes.

As the immigrants waited, new tragedy struck. They recognized it by its first signs, and the dread word spread among them in whispers, none daring to say it aloud: "Cholera."

There was no way to nurse the sufferers, no way to avoid them, and no way to do without infected water. Not one by one, but

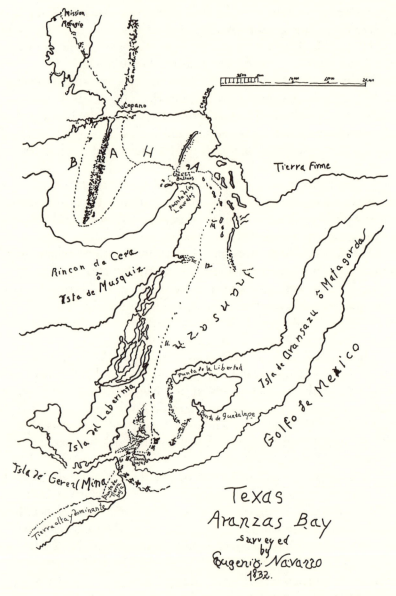

Antonio Navarro drew this map of Aransas Bay in 1832. It shows the treach-
ery of the route from the open Gulf to the relative safety of El Cópano: the
mud flats at the pass, the reefs surrounding Live Oak Point, and the oyster
beds spreading across Copano Bay. Note the projection from the peninsula
shore, likely the first record of the Rocky Point. Published in Texas Irish Empresarios and Their Colonies, William H. Oberste.

scores at a time, Power's colonists fell ill. When they died, those who were strong enough dug shallow graves for them. Other victims were simply lowered into the bay waters.

Mr. and Mrs. James St. John lost a child and could not bear the thought of abandoning their little one to creatures in that murky sea. They were grateful when Thomas Hart and Paul Keogh borrowed a yawl and sailed to San José Island to bury the small body.

While the men were on the island, Keogh fell suddenly and violently ill. Thomas Hart lingered long enough to bury him, too, then returned to the *Sea Lion*.

Although he was weak, Thomas insisted it was only from hunger. Elizabeth hurried to make him tea and toast, but before the food was ready, Thomas was taken with cramps. She warmed salt and applied it as soon as she could, wrapped him up, gave him warm drinks. Her treatment had worked for others, and they had survived. Elizabeth could only pray that her husband would too.

The next day, May 15, when the schooner *Sabine* sailed up from Copano, Thomas Hart was too ill to stand. Two men lowered his featherbed into the boat. Other survivors crowded in around him, fearing they risked infection, but eager to reach the port.

They landed on a sand beach without even a tree to shade them from the sun. Elizabeth stuck spades and hay forks in the ground to make a tent of bedclothes, but her husband begged her to help him walk; he wanted to see what kind of a country he was in, he said.

Too soon, Thomas Hart felt weak and lay down again. Young Rosalie, also ill, lay beside her father on a pallet. Later, when she tried to awaken him, she saw that he was dead.

There was no lumber for a proper casket, so Elizabeth wrapped her husband in a blanket and buried him in the sand. He was one of 250 colonists who found final rest along the shores of San José and Copano or in the Cópanes' Big Field.

Although Power argued against it, Mexican officials held his settlers in quarantine for two weeks. They camped on the bayshore, lost in their grief. When finally the colonists rode ox-wagons to Refugio, the great sorrow that hung over them seemed as plodding and heavy as were their conveyances.

REFUGE

Once James Power's Irish colonists arrived at Refugio, they set up their tents or camped in the old Espíritu Santo mission. Spanish monks had built it a century before, intending to Christianize the indigenes. By the time the Irish arrived, the decaying ruin had little to offer.

The newcomers and the twenty-odd immigrant families who had preceded them to the colony lived simply. They were entirely dependent on the supplies they had brought with them, and on the charity of others. The necessities of life were hard to come by; luxuries seemed impossible to acquire. One way or another, they eked out a living.

The men planted communal crops of corn and potatoes, but after that they were almost as idle as they had been aboard ship. They toured the surrounding territory on horseback, trying to decide on their homesteads. Sometimes they hunted.

Women's work continued as it always had. They cooked bacon, corn cakes, and jerked beef. They bartered for sugar and coffee, bought flour from coastal import traders, accepted gifts of eggs and vegetables from compassionate *ranchero* wives. They learned new ways of cooking—turkey and venison as well as beef; watermelon, squash, cantaloupe, and even small, hot peppers to augment the old standbys of potatoes, cabbages, and tomatoes.

James Power walked among his settlers, hearing the grief of their losses to cholera, their homesickness for green Ireland, their criticism of him personally.

Some colonists still simmered about the extra charge for schooners from New Orleans, and that laid a base for more complaints about uncomfortable conditions in the Refugio camp. But James Power lived no better than his colonists. As Rosalie Hart later recalled, "he dressed and lived and looked like a poor man." She described his house as "about like that of the colonists."

Through endless months of red tape and lack of direction or authority from the Mexican government, the settlers waited for distribution of their lands.

Other colonists came through, unimpressed with subsistence

living in Refugio. Dr. John Charles Beales, who was leading a colony to the Rio Grande, wrote that Refugio had only "five or six miserable huts, built and inhabited by as many Irish families, brought to this country by the Empresario Mr. Power, who could not properly locate them, in consequence of his disputes with respect to the boundaries of his lands. . . . As they imagined their sojourn would be temporary, they made no improvements, not even cultivating a bit of garden-ground! They do nothing but idle about, waiting for Mr. Power to make his appearance with their 'titles'."

Botanist Gideon Lincecum described Power's colonists as "a captious, discontented, quarrelsome, drunken, riotous, bigoted, fanatical, ignorant set of Roman Catholics, incapable of self-government and possessing none of the material for making good citizens."

In retrospect, it's easy to smile at such descriptions. Those Irish did their full share to build the Coastal Bend. And James Power was their trail blazer.

He was a man who focused on grand schemes; details did not seem an important part of his job. If that was a fatal flaw, to cause Power more grief in years to come, neither he nor his colonists had much inclination to think about it. They had enough on their hands, one day at a time.

What rightly concerned Power was news that Santa Anna had repudiated liberalism. The "new Napoleon" abolished all local legislatures and town councils. And in July Captain Sabriego arrived in Refugio with a body of troops, presenting a statement to Power: "Not knowing who has given you, or anybody else, the use of the Church of this ex-Mission, and since it was turned over to me so that it might be used as a barracks by the troops which should be stationed in this place, because water and other resources are lacking at El Cópano . . . I trust that you and whoever else is using it will kindly vacate."

Just in time, José Jesús Vidaurri was appointed land commissioner in Mexico and began distributing town lots to the colonists. Then they learned that their home-building skills from the Old Sod were useless; there was little stone in the fields. Instead, the men made primitive houses of wattle construction—straight poles woven with grass and moss—and dirt floors.

Power's nephew Tom O'Connor built a home on Lot 12, *Calle de la Roca,* just down from Power's little wedding house, now designated Lot 5. Even though Power was building a home at Live Oak Point, he planned to continue using the place in Refugio. With his colonial business offices in the old mission there, the house would be a convenience.

Since *empresários* were also granted "premium leagues" as a sort of bonus, Power sought land on San José and Matagorda islands. General Mier y Terán had denied his earlier petition, growling that "these little islands are not suitable for agriculture but are ideal for pirates and as bases for contraband trade." Power was no freebooter, but he did recognize the value of ports for legal maritime trade, and in time, he got the grants.

As was required of them, the colonists established a militia, with Power as lieutenant colonel. Life got more organized, and the settlers began to feel that they had found home. The houses they built might be of Mexican shellcrete, but the design was that of traditional Irish cottages.

A Fagan descendant wrote—with some exaggeration—that these pioneers "became owners of hundreds, even thousands of acres, more land than much of the landed gentry, earls and lords owned in the homeland and in England." In any case, almost overnight, they had land of their own.

REVOLUTION

AUTUMN

James Power had completed his home on Live Oak Point. It was not grand, but it was comfortable, and the view to the north was spectacular. Only gentle wavelets lapped the base of a twenty- to thirty-foot bluff covered with live oak trees; the prevailing wind was from the southeast.

Power was not lulled by an apparent calm. To the southwest lay Mexico, where recent events threatened his *empresa's* peace. Santa Anna had reversed his position favoring the Constitution of 1824 and was preparing to establish a Centralist government; power and authority would reside exclusively in Mexico City.

The move was designed to curb the exuberance of northern Europeans and Anglo-Americans, who were outnumbering Spaniards and native-born Spanish-Mexicans almost two to one. The *nortes* had taken a wasteland—alternately fought for and ignored under the flags of Spain, France, and Mexico—and turned it into a haven. Santa Anna feared they would inevitably want to join the United States, and he was determined not to let that happen.

Although relations between Mexicans and *nortes* were far from amicable in many areas of Texas, Power and his colonists got along well with their Spanish-speaking neighbors. They had no expectations grander than to be an independent state of the Republic of Mexico. The Power colonists had official support too: The governor of Coahuila and Texas, Agustín Viesca, had joined with several other governors in favor of the Federal system, rather than Santa Anna's restrictive ideas. A loose federation of states, not a strong central government, clearly favored the colonists' interests.

As *empresário*, James Power walked a fine line. He was by nature and heritage in favor of democracy and justice, not dictatorship and tyranny. Many of his friends in Mexico, however, assumed that he was a Centralist and would side with them. After all, they reasoned, he was Catholic, he had lived in the Mexican interior, and his wife was Mexican.

Power used his friends' assumptions to his advantage, and when Santa Anna ordered local militias to disband, Power's colonists complied. Quietly, however, they organized a Committee of Safety and Correspondence as a sort of spy and information network.

But it was Power himself, not the spies, who saw the first hint of war. On September 20, 1835, he stood on his own front porch with his protégé, Walter Lambert, simply admiring the view—and saw a large vessel round the bend of Live Oak Point. As it entered the Copano straits, Power recognized the warship *Veracruzana*, undoubtedly headed for *El Cópano*. He grabbed his telescope to follow the ship's progress.

When *Veracruzana* anchored, Power tried to focus more sharply. He thought—though he could not be sure—that he saw men unloading military supplies, so he spoke tersely to his friend: "Get the skiff."

As their little sailboat neared *El Cópano*, Power and Lambert verified that armed soldiers—probably 500 of them—were milling on the beach. Once ashore, Power learned that Gen. Martín Perfecto de Cós and his officers were meeting in the Customs House.

Power and Cós had a long-standing acquaintance, so the Irishman put a smile on his face and walked inside. He found the young general decked out in gold braid and glittering decorations—regalia befitting a brother-in-law of *Presidente* Santa Anna. Proudly, Cós told Power that he had arrived at the express order of Santa Anna, who was concerned that American interests plotted to take Texas from Mexico.

Cós boasted that his troops would prevent any such possibility. On a march to San Antonio and then east to Stephen Austin's capital at San Felipe, he would remind the northern European colonists that Mexico had adopted them as her children, cheerfully lavishing on them "all its worthiness of regard."

The Mexican general's eyes narrowed as he delivered the main point of his message: If certain ringleaders were delivered into his hands, there would be no war, but Mexico was prepared to repress any of her adopted children who forgot their duties to the nation. Should any colonists be guilty of such lapses of memory, Cós said, "the inevitable consequences of war will bear upon them and their property."

Power, who had listened to silky Mexican words for years, understood the full meaning of Cós' circumlocutions. The young general concluded by asking, "What do you think of my declaration?"

James Power, who knew it was a declaration of war replied, "I think it would be better if you had not come."

Cós seemed not to hear him. The army needed carts, he said, to transport its supplies, and he expected Power to provide them. "Of course. I'll send Walter." Though Power's voice was smooth, Lambert understood the true message he was to carry. He got the required wagons, but more importantly he got the word to Refugio's leaders. They sent riders in all directions, spreading the news: "Cós means war!"

San Felipe, west-northwest of Galveston Bay, 130 miles northeast of Refugio, received the warning within a day.

When Nicholas Fagan saw a horseman racing across the prairie, he gave the event his full attention; no sane man would push a horse that hard without good reason. Dust swirled as the rider reined his mount to a sudden stop and gasped out Power's warning: Cós was on the warpath.

Nicholas had expected the news. He loaned the messenger a fresh horse, sent him on his way and called a family council.

A long road had led them to their bank of the San Antonio River. Back-breaking labor had built their fine home. Patience and skill had developed a good herd of cattle. The family had no intention of losing all that, and it would be sheer folly to wait for war to overrun them. They agreed that Nicholas and his eldest son John would join the fight; the women and younger children would go to Louisiana for safety.

Nicholas Fagan then rode with heavy heart to the home of Carlos de la Garza. Losing the Mexican's friendship would be a great blow. They had shared much over the years, in large ways and small. Carlos had given Nicholas livestock to start his herd. Carlos had been among the *rancheros* who presented Nicholas an old mission bell, though Nicholas had done nothing but bring corn from Caney and set up a mill to help his neighbors. On many occasions, the men had knelt together in prayer.

When Nicholas arrived at Carlos' fine home and his friend greeted him warmly, the Irishman relaxed a little. A servant offered something cool to drink. It all seemed so familiar, and the men exchanged familiar words—how the cattle were doing, what the harvest looked like, when Nicholas might ring that bell again and signal that a priest had come to say Mass.

But then Carlos acknowledged that he had heard about the messenger. "You realize, of course," the Mexican said, "that I must support my government." Both men looked at the floor, and Nicholas nodded into the thick silence that enveloped them. Carlos de la Garza cleared his throat. He said he was raising a company of *rancheros* as an auxiliary unit for the army. Other neighbors would serve as scouts and spies. Less militant but still loyal Mexicans would use his home as a refuge.

Nicholas said he understood.

Each man assured the other that there was no personal animosity between them; each acknowledged that the other had to do as his conscience dictated. The good friends shook hands when they parted, knowing it might be for the last time.

Nicholas Fagan set about the difficult task of preparing his family to leave, but the job was made harder by frequent scares. Throughout the settlement, strange men rode up to houses screaming a warning: Indians and Mexicans were pillaging.

Those more gullible than Nicholas Fagan, those who believed that the men were soldiers, responded to the alarm and fled. When they returned home, they found their houses looted by the very men who had warned them. It was a cruel trick.

The Fagan family packed food, water, guns, and ammunition in their ox-drawn wagon. When the other families had done the same, all assembled for their long journey. Final words of advice and caution were only devices to stall the moment of goodbye. As the wagons groaned slowly east, sad voices called last thoughts across the still air. Then the departing families disappeared beyond the horizon. Resolutely, guns in hand, the fighting men turned west.

At Refugio, Cós enjoyed a full week of festivities hosted by prominent Mexican families. Officials of the San Patricio colony came to pay their respects; officers of the Lipantitlán garrison reported to receive orders.

When Cós moved north to Goliad, Power called his colony's Safety and Vigilance Committee to action. They hastily reorganized the disbanded militia, appointing Power as colonel and Ira Westover as captain; almost everyone volunteered to serve. The colonists elected Power and two others to represent them at a General Consultation scheduled for November.

News of confrontations began to filter in. There had been a skirmish at Gonzales—Mexicans and Anglos vying for an almost-useless cannon under the Americans' defiant "Come and take it" flag. George M. Collinsworth and a group of Matagorda planters intended to capture the Goliad presidio, and Philip Dimmitt had contributed a detachment of Victorians to help. Thirty mounted Federalist *rancheros* had joined the growing brigade, but they needed more help.

Power quickly volunteered and others in the colony did the same. They covered the twenty-seven miles from Refugio to Goliad, approaching the presidio from the southeast, across flat land. The fort commanded an excellent view north and west, where the San Antonio River made a big oxbow away from the fort. Trees along the river hardly obstructed the view of anyone in a bastion or sentry box; the land dropped in all directions, except the way Power's colonists came.

Moving cautiously, the soldiers saw that no Mexican flag flew over the presidio. Someone at the bastion motioned them around the southwest corner to the main entrance. They found Collinsworth standing where the door should have been; he had already claimed the fort.

Texians had taken it with a ruse. Collinsworth told Power one version of the story, but someone else told him another, so he was never certain what the trick was. Some said men broke into a bordello and dressed in women's clothes to fool the Mexicans. Others said local Federalist supporters had staged a dance outside the fortress walls, distracting the guards. In any event, someone managed to chop down the presido door and capture the Mexican commander.

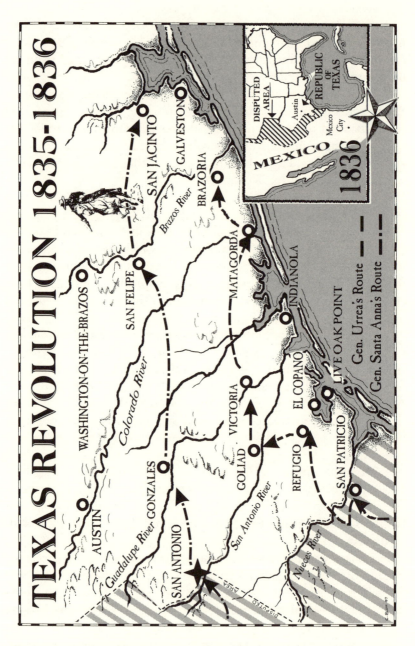

Battle areas of Texas Revolution, 1836. The map illustrates the strategic maritime importance of Aransas as a supply line for military actions across the state. Illustration by Chris Blum.

The battle that followed had lasted less than an hour. It might have gone longer, but the defenders ran out of ammunition. Some Anglo attackers laughed about that, claiming it proved what many of them already believed—that Mexicans were inferior. No American, they boasted, would ever submit to the domination of a race he had no respect for.

Power maintained a grim silence. He and his colonists had always held their Mexican neighbors in high esteem.

Collinsworth said his troops had killed three Mexican Centralists and wounded one. The only injury among Texians was Collinsworth's own freed slave, Sam McCullough, Jr. Sam had been shot in the shoulder, but was recovering.

Many men who fought for the presidio had already moved on, eager to confront Cós at San Antonio. Some who arrived with Power now did the same. Those who remained at Goliad elected Philip Dimmitt as their captain.

Power knew Dimmitt to be a man in many ways like himself. He had come from Kentucky as a trader, learned Spanish and developed influential friends in Mexico. He had married a Mexican, settled in de León's colony and become a successful merchant. Dimmitt had a commissary at San Antonio, and a supply wharf and warehouse near LaSalle's old fort on Garcitas Creek. Now the man was eager to put his energies into the command at Goliad.

Soon word arrived that Karánkawas were raiding settlements along the Guadalupe River and further east, along the Navidad. No one needed trouble from an additional source, so Dimmitt sent James Kerr and John Linn—both of whom had sailed from Ireland on Power's ship — to meet with the tribe. The Karánkawas backed down, even offering to fight with the Texians to get off the hook, but the Irishmen wouldn't agree to it. They advised the Karánkawas to stay away from white settlements as long as the war continued, to live peacefully in their lagoons.

Dimmitt did want support from San Patricio, at the far edge of Power's colony. Two young Power colonists—boys not even in their teens — volunteered to deliver letters there, and Power watched them go with concern and pride.

Word soon came that Mexican Centralists had captured the boys, put them in irons, and forced them to work in the Lipantitlán garrison. Power itched to rescue them, but before he could lay a plan,

Mexicans moved the boys to Matamoros, just inland from the mouth of the Rio Grande. They declared the children prisoners of war.

Power and his colonists pressed for action. On October 31 Dimmitt ordered a detachment of men to reduce and burn "Le Pan-ticlan," as Anglos called Lipantitlán. Dimmitt believed that captur-ing that mud fort would give him arms and position for defense. It should also alarm Mexican Federalists, encouraging counterrevolu-tion below the Rio Grande—and perhaps as far away as Mexico City.

Power rushed to Refugio. Even if Dimmitt was right in his be-lief that the strike on Lipantitlán would provide security, someone had to take care of settler families while their men were off fight-ing. Power sent the women and children of his colony to Victoria for safety; everyone's dreams of homes and crops went on hold for the duration.

Forty Power volunteers, under the command of Ira Westover, were ready to join Dimmitt's force when they arrived at Refugio. Together the band headed for Lipantitlán, thirty-seven miles south-west. They carried the Mexican Federal Flag of 1824 — vertical bands of green, white, and red, with the figure "1824" in the white field. Almost all the Irish thought it was an appropriate symbol; most of them still wanted nothing more than the privileges they had been granted by the 1824 constitution and the probability of living independent of Coahuila, in their own separate Mexican state.

Scouts reported that Lipantitlán was hardly a fort, but only a simple embankment of earth, lined with fence poles to hold the dirt in place. One said it "would have answered tolerably well, perhaps, for a second-rate hog pen." Even better was the news that most en-emy forces were away, looking for Texians. Westover stationed guards all around Lipantitlán and planned an early morning assault.

During the night the guards heard a noise, not stealthy at all, and grabbed their guns. They found two frightened San Patricio res-idents who hastily identified themselves. One thought he could per-suade the Lipantitlán guard to surrender, but his plan sounded too easy. It worked nonetheless. Before midnight, Texians held the fort, two cannons, some old Spanish guns, and a few pounds of powder.

Of course, the Mexican guard's surrender couldn't hold up. The larger Mexican force returned from the north in mid-after-noon, guns blazing. At a distance of 200 yards, their aim was off, but the Texians' was not. Half an hour later, twenty-eight Mexicans were killed or wounded or missing and their commander called a retreat.

No Power colonist was hurt at all and the only Texian injury was a boy who had three fingers shot off. When San Patricio colonists welcomed the Texian troops into their homes for the night, James Power eased gratefully into a good bed.

The next morning was hard. Under a flag of truce, the Mexicans petitioned for medical aid and John Linn found among their wounded a personal friend, Lt. Marcelino Garcia. Although gravely injured, Garcia was loudly denouncing Santa Anna's schemes. He said that he sympathized with the Texians even though, as a regular officer, he had been compelled to fight against them. Linn tried to ease his friend's pain and when Garcia died, the Texians eased Linn's grief. They buried Lt. Marcelino Garcia with full military honors.

Later, Power heard a story he found hard to believe. Some men claimed that a ghostly lady in green had appeared at Garcia's bedside during his final moments. They said she was his beautiful fiancée, come to comfort him. Some asserted that the lady in green continued to haunt Garcia's grave until the exact time of her own death—in faraway Mexico City.

After the victory at Lipantitlán, Power and his compatriots headed home, camping for a night on the bank of the Aransas River. Early the next morning, they watched an approaching company of mounted Mexican soldiers. Men were reaching for their guns when the Mexicans signaled "friends."

The contingent was an escort for Agustín Viesca, deposed governor of *Coahuila y Texas*. He had defied Santa Anna's Centralist government and was imprisoned for it, as had some state officials and land speculators — Commissioner Vicente Aldrete, Dr. James Grant, José Miguél Aldrete, and Dr. John Cameron of Refugio.

As they traveled on toward Goliad, Cameron told James Power what he had learned about Santa Anna's plans for invading Texas in the spring. None of it was good news.

Captain Dimmitt greeted the whole party when they arrived at his Goliad fort, but he was barely cordial to Viesca. Welcoming the fugitive governor, Dimmitt said, might seem an acknowledgment of Mexican sovereignty. That enraged the Mexican citizenry of Goliad, who were eager to meet with Viesca and complain to him that Dimmitt was a tyrant. Everyone got so stirred up that Dimmitt put the town under martial law.

Power was concerned. If Dimmitt alienated the good will of Mexican Federalists, the repercussions could be grave. Gen. Stephen F. Austin ordered him to give up his command and Dimmitt angrily stormed off to the siege of San Antonio.

Power headed in the opposite direction. He and two other Refugio delegates were already late for the General Consultation at San Felipe. With the issues close to home temporarily resolved, the three men hurried to the meeting.

They learned that the delegates had created a provisional government with Henry Smith of Brazoria as governor. The Consultation named Stephen F. Austin as commissioner to the United States and Sam Houston as commander-in-chief of the army—though he had no regular force to command.

Power got a place on the Land and Indian Affairs committee, which put him on Smith's General Council. He nominated John Dunn to purchase supplies for the Texian army and deliver them by way of the port at Copano. That bay at the heart of Power's colony would be a focal point of the war.

When the Consultation adjourned, it left all public affairs to Governor Smith and his council. Power's tenure there was the beginning of a long and sometimes difficult relationship with Smith — one that would have profound effects on Aransas.

Meanwhile, Texians, including a number of Power colonists, had laid siege upon the Mexican Centralists at San Antonio. American opportunists arrived, increasing the total force, but by December, many colonists left to see about their farms and families. Stephen Franklin Sparks, whose descendants still live on Live Oak Peninsula, stayed on to fight under Col. Benjamin R. Milam. Ben Milam was almost legendary. He had sailed to Copano Bay with freebooters in 1821, trying to take Texas. He had operated as a slaver and then as an *empresário* agent. He had fought for Mexico's independence from Spain and more recently joined Federalists defying Santa Anna. For that, Milam had been imprisoned along with Governor Viesca and the others, but he had escaped first.

George Collinsworth's detachment had found him hiding in the brush near Goliad, and he had gone with them to capture the presidio there. Rumor had it that Milam was the man who had suggested the bordello ruse to trick the Mexicans and win the fort.

Now Col. Ben Milam needed another plan. The siege of San Antonio had been long and often discouraging, and the time had come for decisive action. Milam faced his 500 men, took a stick and drew a long mark on the ground. And he asked the famous question: "Who will follow old Ben Milam into San Antonio?" Young Stephen Franklin Sparks and his company were the first to stand at Milam's side.

Even if everyone had been that brave, the battle would have been unequal, but more than 200 men decided to flee. They told Sparks and his fellows that the battle would be suicide; they shook the hands of the volunteers and bade them goodbye.

The assault was a five-day house-to-house battle, 300 Texians against 1,100 Mexican officers and soldiers. Milam died on the third day, shot outside Governor Veramendi's adobe palace. Two days later, Texians claimed the mission-turned-fortress known as the Alamo.

Many believed the time was ripe for Texas to declare complete independence from Mexico. When Goliad's garrison called for a meeting, Nicholas Fagan attended it. James Power's nephew, Tom O'Connor, was beside Nicholas as they stepped inside the gray, stone walls of the old presidio chapel. They paused for a moment beneath the high, shell-shaped arch over the door, then hurried to a pew, knelt, and crossed themselves. Nicholas looked up at the high row of plastered buttresses leading his eye forward, toward the altar.

He saw the *bulta*, a century-old Indian statue of the Lady of Loreto for whom the chapel was named. Propped below her, dramatically lit by candles, was the Goliad Declaration of Independence.

Nicholas Fagan and Tom O'Connor joined ninety-two other men who slowly, almost reverently, walked forward and put their hands to the Declaration. When the meeting adjourned to the presidio parade ground, it was Nicholas Fagan who raised the first flag of Texas independence. On the flag's white field, a bloody arm, severed at the shoulder, held a bloody blade.

Power was not at Goliad and did not sign the Declaration; he was busy at San Felipe, dealing with Governor Smith's captious moods. A man of extreme self-confidence, Smith invariably insisted upon his own way, believing that he knew what was best for Texas. Smith vetoed suffrage for Mexican Federalists who supported the colonists' position. He opposed Edward Gritton's nomination as Collector at the Port of Copano, declaring the man a spy. On both occasions, the Council overrode the governor's objections. Power and Houston consistently sided with him.

The Council established a garrison at Copano and Gen. Sam Houston ordered that "all volunteers arriving on the shores of Texas will . . . proceed to Copano where I designate they be stationed." Copano was the deepest port in Texas. If Texians controlled it and the pass at Aransas, Mexico's army would have to depend on provisions arriving by mule train, while Texas moved its supplies by water with much greater ease.

WINTER
INDEPENDENT SPIRITS

One year ended, another began, and life went on around the world. Young Victoria would not become Queen of England for another two years, Westminster Palace was barely on the drawing board, and the Arc de Triomphe was incomplete. No one had an internal combustion engine, or a telegraph, or pony express. There was no such thing as photography. Sam Colt had not yet manufactured the first revolver and ether would not be used as an anesthetic for another ten years. But twenty-four states had joined the American union, McGuffey worked diligently on his *Readers*, and Texas was producing history's heroes.

On December 30, 1835, a committee from Goliad presented their Declaration of Independence to the General Council at San Felipe. Because the Council still hoped to work out something with

Mexico under the Constitution of 1824, its members dismissed the Goliad document as "inconsiderately adopted." Still, the Goliad signers were heartened that no less a personage than Stephen F. Austin had come out in favor of independence; they knew they had taken the first important step toward a free Texas.

James Power, who had ended his service to the General Council just one day earlier, did not get to vote on the matter. Had he stayed on, Power might have learned to be wary of Henry Smith. As it was, he continued to champion the irascible politician.

Governor Smith went on a rampage when Dr. James Grant and Col. F. W. Johnson, both land speculators, promoted the idea of invading Matamoros. In the resulting confusion, various acts produced four supreme leaders for the Texas military. Enraged by the splits in his government, Smith labeled his opponents liars and conspirators; he charged them with the murder of all they should hold dear. He demanded that the Council apologize for its villainy. If it would not do so, Smith said, the assembly should dissolve.

Instead, the General Council appointed a Special Committee to examine and consider the governor's actions. That committee censured Smith, recommending that he be removed from office. When General Council tried to carry out the impeachment order,

Henry Smith, Provisional Governor of the Republic of Texas and father of Harriet Fulton Smith. Published in Refugio, *Hobart Huson.*

Smith refused to leave. He swore he would shoot "any son of a bitch" who tried to take the official seal of office from him.

Joseph Smith received a letter from his uncle soon after. "I feel extremely anxious," Henry Smith wrote, "to be released and entirely untrammeled from public office. . . . I have in great measure lost confidence in the integrity of public men."

By January 17, the Council could not raise a quorum. For all intents and purposes, Texas had no government and no one knew who commanded the army.

Dr. Grant took advantage of the confusion to pursue his plan to attack Matamoros. He enlisted 200 men from the Alamo and appropriated the fort's vital supplies—gunpowder, small arms, shot, medicine, and blankets. He confiscated food, cannon and all the horses from the presidio at Goliad, leaving it virtually helpless. As volunteer soldiers became aware of what this lack of supplies would mean at their two strongest forts, they began to desert Grant's campaign. But the damage was done.

Power's colony continued to be at the heart of Texas' supply routes for the war effort. Gen. Sam Houston visited Goliad and then Refugio, where he billeted his officers "in the best of the humble homes." He sometimes stayed at Capt. Ira Westover's house, "the most commodious in town," and sometimes at Power's little honeymoon home of palings.

It probably was there that Houston confided a concern: Although he had been made chairman of the constitutional committee, he was not a legal resident of Texas and had no home municipality to elect him their delegate to the Washington-on-the-Brazos Convention.

Power's colony adopted him. When they unanimously elected James Power as their representative, most voted for Sam Houston too. In that fateful moment, they ensured the fate of Texas. Houston, as a protégé of U.S. President Andrew Jackson, intended sooner or later to bring Texas into the Union.

Gen. Sam Houston rode down to the Port of Copano expecting to see troops assembling in accordance with his order. He found no Texians, no volunteer troops from the United States. Col. James Fannin had not arrived; the commissaries had not sent supplies. More than a little dismayed, Houston returned to Refugio, only to find more trouble.

Rebellious troops complained that in many months of service to Texas, they had not received "a single cent, and had no shoes to their feet, also were without even soap to wash their clothes." Houston gave each man five dollars from his own funds. Later, he confided that he would gladly give $5,000 a year to someone who would lead the war and relieve him of that grievous responsibility.

Colonel Johnson and his troops marched into Refugio, bound

for Matamoros. Houston was not at all pleased with Johnson's plan, but he praised the men for their courage. Then he spoke candidly, telling them that their expedition was "an unnecessary sacrifice of the blood of Texians" for a town with no value, beyond the border of Texas territory.

Houston suggested an alternative: The men might wait for Santa Anna to march north. When Mexican troops arrived, tired-out, Texians would prove to them what a small but united number of men could do. Houston concluded with a stirring encouragement that the men would then "rise up en masse and boldly speak out, 'We want to be free!'"

It was superb politics, but it didn't work. Houston's listeners appeared resolute, in no mood to wait idly for Mexicans to arrive. Houston tried again, beginning with words that sounded like capitulation: "Well, then, to Matamoros be it. But at least wait a short time until the troops from Georgia and Alabama land, and, united with them, what power of the enemy can withstand us?"

That speech and another gradually won over Johnson's men. In cool reflection, Texians realized the value of a stronger force; they opted to wait. Grant and Johnson, as leaders without followers, had no choice but to cancel the Matamoros expedition and set up camp at San Patricio.

Houston, expecting Fannin any day, sent five men to meet him at Copano. None had ever been in the region before, and one, Herman Ehrenberg, wrote extensively of his experience.

He was awed by a land so different from his native Thuringia, Germany—forested mountain range and fertile agricultural basin. While his detachment was still eight miles away from Copano, young Ehrenberg wrote that he could hear the surf as distinctly as if he "had been in front of the foaming waves."

To amuse themselves, the young men set fire to dry grass. "Barely had the flames taken hold when they rushed forward with amazing rapidity," Ehrenberg reported. The fire moved so fast, in fact, that he believed "the mighty fire column would soon hurry past our comrades at the mission."

When "screams of the frightened-up winged herds" died down, Ehrenberg could hear the surf again. Soon he and his fellows stepped out of the trees and onto an open, winter-bleached plain. "A lonely, one-story wooden building, which had formerly served as warehouse for the goods of the people moving to San Antonio, stood on this immensely beautiful shore. . . . It was in this old warehouse that we established our quarters. . . . The night was so exceedingly beautiful and we were so thoroughly awake that we sat down on our spread-out blankets near a small group of aloe plants and gazed out on the still restless waves that occasionally threw a fine spray over us."

The next morning Ehrenberg and his buddies found that wolves or coyotes had stolen all their food. "In order to get breakfast we had to use some other means besides to rage," he wrote. The men harvested oysters, a turkey, and two ducks—"a brilliant breakfast, that could not have been served better by Jacob Astor's in New York."

The detachment waited at Copano for a week before seeing Fannin's "two speedy frigates . . . dancing toward the shore." The messenger they sent to Refugio arrived just in time. Dissension and discontent had so grown among idle men that the army had almost dissolved.

Fannin's arrival reawakened the men's hopes for an attack on Matamoros, but he could not find the ships to carry them. Many men left the army again, and Fannin marched the remaining troops to Goliad.

They were still the largest force in Texas—500 men—and, in fact, they were the only real army. But Goliad was, by definition, a defensive post, offering little of the glory of a bold charge. Fannin decided on a new name for the old presidio, an assertive name that would rally the spirits of his men. *La Bahía*, "The Bay," became Fort Defiance.

Fannin demanded that San Patricio send horses and artillery for his use. Johnson and Grant bristled but complied. They realized that plenty of mustangs ran free on the prairie; soldiers could fill idle time by rounding up a new supply.

For James Power, that winter was a family time, a good time. Through all of January and most of February he was at home on

Live Oak Point. James Junior would be three in April; the baby, Maria Dolores, would celebrate her first birthday in only a month.

But James' wife, Dolores, fretted. The *rincón* was isolated. Ships just sailed by and went on. James insisted that was what made Live Oak Point safer than Refugio, safer than Goliad. Dolores was almost mollified when he had to leave again.

The delegates were gathering at Washington-on-the-Brazos. If James Power was to save his colony, it would not be by idling on his lonely point, but by standing for what he believed at the convention.

It was cold inland. The delegates met in an unfinished barn where Noah Byars ran a blacksmith shop. Byars had stretched cloth over the windows to keep out the chill, but that was scant protection; James Power and Sam Houston wore all the clothes they had, trying to keep warm.

On March 2, 1836, the two men shivered as they read the document penned by George C. Childress. It began:

> *When a government has ceased to protect the lives, liberty and property of the people from whom its legitimate powers are derived and . . . becomes an instrument in the hands of evil rulers for their oppression . . .*

How far Power had come from serene Saltillo days and the lonely splendor of Live Oak Point! How far he was from his *empresa* dream!

James Power picked up a pen and signed the document; Sam Houston did the same. The delegates at Washington-on-the-Brazos ratified the Texas Declaration of Independence.

It was a document based on declarations written by the United States and several Southern states, but it had uniquely Texian twists: Texas would be a unitary Republic, not to be divided into smaller states. Each Texian head-of-family was entitled to a league (2.6 miles) and a *labór* (177 acres) of land. No clergyman of any faith could hold office. A president of the Republic could keep his position for three years and no more; he could not lead armies into the field without the consent of Congress. Slavery was legal, but slave-running was censured as base freebootery.

The convention elected an interim government and Sam Houston finally received the authority he'd been waiting for—a commission granting him complete power as commander of all armed forces in Texas, both regular and volunteer.

One day later, William Barrett Travis wrote to Governor Henry Smith and General Sam Houston, begging help for his besieged men at the Alamo. He received no assistance, except from thirty-two gallant men of Gonzales, who, almost at the end of the heroic battle, fought their way into the old mission.

Then all the Alamo's defenders were killed. Sam Houston was at Gonzales, forming his army, when he heard it. He tried to keep word of the tragedy from spreading, but that was impossible.

Capt. Felipe De La Portilla heard the news and hurried to his daughter at Live Oak Point. Dolores Portilla Power was very much alone there—alone with two small children, and pregnant. Already guerrillas had raided her supplies and stock; neighbors were, for the most part, too far away to be much help. Captain Portilla removed his daughter and grandchildren to the care of his son on a ranch near Matamoros.

James Power, still at Washington-on-the-Brazos, received the news and knew that Portilla had made the right decision. When he also heard of Gen. Don José Urrea's troop movements, Power was convinced that it would be useless, and probably dangerous, for him to try to reach his wife, or even Refugio. Instead, he joined the army and went to New Orleans to raise supplies.

THE BATTLE FOR REFUGIO

Urrea. The word is difficult for non-Latins to enunciate. One is tempted to say it in a derogatory way, but the true pronunciation is *oo-RAY-ah*. Or one could simply call the Mexican general "Scourge of the Coast," because that is what he was.

Urrea played a key role in Santa Anna's plan to reclaim Texas, and he did it by ravaging Power's colony. He commanded 1,000 troops that swept up the coast from Mexico, providing an eastern line of protection for Santa Anna's march toward the Alamo. Urrea's goal was to take Goliad and then move on toward Brazoria, between Galveston and Matagorda bays.

By February, he was at Matamoros. Urrea met no resistance there, but when he crossed the Rio Grande he marched into a cold, wet norther. Some of his Central American native conscripts froze to death. And when his cavalrymen reached the Nueces River, they complained of being so cold that they couldn't feel their horses beneath them.

Urrea pressed on to San Patricio. Dr. Grant was still out rounding up horses and Johnson had posted no sentry on that cold, damp night. Urrea crept in, surrounded the town, and demanded that the Texians surrender. As the troops went out to give themselves up, Mexicans shot or lanced them. Fannin was so threatened by Urrea that he felt unable to respond to Travis' pleas for assistance at the Alamo.

Too soon, Urrea was in Power's colony and headed directly toward several homesteads. Each held a shattered family—women and children only; their men were engaged in the war. Even at Refugio, colonists could not abandon their town and flee to safety; the army was using all their wagons and oxen.

Colonel Fannin ordered Capt. Amos King to lead a detachment from Goliad to protect the helpless citizens of Refugio. Nicholas Fagan and twenty-eight others volunteered.

At one ranch after another they found malicious destruction. Although the soldiers had brought ox-carts, the refugees had pitifully few remaining possessions to load on them. As Captain King became angrier, he felt compelled to teach the Mexican force a lesson. With just a few men, he headed toward Urrea's army.

Ten miles south of Refugio and almost at the Aransas River (near the present Bonnie View community), King met an overwhelming force. He rushed back to his refugees and hurried their lumbering ox-carts toward the safety of the old Refugio mission.

Nicholas Fagan and the others tried to form a shield for the families, fighting a delaying action, but Urrea's troops shot at them all the way. Nearly everything the refugees had was damaged by gunfire, and by the time the last of the women and children were inside the mission, fifty-one-year-old Nicholas was gasping.

The refugees and troops were surrounded; they needed more

help. King sent colonist Thomas O'Brien to request reinforcements from Fannin, and he sent Fagan out with another scouting party.

The detail rode straight into a hundred *rancheros* and Karánkawas commanded by Capt. Carlos de la Garza. Nicholas Fagan's old friend took him prisoner along with the others and marched them to General Urrea.

Nicholas knew—everyone knew—that Santa Anna had ordered the execution of any rebel taken in arms. The situation was grim. But Urrea didn't like the policy, and certainly Don Carlos did not. With Santa Anna absent, they contrived a compromise: Mexican colonists would be released. Don Carlos saw to it that Nicholas Fagan was among them.

The Irishman made his way to Goliad—safe, but not for long.

At Power's capital, Refugio, the besieged colonists breathed easier. Col. William Ward and a hundred men of the Georgia Battalion had arrived and would escort them to safety in the Goliad presidio.

By nightfall, some of the soldiers were eager for a fight and even King and Ward quarreled bitterly. Each left the mission with his own troops, heading in different directions. The refugees waited alone.

Ward wasn't gone long. When he saw Urrea's force headed directly toward the mission, he hurried back and began preparations for a siege. The river was only 200 yards away, so Ward sent a detail to fill two barrels of water for the mission refugees.

The men could see General Urrea's army, 1,100 strong, up the far slope. Mexicans opened fire just as Ward's men loaded the filled water barrels onto an ox-cart. The soldiers rushed for their poor fortress. A Mexican bullet released only half a barrel of the precious liquid before Ward's men got it safe inside the walls.

The Mexican force scrambled down the steep river bank and onto the flats. They forded the stream, firing all the while. They passed Power's little paling house and advanced within fifty paces of the mission before Colonel Ward ordered his men to shoot. The Mexicans fell back, leaving the ground "pretty well spotted with their dead and wounded," according to Ward's nephew, who was part of the battle.

Ward sent two messengers to Fannin at Goliad, asking for reinforcements, but while they were gone, Urrea attacked once more. "They were repulsed," an eyewitness said, and "fell back to Colonel Power's cowpen," some hundred yards from the mission.

At dark, Urrea struck for the third time. The officer in charge fell with his head on the church door, but he had no backup. His men were on the run, pursued by the mission defenders.

Ward knew that he had to get out. Under cover of darkness, he sent four men to a heavily guarded spring. They took yellow gourds, long-necked and deep-bowled, and filled them with fresh water, then returned to the mission to slake the thirst of their wounded comrades.

Ward left the women and children asleep, innocent and unaware, while he explained the situation to his wounded men: Retreat was imperative. He planned to head for Copano, but there was no way he could take the disabled; they would have to be left in the church. Grimly, the wounded Texians agreed to his plan. The strong men, as they walked away, blinked back tears and steeled themselves against the sobs of doubly-injured friends.

To his astonishment, Ward met no resistance as he moved his troops right through the enemy camp. But after that he became lost. His troops wandered through the night, only to discover at dawn that they were just a few miles from the mission. Ward decided to head east, toward the Guadalupe River, but a week later he finally surrendered. After Mexicans marched his men to Goliad, they found out what had happened to King's contingent.

When Captain King and his twenty-seven men left Refugio in the opposite direction from Ward, they had found nothing but deserted ranches. Returning to Refugio, they saw that Ward was under siege by Urrea's army; they had to repulse two assaults themselves.

After dark, King ordered his troops to cross the river—not at any expected place but between two fords. They waded chin-deep, then wandered all night. Like Ward's men, they found at dawn that they were about three miles from the mission.

Mexicans attacked and King's men were defenseless, their guns wet from struggling across the deep river. Carlos de la Garza and his *rancheros* forced them to surrender and marched them back to Refugio, tied together in pairs. On the way, Mexicans brought other captured Texians to join them.

During the next twenty-four hours, the soldiers learned how brutal and barbarous their foe could be, but the families in the mission were not injured. Rebecca Ayers even gathered up her four children and called on General Urrea, making a personal appeal for her husband's life.

Urrea did no more than lecture her husband on his hostility and advise him to leave politics alone. "I bowed my head," Lewis Ayers wrote, "and said nothing."

However, Urrea wrote that he later became "unable to carry out the good intentions dictated by my feelings" and allowed his men to rob the women and children in the mission. Then he set the refugees to the hideous task of piling up Mexican dead. Urrea had them drag the corpses to a ditch four feet wide and four feet deep, where they made a stack "as large as twenty cords of wood," according to an eyewitness.

While the women and children were occupied with the horrible task, Urrea marched his military prisoners from the mission in two groups. He halted half of them a mile from the mission on the slope of a hill and sent the rest on some 300 yards, to a mott of oak trees.

"They were all young," a Mexican soldier wrote, "the oldest not more than thirty; and of fine florid complexions. . . . Their lamentations and the appeals which they uttered to heaven . . . with extended arms, kneeling or prostrate on the ground, were such as might have caused the very stones to cry out with compassion."

Urrea ordered his troops to fire and Refugio's defenders "fell dead in heaps." Mexicans untangled them to take their clothes, then left the bare bodies for vultures and wolves.

Nicholas Fagan heard bits of the story while he waited at the Goliad fort, and he learned that a Mexican detachment had captured and occupied the *El Cópano* port: Power's colonists were sealed off and could get no help by sea.

Urrea's advance units came within clear sight of the Goliad presidio, and a Mexican army deserter approached Fannin with an elaborate ambush plan. Fannin vacillated. Sam Houston sent orders for a retreat, but again, Fannin hesitated. He sent his cavalry out in forays against the opposing force, but nothing happened except that the animals got tired. By the time Fannin decided to abandon the Goliad fort, poorly cared for oxen and horses were almost uncontrollable.

Fannin wasn't thinking about animals; he was worried that Urrea's attack would come at night, when he could not see. He ordered his troops to burn Goliad and batter down all the ruined walls. When he left the fort, Fannin had his men set fire to it and to all provisions they could not carry.

On the morning of March 19, the smoke swirled through a dense fog, darkening it as the evacuees crept east. George W. Cash, one of Power's original colonists and a Goliad merchant, rode in a cart, wounded in the head by a musket ball. His wife and son rode with him. The others waded across the San Antonio River, only three feet deep, and then across Manehuila Creek on their way to the Coleto. They were following, almost exactly, the perimeter of Power's *empresa*.

A munitions wagon lost a wheel on the wide, flat prairie, and Fannin was forced to halt his cortege. They were at a bare and indefensible spot—a high, huge circle like an old man's bald pate, and like it, surrounded by brushy fringe. There was no water, no natural cover; every aspect favored an attacker.

Urrea approached from Manehuila Creek, spreading his men four deep in wide platoons. At his order, the pincers met and surrounded the Texians. Fannin hastily arranged his troops in a hollow square three ranks deep. He ordered artillery to the corners; Cash's wagon and others filled the center of the square.

Urrea staged assault after assault. During one lull in the fighting, Mrs. Cash went for water to comfort the wounded men.

As she and her son John walked across the prairie, Mrs. Cash recognized a Mexican officer and asked him to present them to General Urrea.

It was a scenario the commander had played out too many times before, but this time he saw that the youngster carried a shot pouch and powder horn. "Woman!" Urrea said, "Are you not ashamed to bring one of such tender age into such a situation?"

John Cash could speak for himself. In no uncertain terms, he told Urrea that he knew his rights and, like his fellows, intended to get them or die.

In that tense moment, a shout went up; Mexican fingers pointed at the Texians' white flag. They had surrendered.

Two hundred and eighty-four Texian prisoners marched toward Goliad. Nicholas Fagan, among them, had been captured by the Mexicans for a second time within one week.

THE MASSACRE

By March 26, more than 450 prisoners filled the fort—Ward's men, King's men, and Fannin's men. They slept on the ground without blankets. Their rations were skimpy, not much more than a little beef or broth. But some of the boys had flutes with them, and they played in the evenings. In soft voices, other prisoners accompanied them: *"Be it ever so humble, there's no place like home. . . ."*

Lt. Col. Nicolás de la Portilla listened to the music on Saturday night, March 26, as he read a message from his commander in chief, António Lopez de Santa Anna. The general reminded Portilla that "all foreigners taken with arms in their hands, making war upon the nation, shall be treated as pirates." He wrote of his surprise that his previous statements to that effect had not been heeded, concluding: "I therefore order that you should give immediate effect to the said ordinance in respect to all those foreigners who have . . . had the audacity to come and insult the Republic."

Portilla considered the fact that General Urrea, his own immediate superior, had repeatedly disobeyed Santa Anna's execution orders. Urrea had urged Portilla to use his prisoners for rebuilding Goliad, and now Lieutenant Colonel Portilla did not know what to do. To make matters worse, the next day, *Domingo de Ramos*, marked the beginning of the holiest season.

Palm Sunday. Nicholas Fagan thought of it too—the long-ago jubilation in Jerusalem and the great grief that followed. He stared at the presidio flagpole, where only three months earlier he had proudly raised a defiant banner—the symbol of a bloody arm and sword. And now he was imprisoned, his fate uncertain.

A boy tapped Nicholas on his shoulder, breaking the reverie. The young Mexican said that *Señor* Fagan had orders to go to

Miller's orchard and remain until sent for. Nicholas thought the message was a hoax and paid no attention to it. Even when the boy came a second time, Nicholas shrugged him off.

Then armed troops arrived, marching among the Texians, separating them into three sections. Fannin's men, but not the wounded commander himself, were herded through the sallyport in the south wall. Nicholas was among them as they marched southeast and it felt, he thought, a little like heading home. Others whispered of evacuation to the United States through Copano.

Again a messenger arrived, carrying a quarter of beef. He pulled Nicholas from the line of prisoners, saying that unnamed authorities ordered *Señor* Fagan to take the meat to Miller's orchard and stay there until directed to leave.

Nicholas, without understanding the strange command, did as he was told and shouldered the beef. Carrying it to shield his face, no Mexican recognized him, and he easily reached the designated place.

No one was there. He lowered the steer quarter to the ground, then turned to the sound of heartrending cries. The voices spoke English and many had an Irish brogue. They were the voices of his comrades: "Don't shoot; for God's sake don't shoot me."

Nicholas heard deliberate shots, one by one, punctuated by the screams of wounded and dying men. He shuddered in the silence that followed.

The men of Power's colony, and other brave men, had marched out of the presidio. Mexican soldiers had halted them, bandaged their eyes, made them lie with their faces in the dirt. It was a slow thing, one execution at a time. Most men sensed a gun muzzle close to the next man's head before he heard the shot.

Col. William Ward watched all his men die before he was ordered to kneel. He refused. Then he was told that if he would kneel, his life might be spared, but Ward again refused. They had killed his men in cold blood, he said, and he had no desire to live; death would be welcome. The soldiers blew his head off.

Meanwhile, Fannin sat imprisoned in a room in the church. After all the other assassinations were completed, soldiers walked him to the northwest corner of the fort and sat him in a chair.

Someone read a formal message of chastisement; someone bandaged his eyes. The firing squad came within two feet of James Fannin before they fired.

While Nicolás Portilla worked out that careful execution plan, Capt. Carlos de la Garza had been busy with his own arrangements. He had slaughtered a cow on the morning of the massacre as part of a plot to save his friend Nicholas Fagan. He had also devised escapes for young John Fagan, for Anthony and John Sidick, for James Byrne, and Edward Perry.

Nicholas Fagan did not know that until much later. After the massacre was over, he hid until nightfall, then stole to the battleground. Hoping to find someone alive, Nicholas crawled through the clumps of the dead. He discovered Col. William Hunter, very badly wounded, and dragged him to a hiding place.

Mexican soldiers came to the killing field, stripped the bodies of most clothing and all valuables, then burned them. Bones lay across the prairie.

Nicholas tended the wounded colonel through the night, but he feared the man would die without medical attention. The next morning he carried the colonel on his back across the rolling land to Dan Wright's house on Manehuila Creek. Both Mr. and Mrs. Wright were there and Mr. Sidick too. They agreed that Nicholas might safely hide the colonel in a field near the house; Mrs. Wright would nurse him until he was sufficiently recovered to find his friends.

Nicholas traveled on foot and mostly by night, hurrying to his homestead. It was a sorry, pillaged place, and Indians were in the house. Nicholas chased them out. Then he continued east, still on foot, in search of Gen. Sam Houston's army.

SPRING

Nicholas Fagan never caught up with Houston. Instead, he ran into an old friend, scout "Deaf" Smith, and learned that the war was over. On April 21, 1836, the Texians had defeated Santa Anna in bayou-crossed country near Galveston Bay, at a spot named for a meandering river, San Jacinto.

Neither men nor money from the United States had arrived in time to help Sam Houston. American volunteers who had arrived earlier were already dead—killed in the horror of San Patricio, the Alamo, and Goliad. Colonists, almost alone, composed the battle force. Texians won their own independence.

Walter Lambert and Thomas O'Connor were there, along with a number of men from colonist Ira Westover's company. Outnumbered two to one, the Texians crashed into Mexican troops with cries of: "Remember the Alamo! Remember Goliad!" Others, fighting beside them, echoed the sentiments in another tongue: "*¡Recuerden el Álamo! ¡Recuerden La Bahía!*" Mexican Federalist *rancheros* and Texians were one; neither could have been victorious alone.

The revolution was over, but the war was not—even though Santa Anna signed two treaties with Texas. The public one stated that hostilities would cease, that Santa Anna personally would not again take up arms against Texas, and that the Mexican army would withdraw below the Rio Grande. In a secret treaty, Santa Anna promised to work for Texas' independence and Mexico's diplomatic recognition of it. Within a month, the Mexican upper house renounced Santa Anna's agreements. A formal state of war continued, and rumors of new Mexican invasions kept Texians on edge.

Mexican families—even the best and oldest of them, even men like Carlos de la Garza—developed the habit of keeping a low profile. Some moved to Mexico, not to return for many years. And by that time the family story was lost: In the eyes of the Anglos, they were just immigrants, just Mexicans. The old families who did remember preferred to allow the Anglos their mistaken beliefs. More than a century would pass before some descendants chose to make themselves noticed again. They would be, as much as was Carlos de la Garza, heroes in their own way.

Walter Lambert joined Maj. Isaac Burton's cavalry as soon as

COPYRIGHTED 06 BY C. A. MAJOR
GOLIAD, TEXAS

*These old men were mere boys when they fought for Texas' independence in
1836. Franklin Sparks (foreground, just right of the flagpole) started a family
line that continues today in Aransas County.*
                              —Courtesy of the Gordon Stanley Collection

he got back to Copano and before long he saw a suspicious vessel sail into the bay. It anchored just off the northwestern point of Live Oak Peninsula, not far from Power's home.

Lambert and the others paced back and forth along the shore, itching to attack, until finally Burton devised a ruse. He signalled distress and the ship's captain with five sailors rowed to his rescue. The cavalry captured the Mexican ship without firing a shot.

Using the vessel as a decoy, Burton and his men managed to capture two more ships, both laden with provisions and military supplies. After that, people called Burton's company the Horse Marines.

At about the same time, James Power and Ewen Cameron organized a local group of mounted riflemen, the Power and Cameron Spy Company. Power still had business in New Orleans, but he felt comfortable leaving his family under the protection of the firebrand young man from the Scottish Highlands.

Cameron was a cousin of Dr. John Cameron, one of the Power colonists imprisoned along with Governor Viesca at the outbreak of the Revolution. Ewen Cameron knew the border territories well. A natural leader of men, he had enlisted in the Army of the Republic of Texas in July of 1836.

Most of Power's original colonists served in the Spy Company at one time or another, but neither Horse Marines nor spies were what Dolores Power needed on October 2. Her husband was in New Orleans and she was in labor. Twin babies were stillborn and the difficult birth took Dolores' life as well.

Dolores. The word means pains, afflictions, griefs, regrets. James Power stayed in New Orleans for a long time.

BOOK TWO

THE LONE STAR

A Cast of Characters

When the fighting men of Power's colony came home to rebuild their lives, newcomers joined them. Soldiers from Georgia, Pennsylvania, and New York, emigrés from Northern Europe, adventurers from all over had seen Live Oak and Lamar peninsulas when their ships sailed past and docked at *El Cópano*. They knew the beauty of Aransas land, and they were eager to own it.

The old traditions of expansionism and freebooting lived on. Cunning and powerful men took what they wanted on land even more than at sea. Sometimes they called it "speculation."

Most understood that the Republic of Texas would be merely a marker of the transition from revolution to statehood. These settlers, new threads in the old tapestry of European families who created the United States, brought attitudes that still influence the Coastal Bend. A closer look at some of them provides a clue to the continuing development of Aransas County.

SMITH

Joseph F. Smith was much like his uncle Henry, the erstwhile provisional governor of Texas—"caustic in his comments and a stranger to diplomacy." Smith, born in Kentucky, lived in Arkansas territory and moved to Texas at about the outbreak of the Revolution.

As one of a new breed of freebooters, he made his fortune from that war.

Immediately after San Jacinto, Joseph Smith established a base at Victoria. He studied the people of the new Republic, the character of the land, and the titles to it. Then he began to trade in land scrip—the promises of property with which Texas had paid its soldiers. In time, Joseph Smith and his family owned or controlled hundreds of the Texas certificates. He sued for title to undeveloped acreage and even became a lawyer, Hobart Huson wrote, "solely for the purpose of attending to his own large land suits."

Joseph Smith began filing upon Power and other landholders in 1839, after which the county surveyor and his deputy spent several years surveying the locations. The litigation that followed—in the Republic, state, and federal courts—lasted two decades.

Smith was not just an opportunist: he participated in militia actions against the Mexicans and the Indians; he worked tirelessly for land and water service to his town; he donated land to every major religious denomination. In a way, Joseph Smith contributed even more. Without his lawsuits, and the detailed testimonies they elicited, we would not have so many rich stories regarding the lives of Aransas' earliest citizens.

BYRNE

James Byrne, son of an Irish immigrant family, was a successful businessman in Ohio before joining Power's colony. He married Harriet Smith Odin, a relative of the first Catholic bishop of Texas, to whom ownership of the old Refugio Mission was conveyed.

Byrne and his wife arrived in Power country on the heelprint of momentous times, and he volunteered as a private in Ira Westover's company of the Texas Army. When Carlos de la Garza saved men from the massacre at Goliad, Byrne was among them. After the war, Byrne joined the Power and Cameron Spy Company on Live Oak Point. Later, when Power built a town on Live Oak Peninsula, Byrne would build one on the opposite shore—friendly competition between staunch allies.

WELDER

On the very day that James Power signed the Declaration of

Independence at Washington-on-the-Brazos, Franz Welder and his five children arrived at Live Oak Point. They were a pitiful little family, nearly beaten down by colonial disaster and incessant Mexican revolution.

Today the family name is synonymous with baronial cattle ranching and great philanthropy. The Welder Wildlife Refuge in San Patricio County preserves some land as the first family members saw it. The Welders' transition from refugees to benefactors is typical of Coastal Bend stories.

Franz Welder and his wife left Bavaria in 1830. After three years in New York, they joined the Beales colony and soon arrived at Aransas. But the series of comic opera events that followed were not amusing to one with a precise Germanic personality.

The captain of the Mexican coast guard and all his force boarded the ship at *El Cópano*, wishing to salute the colonists. Only one pistol would fire. Embarrassed, the captain told the immigrants they could unload all their supplies without inspection.

Disembarkation was no easy task: the water at *El Cópano* was so shallow that the ship couldn't approach nearer than four hundred yards from the beach. The colonists ran a wagon into the water, lowered possessions to it from the ship, then hauled the wagon ashore with long ropes. They estimated that unloading everyone's supplies would consume five to six days.

While some men continued with the cargo, others pitched tents on shore. They discovered that *El Cópano* had no drinking water. Someone had to sail a small boat to Live Oak Point to get a supply.

Throughout that long December, a series of wet and cold northers assailed the miserable immigrants. Most merely endured *El Cópano*, but the Welders fared a little better. Accustomed to harsh Bavarian winters, they were snug in handmade heavy woolen clothes.

On January 3 Franz Welder led his family inland. For three days they slogged through mud up to their knees; rain and sleet stung their faces. Finally, on the high bank of the San Antonio River near Goliad, the family set up camp on the first dry ground they had seen in Texas.

Even after all the immigrants reached Beales' land on the Rio Grande, the colony was a disaster. Welder moved to Mexico, but found life there just as difficult. When his wife died, he returned to Texas, disconsolate and nearly destitute.

Dolores Portilla Power took the family in, and the Power and Welder fates were joined. Their children would grow up together on Live Oak Point; Welder's eldest son, John, would marry the Powers' daughter, Maria. A new generation would live at the old Mission River homesite. And on the original grant of Felipe Roque De La Portilla, Maria Welder's grandfather, great cattle ranches would begin to grow.

One hundred and sixty years later, the family makes a point of saying that they are still bilingual and still work the same land.

CLARK

Brothers Henry, John, and William Clark, from a family of wine merchants in Montgomery County, New York, were die-hard adventurers. All were experienced frontier fighters who saw duty in the Texas Revolution.

Capt. John Clark, a freebooter in South America before coming to Aransas as a Power colonist, lived near Fagan's settlement prior to the revolution. He served in the Republic's navy.

Henry Clark traded horses on a large scale and made frequent trips to Mexico to acquire them. He formed a cattle business partnership with Franz Welder.

Both Henry and brother William took part in the Mier Expedition, a sad epilogue to the Texas Revolution. For a while, both lived on the island, translating the old Spanish name San José to Saint Joseph. (Although all settlers of the period used this term, we will continue, for clarity and consistency, to use San José.) Both brothers held county offices and helped to build the Copano town of St. Mary's.

Their sister Nancy married Maj. John Howland Wood, another New Yorker who came to Texas for the revolution and stayed to build a cattle empire that included parts of Aransas.

WELLS

James Babbitt Wells became noted in the Aransas cattle business and in politics, but he had started out to be a seafarer. As a boy, he stowed away on one of his uncle's Boston ships.

By the time the Texas Revolution began, Wells was a riverboat captain on the Mississippi. He organized a group of men for the fight and was commissioned a lieutenant in the Texas Navy. At the close of the war, President Sam Houston appointed him first master of the Navy Yard at Galveston, and Wells acquired land there. Before long, he traded that property for acreage on San José Island and began to raise cattle.

In 1844 James Wells—so handsome as to be almost pretty— married Lydia Ann Dana Hastings Hull Pay. A cultured and talented woman, she undoubtedly transformed the barren, barrier island community. Lydia Ann, who had been brought up in the diplomatic circles of Mexico, was a brilliant conversationalist and a purist in English diction who helped translate many Spanish land grants into English. A channel past the Aransas lighthouse was officially named for her.

James Wells served as a justice and a member of the county court for San José Island.

JOHNSON

Capt. Peter Johnson, a Dane, supported the colonists during the Texas Revolution, carrying men and supplies to Texas from southern ports. When the victory was won, he established himself at Galveston and became a citizen of the Republic.

Peter Johnson said he first put to sea on a Danish ship when he was "a mere lad." As he grew to a striking six foot seven inches tall, he looked truly like a Viking and was a man of unusual strength, both physical and mental. In time, Captain Johnson owned a large, three-masted seagoing schooner, the *Belleport*. He carried cargoes around the world until 1832. Then he navigated the coastline between American ports.

Johnson's move to supplying the Texas Revolution was a natural one, and after that, he moved from the open gulf to the bays for good. There he developed and maintained a transportation system along the barrier islands, linking the coastal towns of Aransas.

FULTON

George Ware Fulton arrived in Texas in 1837, leading sixty Indiana men who intended to join the fight for independence. They arrived too late for battle, but Fulton was commissioned a captain and qualified for land scrip. After that, he called himself "Colonel."

When the Texas Army disbanded in June, Fulton became a draftsman for the General Land Office in Houston. Almost penniless, he decided to appeal directly to the Secretary of the Treasury, Henry Smith. Although Smith could not help Fulton officially, the former provisional governor did make the newcomer a personal loan. Fulton and Smith became business partners, and Fulton traveled the coast locating land claims.

Those claims made him rich and famous. The mansion he built on Aransas Bay remains a monument to the era of cattle and speculation.

McRae

Archibald McRae landed at Live Oak Point in 1838. Although he had done well as a carpenter in Florida, economic opportunity in the new Texas Republic intrigued him. Archibald purchased land from James Power—not at Live Oak Point, but on the opposite, uninhabited peninsula. It had a southern view toward Power's home and the second largest live oak in the area. Archibald McRae became, arguably, the first settler of Lamar, and his descendants wrote stories of life there in the old days.

As branches of the family tree spread at Lamar, the McRae name was lost, merged into other trees still shading Aransas. Strong McRae root stock remains, reaching back, by historical fact, to Scotland in the year 1427, and by legend to Ireland and the family of St. Columba or the household of St. Patrick in the year 488.

The great live oak that graced Archibald McRae's yard still stands beside the bay.

Maria Power (daughter of James Power and Dolores De La Portilla) married John Welder (son of Frank Welder). Part of their family lands became the Welder Wildlife Refuge. From History of Refugio County, *edited by Lucile Fagan Snider.*

Peter and Wilhelmina Johnson were early settlers on San José Island. Captain Johnson's stage line ran the length of the island and served the mainland settlements as well.
—Courtesy of the Peter Johnson family Collection

Harriet Smith and her husband George Fulton, seen here circa 1850, later introduced the concept of high society in the small cattle town that Fulton founded and named for himself.
—Courtesy of Fulton Mansion State Historic Archives

Mary Ann Heard and Murdoch McRae lived their lives in Lamar, where Murdoch constructed buildings and boats.
—Courtesy of Virginia Meynard; Mary Ann: published in *History of Refugio County,* Lucile Fagan Snider, ed.

THE STAGE IS SET

In 1840 Texas had only four seaports worth considering—Aransas, Matagorda, Galveston, and Sabine. As Francis Sheridan suggested in his journal, all of these ports were rough and tumble places: "the Bowie knife is in general use among the high and low. They are mostly worn either in the sleeve, or within the back part of the coat collar. As to going about unarmed either with pistols or Bowie knife or dagger stick, it is a piece of neglect unheard of. These knives are a regular article of commerce and . . . are used also for toothpicks."

As more and more energetic citizens arrived in Aransas, land titles became a mass of confusion. Spanish land grants, grants from the Republic, and homestead rights often contradicted one another. Some parcels of land that newcomers purchased from early settlers were heavily burdened with conflicting titles. To make matters worse, "squatters' rights" protected anyone who lived on land long enough; even a person who held legal title could not move a usurper off.

The new Republic of Texas added to this tangled web. Seeking to pay off its notes (the First Texian Loans), the state claimed ownership of all vacant lands and declared *empresário* contracts null and void. The government intended to redistribute these lands by issuing scrip, each certificate worth six hundred and forty acres of vacant land within the public domain. Further, the government offered bonus lands to immigrants and to participants in various Revolutionary battles.

In order to safeguard all valid and legitimate titles, the General Land Office required former *empresários* to submit the records of their land transactions, and James Power promptly complied, but both he and the settlers in his colony were reluctant to bear the expense of new surveys, as requested by the land commissioner. Instead, they swore confidence in "the good old titles."

Power was hardly aware of the problems that were brewing. He had remained in New Orleans after the war, although he wrote to a nephew that money was "very hard to be got" there and that times were very bad. But with Dolores dead and gone, Power wasn't ready to return to his *Rincón de Cera*. Instead, he asked his father-in-law to bring his children to join him in New Orleans. Portilla's own son and daughter, Francisco and Tomasa, came along.

Some men are driven to remarry quickly, and Power, with two toddlers who needed care, was one. On August 19, 1837, less than a year after Dolores died, James Power wed her sister Tomasa, often called by the diminutive nickname Tomasita.

And then he was ready to begin again.

ARANSAS CITY

Power saw that Refugio was desolate; no one wanted to live in the war-ravaged community. The time seemed ripe, at last, to profit from his long-held investment. The former *empresário* decided to sell off some Live Oak Peninsula land and start a town there.

His first partner was an associate in New Orleans, but when nothing came of that arrangement, Power entered into a new agreement with his old friend Henry Smith. Power tolerated the politician's temperamental outbursts, and Smith had already purchased some of Power's Live Oak Peninsula land. He had even built a fine home on property east of Power's own, near old Fort Aránzasu. Since Smith was an attorney, Power trusted him with his personal affairs. That would prove to be yet another mistake born of Power's fatal inattention to the finer points of business.

Power and Smith decided to build their town precisely where their own homes were—on Live Oak Point, overlooking the channel into Copano Bay. They laid off blocks and lots; they named one street Washington and another Market. The town's name seemed a natural, given its proximity to old Fort Aránsazu; Power and Smith called it Aransas City.

Smith described the landscape as comparable to "the haunts of Calypsos," and he predicted that within fifty years (which would have been 1887), the area would contain a greater population "than all the rest of Texas put together."

James Power donated bayfront land for a Catholic church and school—a generous hundred acres that the church could put to other use as well. He started a post office and mail route. He opened a general store adjoining his home and got Walter Lambert to run it. Drawing on long experience in the mercantile business, Power

A modern visitor, driving south on the causeway crossing Copano Bay, still sees this embankment, with newer homes nestled in with the old trees.
—Courtesy of Barker Library,
the Center for American History,
The University of Texas at Austin

stocked the store with groceries, hardware, clothes, liquor, and tobacco. Lambert kept a well-placed personal stock of loaded guns, as bandits roamed everywhere.

Although Refugio had been named the county seat, there were not enough men in that town to operate the government. Nearly all official business for the old colonial region was transacted at Live Oak Point. On January 28, 1839, an act of Congress approved Aransas City as an incorporated town with James Power as its mayor.

Power built a wharf to attract maritime freight and developed a large importing and forwarding business. He used the old Copano customs building as an auxiliary warehouse; his ox carts hauled supplies from there to San Antonio and Goliad. Mexican mule trains arrived laden with silver dollars. Departing, some mules carried tobacco in hundred-pound bales, one on either side of each animal. Other mules were laden with cotton cloth, calico, or other items desired by the Mexican market.

When Power set up a new, temporary customs operation at

Aransas City, Smith recommended his friend George Ware Fulton to run it. Power saw no reason to disagree.

Later, Fulton remembered the events somewhat differently: "Governor Smith saw a great opportunity and a company was formed to build a city. . . . The attorney of the company informed us that the Mexican title was incomplete on account that special assent of the government had not been obtained by Power." By chance, Fulton spoke with a man at the General Land Office in Houston and learned that he was interested in acquiring Live Oak Peninsula. "I at once communicated with Governor Smith, and in fifteen minutes his nephew [Joseph F. Smith] with twelve hundred and eighty certificates was en route to Live Oak Point, and within four days the location was secured to Henry Smith. Six hours thereafter, the party from Houston rode ostentatiously to the surveyor's office in Aransas City, to find they had been defeated."

For a while, Aransas City prospered. In all, ninety-eight families owned property there. Gideon Jaques operated a tavern and public house; Benjamin Neal, Edward Fitzgerald, James Robinson, and Henry Smith hung out shingles and practiced law. Col. Henry L. Kinney, who would later found Corpus Christi, arrived at Aransas City in 1838, attracted by prospects of lucrative trade with Mexican Federalists. He leased all of Mustang Island from James Power and remained in possession of it until after 1850.

No less than seven men registered as Aransas City surveyors. They and others stayed busy, as did George Fulton, locating land certificates. Some were more like freebooters than any of the sea captains or soldiers of fortune.

Differences arose between James Power and Henry Smith, resulting from their confused financial arrangements as partners in the town project. To make matters worse, standing on his own gallery, James Power watched a new settlement grow on the far peninsula.

LAMAR

The rival town was a brain child of Power colonist James Byrne, who had big plans and good backing for his enterprise. Speculator Joseph Smith helped Byrne buy up land certificates. Wealthy friends in Cincinnati invested funds, enabling Byrne to acquire a 1,428-acre survey. But when he tried to take the land of some long-time Mexican settlers, Nicholas Fagan defended them against his old friend Byrne.

James Byrne named his town in honor of the President of the Republic of Texas, Mirabeau Buonaparte Lamar. And Byrne asked the president himself to lay out the town lots. Lamar numbered the streets that ran east and west and named the cross streets for trees. Two streets tracing the shoreline he called Water and Bay.

Anna Catherine Braun, "wife of Frederick Gunderman" (and apparently a liberated woman ahead of her time), bought the first lot from Byrne, and Frederick started making bricks.

Archibald McRae, who had already purchased a nearby lot from Power, was considerably relieved that Byrne recognized his title as valid. The house Archibald built was probably typical of many in the little bay towns. Since his carpentry skills had limited application on the Texas coast—a land with little hardwood—Archibald also learned to make shellcrete bricks.

This photograph may be the only remaining record of an intact shellcrete home at lamar. It was published in the Rockport Pilot.
—Courtesy of the *Rockport Pilot*, April 4, 1940

He used them to build his home, then plastered the walls of the two-story house for a smooth, elegant finish. He whitewashed the walls inside and out. Gentle breezes blew through seven spacious rooms that had high ceilings. Porches with large posts provided shade on the east and west sides; dormer windows in front looked out at the bay. In his loft walls, Archibald McRae crafted square holes to provide rests for rifles, should Indians attack. He built a kitchen for his wife Vincey, separate from the house. It had a fireplace with a deep hearth for cooking and a wide chimney above it.

The land sloped down to the beach, and Archibald planted salt cedars there. He built a wharf, too, for the small boat that was his only transportation.

Behind the house, northwest, lay a barren, sandy plain with a few bushes, a little mesquite, and much grass. Although Vincey had despaired of starting a garden, she learned that the soil was deceptively rich. It nourished every variety of fruit and vegetable, in such large amounts that the McRaes stored a surplus in the cellar beneath their house.

The bay provided oysters, crabs, and all kinds of fish. In winter, when bays and inland ponds were alive with geese, ducks, and whooping cranes, when the woods were full of deer and wild fowl, Archibald hunted. He cured his meat with sea salt collected from the flats.

As more settlers moved in, Karánkawas came to visit. With no idea of ownership, the natives thought nothing of taking horses and cattle for food. "They would descend without warning on the unprotected people," Vincey McRae said, "and no man could hunt, fish or cut a tree without peril to his scalp." All the men of Lamar kept their rifles beside them when they planted potatoes, when they went after the cows.

Any time the McRaes saw Karánkawas headed toward them across the broad plain, they hurried to their loft. Archibald McRae and his sons, John Hardy and Murdoch, stationed themselves at the portholes with guns ready. Although it hardly seemed proper, eighteen-year-old Susan stood there too. She was as true with a rifle as her father. Vincey and her other daughter, Sara, stood ready to supply home-molded bullets, powder, and wad as fast as they could.

For all their preparation, or perhaps because of it, the McRaes were never attacked. But Karánkawas would often appear, quite suddenly, in Vincey McRae's kitchen, demanding food. She quickly gave them sweet potatoes and other produce from her garden, and family legend says the Karánkawas called her a "heap good squaw." Once the Karánkawas presented Archibald McRae with a chief's bow and arrows.

By 1839 twenty families lived in Lamar, and James Byrne petitioned the Republic to move the customs house there. "The owners of the city of Aransas," he wrote in his application, "have made no effort to retain the custom house. Aransas has no more than twelve houses and thirty inhabitants. City of Lamar has twenty houses under construction, and the number of inhabitants more than double that of Aransas."

Aransas City leaders responded that vessels drawing seven feet of water couldn't come within three quarters of a mile of Lamar. Their town had an excellent harbor, sheltered anchorage, and seven feet of water within one hundred yards of shore.

In reviewing the case, President of the Republic of Texas Mirabeau B. Lamar favored the town he had laid out, the town that bore his name. The custom house moved to Lamar, and Aransas City began to decline, but Power's friends in Congress managed to get the office back by year's end.

James Byrne looked to other enterprises, including a salt works. Lamar marshlands flooded and drained periodically, leaving behind crusty deposits of sea salt. It was a precious commodity, so Byrne simply capitalized upon the natural process. He ran bay water into evaporation pits beside St. Charles Bay, near the Big Tree. When the salt was dry, he scooped it from the pits, broke it up and ground it, either coarse or fine, at a wind-powered mill.

Settlers from the United States continued to arrive regularly, needing supplies, and that gave Archibald McRae the idea for a new business. He purchased a part of the old Aránzasu fort and got its lumber across the strait to his front yard. There Archibald built his first large boat, the *Belle of Lamar*. That single-masted sloop carried him and his cargo to settlements all around the bays. It proved a blessing, too, when the family became more frightened than usual by a band of Indians; the McRaes all boarded the *Belle* and sailed to the comparative safety of Aransas City.

Archibald got his wares at John Linn's settlement, Linnville. Inland of the present Port Lavaca, Linnville was, at the time, the most important port south of Galveston. That ended abruptly on

August 14, 1840, when six hundred Comanches swept through. Archibald McRae was there to see the town's death.

Two years later, when Karánkawas stood in Vincey McRae's kitchen, they, too, were dressed in war costumes and had their bows strung. Vincey's heart almost stopped; she had never before seen them look so threatening. When she gave them the food they wanted, the Karánkawas went on their way. That night, though, they stole the *Belle* and sailed it across the strait to take part in a raid on Aransas City.

Seth Ballou established a steam ferry—the first in Power country—shuttling from Lamar to Aransas City. James Byrne built wharves and warehouses.

His goal was to make his town the prominent port south of Galveston. Although Indianola was growing on the south shore of Matagorda Bay, replacing Indian-ravaged Linnville, Byrne believed Lamar could be a strong rival. He decided to promote an island community as well.

Saint Joseph

San José Island guards all of Aransas. On its eastern side, Gulf waves roll to a smooth strip of sand. Behind that, dunes rise and then the land becomes flat once more. Much of the island's bay shore is so subject to inundation that it's difficult to imagine a town there. It's surprising to see that cattle prosper, even now, between dunes and the ragged, marshy shore.

The village was on William Little's survey, north of Lydia Ann Island. It was called Aransas at first, but later Saint Joseph. Most of the town's earliest inhabitants were "seafaring men"—that handy euphemism that generously includes adventurers from the Texian navy, privateers, and pirates from Lafitte's old gang. Which men were what is information often lost, blurred, or conveniently forgotten, but some family records are clear.

Young George Brundrett, a Scots orphan from the poorest class, came to America with the Peter Holinworth family, of England, in 1828. They settled in Michigan, and in 1835 George Brundrett married Peter Holinworth's daughter, Mary Hannah. The young couple came to the Texas coast in the 1840s. According to some sources, George worked as a machinist and boilermaker in Corpus Christi; others say he may have been a gunsmith.

In 1848 George bought a schooner to haul freight along the coast. He was sailing off Mud Island one day when the boom of the mainmast swung and hit him in the head, knocking him over the side. Maybe the blow killed him; maybe George drowned. No one ever knew for sure, as his body was never recovered. Some whispered of foul play. The crew denied all knowledge of money that was missing from the boat when it came to shore.

Hannah Brundrett remarried, moved to San José Island, and raised seven Brundrett children, plus another from her second marriage. When that husband died of pneumonia, Hannah married again and had two more children. Hannah Holinworth Brundrett Thompson Gaston had started an enduring Aransas line.

During the time Hannah lived on San José, James and Lydia Caroline Stephenson had a home there, too. On the morning following a terrific storm, James found Capt. Francis Mackenzie Smith on the beach. The young man appeared to be more dead than alive, but the Stephensons nursed him back to health. In the process, they learned that Frank Smith had run away from his Iowa farm home in 1837—when he was only twelve—to go to sea. Now he had lost his ship, but he won the Stephensons' daughter, Arminda Elizabeth, and married her in 1856.

But Frank Smith, like George Brundrett, would die at sea; another widow would raise children alone.

Still, seafarers and ranchers—Littles, Pauls, Plummers, Wellses, Collinsworths, and others—spread out along the island. Dr. Joseph Austin Seward provided medical services to the small but growing community, often assisted by his wife, Eliza.

Cedar Bayou was no barrier to him, nor to any of the settlers; most of the time a man could wade across its winding path without wetting his armpits, so San José and Matagorda seemed one land mass. People and cattle ranged the open land, back and forth between islands and to the mainland peninsulas.

And they learned what the Karánkawas had known: a well four feet deep anywhere on San José, even near the shoreline, reached a shallow fresh water table.

CRITICAL EPISODES
TEXAS RANGERS

As late as 1842, the war with Mexico had come to no clear end; border skirmishes persisted. Opportunistic thieves and Indians took advantage of those distractions to impose their own challenges on the new Republic of Texas.

Citizens desperately required protection, but the Republic could not afford a regular army. Instead, local communities recruited ranging companies of men on horseback to provide security. Over time, these rangers became the famed Texas Rangers—colorful, efficient, and deadly. They placed their confidence in a new weapon—Samuel Colt's revolving six-shot pistol.

Ewen Cameron, co-organizer of Power's Spy Company, seemed born to be a Ranger. He exuded a magnetism that few could ignore, and his bravery was beyond question. When the Mexican civil war between Federalists and Centralists flared up in 1838, Ewen Cameron and other Rangers joined in on the Federalist side. Mexican Centralists called them *Los Tejanos Diablos*, the Texas Devils, or *Los Tejanos Sanguinários*, the Bloodthirsty Texians.

Federalist Gen. Antonio Canales used San Patricio as a refuge and staging area. James Power and Philip Dimmitt (the former Goliad commander) gave him letters of introduction so that he could call on key Texians for assistance.

Then Federalists betrayed the Texians who had come to their aid. By secret agreement, they ended their differences with the Centralists, promising to "separate from, and abandon to their fate, the adventurous strangers at present among them." The Mexican government marked James Power, Ewen Cameron, and Phillip Dimmitt for special vengeance—when the opportunity arose.

One year later, a Mexican cavalry raided Dimmitt's trading post on the Nueces River, inland from the present city of Corpus Christi. They sent Dimmitt and eighteen of his workmen to Monterrey, where the men were put in irons. People in Power country rallied in support of Dimmitt, their admired revolutionary commander, but to no avail. Dimmitt wrote to his wife that he preferred "a Roman's death to the ignominy of perpetual imprisonment," then took a lethal dose of morphine to end his life.

In August the same troops pillaged Refugio homes and scattered the town archives to the winds. They took eight captives, including James Power, and sent them to Monterrey. But that time James Hewetson, Power's old partner who had lived in Mexico all along, used his political influence to free all the Texians.

THE INDIAN PROBLEM

Concurrent with threats from Mexico, Aransas settlers faced continuing Indian raids. President Sam Houston, however, was determined to defend the welfare and security of the native people of Texas, not destroy them. He named James Power his deputy to work out a treaty with the Lipans, local tribe of the widespread Apache nation.

Most settlers considered the Lipans cattle thieves, plunderers, murderers of traders. When Chief Cuelgas de Castro and his tribesmen arrived at Aransas City in January 1838, however, Power welcomed them with honor.

The Lipans wore full ceremonial dress and offered gifts according to tribal formality. Power responded in kind. Both men expressed friendship and the fervent hope of mutual understanding. When they signed the peace treaty and the Lipans departed, Power had good reason for guarded optimism.

The peace lasted less than two years. And, of course, it had involved only Lipans. During the time of Lipan peace, other tribes raided.

James Power got word that nearly 1,000 Comanches had assembled in Mexico and were heading into his country. Half the Comanches split off at the Rio Grande, but the rest continued to Refugio, then on toward Fagan's Settlement.

Nicholas Fagan was in his wagon with a small child when a riderless mule ran up and followed them. The old settler sensed at once that the rider had been killed, that the rumored Indians were near. He had little choice but to continue calmly with the child, and the Indians crossed the river ahead of him.

James Power's posse finally confronted the Comanches in a bloody battle. He defeated them, but at the cost of several colonist lives.

Late that year, Houston's term as president of the Republic ended and Lamar's began. In his inaugural address, Lamar abrogated Houston's lenient policy, declaring that all Indians should be expelled from Texas.

Congress cheered. It was clear that the new Europeans in Texas believed they could not achieve their manifest destiny while attempting to coexist with a culture so different from their own.

In order to appropriate land that was not theirs, in order to slaughter the natives, settlers adopted an age-old formula: They thought of their enemies as beasts. They found it comforting to believe that the people they exterminated were inferior, barely human. New Texians created stories of Indian ignorance, indigence, and cannibalism.

The days of innocent Fagan children sharing Karánkawa beer, the days of honoring an Indian girl in a Spanish carriage, were over. Battle lines were drawn.

POWER IN PRISON

Most thieves who ran rampant throughout this chaotic period could hardly be identified as coming from one group or another. Some were out-of-work mercenaries; some were Indians; some were resentful Mexicans. The majority seemed to have mixed, or shifting, allegiances.

On March 3, 1838, robbers accosted a businessman near Power's Copano warehouse. They carried off most of the tobacco stored there, and the man, under duress, went with them as far as the Nueces River. Word of it spread throughout the colony.

A few days later, Lt. Col. Antonio de los Santos and forty-five Mexican troops arrived at Live Oak Point. Power assumed they had come to trade, and as traders he welcomed them—but in the end he knew them as bandits.

They took everything of value from his store. They took what they wanted from his home. And then they took Power as their prisoner.

As the troops marched James Power away, he shouted to his wife Tomasa and to Walter Lambert: "Close the business; lock all the doors. Don't let any Mexicans in."

Power was hardly out of sight when another band of robbers appeared. Walter reached for a gun, but Tomasa stayed his hand. If he shot, she feared, the other marauders would murder her husband.

For three agonizing days the Mexicans terrorized Tomasa, the children, the neighbors. Walter bargained, at last persuading them to leave with twenty-two bales of tobacco. The thieves took cattle and oxen too—not a part of the negotiation.

Meanwhile, James Power paced in the Matamoros jail. Finally, influential friends arranged his parole, on condition that he not leave the city. Five long months later, the parole was broadened: Power might return to Live Oak Point so long as he promised to deliver himself to the Mexican government whenever they demanded it.

THE PASTRY WAR

Mexico's harassment of the Texas republic was interrupted by France's harassment of Mexico. That finally erupted in an armed dispute and Aransas City customs officers took part in it, almost on their home turf.

Because Mexico had never developed an effective number of citizen scientists and merchants, foreigners controlled most trade. They were continually irritated by Mexico's general disorder, and when riots damaged their shops, they filed claims in Mexican courts. Unable to collect on those petitions, the investors turned to their homelands for help.

France asked for a grand total of 600,000 pesos, but Mexico declined to pay. When the French responded by blockading Mexican ports, Mexico declared war. Some called it, derisively, "the Pastry War," since one of France's claims involved an incident in which drunken Mexican army officers had demolished a French pastry shop.

Mexican Centralists tried to bypass France's blockade by landing supplies all along the Texas coast, but the Republic declared that smuggling. Aransas City's Customs Service conducted a series of raids, culminating with the storming of a high ridge on the southeast shore of Corpus Christi Bay. Mexicans there scattered, leaving behind one hundred barrels of contraband flour. Aransas Customs officials confiscated it and gave the spot its enduring name, "Flour Bluff."

The Republic of Texas was naturally more lenient toward Mexican Federalists. When the French blockade kept them from receiving military supplies, Aransas City became the Federalists' port of choice. Legitimate trade with them—and smuggling—turned a fine profit for American entrepreneurs like Capt. John Clark, Col. Henry L. Kinney and Capt. John C. Pearse, who helped John Linn land contraband tobacco.

THE MIER EXPEDITION

At least five men of Power country—Ewen Cameron, John Cash, Henry Clark, Edward Linn, and Joseph Smith—participated in an ill-advised and tragic military expedition into Mexico. The fiasco was known for the town where its major action took place— Mier. When the mission failed, an original Power colonist, José Miguél Aldrete, helped the Texians interpret the terms of their capitulation.

President Santa Anna intended to execute the Texians, but American and British ministers protested. As a compromise, Santa Anna issued a decree that followed an old formula: Shoot one man in ten. The Texians' fate was decided by lottery—black beans and white in a handkerchief-covered jar.

Ewen Cameron pulled out a white bean. So did Joseph Smith and Edward Linn. John Cash drew black. "Well," he said, "they murdered my brother with Colonel Fannin and they are about to murder me."

After the executions were carried out, Ewen Cameron implored the officers to execute him and let the rest of his men go free. His wish was granted and a priest offered confession.

The Scotsman declined it, because he had "lived an upright life." He refused a blindfold, declaring that he would do as he had "often done before for the liberty of Texas, look death in the face without winking." Ewen Cameron threw his hat and blanket to the ground, opened the front of his shirt and gave the order himself. "Fire!"

Much later, when Joseph Smith was released, he returned to

Aransas and resumed a quieter battle—one involving deeds and documents which could gain him Power's *empresa*.

The Mexicans never made another purely military raid against the Republic of Texas, but men of the Texas Rangers marched to Mexico in another war before too long.

TO PLEDGE ALLEGIANCE

THE AMERICAN FLAG

In June 1845 San José Island sweltered beneath the summer sun. The bay lay flat as glass. The Gulf heaved only in lazy swells; no whitecaps relieved the sameness of waves that seemed little more than ripples. No wind filled sails or refreshed housewives in Saint Joseph homes. No cloud relieved the perfect blue of sky or gave one moment of shade to cattlemen on the range.

Agitation for the Republic of Texas to join the United States of America had reached fever pitch even before the weather turned warm. On March 1 both parties had signed a resolution agreeing to their union. Some loyal Texians saw great irony in that: Just nine years less one day earlier, they had declared independence—from Mexico then, but nonetheless, a hard-won freedom well worth preserving.

The tide of sentiment ran against these libertarians and on June 26 the Ninth Texian Congress consented to annexation. The President of Texas called out volunteer Texian militia to repel any Mexican troops attempting to invade Texas. And he invited the Executive of the United States to occupy the frontier with whatever troops were necessary for the defense of Texas.

When the voters of Refugio County turned out to choose their delegate to the annexation convention, they voted for Col. James Power. It was to be his last public office.

Power went to Austin for the convention when it met on July 4, 1845, and on that most appropriate day Texas adopted as its own the Independence Day of the United States.

American Army troops, under the command of Gen. Zachary

Taylor, sailed from New Orleans aboard the *Alabama*. They arrived at the Aransas pass early on the morning of July 26. Troops went ashore on San José Island, and a Lieutenant Chandler scrambled to the top of the highest dune. There he stabbed a pole into soft sand and unfurled—for the first time on Texas soil—the American flag.

No trumpets blared, no drums beat a stirring tattoo, no pipes trilled with joy, but a fifth flag flew over Aransas. No crowds were there to see it, no speeches were made, but everyone who later heard the news believed that flag would be Texas' last.

The ensigns of Spain, France, Mexico, and the Republic of Texas had fallen. With the twenty-seven-starred banner stuck firmly in the sand, Capt. W. S. Henry reported: "It floats over a rich acquisition, the most precious Uncle Sam has yet added to his crown." Soon the flag would add a twenty-eighth star, representing Texas.

Eight companies of the Third Infantry established temporary quarters on San José, although Zachary Taylor planned to remove his troops to the mainland almost at once. "The position will probably be Live Oak Point in Aransas Bay," he wrote. The site was under consideration as the principal rendezvous of the American Army of Occupation.

Troops of the Third Infantry sailed along Live Oak Peninsula to the spot where a rocky point projected into the bay, providing a good landing. Cavalry Commander Kirby Smith jumped war horses from the ship deck and swam them ashore. As the men disembarked, they saw a large oak tree about half a mile southeast. When they marched to it, they made camp in its shade. Between the oak and the rocky point, the town of Rockport would later grow.

But at that time there was only the tree, only a campsite, sheltering twenty-four-year old 2d Lt. Ulysses S. Grant and other young officers, yet untried. Robert E. Lee, William Sherman, Jeff Davis, Braxton Bragg, Philip Sheridan, Thomas Jackson (later called "Stonewall"), Joe Hooker, and Franklin Pierce would prove their worth in Mexico. Undoubtedly, many of them sailed through Aransas Bay on their way to launch a string of fateful events: aquisition of new western territory, establishment of a new principle for the control of slavery, the repeal of the Missouri Compromise, the formation of the Republican Party, the election of Abraham Lincoln to the presidency, the secession of the South. The tactics these young officers learned together in Mexico would affect the battles

GEN. ZACH. TAYLOR PITCHED HIS TENT UNDER THIS
LIVE OAK TREE DURING THE TEXAS-MEXICAN REVOLUTION,
MEASURING 100 FT. FROM TIP TO TIP.

The Famous Taylor Oak, near the present intersection of Rockport's Pearl and Bay streets, was Zachary Taylor's first mainland campsite as he began the Mexican Campaign. Postcard from Gordon Stanley collection. Photograph by W.D.L. Dye.

of the Civil War, when they commanded opposing sides. Their decisions then would mark the nation forever.

It was only for a moment that Aransas drew them—as it had drawn early explorers, supply ships for Spanish missions, settlers from Europe, and the colonists, patriots, and speculators favoring revolution. At Aransas, once more, the world turned.

James and Tomasa Power invited Gen. Zachary Taylor to dinner and included John Howland Wood on their guest list. In the course of the evening, Taylor talked about the rocky point, and Wood began to see that the spot offered strong possibilities as a port. The solid foundation could carry a rail line to deep water, and the location was much nearer the Gulf than Aransas City, Lamar, or Copano.

The time for that was not yet ripe. For the present, Wood simply negotiated with General Taylor and obtained a contract to furnish the troops with beef, transported by his fleet of carts and teamsters. Eventually, Wood earned a commission as lieutenant colonel in the Coast Guard. And as he secured his place as an Aransas cattleman, Wood developed his ideas concerning the rocky point.

Texas' annexation process continued unimpeded. On October 13 approximately 4,000 Texians voted for the state constitution drafted by chosen delegates including James Power. About 2,000 men opposed it.

A month later, the people of the state of Texas elected their first governor, Pinckney Henderson, and two United States senators, Sam Houston and Tom Rusk. Col. Henry Kinney was elected to the state senate from the Refugio district, including all of Aransas. On December 29 U.S. President James Polk signed the act making Texas a state. Two months later, February 19, 1846, the Stars and Stripes became the official banner of the land.

But the Lone Star still waved as well. In April, when Gen. Zachary Taylor marched south into disputed territory between the Nueces River and the Rio Grande, Texas Rangers marched with him.

By May, President Polk had accepted a hard fact: Mexico still considered Texas its province and was willing to fight to keep it. The United States officially declared war.

Although the battles were all fought far to the south, Aransas played an important part in military staging operations. Archibald McRae continued to work the bays with his *Belle*, providing the army with beef and other supplies. Aransas whooping cranes became a valuable commodity: eggs, fifty cents; skins, two dollars.

The American force faced a Mexican army four times its own size, a courageous army strong in engineering and artillery. American victories were a triumph of skill over numbers, and the war wound down.

Jonas Casterline, infantry, received his release from duty in November 1846, having served out his five years. Jonas had been a carpenter in Seneca, New York, but once he had seen Aransas he decided to make it his home. So began another Aransas lineage.

In July 1848 Mexico and the United States ratified the Treaty of Hidalgo: Mexico would relinquish all claim to Texas and recognize the Rio Grande as the state's southern boundary. The United States would purchase from Mexico, for $15 million, lands now known as California, New Mexico, Arizona, Utah, Nevada, Wyoming, and part of Colorado. The war accomplished even more than U. S. politicians had hoped for.

Aransas remained an entity unclearly defined. When Texas joined the Union, the "precinct" of Refugio had been assumed to cover the same land as Power's original *empresa*—ten littoral leagues between the Nueces and the Coleto-Guadalupe, together with the barrier island areas that fell within the extended lateral lines. As Goliad and San Patricio and Bee counties were delineated, Refugio/Aransas began to take on its present shape.

The people of Lamar and Saint Joseph complained that the town of Refugio was too far to go to vote or settle minor court issues. By public demand, Refugio County (population 127) was divided into Election and Justice of the Peace Precincts in 1848. James Byrne served as judge of the Lamar Precinct and James Wells had the same job on the island.

Transportation issues intrigued a former Tennessee congressman, Pryor Lea. He envisioned a great western port at Lamar, connected by rail lines to Goliad and even on to San Antonio. With James Byrne and others as his partners, Lea even gave Lamar a new name, Treport, but it didn't last.

The men first planned a turnpike road with bridges and causeways and obtained the right to charge tolls for using it. By 1856 the resulting Aransas Road Company had rights to construct and maintain a road or rail line—and to improve navigation at the Aransas pass.

The company was also empowered to tackle the problem of the Corpus Christi mud flats just inside the pass, a sticking spot from days of earliest Spanish and French exploration. To solve the blockage, they received permission to close every tidewater channel between Aransas and Corpus Christi bays, except the main ship channel. Even Cedar Bayou, many miles north, could be closed to improve tidal flow at the Aransas pass.

Nothing much came of Lea's endeavor, except to spur the growth of Lamar—and to plant ideas of rail lines, ship channels, and a new harbor site in the minds of a few influential men.

CULTURE AT THE END OF THE ROAD

Viktor Bracht, a well-educated German physician, immigrated to Aransas in 1845 and described Texas as "the Italy of America." He was most likely thinking of geography and climate rather than of the arts. Viktor was twenty-six years old, a man fluent in many languages and given to rhetoric.

Nothing seemed that fancy to the plain people of the Lamar peninsula, but their work produced the beginning of intellectual and artistic achievement in Aransas.

It began simply enough: Murdoch McRae inherited his father's thriving coastal trade business, including stops at the growing community on San José Island. Because he transported so much lumber, it naturally followed that Murdoch became a building contractor as well.

Henry Ludwig Kroeger, recently arrived from Germany, lived in a rawhide house in the McRae backyard while he built the hotel that he would operate for years. At about the same time, Anton Strauch, a Prussian, purchased a farm on Salt Creek, about twelve miles from town. There he grew and processed tobacco. The cigars Strauch didn't smoke himself, he sold to others.

Captain and Mrs. James Byrne donated two lots—1,088 feet of Aransas Bay frontage, 223 feet deep—for a Catholic church. They hired New Orleans architect M. D'Alsure to design it. Slaves, including Seth Ballou's Moses, did much of the work, but Murdoch McRae and the whole town pitched in, without pay, wherever they were needed. When the chapel was completed, the citizens christened it *Stella Maris*, Star of the Sea.

In 1855 Jane Gregory O'Connor arrived. She was a young widow and a school teacher accompanied by her baby son, her mother, and her sisters. She opened a school, the Lamar Academy. As its success grew, boarding students came from Refugio, Victoria, and Copano. Some families moved to Lamar to allow their children an education there.

Jane O'Connor's sister, Caroline "Carrie" Gregory Byrne, taught music on a fine, big rosewood piano in the family home. Lydia Ann Wells contributed her talent, high culture, and refinement. Ultimately, her relative, Edward Dingle Hastings, of Laurel, Delaware, taught music and dancing at Lamar and raised a family

Viktor and Sybil Shaefer Bracht with their infant son Roland Prosper. Bracht wrote a book describing Aransas for fellow Germans still in the homeland. He later founded a Rockport dynasty. Published in Texas in 1848, Viktor Bracht.

A handmade frame of yarn-wrapped cardboard embellishes this photograph of Jane Gregory O'Connor, founder of the Lamar Academy.
—Courtesy of the Caroline Williams Collection

The cactus plants in the foreground of this photo show Stella Maris Chapel as it may have appeared to the early settlers who built it. The renovated building has been moved to a new setting.
—Courtesy of the Peter Johnson family Collection

there. For newcomers in Aransas, his music brought the comforting sounds of home, breeding, and gentility.

In 1860 Murdoch McRae went to do some cabinetry at the Heardsdale compound on the north side of Copano Creek. There he met Mary Ann and invited her to a barbecue at Lamar. Mary Ann accepted.

She later wrote: "He took me out sailing in his little boat in the bay. While sailing around he took my hand in his and says 'Will you be mine?' I trembled and said nothing. He says, 'If you do not say yes I will throw you overboard.' I was only sixteen and you know how foolish girls are at sweet sixteen. He was a man of twenty-nine. Mr. McRae says, 'Do not be uneasy. You are mine and I will take good care of you.'"

They married at Heardsdale on August 13, 1860, and Mary Ann moved to a vital, successful Lamar community of 120 people in forty-four houses. But she had no home of her own. Mary Ann moved into the house that Murdoch shared with his mother, the very house that Archibald had built for Vincey when the land was wild.

John Jacob Thommen, his wife Verna, and their five children lived some miles inland from the spot where Salt Creek empties into the northwest reaches of St. Charles Bay.

Late one October afternoon, the Thommen daughters, Eve and Sarah, were driving the milk cows home. It was the best time of the year, still warm, but past the summer's searing heat. October in Aransas seemed gentle.

John Jacob was watching his girls when he saw the Indians. He tried to warn them by blowing his Alpine horn, but it was too late. The Comanches scooped Eve and Sarah up onto their horses. Jacob got his gun and drew a bead on one Indian, but Verna begged him not to shoot. The Indians might kill the girls, she said—or even massacre the entire family.

Helpless, John Jacob and his wife watched as the Comanches rode swiftly away. Eve was struggling. Sarah's flaming red hair was blowing in the wind.

The Indians traveled all night, while Eve tried again and again to escape. Disgusted with her, one Comanche finally threw the girl to the ground. The others rode past and stabbed her with their spears. One cut off her hair but did not scalp her. They tied Sarah firmly to her mount before they finally rode away, leaving Eve unconscious on the ground. Her brother found her shaken and bloody the next day.

The chief loved Sarah's red hair and ordered his braves to take care of the girl. She rode with them all the way to San Saba, more than 190 miles northwest. She was there for several weeks, until the U.S. government traded an Indian boy, a few blankets, and some other articles in return for her release.

Despite the incursions of Comanches and others, many Lamar residents continued to have pleasant dealings with the Karánkawas who had always inhabited the coast. On particularly cold winter nights, the people of Lamar opened their front doors so that Karánkawas could creep in for a warm sleep. The visitors were always gone when the families got up in the morning, but they came back later in the day, bringing baskets of oysters in thanks.

Across the channel on Live Oak Point, Tomasa Portilla Power had a soft heart for the sad beggars and never sent one away hungry. In time, she and James Power took in two orphaned Karánkawa children, Domingo and Mary Amaro.

Mary had "a certain native wildness," Philip Power later wrote. Often, when the family looked for her, she could be found hiding high in the branches of a tree.

The last time that people of Power country had any dealings with unacculturated Karánkawas was in 1851, when the dispersed tribe regrouped. From a base at their old camping ground near the mouth of the Guadalupe, they began stealing from the white families. The Karánkawas became such a nuisance that a posse led by John Hynes determined to rid the community of them once and for all.

The Karánkawas put up a stiff fight and wounded some members of the posse. But when Hynes' men killed several Karánkawas and wounded more, the Indians fled the battlefield in disarray. They moved south along Padre Island and into Mexico. For a while, authorities on both sides of the Rio Grande hunted them like animals. And then, everyone believed, the Karánkawas were gone.

It was one more step in the great American genocide which had begun with Chief Pontiac in 1763. The technologically superior whites believed in their hearts that they had every right to kill off "red vermin." And they very nearly did.

But Domingo and Mary Amaro remained safe in the heart of Power country. Mary made friends among the Plummer and Welder families, and on January 19, 1859, she became the bride of Charles Frederick Pathoff, a citizen of Copano.

SMITH V. POWER

In 1848 Viktor Bracht had written: "Looking at the weaknesses in the character of a Texan, one finds an inclination in many of them to employ their native shrewdness in dealing with others, and to use this cunning in every possible way to cheat in business dealings. Furthermore, his stolid repose and self-possession, when thoughtlessly insulted, too easily give way to that passionate and vehement excitement which often bring about unexpected bloodshed. It is dangerous to provoke a Southerner."

Bracht also noted that "Mr. Power does not seem to have gained any considerable wealth from his undertaking as empresario." Power's situation became particularly difficult when his land titles were called into dispute.

Joseph Smith had been making careful inquiry into the nature of Power's land titles and surveys since the early 1840s. He came to the conclusion that Power held no valid title to the coastal lands he purchased outright. Such littoral leagues were reserved by the national colonization law of 1824, and Power had failed to obtain the explicit consent of the Mexican Federal government as was required for him to hold those lands. Smith argued that Power had title only to land he acquired as *empresário*.

Then Smith went even further, concluding that almost every Mexican grant in the area was void. None, he said, had a definite legal description or provable corner markers.

These two opinions effectively dispossessed every family who

Nephew of Provisional Governor Henry Smith, Joseph F. Smith was a land speculator who used his legal expertise to acquire colonial titles. Published in Texas Coastal Bend, *Alpha Kennedy Wood.*

had settled in Power's colony. If the grants were no longer valid, it logically followed—according to Smith's position—that all of Power country was public domain. Anyone with a legitimate land certificate could locate a claim there.

Smith's action was a signal to honest and unscrupulous land speculators alike: They could locate their certificates on Copano and Aransas bay lands without considering the *empresário's* rights.

Power responded by filing suits of his own, but he had learned to be a realist. Power accepted the fact that he might lose Live Oak Point, and he was well aware that Aransas City was unlikely to become prominent. He began to develop a town on land to which he had a more secure claim—Copano, site of the old port settlement.

Power started work on a home of his own, a two-story shell-crete house on Power Point. Walter Lambert built a two-story emporium at Copano; Henry Norton built another. He had a lumber shed between the store and the bay, and his wharf extended from that. There was another wharf in front of Moses Simpson's story-and-a-half home. The town had a school and a post office—twelve buildings in all, but no church.

Power, the visionary who had seen promise in the wild Texas coast, had not lost his ability to sense the temper of the times, to grasp new opportunity. He even gave some consideration to a railroad, and it was he who started the town of Saluria on Matagorda Island.

By that time, Power's original colonists finally understood the seriousness of not having proper surveys. Infuriated by Joseph

Smith's legal shenanigans, they held mass meetings and adopted a resolution: They would "if necessary . . . oppose and repel by force of arms any such persons as are disposed to make locations and surveys on our old titled land."

Smith argued that "Power acted upon the philosophy that the end justified the means, and made heads of families of single men, and made suckling children single men. To such heads of families he issued titles."

But then Smith went too far, adding a postscript to his declaration: "I had forgotten the best part of those who seek relief, and that is, that about one-half of these colonists were traitors in the revolution and many fought against us."

The Supreme Court struck the name of Joseph F. Smith from its role of practicing attorneys, for behavior unbefitting the legal profession. Still, the final result of Smith's lawsuits was to declare void all titles which Power and Hewetson, or their transferors, had purchased directly from the state of *Coahuila y Texas*, without the consent of the Supreme Executive. That vindicated the titles of the individual colonists, but everything Power owned outright was still in jeopardy.

POWER'S PASSING

Throughout the 1850s new generations of the old families came into their own. Influential newcomers arrived. Fresh hands grasped the reins of county government, and novel ideas became the norm. Not everyone liked that; some longed for the old ways, the better ways. They were realists though: People died. Things changed.

Nicholas Fagan passed peacefully away at his ranch in 1851. Perhaps that event prepared the people of Aransas, if anything could, for the loss of their *empresário*.

In August of 1852 James Power lay dying. He was still on Live Oak Point; the new house at Copano was incomplete. Power was sixty-three years old, worn down by years of hard work, worry, and disillusionment. As the sad news of his serious illness reached even the most remote ranches, James Byrne and Walter Lambert witnessed Power's will.

The *empresário* called loved ones to his bedside—wife Tomasa, son James, friend Byrne, and a priest. Death came quietly on August 15. Tomasa buried her husband in a brick vault on the grounds of their home, well back from the water and shaded by live oaks.

Many eulogies honored James Power, the founding father of Aransas, leader under three flags. One such statement sums up both his life and his times: Power was "the last of a breed of statesmen, men sometimes not well educated, often unmannerly and unpolished, but men dedicated to causes, willing to sacrifice their lives, their liberty and fortunes."

None of this deterred the grinding due process of law. When the courts finally decided the *Power v. Smith* suits in favor of Smith, James Power's heirs lost their home at Live Oak Point. A grieving Tomasa moved with her children to the Copano house, suddenly less grand than her dream of it—and so empty without her husband there.

THE LIGHT

Even as Power buoyed his last days by building Copano and Saluria, other towns competed for the growing number of new citizens.

Joseph Smith had been wanting to build at Black Point, near the mouth of the Aransas River, since before his capture during the Mier Expedition. Subsequently, he and his investors developed St. Mary's, between Black Point and Mission Bay. The histories of the two towns blend into one, but in both cases Smith needed Maj. John Howland Wood to accomplish his goals.

Wood had served at San Jacinto and remained in the Texas Army as quartermaster at Victoria. Since the government's sad financial state required him to accept livestock and cattle as partial payment, he gradually accumulated a decent herd. And when his military scrip provided land for the animals, the astute and practical-minded Wood became a rancher.

Shortly after his marriage to Nancy Anna Clark (sister of his army buddies Henry, John, and William Clark), Wood made a trip to New York to receive the first of a series of inheritances. He returned to Texas with wooden kegs full of gold coins and the capacity to establish a Texas dynasty.

Joseph Smith, heavily in debt from his long litigation with Power, appealed to Wood to be an investor in Copano development. Wood hesitated, wary of the shallow reefs in Copano Bay, concerned about the distance to the Gulf. He would have preferred the rocky point of Live Oak Peninsula. But he had agreed, long before, to help Smith develop a townsite, and he felt obligated to honor that promise.

He even built a home of his own during the town's development. It still stands—a grand house of Florida longleaf pine, not shellcrete, and three stories tall, plus the full attic. It was a gracious home for entertaining ladies in fine dresses, accustomed to the elegance of Eastern seaboard living. Wood's home, as much as anything, marked the ways in which Power's country was changing.

Lack of water was a problem at Black Point and St. Mary's, as it had always been at *El Cópano*. Judge Charles Arden Russell wrote that "the only supply they had was rainwater cisterns, some below ground, but mostly cypress tanks above ground. There wasn't a single well or spring anywhere near. The water in abundance at about fifteen or twenty feet was as salty as concentrated brine."

Developers were confident they could overcome the problem, and pretentious homes sprang up at an impressive rate. A Masonic Lodge was founded, demonstrating that Power country had truly spread beyond its Irish Catholic roots. As three-masted schooners brought in Florida longleaf pine, the port became, almost immediately, the largest lumber and building materials center in western Texas. A good road ran to Beeville and a better one to Corpus Christi.

John Howland Wood, from a prestigious East Coast lineage, brought wealth and business acumen to Aransas County and the surrounding area. Published in Texas Coastal Bend, Alpha Kennedy Wood.

To the north of Aransas, Germans were entering Texas

through Lavaca Bay, although Power had tried to interest them in Copano instead. Viktor Bracht's book dissolved any illusion that new port towns were always fine ones. He wrote in 1848:

"The great mortality during the past year among the immigrants of the Verein encamped on the Lavaca Bay was inevitable, and was predicted by everyone acquainted with conditions. There was apprehension concerning the danger of crowding so many people from a northern country, during the heat of summer, on a flat coast with numerous bayous and swamps of stagnant water, and barren of trees and shrubs or good drinking water.

"This danger was immeasurably increased by the absolutely filthy living in musty mud huts. . . by a voluntary rather than enforced idleness of mind, in a word, by complete demoralizations of the mass of the immigrants, together with inexperienced and inadequate medical aid. . . .

"It is simply quite impossible, for anyone who has not seen it with his own eyes, to form any conception of the carelessness with which the stupid German farmers expose their bare heads, even after repeated warnings, to the rays of the noonday sun in the twenty-ninth latitude. The sun kills most of the careless newcomers who will not listen to friendly advice."

With the rapid growth rate at Aransas, the need for a well-marked pass became more and more essential. For years, the best landmark for ships nearing the pass was a "very conspicuous" large frame warehouse on San José, probably Capt. Peter Johnson's.

By that time, Captain Johnson had won a U.S. government contract to carry the mails from Indianola to Corpus Christi and all the ports in between. He developed a route for passengers as well as mail, moved his headquarters to Saint Joseph from farther north and built a large, two-story station house. Upstairs, where his family quarters were, Captain Peter offered lodging for passengers; down below, he maintained a commissary and warehouse.

The investment required by such an enterprise was large: Captain Johsnon had two stage coaches, three stage station houses, a ferry boat, relays of mule teams, the sloop *Belleport,* and the schooner *Fairy.*

His route began with a boat from Indianola out to Saluria, the thriving customhouse at the northern tip of Matagorda Island. Stagecoaches ran the barren bay shore from Saluria south to Cedar Bayou. They crossed by ferry to Vinson's Slough, where passengers could spend the night at another stage station. The next day travelers could continue by coach along the San José beach to the town of Saint Joseph's. From the island, boats carried passengers and supplies to Aransas City, Lamar, the far western Copano shore settlements, and Corpus Christi.

Obviously, Captain Johnson couldn't handle all this alone. His assistant in the enterprise was Capt. Theodore "Charlie" Johnson, no relative, but close enough in affection to be one.

As early as 1847, the U.S. government located at Aransas three of its first buoys to mark Gulf passages. But establishing a light there was, indeed, something else.

The points of San José and Mustang islands alternately grew and diminished, changing the location of the pass. Constant erosion also showed that neither island's end could provide sound footing for a lighthouse. That issue was resolved when the United States government acquired Harbor Island, just inside the pass.

After some discussion of various lighthouse designs, government officials decided to build a brick tower. The ship carrying those bricks went aground just as had so many others negotiating the Aransas bar, but work finally began late in 1855.

The work was miserable. Day laborers toiled on marshy land, cold and damp, or hot and humid. By slow but steady progress, they completed the tower in February 1857. At its base, the brick walls were four feet thick. Sixty-nine wedge-shaped steps circled upward to the light.

For over a century, the principal lighthouse illuminant had been an oil lamp with a circular wick, protected by a glass chimney. That was coupled with silvered copper reflectors set in a parabolic curve, but the beam had to be rotated for visibility from any direction. Then a revolving light, operated by clockwork, was developed.

The Aransas light was different; it was state-of-the-art, utilizing the work of French physicist Agustin Fresnel. He had devised a means of reflecting, refracting, and magnifying light with a curtain of prisms around a bull's-eye lens. More reflecting prisms above and below created a lens somewhat like a glass beehive, refracting light in a narrow, horizontal beam. The Fresnel lens purchased for Aransas was three feet tall with an eighteen-inch diameter and two concentric wicks. Installed fifty-five feet above the tower base, sixty feet above mean sea level, it had the power of 490 to 520 candles.

With the beam shining across Saint Joseph, citizens knew they had entered the modern age. And ships could see the Aransas light from eighteen miles out in the Gulf.

Elmason Lewis, the first Aransas lighthouse keeper, had been on the payroll since October 30, 1856. The laborers who built the lighthouse constructed his residence too.

CIVIL WAR

All Sorts and Conditions of Men

The new light shining at the Aransas pass, installed through Federal action, illuminated more than a waterway; it brought new attention to the entire area. Newcomers spread across the Aransas bay system, creating an increasingly diverse population. For better or worse, Aransas gained both the assets and the liabilities of the United States.

The old settlers replaced their primitive houses with substantial homes. Men who had learned to plant watermelon and squash now learned about cotton. And their herds of livestock grew. By 1861 Aransas/Refugio ranchers looked after almost 130,000 head of cattle, 6,000 horses, and more than 2,000 head of sheep.

Though most families were large, they often needed help to tend these extensive and varied crops, these herds of animals. Some men bought slaves. No one in Aransas had many—not by the standards of the Deep South, where a person had to own at least fifteen slaves to be considered a slaveholder.

The rationale for slavery seems ridiculous today. We understand that even the most paternalistic ownership warps not only the slave, but the slaveholder as well. We can hardly imagine a world like that. We can see it, though, through the eyes of its residents.

Mary Ann Heard McRae didn't think of herself as owning a slave. She and Murdoch just had Aunt Phoebe, who had cared for Mary Ann since she was a small child in Alabama. Phoebe was part of the family—a second mother—and Mary Ann depended on her.

Back in Alabama, Mary Ann's father, Humphrey Heard, had been overseer of one hundred slaves on his father's plantation.

121

Mary Ann, like others of her day, did not think of them as slaves, just as "the Negroes." She remembered that "the oldest Negro woman on the farm had to take care of all the little children while their mothers were at work in the fields. They would come home at noon and night. The ones with little babies would [also] come at ten and three o'clock."

Mary Ann saw herself as a benefactor of these workers. She wrote: "After I was large enough and my father became owner of slaves himself, I would go around and see if the little ones were in need of any clothes. If so, [I] would get all my old dresses and make little dresses out of them for the poor little Negroes and also make quilts for the old ones so that my father did not have to buy but one blanket a piece for each Negro."

In Texas, the largest slaveholders that Mary Ann knew about were planters and ranchers along the San Antonio and Guadalupe rivers. Many of these had come from other areas, bringing their slaves with them—a Dr. Wellington owned eighteen—but most old families had at least a few slaves too. Henry and Joseph Smith did. Tom O'Connor owned fourteen; John Wood had ten and James Wells, five. James Power, Jr., and John Fagan each had one. John's sister Fannie Fagan, orphaned at twenty-one, bought a woman named Hannah from her mother's estate.

Throughout the South, slaveholders were concerned about runaways. They organized and maintained volunteer patrols to watch for slaves whose owners had not given them permission to be abroad. By 1860 even the areas around Lamar, Salt Creek, and St. Mary's took advantage of such spotters regularly.

Throughout the South, women managing large plantations alone found the patrols a blessing: They provided a means for "chastizing obstreperous bucks." However those good Christian ladies rationalized it, the thought now appalls.

By 1861 Aransas/Refugio County had a population of 279 blacks, with their own viewpoints, memories, and traditions. Will Duke's father was an Arab, while his mother, Emily Jones, was African. When she died young, Will was raised by an aunt who brought him to Texas and made a home in the Blackjacks. In time,

Will married Caroline Ennels, who worked for the Johnsons at Lamar, where they provided her with some education.

Ellen Heard got a last name from the family that transferred her from Alabama to Indianola, then settled on Live Oak Peninsula. There she married Grant Richardson, also of Alabama, who had taken his name from the Richardson family at Indianola. The Huffs of Rockport got their name from Ransom Francis Huff, who lived on Matagorda Island before the Civil War, but then moved to Hynes Bay for safety.

In France, a master named his slave Thornton. Later, in Virginia, that slave got a last name from another master, Williams. Thornton Williams became a horse trader, and in his travels he met and married a half-blooded Indian named Fanny. She and her full-blooded Indian brother, Mankin, had been taken in a raid. Fanny would go out for days at a time, collecting roots and plants; people praised her as a fine "medicine squaw."

Butler Williams, son of Thornton and Fanny, married a girl of the Weathers family. Theirs was a family tree including tall Watusi tribesmen and a light-skinned woman.

All the men kept the name of their slave owners. Their families grew up and scattered, but when anyone met another with his name and both spoke of the San Antonio River, they knew that they were kin.

Viktor Bracht reported of the Texas "Negroes" that "almost without exception they are well treated, and, aside from the thought of perpetual slavery, their lot is undoubtedly far better than that of many servants and most factory workers of Europe."

That one exception, the thought of perpetual slavery, was more than some people could easily shrug off. One of these was George Fulton, who had moved back North as early as 1846. By then he was married to Harriet, daughter of his friend and benefactor Henry Smith, and had three children.

Jane O'Connor had not yet established her Academy, and the Fultons wanted a good education for their brood. That was the reason they gave for moving North, but Fulton knew well the view of slavery held by his new relatives on the rich plantation lands of Brazoria County. He was acquainted with men who dealt in slave trade, yet earned positions of respect in their communities.

In 1850 Texas enacted a new law prohibiting the sale of slaves. However, immigrants were still allowed to bring in any slaves they already owned, and the numbers of slaves grew by leaps and bounds.

The population of Aransas/Refugio was 288, with 19 slaves. Five years later, the area registered 148 slaves. By 1856 that number had risen to 185, with a white population of 959. And in 1860, Aransas/Refugio boasted 1,600 residents owning 200 slaves. The white population was five and one-half times what it had been just ten years before—and they owned ten times as many slaves.

THE SIXTH FLAG

While Texas, like the rest of the South, was building an economy based on agriculture, the North was becoming ever more industrialized. Interests there required broad economic policies as much as the South depended upon states' rights and a worker population.

Many slaveholders believed in their hearts that slavery was wrong, but they were caught in an economic trap. Northerners—who may not have considered blacks their equals any more than Southerners did—were involved in a wide range of businesses that did not depend on slavery. As the two economic positions polarized, slavery became an emotional issue that both sides used in rallying support.

When Abraham Lincoln was elected president of the United States in 1860, Southern planters sensed disaster. Secession from the Union seemed the only answer.

On the Texas coast, St. Mary's was a hotbed of secessionism. Joseph F. Smith and Youngs Coleman led the pack. The Hobby brothers, Alfred Marmaduke and Edwin, were loudly in favor of leaving the Union. The Woods, like the Heard brothers of Copano Creek, agreed with them. So did Pryor Lea, now in Goliad, and many others.

The men of Lamar discussed secession everywhere: in Richard Jordan's stores, outside *Stella Maris*, at the post office. James Byrne and James Wells were against it, and they knew that Tom O'Connor and Thomas Welder shared their sentiments. So did Governor Sam Houston.

Secessionists petitioned Governor Houston to call a state convention to discuss the issue, but he refused. When he was finally forced to give in, a sort of compromise allowed each legislative district to elect delegates for a convention. Houston saw to it that their action would be clean-cut and decisive. He drew a line for Texas, as surely as Ben Milam had done in the early days of revolt against Mexico: Sam Houston mandated that unless the referendum defeated the secession ordinance, Texas would leave the Union on March 2, 1861—the twenty-fifth anniversary of her declaration of independence from Mexico.

Alfred Marmaduke Hobby and Pryor Lea represented the district of Goliad, Refugio, and San Patricio counties. They voted in favor of secession, speaking not only for its strong advocates in towns like St. Mary's, Copano, and Saluria, but for moderate settlements like Lamar, Live Oak Peninsula, and San José Island as well.

That convention, however, took a step no other southern state offered—it gave the citizens of Texas the right to vote directly upon the secession question. On February 23, 1861, only a small percentage of Aransas/Refugio men turned out to vote, but those who did chose secession—125 for, 70 against.

By then, delegates from Texas had already joined South Carolina, Mississippi, Florida, Alabama, Georgia, and Louisiana to form the Confederate States of America with Jeff Davis as president. By then, Rebels had engaged Yankees at Fort Sumter. Soon, Virginia, North Carolina, Tennessee, and Arkansas joined the Confederacy.

On March 2 Texas officially seceded from the Union. But on March 16, when state officers were to take the oath of allegiance to the Confederacy, Governor Houston refused to raise his hand. His office was declared vacant and Lieutenant Governor William T. Clark was appointed in his place. A sixth flag flew over Texas.

The men of Aransas/Refugio who had fought against secession were gracious losers; they did nothing to retard Confederate efforts. Some, like Thomas O'Connor, saw their sons serve active duty for the Confederacy.

Capt. Edward Upton, a Northerner and staunch Unionist, accepted the situation; as the old patrol system evolved into home guard units, he led the Lamar Guards. Murdoch McRae and Richard Taylor Byrne were among those who served under him, maintaining coastal defense and keeping lines of communication open to Mexico. Each home guard member furnished his own weapon and ammunition. To support the war, Murdoch McRae also exchanged $10,000 in gold for Confederate currency.

WAR IN THE GULF

In November 1861 the governor of Massachusetts reminded the United States government that it had "virtually bought" Texas after the war with Mexico; the state was, he believed, the property of the Union. Because of this special status, the Massachusetts governor suggested, Texas should be reduced to submission ahead of any other southern state.

The United States did not put all of that governor's suggestions into effect, but it did take an active interest in Texas and blocked the passes from the Gulf into the bay systems. Since the Confederacy held the barrier islands, however, bay navigation continued unmolested. Everyone realized, of course, that if Federals took the islands, even Texas' land routes would be within striking distance of enemy forces.

Two days after Christmas, the Texas Legislature created thirty-three brigade districts. The Twenty-ninth Brigade included Aransas/Refugio, San Patricio, Nueces, Goliad, Bee, Live Oak, Karnes, McMullen, LaSalle, and Dimmitt counties: Gen. Hamilton P. Bee was its commander.

When the Legislature adjourned, Alfred Marmaduke Hobby resigned his seat in the House to raise an infantry battalion for General Bee. Second Lieutenant Charles F. Bailey, who would later have a role in the development of Rockport, served as chief of staff and quartermaster.

Benjamin F. Neal headed a heavy artillery company headquartered at Camp Semmes on the northeastern tip of Mustang Island, facing the Aransas pass. John and George Brundrett, Jr., were transferred there from Saluria. The camp was little more than a cluster of sand embankments, with artillery mounted on wooden platforms.

Across from it, on San José, Neal established a depot, or storage area, near Lafitte's old pirate fort.

He established another garrison on Shell Bank Island, guarding the narrow channel winding from Aransas Bay toward Corpus Christi. Other men of Neal's battery were stationed at Corpus Christi.

At Pass Cavallo, the other main entry to the Aransas bay system, ill-clad and poorly-armed Texans camped near the lighthouse on the Gulf side of Matagorda Island. The remains of Fort Washington, one of Zachary Taylor's unloading posts, served as their base. In January 1862 U.S. gunboats attacked and captured the schooner *McNeill*, taking prisoners.

Before the end of the month, the first units of a Federal blockading squadron appeared off the Aransas pass. Lt. Cmdr. J. W. Kittredge was aboard the flagship *Arthur* as his Marines on the *Afton* captured Benjamin Neal's patrol sloop there. The Marines burned the Mercer and Clubb homes on Mustang Island, then moved on to San José and burned the Aransas Wharf there.

No cannon batteries protected Aransas shores; otherwise, this painting of the Battle of Corpus Christi depicts the threat of federal ships that attacked unprotected San José and Lamar.

—Courtesy of Corpus Christi Public Library

But Confederates had a strong base to the north. On Matagorda Island, Maj. Caleb G. Forshey had set up his command in the old pilot station's pine buildings, facing Pass Cavallo. He reported: "The rumor which you may have received of the landing of 1,200 (or any other force) in the region of Aransas for purposes of occupation is false." Forshey also made clear that the three-masted schooner that went down had taken up her position with the bark *Arthur*, not the *Afton*. The *Arthur*, with a fourteen-foot draft, was unable to cross the bars into the bays.

That Yankee schooner carried a reinforcement of some 200 men, but strong north winds delayed her outside the pass. Forshey pressed to take advantage of "the last opportunity to save the pass and the bays and interior navigation."

He wrote that Captain Neal's companies had moved twenty miles inland and "render no service to the inhabitants [of San José Island] in their attempt to save their property and escape. They are leaving as best they can, leaving all their stock and their homes at the mercy of the enemy."

Peter Johnson, Jr. was only four years old, but he wrote later of a life on San José that "became unbearable and extremely dangerous." Ships shelled the little Saint Joseph settlement from a distance of three miles, he remembered. After one particularly fierce bombardment, almost the entire population decided to abandon their island homes and go to the mainland for safety.

Peter watched as his papa, Capt. Peter Johnson, hitched the mules, Susan and Sally, to the stagecoaches. The child carried what he could as his sister Louisa and brother William hurried with their parents to load up all the family's portable possessions.

Some families had already abandoned their homes, their sheep, their cows; they had fled in different directions. Hannah Gaston stayed. The widow of George Brundett, estranged from her third husband, refused to bundle up her children and leave.

The Johnsons headed north along the island, urging the mules almost beyond capacity. At Cedar Bayou, Peter watched as everything was unloaded from the coaches, then loaded onto the ferry boat. He watched his papa tie the ferry to one of the sailing vessels. All the family got aboard the sailboat and towed the ferry behind them into St. Charles Bay.

The Johnson family and other refugees had hardly reached

safety when fifty Marines landed near their abandoned homes and "wreaked havoc," according to young Peter. "They burned many of the buildings, and what they did not burn they demolished. The great station-house of Captain Peter Johnson disappeared in this work of destruction." The Marines remained on San José for several days.

Major Forshey wrote that "the conduct of Captain Neal and of his Lieutenant Maltby have been made the subject of very severe animadversion by the citizens of Aransas and vicinity. They are charged with cowardice and indecorum to an extent scandalous to the public service."

Forshey added that Capt. Peter Johnson, worried that his mail-route boat would be captured, would make only one more trip from Aransas to Corpus Christi. Forshey also requested permission to dismantle—rather than blow up—the Pass Cavallo lighthouse and save the materials for future use.

The Union ship *Afton* continued to lie in wait off the pass at Aransas, seizing vessels laden with merchandise for the Confederacy. On February 21 she captured a vessel carrying medical supplies. Confederate Captain Neal almost turned the tables on the *Afton*, but failed to save the medicine so needed by the Confederacy.

Five days later, Forshey complained: "I had received orders to mount guns at Aransas pass some time since, but had not yet received the guns." Although the *Arthur* had possession of the pass at Aransas, Union troops had not yet planted guns on shore. But Capt. Peter Johnson's mail run had ceased operation and "the line of trade, from fear of capture, has entirely ceased."

Forshey also reminded his superiors that he had asked for authority and orders to destroy the lighthouse at Aransas.

Hannah Gaston had remained in her Saint Joseph home, but it hardly seemed to be hers. Federal officers commandeered the house for their quarters. The Yankees were friendly enough: They held her daughters, Sarah and Capitola, on their knees; they entertained the girls and gave them candy. But everyone knew the Yankees were destroying the ranches and killing the livestock.

Hannah, who was about forty-five at the time, rode north along San José, then waded neck deep across the Cedar Bayou channel to warn the Hawes family and the men in the Confederate installation that Yankees were coming.

The Federal gunboats moved north through Aransas Bay. To keep Murdoch McRae's *Belle of Lamar* out of Federal hands, Confederates set fire to her sails and then sank her.

Federals arrived off Lamar in February 1862. They shelled boats at anchor, tore up Byrne's wharves, raided his warehouses, and destroyed the salt works. As Yankees departed with all the supplies they could carry, they fired a few last shells into town, setting all the frame and log buildings ablaze.

In their fine old shellcrete home, the McRaes were as safe as anyone could be. The house survived, along with the other shellcrete structures. The Peter Johnson family lived in one of them—a warehouse owned by James Byrne—until the end of the war. Most experienced salt-makers were away in that war, slowing restoration of the much needed salt works.

On April 22 Federal commander Kittredge adopted one of Lafitte's old tricks: He used two launches to enter the bay through Cedar Bayou, passed Lamar and ran the length of Aransas Bay— more than twenty miles—to attack three blockade runners near the Shell Bank fort. Kittredge put his prisoners in irons and looked toward the Aransas pass. He saw no reason why he could not sail the captured sloops out into the Gulf, "under the very noses of the Confederates."

Word reached Confederate forces in time, and stopped Kittredge short of his goal. Abandoning his prizes, Kittredge ordered his men back into their launches, hoping to escape through Blind Bayou. There the launches ran aground and the Yankees abandoned them too. As they ran across the dunes, Confederates pursued them. Before they could be caught, all the Yankees managed to wade out into the Gulf, where launches from the *Arthur* waited for them.

HOMEFRONT

By the end of May, all of Texas was under martial law. The Confederacy took over everything—the Lamar salt works, the postal service, the flow of supplies. Murdoch McRae, who had seen so much turmoil in his bay, could be content with home guard duty no longer: He enlisted for service in the Confederate Army.

But there was his family to consider. Murdoch's mother, Vincey McRae, staunch pioneer, refused to leave her Lamar home. Other old-timers felt the same, so Capt. James Byrne, at age sixty-eight, promised to look after them.

But Murdoch's young wife Mary Ann was pregnant, and Mary Emma, their first child, was only a year old. Murdoch couldn't leave them on vulnerable Lamar Peninsula. Instead, he took his family to the Heards in Mission Valley. After a sad goodbye, he rode to Goliad. There, on May 14, 1862, he enlisted in Major Hobby's Battalion. "So," Mary Ann wrote later, "we had to give up our good man to go to war. I thought I would never see my good old man anymore."

By October James Byrne lay dying. In the delirium of his last hours, Byrne implored his granddaughter to burn ten or twelve barrels of his papers so that Federal troops would not get them. She complied, and so were lost invaluable records of an old speculator and contemporary of *empresário* Power.

Ann Willie Byrne Vineyard reported that her grandfather's last words were: "I have seen the brightest side of life; I have seen its dark side, too. . . . I have no hope . . . left; but the thought of a clean record and a clear conscience. Altogether, life is scarcely worth the living."

Up at St. Mary's, Joseph Elton Plummer, Jr., Charles Pathoff, and Domingo Amaro had enlisted too. One nineteen-year-old Karánkawa girl felt very alone. Mary Amaro Pathoff was losing both her brother and her husband to the war—and like Mary Ann Heard McRae, she was pregnant.

Mary Pathoff's friends, the Plummers, lived some distance from the settlement at Copano, unprotected by any men. They decided to move to St. Mary's for the duration of the war, and Mary "went partners" with them on the purchase of a house there.

But the town was almost unrecognizable. Federal blockade had halted the lucrative maritime commerce that nurtured St. Mary's and other towns like it. Only a few privateers braved the web of Federal vessels and reached the town. Once-crowded wharves and warehouses stood silent. All the long rows of Mexican ox-carts that had lined the waterfront were gone to serve the Confederacy.

Now there were only county court officials who took inventories, made reports, and tried to supply soldiers' families with the necessities of life. At first, they provided rations based on the number of mouths to feed: Mrs. Lambert, with two children, received three bushels of corn each month and twenty-five pounds of beef per week; Mrs. Pathoff, with no child yet, received one bushel of corn and ten pounds of beef.

But Refugio had never grown much corn, and a three-year drought had greatly reduced the ordinary crop. Corn had to be hauled in, or carried on barges. And sometimes those barges were captured.

Occasionally, an enterprising speculator was able to exchange salt for flour, but rarely did anyone succeed in getting enough Confederate money to pay for a sack. When someone did, family and friends enjoyed Sunday morning biscuits for a while. Mostly, soldiers' families made do with bread from the yellow meal parceled out by county courts.

Then the commodities distribution process became so onerous that the courts decided to give families money instead. Mrs. Lambert received thirty-six dollars; Mrs. Pathoff, twelve; Mrs. Brundrett, with five children, seventy-two dollars. As money depreciated, the courts were forced to change back to rations again.

Although there was very little bread, there was always plenty of beef—Aransas/Refugio was cattle country. For a while, John Wood furnished meat on contract, as some others did, and there was a packery at Mission Lake. By the end of the war, though, court officials just went out on the prairies and slaughtered the cattle they needed for the families, carefully recording the brands so they could pay the owners later.

The Texas Military Board provided tax relief to promote private industry producing war materiel. Business opportunities flourished, but illicit practices—counterfeiting, illegal contracts, and price fixing—plagued the system.

Since cloth was in short supply, the State Penitentiary turned into a manufacturing plant. It provided soldiers' families with short-hair wool, not the most desirable for weaving cloth. Some manufactured goods were shipped in from Brownsville, so those who could afford it bought French and English calicos. But "the generality of mankind," Lyman Russell wrote, "didn't have money enough to pay for a shoestring."

It was as though they had stepped back in time and become primitive again. But people found that they had lost the old skills. Lyman's father figured out how to make a loom complete with shuttles, but not the sley and harness.

He found someone who lived where cane was abundant and still knew how to make a sley—the movable frame, or batten, needed to carry the weaver's reed in a loom. After Mr. Russell bought or bartered for one or two, women spun cotton and made it into fishline thread to serve as heddels—a set of parallel doubled cords—for the harness. The completed harness guided warp threads to the batten, alternately raising and depressing the threads of the warp.

Lyman Russell later wrote that "the two Negro women, with my mother, could card and spin the woof and warp pretty fast; and after sizing it and reeling it, and putting the warp into the loom, it fell my lot to do the weaving. I wove something like a thousand yards of homespun during this time, getting so expert that I could turn out ten or twelve yards a day."

Pecan and oak bark dyed the cloth in shades of tan. Blue came from wild indigo plants. The women or children went to low, moist or marshy areas, seeking the knee-high weed. Even babies could spot it in early spring, when drooping sprays of bonnet-shaped flowers, soft yellow, adorned the branches.

The women gathered wagon loads of indigo, then packed it in whiskey barrels and let it steep a few days. When they removed the weed and drew off the water, indigo dye lay in a cake on the bottom of the barrel, half an inch to an inch thick.

Yellow dye came from copperas and a beautiful green resulted from mixing the copperas with indigo dye. The spectrum was limited, but it would do.

Like the St. Mary's residents, Mary Ann McRae learned that spinning "had to come back to me again." Waiting out the war in Mission Valley, she dreamed of the easier years of her childhood. Then Mary Ann had "thought it very hard" that her father expected her to make cloth even though he had slaves to work. She had complained and Humphrey Heard had regularly said, "Daughter, if you never have it to do you will [not] know how to have it done. Also, work never did kill anyone yet. . . . All play and no work made Jack go without a shirt."

In the difficult days of the Civil War, Mary Ann came to acknowledge that "This was a true saying."

And she found that spinning "was not quite so awkward to me as when a child. I spun and wove cloth to clothe myself and child and sent my soldier a suit and had one ready for him when he returned from the war. In the meantime my father gave me a fine Negro woman to help me work and we made a good living all through the war."

Franz Josef Frandolig, who had provided Zachary Taylor with horses during the Mexican War, now responded to a new need. He delivered cotton to Bagdad, a large town that had sprung up, almost overnight, on the shore south of the Rio Grande. The cotton brought one dollar per pound in cartwheel silver *pesos*, or traders could exchange the cotton for arms, munitions, coffee, food, and imported goods.

Hundreds of steam and sailing ships moved along the river, crowding the port; twenty restaurants and an equal number of bars and saloons catered to a rough crowd. Businessmen, speculators, drifters, and prostitutes all sought the benefits of war that Bagdad offered. A priest described the place as "a veritable Babel, a Babylon, a whirlpool of business, pleasure and sin."

Franz Josef functioned equally well in two worlds—raucous Bagdad and serene Aransas.

Throughout the Confederacy, salt, like cotton, became a medium of exchange. It was easily traded for Mexican *pesos* and always in short supply. Special legislative action increased the production from domestic salt works like James Byrne's and Murdoch McRae's at Lamar. On January 11, 1862, the Legislature had also incorporated the Aransas Salt Works Company, near the present town of Rockport. Pryor Lea was commissioner of the operation, since it would utilize his Aransas Road Company.

Mrs. Thomas Clubb, an ingenious and energetic woman who had been burned out of her Mustang Island home, supported herself by manufacturing salt on the mainland. She earned the equivalent of six dollars in *pesos* for twelve bushels of salt.

Communications continued to be a major problem. "Finally," Philip Power wrote later, "the manpower [at Copano] was reduced to Judge [Walter] Lambert and myself. . . . I was about fifteen years old at the time, but a good, strong, sturdy lad . . . thrilled with the idea of carrying the mails and the large salary incident to the position."

Philip rode horseback, circling the beach from Lamar to Copano. There he received mail that had come in by ship or overland from Refugio. He carried the mail sacks on his shoulders as he continued the circuit to Mission Bay where he kept a skiff. Philip rowed across the pass, then walked on with his sacks, down the beach to St. Mary's. After he delivered the mail, Philip retraced his entire route, carrying letters the other direction.

Perhaps one of the letters that passed through his hands was from teen-aged soldier Aransas Prescott, who had been born on San José:

"Dear Father and Mother: I take the pleasure of writing you a few lines to let you know that I am well. . . . There is fifteen men and one Lieutenant here on Padre Island and the rest on Mustang Island."

Prescott complained that an infantry company near the channel had only one twelve-pounder gun—a gun firing twelve-pound projectiles. His group was camped two miles from them, anticipating the Yankees' landing. "We are on the lookout all the time. There is only four men on guard every day. We come on every fourth day and night, and that is not very hard on us.

"As we expected, we have good water here; we only have to dig two and one-half feet to get water." They sunk flour barrels in the water holes to keep them from filling with sand.

The boys had fun too: "We go swimming every evening in the ocean . . . about 200 yards from the shore." They caught fish until they were tired of eating them. "There is no grass here but this tall salt grass," Prescott continued. "We got a load of corn yesterday for the first time since we have been here. I have got a small box of nice shells assorted for Mary if I can get them home.

"My love to all. . . . P. S. Please send me some stamps."

Harriet Smith Fulton, daughter of the staunch secessionist and former Provisional Governor of Texas, Henry Smith, waited out the war with her Unionist husband, George Fulton. Safe in Covington, Kentucky, Harriet thought often of Texas. When her husband George was away on business, Harriet wrote to him: "Suddenly I heard the bugle at the barracks. What a thrill it sent through me; it reverted me back years ago, when I was a thoroughly happy child [in Brazoria, Texas], surrounded by dear friends, father, mother, sisters, brothers, and many others whom I dearly loved. Where are they now? Echo answers, 'Where are they?' I felt, oh, so sad."

Battles in the Bays

July 1862. When the Federal fleet sailed up to Lamar again, three Confederate vessels and a barge were in port: the *Belle Italia* carried corn and bacon; the *Monte Cristo* was loaded with powder and supplies; the *Reindeer* bore fifty-two bales of cotton; the barge had a cargo of corn. Yankee Lieutenant Commander Kittredge captured it all. His landing party found another 300 bales of cotton in storage: Kittredge seized those, too, then destroyed the warehouses.

He ordered his ships on to Copano, and they anchored there while the residents fled into the brush. After a while, the Federals moved on to St. Mary's.

The town's residents—women, children, old or disabled men, a few wounded soldiers home on furlough—had heard of Federal raids all up and down the coast. Although they had expected to see Yankee ships some day, the arrival still came as a surprise.

Clara Lemore saw them from her home on the bluff overlooking the bay. The nine-year-old felt half an orphan, with her papa a prisoner of the Yankees. Later Clara recalled:

"It was about noon, or perhaps a little after noon, when two Federal sailing vessels unexpectedly made their appearance in the bay in front of the town. Before the people were aware of their presence, the town was alive with Union soldiers. . . . They did not shell the town, but landed quietly and without resistance. The wounded soldiers went to the brush to avoid capture."

When the Union captain and some others came to Clara's house, Mrs. Lemore "was much alarmed and appealed to the captain for protection." She told him that her husband was a prisoner of war—and that Mr. Lemore was a Free Mason.

All Masons take an oath to protect the wife, widow, orphan, mother, sister, or daughter of any other Mason. The Yankee captain, in accordance with that oath, instructed his men not to disturb the Lemore family.

The raiders did not leave St. Mary's until they had searched through every house. They did it "in an orderly manner," Clara recalled, "and did not harm the inhabitants. The soldiers took chickens and some provisions, but did not steal much else."

Yankees destroyed two large warehouses at the wharf; other soldiers raided out in the country. They went south of St. Mary's a mile or so, approaching Major Wood's home at Black Point. The fences around the Wood place were palisades—logs set upright in the ground—and in the enclosure some cattle moved about.

From a distance, the raiders saw those palisades as soldiers and hurried back to St. Mary's. They informed their captain that a large body of men was coming up from Black Point to attack them.

One of the Federals climbed to the schoolhouse roof to take observations. He seemed such a good target that a wounded Confederate soldier chanced a shot from his hiding place in the brush. The Federal, out of range and not hurt, dropped off the building and came running to the business district, sounding the alarm.

"Whether the Federals feared an attack or whether they had finished their business at St. Mary's, I do not know," Clara said later, "but shortly afterwards, they took to their boats and left the place and never again returned."

The Union troops sailed back to Lamar, loaded their confiscated cotton, and transported it to the Aransas pass. There Union Lt. Cmdr. J. W. Kittredge saw that he had more cotton than he could safely ship. He stored part of it in the nearly-ruined remnants of a Saint Joseph warehouse.

All passes between Aransas Bay and Corpus Christi Bay were

blocked, and Aransas Bay belonged to the Federals. Kittredge armed his Lamar prizes, the *Reindeer* and the *Belle Italia*. He had two sailing vessels—the bark *Arthur* and the yacht *Corypheus*—long since fitted out as men-of-war. He also had the gunboat/steamer *Sachem*. Kittredge's next goal was Corpus Christi.

Confederates had sunk pilings in the passes. It took Kittredge's troops a while to remove the obstacles, but they did it. And then the ships penetrated Corpus Christi Bay.

The captain of a Southern schooner, *Breaker*, saw the Federals coming and tried to outrun them. When that failed, he ran his ship aground on a reef near the entrance to Nueces Bay and set fire to it. His crew intended to leave a bag of powder aboard to blow the ship up, but when they reached shore, they discovered that they had brought the powder with them and left brown sugar on the ship instead.

Yankees put out the fire and added *Breaker* to their fleet. The next day they chased the *Hannah* south along the bay and set fire to her. Then the Yankees were free to bombard Corpus Christi, but they gave women, children, and other noncombatants two days to get out of town.

General Bee had put Maj. Alfred Hobby in command of all military units along the bays. One of Hobby's first actions was to request organization of one company entirely of Mexicans. Otherwise, he wrote, "orders have to be repeated in both languages." Hobby knew the men were good soldiers; he wanted to use them in the most efficient way possible.

August 16, 1862. The Battle of Corpus Christi began at dawn and Maj. Alfred Hobby's men battled the Yankees all that Saturday. Although both sides declared a truce for the Sabbath, another Confederate ship fell into Yankee hands that day.

On Monday, Kittredge resumed his bombardment; Tuesday he landed a cannon and forty men on the north beach. Major Hobby and his men repulsed them with two pieces of heavy artillery.

When the Union fleet withdrew, both sides claimed a glorious victory. Kittredge, who had fired a total of 452 shells at Hobby's shore batteries, made no further demonstration against Corpus Christi, but he did capture the English ship *Water Witch* at the

Aransas pass. Its cargo of gunpowder and supplies was valued at $10,000.

Four weeks later, when Kittredge was exploring at Flour Bluff, Hobby's men lured him into a trap and captured him. That early in the conflict, the rules of gentlemen-at-war prevailed. Hobby released Kittredge on his own parole, and the Union commander promised to return home.

Throughout the fall and winter of 1862, rumors persisted that the Federals would utilize Aransas bays as part of a grand plan to invade all of Texas from the sea. Since Pass Cavallo gave access not only to Aransas, but to Indianola, even more directly, and to points north, improvements to its fortifications were vital.

On a rise facing the pass, Maj. Caleb G. Forshey and Pryor Lea directed the labor of 500 slaves. They built an impressive earthwork—a real fort—and the Major named it *Esperanza*, Fort Hope.

The largest gun mounted on a Texas garrison wall during the war was there, a Columbiad that could hurl ten-inch solid shot, weighing 128 pounds, an amazing 2,000 yards. There was another cannon just as large, equipped to pivot. And eight twenty-four-pound smoothbore cannons stood on crude protective walls of heavy upright timbers.

A wide web of temporary fortifications, scattered among the sand dunes, further protected Fort Esperanza. Heavy rifle pits, their palisades dotted with openings for the guns, extended south along the beach for a full mile. Across the channel, on Matagorda Peninsula, Decros' Battery furnished additional protection.

A twenty-four-pound cannon was mounted on earthworks at the inland tip of Matagorda Island, but Forshey ordered that the town of Saluria be burned and the lighthouse on the Gulf shore blown up. The order further stated that cattle on the island should be driven to the mainland, if possible.

By early 1863, Col. Alfred Marmaduke Hobby and the Eighth Infantry regiment were responsible for the defense of the entire area between Indianola and Corpus Christi, including the outlying islands. Hobby established a permanent garrison on Shell Bank. At the south end of San José, he stationed the company commanded by his brother Capt. Edwin Hobby. He based Capt. B. F. Neal's heavy artillery company on Mustang.

When Neal received orders to destroy the Aransas lighthouse, Confederate sympathizers buried the lens. Neal's soldiers used dynamite to try to destroy the tower, but only damaged it.

April 30, 1863. Union forces captured Capt. Peter Johnson's *Fairy* in Matagorda Bay.

May 3, 1863. Officers and twenty-eight men of Capt. Edwin Hobby's command, unsheltered from rain and short of provisions, were determined to hold San José Island until they found an opportunity to attack the enemy. When three Federal launches arrived, containing forty soldiers, the Confederates had their chance.

They captured one launch, five men, six new Sharps rifles, five cartridge boxes and one ammunition chest. Another launch, 300 yards from shore, also surrendered, but then opened fire. Hobby's response resulted in a number of enemy deaths, but his Confederates suffered no casualties. Captain Neal summed up the battle as "quite a brilliant little victory."

Captain Hobby also retrieved ten bales of captured cotton and carefully concealed them on the shore of San José, awaiting transportation.

Col. Alfred Hobby ordered the Sharps shooters repaired and turned over to his brother's company: "They are greatly in need of guns," he explained, "having sixty-four men and only forty guns."

Rumors ran wild regarding Federal plans for a major attack. Gen. John Bankhead Magruder, now in command, believed that enemy naval forces would attack Aransas Bay and move inland from St. Mary's to San Antonio. He said the city should stand ready to move all military property—and all civilian shops and machinery—to Palestine, 250 miles northeast.

Reasoning that "Saluria must be defended, otherwise Galveston will be turned," Magruder was prepared to "give up, in case of necessity, the Rio Grande and the coast as far as Saluria, the entrance to Lavaca." He gathered his troops in the Coastal Bend and even withdrew defenses from the islands to better fortify the mainland. Magruder suggested only Quaker guns—dummies made of wood—in the dunes at the Aransas pass.

October 26, 1863. Maj. Gen. Nathaniel T. Banks sailed from New Orleans with a Federal army of 7,500 men on thirteen transports and three gun boats. They arrived not at the Coastal Bend, but at Brownsville. After taking the ill-prepared and poorly defended town, the Federal troops moved methodically north.

November 16, 1863. Banks and his men arrived at the Aransas pass, and the small Confederate garrison yielded to superior force. The men were captured, taken to New Orleans and held prisoner until the end of the war. Joseph E. Plummer, of Copano Bay, was among them.

Banks then focused on Corpus Christi, and Hobby ordered all noncombatants to leave the city. Most went to a refugee camp in a grove three miles west of town.

At least two citizens, however, did not. One was Rosalie Hart, who as a little girl had lost her sister to heat stroke sailing from Ireland in 1833 and her father to cholera on the shore of Copano. Rosalie Hart had grown up through the Revolution, and was by this time a married lady, Mrs. Priour, with Corpus Christi as her home. From her own kitchen, she and her husband fed Confederate cavalrymen throughout the day.

A terrific bombardment, lasting several hours, damaged many houses. Confederate batteries returned fire but were no match for the long-range Yankee naval guns. Colonel Hobby realized he could not prevail against the larger Federal force and surrendered Corpus Christi at the end of one long day of fighting.

After the battle, Confederate General Bee reported: "It is essential to keep the State troops . . . on the outer edge of the settlements until, at least, the stock can be driven in, and to prevent depredations by the guerillas. . . . I shall virtually abandon this place [Corpus Christi] tomorrow. There is nothing for the cavalry horses to eat, and, from the latest developments of the enemy, he will either march up Saint Joseph's Island and attack Saluria, or he will land at Lamar, and cross over to Indianola, thus cutting off Fort Esperanza."

In the area of the King Ranch, state troops requested that stock owners drive their animals, especially the horses, east of the Nueces. Those troops also understood that "under no circumstances" should "Negro" men be left behind; like the horses, they were too valuable. If owners showed no disposition to move their

"Negroes," the troops had explicit orders to "take forcible possession of them, or, in the last alternative, shoot them, for they will become willing or unwilling soldiers against us."

Some Federals tramped up San José Island while two of their large transports crossed Aransas Bay. A smaller ship landed cavalry at Live Oak Point, but found no settlements on the peninsula. The land troops crossed Cedar Bayou and moved north along Matagorda Island.

November 29, 1863. In a morning attack 2,800 Federals approached Fort Esperanza from the rear. Although 500 Confederates repulsed all attacks, the commanding officer decided to evacuate the fort and withdraw his men to the mainland. It was a serious loss.

December 17, 1863. Federals captured 110 Confederate artillerymen on Mustang Island and took them to New Orleans. Five days later, Confederates patrolling from Fort Esperanza got involved in a heavy skirmish at Cedar Bayou and lost one man. Then Union forces held all of Aransas.

General Magruder ordered Hobby's regiment to Caney, but some of the troops "expressed a determination not to come east." One Confederate commander wrote: "Some sixty men . . . deserted their colors this morning, taking with them their arms. One company will await their arrival at Wharton and the other at Elliott's Ferry. You will instruct the commanding officers of companies to arrest the progress of these deserters . . . and bring them, with their hands bound, to these headquarters. You will instruct the commanding officers of companies to shoot them down to a man, should they resist or refuse to surrender, or attempt to make their escape after being captured."

One entire cavalry regiment—700 men—joined the rebellion, intending to head west and home. How it came to be, then, that by year's end the Eighth Regiment was at Galveston, is not fully understood. Wartime reports were often sketchy, some resolved issues left unexplained. It is clear that Richard Byrne was at Galveston and that Murdoch McRae, assigned to the Galveston Observatory Signal Corps, interpreted messages from Federal gunboats hovering off the coast.

December 23, 1863. Federal troops moved from Saluria to the mainland, occupied Indianola and Port Lavaca, then moved northeast to bombard Caney. By mid-January they abandoned the Matagorda peninsula, but not before tearing down every building at Pass Cavallo. They did the same at San José and Mustang islands.

CAMELS

During the last days of 1863, a Confederate colonel outlined an elaborate plan to regain Texas ports, beginning at the Rio Grande. He applied for and received permission to use an innovative means of transportation—camels.

The exotic beasts had been Jefferson Davis' inspiration ten years earlier, during the Mexican War. Davis had insisted that camels could most effectively transport army supplies across the "deserts" of Texas. When three shipments of them arrived at Indianola, townspeople from as far away as Refugio had traveled to see the novelty.

Arab and African handlers drove the camel herds to a station especially provided for them at Camp Verde—west of San Antonio—but the hooves of heavily-laden camels were ill-suited for the rough terrain. When the camels became footsore and useless, the Army left them to roam at will.

Over the years, the herd increased and parts of it wandered to Aransas, multiplying further. Some handlers, wanderers too, came to intermarry with Aransas slave families.

Now pressed into Confederate duty, the camels were sent to the Guadalupe for corn, but two died on the trip. A report read: "They can live best on grass, and it is not certain they will live on corn."

Horses hated the camels' scent and became unmanageable any time they were near. Oxen feared them. In the end, the camels proved of no use to the military, or to anyone else in Texas. Some were sold to circuses, others to a Frenchman who got so disgusted that he turned the unfortunate beasts loose to fend for themselves. The ranging camels then became Aransas' misfortune. They broke down fences; they ate and trampled crops. A provoked mother camel attacked a young boy near Hynes Bay.

Philip Power, whose duty it was to haul women and the community wash from Copano to Melon Creek each week, had his own problems with the camels. He later wrote: "We were en route to the creek, with the wagon piled with dirty clothes and empty barrels, and the women seated on top of the bundles of clothes. . . . I was prodding along a yoke of stubborn oxen. Suddenly and unexpectedly some camels appeared out of the brush and frightened the oxen, which ran away with the wagon. The women were spilled and the clothes and barrels were scattered all over the ground. . . . The women were as scared as the oxen, as a camel was something unusual in the vicinity. When the washing was done and we started back to the village, I could not get the oxen to return over the same route."

The last camels at Lamar were driven off from Barrel Tree Bend on March 20, 1868, and sold to a man who put them in a pasture with his mules. The next morning he found some of his mules draped all along the barbed wire fence; the rest had spread over the surrounding country.

During the next few years, hunting parties systematically tracked down and killed all the camels in Aransas.

The End

While the struggle for the Rio Grande Valley raged on, Union ships again assailed Lamar. Captain Upton's Lamar Home Guard fired at them, and the Federals responded with cannon shot, but no one in town was hurt. On February 11, 1864, seventy-five Yankees raided the salt works and tore down some warehouses and wharves. They removed all the lumber they could carry, loaded it on a large scow, then appropriated a blockade runner filled with cotton.

The commander turned his men loose to raid, and they entered almost every house, taking what they wanted. Some Lamar residents recognized men they knew—turncoats from Corpus Christi, Bee County, St. Mary's.

Henrietta Little wrote: "We were badly frightened, although they were polite to us and we were to them. Before the war we had a sack of coffee in the house, but the war lasted so long it gave out, and we could get neither coffee nor tea. We did not care for ourselves, but we felt sorry for our poor mother. There was no flour either. We had to eat cornbread, which we did not relish. We had no lamp oil. We had a sardine can in which we put melted grease, with a rag sticking up in one corner and that was all the light we had which indeed was very poor."

Captain Upton sent James Wells to talk with the Federal officers, playing the role of an inoffensive citizen, listening to the enemies boast. Wells did not like the stories those Yankees told: that all the citizens of Corpus Christi had gone over to the invaders; that a Texas regiment, enlisted in Corpus Christi, was stationed on Mustang Island; that Union General Banks had 25,000 men heading toward Galveston, where they would join an even larger force. The Yankees bragged that Texas would be overrun by spring.

The Federal ships sailed into Copano Bay and again harassed the towns of Copano and St. Mary's. On February 24 the Union commander of troops in the Matagorda Bay region extended conditional amnesty to all residents of the middle coast of Texas.

Ardent Confederates accused Upton and Wells of disloyalty for their fraternization with the enemy. They had Upton removed from his command; they confined both Upton and Wells at Gonzales for the remainder of the war. Wells' health failed in prison.

But the information Upton and Wells had passed on allowed Confederate generals to plan moves countering the Yankee onslaught. Men of Aransas/Refugio arrived at Louisiana battle lines just in time to keep Texas free from a massive ground invasion.

By the beginning of 1865, the Refugio County court was having great difficulty finding anyone to haul breadstuffs from the Colorado and Brazos rivers. George Brundrett, Jr., of Colonel Hobby's regiment, who saw it a good opportunity to check on his family, volunteered for the job. The Commissioners Court ordered Brundrett's commander to detail him to delivery service.

Meanwhile, Murdoch McRae had been named boatman for the schooner *William*, a three-masted ship working the channel between Galveston and Bolivar Point. Its primary function was to deliver supplies to families of soldiers and bring back plantation corn for the army.

By February 1865, Murdoch began to bleed from the lungs and

the army physician said he was suffering from exposure. Murdoch was incapacitated for two months and on April 8, still unfit for duty, he was furloughed.

But since Murdoch had not yet left the fort on April 9, he was the first man to read signals from a New Orleans dispatch boat: At Appomattox, Confederate Gen. Robert E. Lee had surrendered to Union Gen. Ulysses S. Grant.

AFTERMATH

Col. Alfred Marmaduke Hobby's regiment received orders to muster out of service May 22, 1865. Murdoch McRae went immediately to Mission Valley where Mary Ann, daughter Mary Emma, and the new baby Josephine awaited him. The reunited family remained briefly with the Heards, then returned to Lamar.

Vincey McRae greeted them with a surprise both happy and sad. Her daughter Sarah had died in 1863, followed by Sarah's husband George Little, just two years later. They left a son, Hally. Vincey had been taking care of the boy, but now he would be Murdoch's responsibility, his stepson. Hally was the only son that Murdoch would ever have.

Mary Ann's former slave Aunt Phoebe had accompanied her to Lamar from Mission Valley. Phoebe's daughter Louise and Louise's children came too; they all took up residence in a little house behind the McRae home. Then, on June 19, 1865, Union Maj. Gen. Gordon Granger stepped onto a platform on Galveston Island and read the Emancipation Proclamation. Abraham Lincoln had first issued it two and a half years earlier, but Granger's reading was the first time Texas slaves heard officially that they were free.

Murdoch's Confederate money was worthless and his *Belle of Lamar* lay at the bottom of the bay. As soon as he felt healthy again, Murdoch accepted the post of captain of the *William*, the same supply boat he had sailed near the end of the war.

When one of the Ballous returned to Lamar, he told a friend that he had gone off to war a carefree sixteen-year-old boy and he came home a saddened man.

Capt. Peter Johnson never resumed his island transport business, but remained at Lamar. He traded his last boats for the schooner *Frances*, then sold it to Capt. Charlie Johnson. Peter farmed a little, traded a few cattle and some salt, held public office from time to time. Charlie, on the *Frances*, worked the coast as his mentor/father-in-law had done before.

The Union detachment that had taken possession of Lamar remained there for several months after Lee's surrender.

At the far reaches of Copano Bay, James Power, Jr., who had been wounded in service, was home and serving as postmaster.

Mary Amaro Pathoff learned that her husband Charles had been killed in the war. She had a son by then, young Tom, named for her father, and when the Plummers moved back to their Copano home, Mary stayed on at St. Mary's.

She never wed again, never had another child. Her half-breed son remained single all his life. Eventually Mary and Tom moved to Beeville and there Mary died. The last full-blooded Karánkawa is buried beneath a simple marker in Beeville's Catholic cemetery.

A small community formed in the Blackjacks, made up of freed slaves. The genealogy of their former owners explains their surnames. A white couple, John and Sarah Huff, gave their slaves freedom, land, and a house in 1863, when they first heard the Emancipation Proclamation. Their son Ransom Francis Huff married Kate Jane Tucker, daughter of Mary Frances Duke. After the war, the freed Tucker and Duke slaves and a family named Joshlin joined the black Huff family. All were hard workers and soon had crops in and gardens growing. Their descendants live in the Blackjacks still and in Rockport as well.

Throughout the Civil War, professional photography had brought images of conflict into ordinary homes. In the years that followed, photographs brought the world together; they set standards for the way things should look; they provided undisputed truth of how things were.

In general, there was an explosion of technology and information after the war. In 1876 the State of Texas established its first public institution of higher learning, the Agricultural and Mechanical College of Texas, on broad farmlands near Bryan. In 1881 the main campus of The University of Texas was located at Austin, with a Medical Branch at Galveston. The universities had been preceded by a few colleges. Some of them—and more that would follow—eventually became a part of the great university systems of Texas. Other church colleges grew to significant stature in their own right.

During the late 1800s, Thomas Alva Edison patented one invention or improvement every five days for four years—the phonograph in 1878, the incandescent light in 1879. The first long-distance telephone call linked Boston to New York in March 1884.

That same year John Albert Brundrett, first child of John and Hannah Wells Brundrett, went to St. Mary's College in San Antonio. He had a hard trip—first by boat from Lamar to Corpus Christi, then by train to Laredo, where he caught another train to San Antonio. Travel for Aransans would not be so difficult much longer.

In 1845 the Eastman Dry Plate and Film Company of Rochester, New York, manufactured the first commercial motion picture film. In 1887 Edison received a patent for his Kinetoscope, a device producing moving pictures.

A year later George Eastman registered the trademark "Kodak" for a camera that used flexible roll film. Photography was then available to anyone who could press a button.

The period was distinct from any before in Aransas. It was characterized by great variety, activity, and change—attributes that became the shapers of the county.

Familiar faces remained, but newcomers outnumbered them. Families from the Old South, wiped out by the war, came to Aransas to start again. Soldiers from both sides who had sailed past Live Oak Peninsula on troop ships returned to enjoy its beauty.

Reconstruction governments believed that the only men safe to hold local political offices were those who had never favored secession. In Aransas/Refugio that list included men like James Wells, Thomas Welder, and James Power, Jr., so affairs of the county remained in the hands of old, familiar citizens. These men were able to save their county from the worst abuses resulting from Reconstructionists' control.

Charlie Johnson served as election officer for Lamar, while William Smith held the same post at Saint Joseph. Edward Upton, who had led Lamar's Home Guard before languishing in jail as an accused Yankee sympathizer, was Refugio's first county judge. He headed a family that dominated early Aransas/Refugio County politics.

Ranching continued to be the mainstay of the community, even as Northern promoters in Aransas elevated the work to new levels of vigor and power. Larger towns demanded more merchants and wider selections of merchandise. A multifaceted population required more and better government. Old settlers who could not keep up fell by the wayside.

An artist's conception of the early Rocky Point wharf that enabled men to transfer cattle directly from pasture to ship. Original painting by Thom Evans.

BUILDING BLOCKS

ROCKY POINT

The history of Aransas in the last quarter of the nineteenth century is a study of contrast. We consider its elements individually to understand the whole.

Five years after the Civil War, John Howland Wood's ranching empire covered a large section of Refugio County. Wood realized that if his herds went by ship to spring markets, they could arrive ahead of cattle driven overland, giving him the advantage of early high prices. But Wood could not ship from his ruined wharf at St. Mary's. And even if Federal troops had not destroyed it, large, modern steam vessels would have been unable to navigate shallow Copano Bay.

John Wood remembered the conversation with Zachary Taylor that had taken place that long ago evening at James Power's home on Live Oak Point. The general had spoken enthusiastically about a rock projection at Hackberry Ridge, where his men had disembarked. The ledge, reaching all the way to the deep-water channel, formed a natural harbor.

Wood talked about that rocky point with his son Richard, who discussed it with his partner and longtime Refugio friend, James Murray Doughty. A wharf on the rock could be the key to successfully marketing their cattle.

Doughty got his brother Captain Dan and his half-brothers Jeremiah and Robert Driscoll to join the partnership, and the men purchased 640 acres of Live Oak Peninsula. They built warehouses and cattle chutes on the rock and drove cattle directly from their pastures onto ships. James Doughty advertised the enterprise as

150

shipping "beaves, wool, hide, and such other freight as our County has to export."

When word came that a new Fresnel lens was going in at the Aransas light, the partners felt confident that shipping would be safer and more successful than ever before.

Richard Wood formed a separate partnership with Samuel B. Allyn, a ship captain from Boston. They planned to operate a cattle ranch on San José Island and gradually acquired, from its various owners, all of the land there.

Thomas Henry Mathis arrived soon after. A well-educated man, he had been a schoolteacher in Arkansas and Tennessee, then moved to Texas in 1859 and engaged in trade. The Civil War ended that enterprise, so Mathis began forwarding supplies to soldiers.

Thomas Mathis welcomed the arrival of his cousin John M. Mathis in Aransas. Both men saw great possibilities for the port at Rocky Point and for the area at large. They bought Doughty's warehouse and wharf facilities, then reconveyed a third interest to him.

To ensure regular service to their port, the Mathises purchased a steamship, the *Prince Albert*. It was wrecked on an early trip, and the Mathises became agents for the Morgan Steamship line. Morgan agreed to furnish three ships a week to handle cattle from the Rocky Point wharf.

Only about 1,000 people lived in all of Aransas/Refugio, but Doughty and the Mathises could see that a shipping boom would mean workers, families, and businesses. It was time to promote a town, and they decided to name it for the limestone ridge. They called their enterprise the town of Rockport.

While Doughty and Mathis platted and surveyed one site, Joseph Smith and John Howland Wood laid out another to its north.

William Caruthers was one of the early arrivals. He wrote that in the summer of 1868, Rockport consisted of "two small wooden buildings, a cattle chute and wharf and acres of live oak bush and sage." From that humble beginning, according to Caruthers, Rockport "came as a mushroom in the night and at its first anniversary numbered not far from 1,200 inhabitants." This number exceeded the entire county's population when Doughty and Mathis first began to promote their town.

Viktor Bracht had left Texas for Mexico before the Civil War. He prospered there as a merchant until 1867, when Emperor Maximillian was assassinated and the French invaded. Although General Zaragoza had repelled French troops, Bracht lost everything in the melee. He hurried his wife and eight children aboard a steamship where the family was fed only pea soup during their hard journey to the Texas coast.

Almost as soon as they arrived at Rockport, Bracht found work as postmaster. He also served as Rockport's first agent of the Morgan Steamship Line. Morgan had ships in Texas as early as 1837 and was the first line back in service after the Civil War. Bracht operated the only regular steamboat service along the coast and subsidized it with mail service. He now spelled his first name "Victor."

Simon Sorenson sailed in on the schooner *Alfred and Sammy*, where he was mate to Capt. Charlie Hughes. When Hughes fell overboard and drowned, Sorenson quit the sea to work on land and settled at Rockport. After a while, his brothers Andrew and John joined him.

Terrill Bledsoe, another early arrival, described Rockport as a town of "waterfront characters, frontier merchants, booted and spurred *pisteleros* from the brush country, cattle barons, working cowboys and uprooted farmers and tradesmen from the states of the South."

Rockport's bustle was a Babel of languages, dialects, accents: Mexican *braceros* chatted in familiar Spanish; wagon freighters from the Texas Hill Country spoke German; fishermen from Louisiana bayous conversed in a Cajun slur; East Texans had a nasal twang; former plantation owners still carried the soft, cultured accents of the Old South.

Most newcomers found temporary lodging in Mrs. Conglon's hotel at the southwest corner of Water and Market streets. When rancher Robert Driscoll and his wife Julia Fox boarded at Conglon's, their tiny daughter Clara was the subject of much attention. If anyone asked the tot her name, she replied naively, in lisping baby talk: "I'm the black-eyed beauty, the belle of Rockport." When she grew to adulthood, Clara Driscoll's philanthropy would outshine even her remarkably good looks.

No one stayed long at Conglon's Hotel; houses were going up at an amazing rate. Judge Williamson Moses and his wife Victoriana built a small cedar cottage on the shoreline. From its rustic front porch, they looked out across salt marsh and bay, well north of the wharf area.

Dr. John W. Baylor built another cedar house on the beach, equally distant from the busy port, but to the south.

John Mathis, wealthy from the wharf, erected Rockport's first mansion. He had cypress shipped in and built the house on a seven-foot foundation of brick arches. The style was Greek Revival for beauty, but ship's carpenters pegged and joined the planks for stability.

No one built particularly close to anyone else; most homes were scattered among the oaks. But in other ways the citizens were uniting. By the end of 1869, Free Masons had formed Rockport Lodge No. 323. Two years later, Rockport had an Episcopal church, appropriately named St. Peter's, for the Great Fisherman disciple. The twenty communicants at the church included Sorensons, Deans, Fultons, and Sheltons.

Mrs. D. D. Scrivner, living in the ninth house built in Rockport, gave birth to the first white male born in town. She and her husband named him David Rockport. If a girl, or Mexican or black baby of either sex, preceded David, it was the character of those times that no special note was made of it.

Capt. Charles Francis Bailey and Geraldo Alonzo Beeman started a newspaper, the *Transcript*. They brought the printing plant from St. Mary's, where their newspaper, *Vaquero*, had been the first in the county. But prospects at St. Mary's had seemed limited compared to the promise of Rockport.

Still, Beeman returned to St. Mary's, so Bailey hired Lyman Russell and Emilie A. Perrenot, who had worked for him at the *Vaquero*. He put his son Henry to work on the paper too.

Lyman Russell wrote later: "The office was on the lower floor of a two-story frame building, and above I had a sleeping room all to myself. . . . I boarded with Bailey and family, and got twenty dollars a month besides."

Like any boomtown, Rockport had its saloons and gambling houses. Oliver Reed and Maj. Andrew Hogan ran one called "The Finish." Right on the bay shore, and nearest the wharf, it was well known to ranchers all over South Texas; many a cattleman's herd was "finished" there.

Across from The Finish, Capt. E. L. Snow set up a stand on the bay shore and sold raw oysters on the half-shell.

Rockport became the distributing office for mail addressed to St. Mary's, Refugio, and Beeville. Charlie Johnson still sailed the mail route on his schooner *Frances,* and he knew Rockport to be a rough place. Once, when some of the tough, new crowd instigated a scrap, he licked the whole bunch, wrote Lyman Russell, "fighting with both hands and feet, tooth and toenail."

On August 13, 1870, the Texas Legislature officially incorporated the Town of Rockport, with appointed officers who would preside until the next regular election. Governor Edmund J. Davis named John M. Mathis as mayor, George Dye as secretary, and as aldermen Edward Moffett, S. D. Robb, Charles L. Dean, Richard H. Wood, Victor Bracht, and W. R. Archer.

The town council met for the first time December 20, 1870, and passed three ordinances: to prohibit discharging firearms in the city, to prohibit reckless riding, and to prohibit drunkenness and disorderly conduct in the city. For public meetings, the council rented Mehle Hall, using money loaned them by Richard Wood.

James Hewetson, who had conceived the *empresa* with James Power only forty-eight years earlier, lived just long enough to hear how the place had grown, then died in his Saltillo home.

THE FULTON FAMILY

Harriet Smith Fulton was in Ohio, hardly aware of what her old home was becoming, but yearning for it nonetheless. She wrote to her business-traveler husband: "Oh, Pa, how I should like to take a trip to Texas this fall. (Texas—there is something fascinating in that name. Oh, how I love it.) Suppose after you come back from Baltimore, we pack up and store our furniture . . . take Georgie and go to Texas. What a treat it would be."

If Harriet envisioned recapturing her bucolic youth on the Brazos, she would not find it. If she imagined that a new Aransas would offer her the amenities of Ohio, her dreams ran ahead of reality. In any case, George Fulton did not act on his wife's wishes right away. But he saw that she had made a suggestion well worth considering.

George believed his wife might be the sole heir of her father, Henry Smith. Harriet had received no communication from her two half-brothers for many years and suspected that they were dead. George made inquiries of old friends, attempting to verify that. Now that Smith litigations against the Power family were successfully concluded, Harriet's fortune in land might be considerable. The Smiths' large blocks of property on Live Oak Point, combined with Fulton's own, would offer a significant business opportunity.

In the summer of 1867 George Fulton sent his son James to Texas on a scouting expedition; a few months later, the entire family sailed down the Mississippi to New Orleans, then traveled on to Aransas.

Fulton settled them into the modest house he had built just after the Texas Revolution. He had wanted no mistakes in the construction back then, so he ordered wood from Cincinnati and had the boards already numbered. Harriet had remembered the place fondly as her honeymoon home, an old-style dogtrot house, with a wide hall down the center. Now she saw that it was much too small for her grown-up family.

George William was fourteen years old; Hattie, sixteen; James, nineteen; and Annie, twenty-two. Poor Henry, age twenty-three, was weak in both body and mind. A doctor in Ohio had warned Harriet that the boy would not live much longer. Another son, George Ware, Jr., had been born the same year as Henry, but only lived a decade. Harriet focused all her homemaking skills on creating a comfortable, familiar environment for her children—however cramped their home might be.

George Fulton saw the house differently. He appreciated the fact that it was strategically located. To the north was still-beautiful Live Oak Point, where Aransas City had once prospered; to the south, on the Rocky Point, rose the new promise of Rockport. Still, Fulton was not at all sure that he wanted to remain in Texas permanently, so there seemed little point in improving the old homestead.

As Fulton settled down to business, he realized that his land was not likely to turn a good profit until Aransas developed further. Although he was already fifty-seven years old, Fulton prepared to make that progress happen.

In August, George Fulton received a letter from James

Doughty, who was interested in building a railroad from Rockport to San Antonio. "A number of persons," Doughty wrote, "have promised to donate one half of all the lands that they own near where the said railroad will run." Doughty felt confident that, with Fulton's monetary and management assistance, "the half part of your lands will then be worth dollars where the whole is now not worth dimes." He concluded with comments that someone else planned a connecting rail line to Mexico.

Fulton must have smiled as he read the eager words of such a promoter. If there was a railroad to be built, he would prefer to build it himself—and keep his land.

By the end of the year, George Fulton had organized the Fulton Town Company. In what must have been a paper transaction, he sold his company 1,100 acres at two dollars per acre. Not all the property was in Aransas; the Smiths held acreage in San Patricio, Jackson, and Galveston counties as well.

George Fulton platted the town bearing his name just three miles north of Rockport. It would depend, as Rockport did, on the cattle industry. As soon as his wharf and warehouse were complete, Fulton sent several shiploads of cattle to New Orleans.

Cowboys

Large bovines had historically fared well at Aransas. Paleo-hunters chased vast herds of bison across its plains. Hernán Cortéz imported Spanish cattle to grow fat on its rich grasslands. By 1761 Don José Escandón was able to report that ranches along the Rio Grande were "very large." Fifty years later, huge herds had spread up the mainland and filled the islands too. A storm surge in 1808 drowned 50,000 cattle on Padre Island alone.

Power colonists brought oxen to do their heavy work. Carlos de la Garza helped Nicholas Fagan start a cattle herd, as Nicholas later helped his son-in-law Tom O'Connor.

The Texas Revolution provided an opportunity for large sales of beef to feed the military, as did the Mexican War that followed. Men like John Howland Wood, who were extremely successful as suppliers then, carried their expertise forward during the Civil War and after.

Aransas/Refugio ranchers had always allowed their cattle to range freely and to intermingle, identified only by their brands. As the area became more developed, the design of these brands became more ingenious. Each had to be easy to distinguish, but difficult to alter. If the simple addition of a mark could convert one brand into another, a man might lose his herd to an unscrupulous dealer.

By common agreement, new calves were assumed to carry the brand of their mothers, but any unbranded yearling could legally belong to the first person who marked it. Owners worked together to track down rustlers and to sort things out at roundup time.

Brandings took place each spring and fall, when ten to fifteen neighborhood men—a "Crowd," in their parlance—combined forces, prepared to spend several weeks on the hunt. Each man carried a lasso at his saddle-bow and armed himself with a quality six-shooter and a Bowie knife. Each brought along two or three spare horses.

Additional pack horses carried provisions—blankets, coffee, sugar, bacon. When the men were hungry for fresh meat, they found plenty of unbranded yearlings to slaughter—not to mention deer, prairie hens, and other game.

Contrary to persistent images of cowboy life, whiskey was excluded from these roundups. It was regarded, George Fulton's brother Charles wrote, "as rather dangerous in companionship with six-shooters." Many men of Aransas, in fact, boasted that they would "never touch, taste or handle" any sort of liquor. Those who did indulge, abstained for the duration of a roundup.

Charles Fulton admired the young cowmen and wrote that they "evince splendid horsemanship, indomitable courage, great capacity for endurance, strength, activity, and a ready presence of mind in times of great danger."

Hobart Huson wrote that "to go up the Chisholm Trail at least one time in his life was the ambition of practically every cowman and cowhand in Texas." The prestige of such an adventure, he added, was "secondary only to having served as a Texas Ranger."

PACKERIES

Over the years, South Texas cowmen did well—too well. Vast

cattle herds far exceeded the market for meat. Since ranchers couldn't sell cattle, Rockport and Fulton couldn't ship them. It appeared that the towns would fail, along with the ranchers.

Ironically, it was cattle thieves who came up with a solution: They killed and skinned the animals on the open range, then took the hides to Mexico, where there was a ready cash market. Legitimate owners learned the lesson from them and began to look at a lucrative profit in cattle parts.

The first hide and tallow packery in Rockport began business in 1867. John Brundrett operated another at Lamar. Mr. Cushman set up business operations on a triangular point of land between Rockport and Fulton. It would later be known as the prosperous canal community of Key Allegro.

George Fulton consulted old acquaintances in the slaughterhouse and meat packing businesses around Cincinnati. He found markets for beef and by-products, including sinew. He elicited capital investment.

By the end of 1868, Fulton and William Caruthers joined forces to establish the Caruthers-Fulton Packing Company. Soon half a dozen other packeries located near it, focusing almost exclusively on cattle hides, with only nodding attention to tallow. But that would change.

New settlers, eager for work, took on ugly jobs in slaughterhouses. Young Robert McHugh was one of them, and from the first day he found the work harsh and unpleasant. But Mr. Cushman, the owner, humored the boy. He put a half-dollar on a rafter and told Robert he could have it at the end of the week; Robert showed up again the next morning. Later, Robert McHugh said that he had never worked so hard for fifty cents in all his life.

At the slaughterhouses, men and boys drove four or five cows at a time into a chute so narrow that the animals could not turn around. Above the chute, a "sticker" walked his platform, wielded a long lance and deftly severed the spinal cords of the cows. After all the cattle had fallen dead, men bled them; another crew hauled the carcasses to the skinning floor.

A skinner did his job faster than words can describe it. He ripped the hide off a cow's head first, but left it, like a grotesque mask, flopping along the animal's neck. He cut the feet off, then made a slit in the hide on the inside of the four legs and along the belly. He grabbed the cow's long horns and used them to fasten the skull to a ring in the floor. He passed a steel hook through the nostril openings in the loose skin from the cow's skull. A rope in the hook's eye ran to a crossbar, harnessed to a mule. The mule pulled and quickly shucked the whole hide from the cow's body.

As the skinner turned to the next carcass, a court-appointed inspector looked at each branded hide. He certified the brand as authentic, made out a bill of sale and received twenty-five cents for his effort. Since he could do that 400 times in an average day, an inspector had the opportunity to make a significant amount of money. Such a job, therefore, generally went to the sort of man most favored by the Reconstruction government. It was just another example, unreconstructed Rebels muttered, of how things ran against them.

The hides, dry or salted, were rolled and tied in bundles, awaiting shipment as soon as possible. Work progressed on the skinned carcasses. A marking man cut the hams and shoulders; the axe man severed all bones at the marks. Someone cut choice sirloins into five- or six-pound chunks for the army.

It would not be sold as fresh meat; that was impossible without refrigerated transportation, a limited option in 1868. Instead, a careful conversion process turned those sirloins into "mess meat"— pickled beef. The meat steeped in large steel vats filled with the "three fours" formula: four pounds of brown sugar, four pounds of salt, four ounces of saltpeter.

Packers cooked the rest of the meat in steam vats, rendering the fat. No one thought the cooked meat was good for anything other than hog food; they dumped much of it into the bay. The tallow—huge 1,100-pound barrels of it—was considerably more valuable.

In one year over 100 million pounds of tallow were shipped from the Texas coast, along with hides valued at over $2 million. A typical schooner might carry almost 2,000 hides, nearly 4,000 horns and twenty tons of bones, unbaled, tossed in a wild jumble. These would become buttons, combs, or handles for tools.

Robert McHugh saw one huge steer brought to Cushman's with a spread of horns nine feet wide. Cushman ordered those horns mounted and sent to President Grant. His accompanying letter suggested the horns might serve as a reminder of Grant's early days camping in Aransas, when he served in Zachary Taylor's army.

The men and boys who worked in the packeries needed few clothes and they had plenty to eat—too much meat, in fact. On weekends, they tended to spend their earnings in the saloons, but were usually sober enough for work on Monday mornings.

Billie Silberisen came looking for work and got a job with Mr. A. W. Clark, a packery foreman. Clark had 175 cattle in the pens and no one to slaughter them because the crew was on a drunk. Billie assembled a crew for him and soon they finished the job.

Meat continued to pile up. Hammond G. Smith, whose father had been born in New York but married a Texas girl, remembered this of his Aransas childhood: "You could go by the packery and cut off a chunk of meat and take it home with you, and nobody minded. . . . When the lard was rendered, you could fill a fifty-pound can for your own use. It didn't cost you anything."

Except, perhaps, the indignity of living within breathing distance of a growing mound of rotting flesh. A five-square-acre hill of spoiling beef accumulated, attracting flies, growing maggots, fouling the air with its stench. Some people today point to a certain rise in the land and identify it as that hill. Folklorist J. Frank Dobie reported: "It stank to high heaven. Flocks of seagulls and other birds gorged on it. Those must have been the fattest seagulls in Texas!"

Visitor Louis Ratisseau said that at night the hogs, raccoons, and opossums feasted early. Packs of wolves and coyotes arrived around midnight. His granddaughter Shirley Ratisseau wrote: "The wolves and coyotes howling at night over the refuse, and the smell of it, all stayed with my grandfather forever. Later, when my father, George Albert, would invite his father Louis to come visit us, Louis would shake his head and reply in three languages (English, French and German) just to make sure we understood he was never going to visit and smell Rockport again!"

The smell wasn't too bad when the wind was high and odors dissipated inland, but on calm days—the hot, flat days of summer—that reek of rotting flesh was everywhere. It penetrated solid walls; it lived in the nostrils. Putrefaction seemed to affect the very soul of the towns. It was the price they paid for commercial gain.

Finally, Yankees Sharpless and Carpenter organized an extensive operation to salvage the decaying cow carcases. They bought the rank meat for almost nothing, made it into fertilizer, and shipped it north.

It seemed, then, that Aransas could make something good out of anything. It could take the best and the worst parts of a cow, the finest and the lowest kinds of people, the brightest promise and harshest reality of a boomtown and turn it all to money.

THE LAMAR COMMUNITY

Lamar was older and more like Refugio than other parts of Aransas. Changes there were subtler. Richard T. Byrne opened a store. Capt. Peter Johnson took on the job of postmaster.

Up until 1869, visiting Presbyterian preachers held services in Murdoch McRae's home, and he laid planks on kegs to seat the worshipers. Then Lydia Ann Wells donated land for a church and Murdoch directed its construction. "Every man or youth of Lamar who could drive a nail assisted," according to Josie McRae. Each afternoon, Mary Ann McRae and Lydia Ann Wells' three daughters— Hannah Wells Brundrett and Misses Joe and Susie Wells—served cake and coffee under the spreading McRae oak, refreshing the workers.

"Both Catholic and Protestant worked side by side until the little church was finished," Josie wrote. "It was hard to tell who was prouder . . . when it was painted both inside and outside and services held. . . . All denominations were gladly welcomed to hold services . . . and were entertained in the homes of the McRaes and Captain Wells."

Visitors came to Lamar for its healthy, relaxed living, but often found the amenities few and the competition for them fierce.

One spring, Martha Foster Wellington checked into Henry Kroeger's hotel for a period of recuperation from an infectious virus. Rain woke her in the night and she got up to close the window. Mrs. Wellington fell, gashing her right brow, and Mrs. Henrietta Little put on sticking plaster. Mrs. Wellington wrote to her daughter that she looked "a perfect sight." She said she hated to appear at breakfast "before so many men (and all strangers)." Still, she realized that she "had to be at the first table" or not "fare as well as the rest."

Richard Byrne, "Dick" to his friends, sketched a simple house on the back cover of his account book and whimsically labeled it "Byrne Mansion." Another account book detailed costs of the house at $3,983.75. Then Dick contracted with Murdoch McRae to build a sloop, the *Rob Roy*.

They began work December 16, 1867, and Dick carefully tallied the number of hours that he and Murdoch each contributed to the project. In March 1868 Dick went "to Island for Mast," and on the 21st he "got lumber at Copano." On March 23 "McRae made coffin for Power." On April 21 Dick recorded "no work on boat by McRae—planting." At the bottom of one page, Dick wrote "I'm amighty hungry."

By July 24 the men had completed rigging and caulking and launched their boat. By this time, Dick had married Caroline Sarah Gregory, sister of Jane Gregory O'Connor, the schoolmistress.

The U.S. government ordered another boat from Murdoch McRae. He named it for his daughter Ella and launched it onto St. Charles Bay with great fanfare. Following that boat came others for the growing coastal communities, and Murdoch named most of them for his girls—the *Mary*, the *Belle II*, the *Hannah*, the *Susan Emma*, the *Josie*, and the *Mattie*.

Murdoch made parts for the boats on his front lawn, in the old shop where each of his bright saws and tools hung on its own particular nail. Hally Little, almost always at Murdoch's side, handed him what he needed. Murdoch's daughters vied for the honor of turning the grindstone when their father sharpened his tools. Mary Ann made eyelets in the sails, sitting on the porch Murdoch had built in front of Vincey's kitchen.

There Vincey continued to bake her famous corn pone and roasted ribs at the wide hearth. When she made pies, Vincey cut dough in fancy oak leaves for the top crust. Her young granddaughter Josephine thought they were beautiful.

Vincey showed Josie how to skim rich cream and churn slowly, turning the dasher each time she lifted it. When the butter was ready, Vincey gathered it into a bowl, using a cedar paddle she had

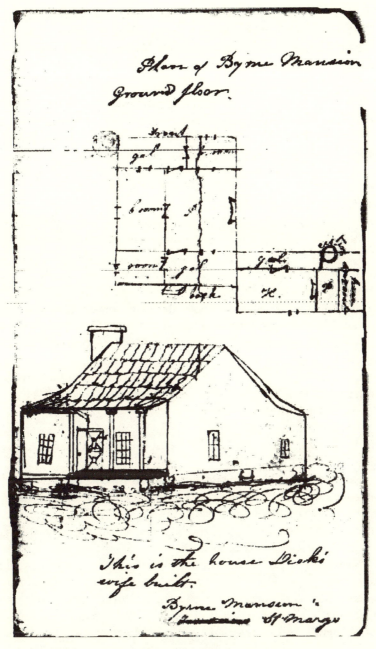

Dick Byrne's drawing was restored by computer technology.
—Courtesy of Caroline Williams; computer-enhanced by Chris Blum

rubbed with mulberry leaves. Then she patted and worked the butter into a pineapple shape magnificent to behold and sweet to eat.

But Vincey's skills represented the past, not the future. Aransas was changing before her eyes.

Tangled branches of another family tree spread on the west side of Live Oak Peninsula and became the basis of Sparks Colony. Most of the residents were, in one way or another, descendants of Stephen Franklin Sparks, Texas Revolution hero and chronicler.

THE NEW COUNTY SEAT

A Constitutional Convention met early in 1869 and moved the county seat from Refugio to St. Mary's. Judge Edward Upton ignored the ordinance, so most of his associates did too. St. Mary's had the honor in name only.

Still, progressive newcomers—and even some established families like the Woods, Driscolls, Aldretes, and Doughtys—recognized that the coast, not Refugio, had clearly become the population center. By 1870 over half the county's 2,320 people lived in Rockport and nearly all the rest were in other bay communities. The time had come, businessmen claimed, to move county government away from the dying, inland town of Refugio.

They took note that investors in Atlantic City, New Jersey, were building a boardwalk, and they observed that warm Aransas could easily rival the cold northern shore.

Rockport, St. Mary's, and Copano all made proposals to the legislature, seeking the county seat. Some men of Rockport, Lamar, and San José signed all three petitions—hedging their bets against an inland site—but Rockport, the "seaport of the County of Refugio," was clearly the best choice.

Nearby Fulton, with numerous packeries and semiweekly steam ships direct from New Orleans, was "mart and market of a large surrounding country." It was a successful town, but much too industrial for the county seat. Rockport remained comparatively pristine, while Fulton carried on the dirtiest work. Whether by chance or by design, this is the shape the two towns took, and in some ways they carry it still.

The Rockport Town Council adopted a resolution urging senators and representatives to advocate transferral of the county seat; the district judge and members of the bar of the Tenth Judicial District did the same. Since most of these men had remained loyal to the Union during the late war, the Reconstruction government in Austin looked favorably upon their desires.

On March 15, 1871, the Twelfth Legislature approved an act transferring the county seat—permanently—to Rockport.

Almost immediately, Mathis and Doughty informed the County Court that they had already designated a parcel of land for official county buildings. "At the time the map of the Town of Rockport was made," they said, "we contemplated that . . . the County seat would be located at this place." The partnership had also established a steam ferry between Live Oak Point and Lamar, simplifying transit from more distant portions of the county.

On May 26, 1871, an Act of the State Legislature officially elevated Rockport's status from town to city. The town council had already started the work of a city—building streets, passing a poll tax for every male over twenty-one, considering a petition "for the removal of houses of ill fame," and enacting an ordinance that required every house to keep a ladder long enough to reach its roof. Fires could be a problem.

Citizens in the town of Refugio were stunned by all this activity. Easy-going and complacent, they had done little to prevent the loss of their county seat. Even though many were kept out of politics as unreconstructed Rebels, they believed to the end that they would retain their dominion, just as they had believed, to the end of Smith's litigation, in their "good old titles."

Finally stirred to action, Refugio's leaders met with the "live wires" from the coast. It was true, the Refugians acknowledged, that the county covered a large and unwieldy area. It was understandable that Rockport and the island people wanted a county seat closer at hand. Refugio was ranch country; Rockport and Fulton were interested in business and maritime opportunities. Only one course could solve the dilemma: the county should be divided.

The two factions agreed that Cedar Bayou and the Aransas pass, from the Gulf shore inland, would mark the new county's north, south, and eastern limits. The county would appropriately include all of San José Island and bay-bordered Live Oak, Blackjack, and Lamar peninsulas—but how far inland should it extend? The Upton families, on Copano Creek, wanted to be part of the new county, and old-timers in Refugio were not overly sorry to have the Yankee upstarts out. A gerrymandered county line ran up the creek just far enough to include Judge Upton's ranch. The remaining portion of Power's old *empresa* would continue as Refugio County, with the town of Refugio as its county seat.

(Almost a century later, county officials negotiated a boundary dividing the waters of Copano Bay and jagging a little at the Aransas River. Another, larger gerrymander gave most of Harbor Island to San Patricio County.)

On September 18, 1871, the Texas Legislature made it official: Rockport had the seat of government and Texas had a new county with a grand old name—Aransas.

That word had originally meant a place of thorns. It suggested a complex situation, a difficult path. It evoked all the history of Aransas—and perhaps its future too.

When quiet, insular Refugio heard the news, the town went wild. Spontaneous celebrations turned into "the biggest Irish wake ever held in this county," according to Judge William Rea. The merrymaking went on and on; liquor flowed. The men of the coast "were roundly cussed, individually and collectively," Rea reported.

Near the end of that rowdy celebration, an Irishman jumped up on a table and offered a toast that was really a curse: "Faith and bejabers, and the dam-yankees got all the water there was in the county, and, begobs, it is me that hopes they all will drown their damned selves in it!"

Mehle Hall, acquired by Aransas County in 1881 for use as a temporary courthouse.
—Courtesy of Aransas County Historical Commission Archives

BARONS

PARTNERS

George Fulton was, of course, one of the "damn-yankees" Refugio's Irish excoriated, but he had little time to notice, much less to care. Fulton had businesses to run. Texas-packed beef had become so popular that some parts of the South used it even more than salt pork and bacon, longtime staples of the region.

In response to the demand for fresh beef, George Fulton organized a new company that became as important to the development of Aransas as any one event before or since. Some of Fulton's land, combined with acreage belonging to Youngs Coleman, his son Thomas Matthew Coleman, and cousins John and Thomas Mathis, created a giant ranch—115,000 acres across San Patricio and Aransas counties.

The territory ran from Copano Bay to Corpus Christi Bay and up Chiltipin Creek, where Youngs Coleman had a home. A thirteen-mile-long fence on the west side of the great ranch completed its borders. Other land acquisitions followed and CMF became the largest cattle firm of its time.

Although ranch headquarters were in Rockport, daily operations centered at Rincón Ranch, across Port Bay from Live Oak Peninsula. With ranch houses and quarters strategically located, management was state of the art.

But "Coleman, Mathis, and Fulton, Dealers and Shippers of Live Stock" was more than a ranch, and the name said it all: CMF was a trading company. In 1875 alone the partnership acquired 274 brands through purchase.

The CMF partnership also purchased an interest in the Rock-

167

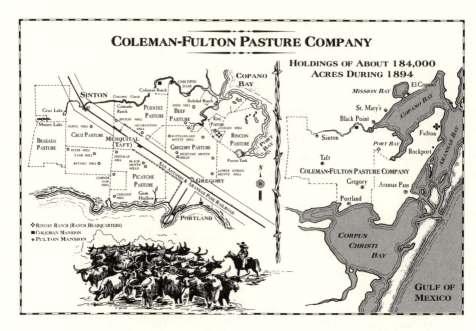

COLEMAN-FULTON PASTURE COMPANY

HOLDINGS OF ABOUT 184,000 ACRES DURING 1894

Sprawling from Copano Bay south to Nueces Bay, and inland some thirty miles from Aransas Bay, the Coleman-Fulton Pasture Company succeeded CMF. Illustration by Chris Blum.

port wharf and, as agents for the Morgan Steamship Company, the partners controlled maritime cattle shipment for the entire area.

Soon CMF constructed a larger wharf on the old site, with improved warehouses and shipping facilities. When completed, the wharf was thirty-five feet wide—space enough not only for a high, six-foot-wide cattle chute, but also for two lanes of freight wagons. The wharf extended 1,100 feet out into the bay, ending in a 400-foot-wide T-head supporting two big warehouses. Any commodities bound for Corpus Christi came first to Rockport, where dockmen transferred the load to smaller ships that could navigate shallower bays.

Between October 1872 and July 1878 CMF shipped from Aransas to New Orleans 104,600 full-grown steers, cows, calves, and yearlings. This impressive number represented only a third of the company's deliveries; the rest went from Indianola to Havana, Cuba.

As many as six ships might be tied to the wharf at one time, and bags and barrels of silver, commonly referred to as bland money, sat on the floor of the CMF office. There was so much silver that no one even counted it; someone just measured it out.

Andrew Sorenson never forgot that. Fresh from Denmark, he promptly fell in love with the cattle business and went to work as a CMF cowboy. At the close of one business day, Andrew Sorenson rolled fourteen barrels of silver from the dock to the office. As the story is told, Sorenson could have left the silver outside overnight and no one would have taken a dime.

Sending cattle to northern markets by ship was a big improvement over land drives, but George Fulton yearned to bring a rail line to Aransas. He dreamed of providing his cattle country with the transportation benefit that other parts of Texas enjoyed. Railroads were moving cotton and other products to northern markets with much greater ease than steamships could offer. In 1871 Fulton had received a state charter for the Rockport, Fulton, Laredo, and Mexican Pacific Railroad, but his project never drove a spike.

That same year, though, a telegraph line had gone up, designed to assist the scheduling of steamer traffic along the coast. It just missed Aransas, running from Indianola to St. Mary's and on to Corpus Christi and Brownsville. Within a year or so, Rockport raised $6,000 and connected to the line.

By this time, George Fulton's daughters Annie and Hattie had married the brothers Eldridge and Charles Holden. Hattie and Charley lived sometimes in New Orleans and sometimes in Fulton, where he ran a mercantile store; Annie and Ell lived with her parents for extended periods as Ell managed various family businesses. A third Holden brother, Daniel Livingston, developed a compression ice-making system and installed it in Fulton's slaughter house.

ISLAND FORTRESS

In 1874 an enterprising Bavarian obtained a state patent granting him the acreage on a triangular peninsula between Rockport and Fulton. Often, a slim flow of salt water separated the point from the mainland, so his family usually got home by wading. Much later, his Frandolig Point would become Key Allegro.

Franz Josef Frandolig pronounced his name softly, like a palm frond, and ending with the *g* sound of *knowledge*. Italian, French and German branches of the family had other variations of the name. Frandolig kept to old, European ways, bossing his family, keeping the best of everything for himself. But he worked hard, as hard as his wife, Anna Swander, or any of his children.

In the 1840s Franz had caught and broken wild horses that he sold to Zachary Taylor as cavalry mounts. During the Civil War, he delivered cotton to Bagdad. Later, Franz moved his family to Duval County, west of Corpus Christi. There they gathered wild cattle and drove a herd north along Kansas and Nebraska trails.

But cattle drives were too hard with a family. Franz drove a herd of cattle to Rockport one day, sold them all, and made the town his home. He had decided he could use his children more effectively in working the land.

Franz Josef Frandolig, Bavarian immigrant, had a knack for being at the forefront of each new business opportunity. His bay island farm became known as Frandolig Point.
—Courtesy of James Frandolig Collection, Aransas County Historical Society Archives

Franz received a patent for a Triangular Bay Island where he raised "wonderful" vegetables and fruit to sell in town. The family planted fig trees among the mesquites, and they had a vineyard too. They made wine by the barrel and sold it to fishermen who put in along their shore.

Franz also built and ran a salt works, despite the fact that his children and grandchildren hated the hot, harsh job, hated the sores they got from the work.

Franz watched them from the house. He had built it to look

like a fortress. And he thought of himself as a baron, as much as were those wealthy people north of him.

MANSIONS

Halfway between Frandolig Point and Fulton, William S. Hall built a two-story colonial mansion. He owned one of the Fulton packeries, so he could easily afford fluted pillars, eight high-ceilinged rooms, two baths, and a wide, winding stairway. His spacious grounds, full of oak trees, were a favorite strolling place for romantic couples. Morgan steamers from New Orleans brought in orchestras for dancing; delicacies for fine dinners came on the same ships.

Even without such splendor, Harriet Fulton had become painfully aware of the inadequacies of her honeymoon house. She had already added some rooms, but as she prepared to take in her two half-brothers, John G. and James Smith, she needed still more.

The addition of her brothers to the household was something of a shock. Harriet had received a letter as though from the grave, learning that they were still alive in California. Neither man had prospered there, but they made a living herding sheep and taking odd jobs.

George Fulton had fired off one letter after another. He had sent money. He financed small business schemes for the men. Finally, he and Harriet welcomed her brothers to their home and promised to care for them the rest of their lives. In return, the men signed over to George and Harriet the deeds to all their property.

Harriet's home renovations ultimately created a very long ranch-style house—a full seven bays—with a front porch extending its length. George Fulton appreciated her work, but he needed a place where he could entertain influential Texans from around the state. Fulton decided to build a home befitting his new stature as a cattle baron, a place like nothing that had ever been seen on the South Texas coast. He would bring the best of Midwestern and Eastern seaboard cities to his little town.

Fulton thought he should have a fine house right on the bayfront, and he chose a site just slightly south of the crowded home where his family was living. He determined to bring all his engineering skills, all his ingenuity, to bear on the job. His house would include every possible modern improvement. It would be a symbol of progress, a model for all of Aransas.

George Fulton started work on the grand design in 1874. That year, the CMF dividend was only $67.50 a share, down from $200 a share the year before. The partnership had to borrow $100,000 from Tom O'Connor of Refugio. Fulton must have winced at the bad economic news, but he didn't stop work on his mansion.

Its finishing touches were finally completed in 1877, and George Fulton moved his family into their grand, new home— twenty-nine rooms covering 6,200 square feet. It had cost him $10,371 for materials alone.

Fulton called the place Oakhurst, and it was extraordinary. Sixty acres surrounded the house—plenty of room for the stable, a carriage-house with servants' quarters above it, vegetable gardens, an orchard, a vineyard. Immediately south and west of the mansion, flowers filled landscaped formal gardens.

A broad and elegantly ornamented front lawn extended to the bay shore. Visitors approached Oakhurst along the beach, then turned into a circular shellcrete drive. It looped around a fountain that bubbled spray through the mouth of a crane. Outside the drive, rare trees shaded luxuriant flower beds.

The style of the house was French Second Empire. Although the exterior was finished with cedar slats, it was decorated to mimic stone. The mansard roof gleamed with ornamental slates, and a majestic three-and-one-half story tower rose beside a distinctly American veranda. As elegant as the house appeared, George Fulton had built it to withstand any storm that the Gulf could deliver; every wall was solid—built of stacked and staggered planks.

The full basement was only half below ground. In summer, bay winds blew through, cooling the kitchen and laundry. Vents caught the breeze and swept it upward to freshen the living areas of the house. A great furnace delivered heat to all the rooms in winter.

Fulton installed gas light fixtures and a bathroom with a flush toilet on each floor of the house. He designed the water lines himself, as well as a pressure system that brought hot water to some of the faucets. He also designed a dumbwaiter to lift platters of food from the basement kitchen to the dining room.

Harriet purchased a wide variety of fresh meats and fish; she could even have lobster shipped in. She had fresh fruits and vegetables grown on the property or purchased locally. She stored them in her basement larder, where troughs of running water kept things cool. Harriet raised chickens, geese, ducks, and milk cows. She could get canned goods at the Holden store.

Most of the house furnishings had come from the Meador Furniture Company in Cincinnati, at a total cost of almost $3,600. Harriet chose wall-to-wall carpet, up-to-date complicated color schemes, and popular bric-a-brac for every available surface.

A woman was measured by the state of her home, and visitors were frequent. Prominent South Texas families often crowded Harriet's eighteen-seat dining table. The Driscolls were there. Mifflin Kenedy and Richard King came from their growing ranch lands south of Corpus Christi. The McCampbells, wealthy from ranching and mercantile, joined the family of George Brackenridge, who had founded the San Antonio National Bank. Occasional guests also came from the East Coast and from Europe.

After Charles Fulton, George's brother, paid a visit, he wrote in his *Baltimore American* newspaper: "In the homes of Texans—those of the class who control business operations—there is as much refinement and cultivation as is to be found in the best society in our Northern cities." He stated proudly that the Fulton mansion and grounds were "not surpassed by those of the finest country residences around Baltimore."

George Fulton continued to travel. Harriet wrote to him, sitting at her little desk in the master bedroom bay window. As she looked out over the water, she evoked images of daily life. Harriet had an eye for the unusual, the entertaining. She described things in compelling detail, as though offering her husband snapshots of home.

"The hawks are taking all of my little chickens," she complained in one letter. "The little things . . . are so exposed. . . . Hattie thought there ought to be brush . . . to protect them, so this morning I had the large branches of the oleanders taken out and scattered around."

In that same letter Harriet wrote: "Jackson's wife died about a week ago, about two years ago she swallowed a five-dollar gold piece accidentally. Since that time she was troubled with a cough, the doctors thinking the money had lodged in her lungs thereby causing the cough and finally her death. They decided to make a postmortem examination. Mrs. Woods witnessed the operation. They cut her breast open and laid the bone back over her face, while they examined her lungs. They failed to find the money. How Mrs. W. could have the nerve to look on such an operation is strange to me."

Harriet signed that letter "Goodby God Bless and protect you my darling husband," but she wrote "husbang" by mistake. She scratched through the misspelling and added: "I was not thinking of bangs. Why should I have added a g instead of d."

Harriet Fulton was fifty-four years old, with a husband twelve years her senior, but she wrote to him in a voice of charming flirtation. One letter included her dream of a long-ago day when she had been a student and George Fulton her teacher. "The next morning in thinking how you looked in my dream, how vividly, oh how vividly your looks brought to my mind that memorable morning . . . in the little school room in our dear old home on the Brazos. Your head ached and . . . a little vixen treated just as meanly as I was going to treat in my dream. But you didn't put your arm around me and kiss me then. But I am sorry now that I didn't let you. Aren't you. ha. ha."

Rivalry

Shortly after Oakhurst was completed, the Fultons held a grand housewarming party. Mrs. Thomas Coleman was hardly in her carriage on the way home from it when she began to complain to her husband. There was no reason, she believed, why the Fultons should have a finer home; as business partners and equals, she and her husband could afford to be just as impressive.

Three years later, in 1880, the new Coleman house was complete. According to one story, Thomas Coleman "tallied up to eighty thousand dollars and then quit counting." Another report set the final cost at $150,000.

Landscaping extended for a full mile from the house in every direction. There were fountains and statues, stables, hunting dogs, and pens. By the early 1890s, the Colemans had a private telephone line running from their house to the Rincón Ranch. It was the good life, in high times.

But by then, John and Thomas Mathis had dropped out of the

CMF partnership. George Fulton and his son James formed a new enterprise with Youngs and Thomas Coleman: The Coleman-Fulton Pasture Company.

A need to retire old debts—coupled with Tom Coleman's ambitious improvements to the ranch—exceeded income, so the partnership elected to make payments in shares of stock. Among the moneyed men in Baltimore and Cincinnati who purchased it eagerly was David Sinton. An Irish immigrant, he had become wealthy manufacturing pig iron during the Civil War.

As the largest buyer of Coleman-Fulton stock, Sinton soon found himself the unwilling arbiter in a growing power struggle between the partners. Ultimately, Coleman declared if he couldn't hold high office in the organization, he would leave it entirely. Sinton saw no option but to purchase all of Coleman's stock; he became the company's largest shareholder and principal mortgage holder.

David Sinton assumed veto power over ranch operations and put his son-in-law, Charles Phelps Taft, in Coleman's seat on the Board of Directors.

It was a bad time for the cattle business; livestock prices were depressed throughout the area. Cattle exports had dropped every year since 1873. In 1878, when shoaling closed the Aransas pass, only one load of cattle went out. The next year there was none.

Sinton appreciated Fulton's skills as promoter, imaginative innovator, and risk-taking entrepreneur, but his own focus was on the bottom line. He took all decisions regarding the business out of Fulton's hands.

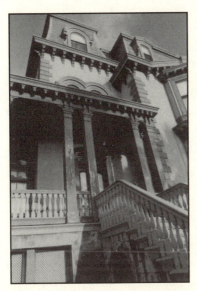

George Fulton's 1877 home reflected the style of elite houses in the Northeast; his innovations introduced conveniences new to Aransas. The mansion continues to attract attention from worldwide visitors.

—Photo by Thom Evans

HARSH REALITY

LOSSES

Emma Fulton died in 1876. Just past her second birthday, she was the second child of James Charles Fulton and bore the sad distinction of filling the first grave in the new Rockport cemetery. The land had been deeded to Sam Smith, Henry Smith's nephew, for a burial ground. He would never have imagined that Henry's great-grandaughter would be the first to lie there.

The Fultons chose the cemetery's finest plot, on a slight rise, looking out across the marsh toward the bay.

On November 30, 1876, an aging but still popular sidewheel steamship, the *Mary*, sank as she entered Aransas Bay. Her wrought iron hull remains there, between modern jetties. Following investigation by divers in 1990, the wreck of the *Mary* was designated a State Archaeological Landmark.

She sank where Béranger ran up on the shoal in 1720, where James Power's Irish colonists came to grief, where a load of bricks for the lighthouse went down.

She had a crew of thirty, eight passengers, and a load of general cargo—grain, flour, fabric, wagon wheels and crosstrees, bottles of medicine, and a dentist's chair. When the ship first hit the shoal, John and Ned Mercer, Tom Brundrett, Tom Lacy, and Parry Humphrey started for her in the pilot schooner *Doaga*. It took three hours of tireless effort to get a line to the *Mary*; then they took her passengers to the home of bar pilot Capt. Robert Mercer.

The next day, Mercer wrote in his typically terse style: "Ned took the passengers on the *Doaga* and put out for Rockport. So ends the day. Wind N.E." On December 2 Mercer noted that "boats of spectators are commencing to arrive." For days after, he recorded the slow breaking up of proud *Mary* and "people on the beach all the time."

The tourists watched Mercer's crew salvage what they could. The Corpus Christi paper warned everyone not to taste unlabeled medicine bottles; *Mary* had carried a supply of strychnine.

Those tourists may have seen the wreck of the *Mary* as a curiosity—an entertainment even—but it was far more than that. The event represented the continuing struggle for survival on the coast—a struggle with no certain outcome.

In 1878 the second of two fierce epidemics, now unidentifiable, swept Lamar. During a nightmarish forty-three days, three of Lydia Ann Wells' children had died. In this new outbreak, Lydia Ann, who had always "kept medicines of all kinds and doctored people," naturally volunteered to assist the local physician, J. A. Clark. He could not otherwise have kept up with the caseload.

Then the illness gripped Lydia Ann too. As she lay dying, she overheard friends express regret that they could not relieve the gentle, cheerful woman who had been so helpful to others. Lydia Ann remonstrated, asking, "What good have I ever done?"

The whole town had experienced the answer. They crowded the church at her funeral and, according to one newspaper report, "followed her remains with sorrowful hearts, in testimony and homage to her memory, worth and work."

Seventeen months later, those same mourners laid James B. Wells to rest beside his wife. By that time, only 129 people lived in the village of Lamar. In 1882 Richard Byrne moved his store away. No one at all lived at Copano. From that time on, Rockport and Fulton would be the only real towns on Aransas bays.

THE BLACKJACKS AND THE ISLAND

East of Lamar, across narrow St. Charles Bay, lay another peninsula twice as large. The Blackjack Peninsula was so dotted with ranches that sometimes it seemed just one large spread, and eventually that is what it came to be.

In the quarter century following the Civil War, displaced San José settlers—and some other families—claimed over 34,000 acres of ranch land on the Blackjack Peninsula, land that had once been part of the vast Power and Hewetson estates. In addition to cattle, the families raised sheep, goats, hogs, horses, and mules. They maintained small farms—just large enough to supply their own needs—and by the simple expedient of reference points, ranchers gave their names to the land: Big and Little Brundrett lakes, Jones Lake, Spalding Bight, McHugh Bayou, Ballou and Bludworth islands, Webb's and Meile Dietrich points.

Emeile Dietrich was a second generation Texan, son of an Alsatian father and a San José Island girl. Meile's father, Joseph, had arrived at Matagorda while Texas was still a republic. When he fell in love with fourteen-year-old Ann Jane Seward, Joseph had to get her father's permission to marry the young girl.

Meile married Dora Casterline, descendant of Jonas, who had arrived at the end of the Mexican War. Meile and Dora raised three children in the Blackjacks.

John Lane DeForest lived in a colony just a mile south and inland of the head of St. Charles Bay. John could hear whooping cranes "holler" for miles. Often, when he was out hunting them, he saw twenty or thirty of the great birds at a time. The cranes were wonderful eating, he said.

Bernard Leonard Bludworth and his wife Mary Brundrett had nine children to provide for. Bernard got a contract to provide venison to a butcher in Indianola, and he killed his deer with a shotgun. He harvested so many of them that the butcher canceled the contract.

Ann Jane Seward Dietrich lived all her life on San José and Blackjacks ranches. Her eyes give haunting testimony to the hardships of every early settler.
—Courtesy of McHugh-Dietrich family Collection

In 1881 on a neighboring ranch, Hannah Wells Brundrett kindled a fire with kerosene oil. That was her usual routine—but the can exploded. In no time at all, Hannah and her fourteen-year-old daughter Lydia Ann were covered with flames. Albert, age fifteen, fought heroically to save his mother and sister, but no one thought either victim would survive. Hannah died after thirty-four hours. Lydia, who must have had the spirit of her Grandmother Wells, overcame her injuries. Still, the burns on her stomach and chest were so severe that Lydia Ann always wore high-necked dresses to hide the scars.

Widower John McOscary Brundrett soon remarried, much to his children's dismay. Lula Hastings was only sixteen—a year younger than John's son Albert. But she proved a devoted wife who bore her husband another twelve children.

Perhaps because he had so much experience caring for his own family, John served as unofficial doctor for the Blackjacks community at the turn of the century.

James William Brundrett, John and Hannah's son, moved to the Blackjacks after he married Lydia McRae, Murdoch and Mary Ann's sixth daughter. For a period of six years, their nearest neighbor was six miles away, though they could look across St. Charles Bay and see Lamar. Later, Charlie Casterline was their nearest neighbor, just across Bill Mott Bayou.

The Brundretts had a mott of anaqua trees, a big iron cistern, and, of course, a wood barn. They lived a "do it yourself" life. Lydia ground her own corn, milked twenty-five cows, churned butter in a crock. Each year she put up "hundreds of pounds" of green grapes, huckleberries, dewberries; she canned corn and other vegetables. People passing through the country often stopped at her house for the night and remained for several days. Once a week, the Brundretts sailed to Lamar or Rockport to buy staple groceries.

John McOscary Brundett made a pleasant pond out of the marshland at his "Gables house" in the Blackjacks.
—Courtesy of Aransas National Wildlife Refuge Collection

Lydia helped her husband round up cattle, sitting sidesaddle with her long riding habit touching the earth. One year they branded 900 calves. During hunting season, Lydia and James roamed with a big feather bed in the wagon for their ten children, along with plenty of food and the wash pots.

The peninsula was mostly pasture—not thick brush as now, but only a scattering of tree motts. All the ranching families in the Blackjacks, and on Lamar as well, used those trail-lined motts to advantage when rounding up cattle or wild horses. While some boys drove the animals into the motts, others climbed trees with wide branches over the trails. When an animal passed under the tree, a boy could just drop a noose over its head.

Settlements developed throughout the Blackjacks. Carlos City, halfway down the eastern shore of the peninsula, and Faulkner, on the northwestern side, had post offices where mail arrived by horseback once a week. Teachers came by boat from Rockport to work at community schools; sometimes they took board and room with the families. The Brundretts even ran a school in their home for a while. Schoolhouses were little more than shacks with homemade desks and school benches furnished by the families.

Other Brundretts still ranched on San José. Unlike many residents who had deserted their island homes during the Civil War, they had never left. Jed and Tom Brundrett traveled from their home to Mustang Island for Capt. Thomas B. Clubb's remarkable fifty-fifth birthday celebration. The party began on December 26, 1872, and went on for two days and nights.

Robert Mercer, whose family operated a wharf on San José, facing Lydia Ann Island, was Clubb's Mustang Island neighbor and the island pilot. Of the birthday party, Mercer wrote in his log that the weather was so cold the guests had to keep dancing or else they would freeze.

Marion and Mary Ann Seward moved back to their San José home after the Civil War and their family grew. But when the island community did not prosper, Mary Ann wanted to move to the new town, Rockport. She said she feared that a great storm would come and blow them off their fragile isle. But Marion was an island man; there was no moving him. Mary Ann made do with an occasional day of shopping in the mainland town.

LAST OF A BREED

When Murdoch McRae completed the *Mattie* in 1883, he knew she was his last boat; Murdoch's lungs had begun to trouble him, just as they did near the end of the Civil War. A receipt tucked in the back of Murdoch's account book showed purchases made at an Indianola drugstore: whiskey, brandy, and plaster.

Mary Ann wrote later: "I nursed my poor husband six years and then he died and left me with seven children, all girls, and his poor old mother."

Murdoch McRae was fifty-seven years old when he died December 5, 1889. An obituary praised him as a prominent resident who "built the finest vessels that sailed the waters of the coast." His daughter Josie noted that he was a "good man and never even sailed his boat on the Sabbath."

Tough, old pioneer Vincey Williams McRae outlived her son by five years, but in the spring of 1894 she was buried beside him. They rest beneath an elaborate marker eternally joining Vincey to Murdoch in death, as she had held to him in life. Two years later, Mary Ann Heard McRae moved to Cuero with her younger daughters.

There she had time to write a short biography. It concluded: "I am now fifty-two years of age and can do a good days work. Never was sick any to hurt. I have done two weeks washing this day and wrote and composed this, being the twenty-sixth of October 1896, at Refugio where I visited long years ago when I was a young lady."

At Lamar, an old oak tree in a yard and salt cedars along the bay remain as a fitting memorial to hardy pioneers.

WEATHER

Anyone who had been in Aransas long knew when hurricane season was. A storm might come as early as the first soft days of June, or as late as expectations for a first November chill. Generally, the worst hurricanes hit in September.

People learned of building winds first from boats that radioed what they saw. Then seaports watched the approaching storms and telegraphed detailed descriptions. Towns that escaped the brunt of a storm felt some compassion for stricken neighbors, but mostly they felt relief that they were spared.

In 1875 a big storm struck Indianola. Ten percent of the population died. Three-fourths of all the town's buildings disappeared without a trace and most of the rest were in ruin. Where buildings had stood only a day before, twelve bayous cut through the town. People began to rebuild, but only eleven years later their town was hit again and no one had the spirit to start over. Aransas suffered from these storms as well, but to a lesser degree.

A year without a storm could be a year of drought. That happened in 1898. Lack of rain withered grass on the range. It seemed to dry up the tourist season as well—or maybe visitors couldn't afford to come because of the economic depression.

The bays froze over in 1899. On February 11 the temperature dropped to twenty-four degrees; the next night it was down to eleven degrees. Fish died. Everyone suffered, the fishermen most of all. The following November, "a wildcat-killing hail" fell on Lamar for more than ten minutes. James C. Herring said that ice balls, "bigger than hens' eggs," stripped the oak trees of their leaves and picked clean 200 chickens.

On September 8, 1900, hurricane winds swept Galveston, Texas. That storm remains the worst weather disaster in United States history. Afterward, someone wrote a song with this chorus: "Wasn't it a mighty day, when the storm winds swept the town?"

It was a terrible day, and Galveston was never the same again. Too many people had died, too many beautiful homes had been turned to kindling wood. Galveston, one-time home base of the pirate Lafitte, later the grandest port on the Texas coast, would fade from its glory days. Houston, across the bay and up the San Jacinto River, would become Texas' major shipping center.

THE CITY OF ROCKPORT

HOMES AND BUSINESSES

Rockport had grown indistinguishable from a small town anywhere—except for its special grace, the waterfront. Aransas Bay
controlled everything; it gave the town a focal point.

When Joseph Smith's will left a full city block to his nieces,
Janie, Alpha, and Lizzie Kennedy, they ran a pier past Victoria and
Williamson Moses' beach cottage, across the marshes and out to deep
water. Their house had a third-floor turret for the spectacular view,
as did the James Hoopes' and even Leopold Bracht's, although the
latter was somewhat inland. The John Hynes' house, and the Albert
Bruhl's, also faced the bay. South of them there grew, gradually, a
long line of homes on Water Street, stretching all the way to the cove.

Seafaring men seemed to favor those houses, but others lived
there too. Widow James took in sewing. She thought of the brush
families, inland, whose protected sewing machines remained well-
oiled. She thought of them every time she had to sandpaper her needles and pins. But Mrs. James relished her breeze.

In 1877 Leopold Bracht and his brother Roland started a mercantile business, appropriately named Bracht Brothers. A younger
brother, Adolph, went to work at the Kohler Lumber Company in
1890. So many people wanted to build that he checked lumber directly from rail cars to the purchasers; it never went to the lumber lot.
Just three years later, Adolph started a mercantile store of his own.

Simon Sorenson built a ship's chandlery and grocery on Austin
Street. Its dark brick walls rose from a simple dirt floor, but sturdy
ceiling beams recalled the shipbuilding background of the store's
designer. Just south, another store had a pretty canopy. Eventually

"Main Street, USA." Looking north on Austin Street, note the stair-stepped roofline of Sorenson's Chandlery and, behind it, the towers of Aransas Hotel.
—Courtesy of Jackson family Collection

A view from the water, looking south along the Water Street ridge. From right, Mason, Norvell, Simon Sorenson, Sedan, and Gruey homes. In the distance is Bayside Inn. Some of these houses remain today.
—Courtesy of Aransas County Historical Archives

horse ties were embedded in a sidewalk to make shopping convenient for customers.

A Presbyterian congregation started and failed, but both Baptists and Methodists had built churches. The Methodists needed money for an organ, so their minister, blind "Uncle" Myers, went down to The Finish and appealed to the gamblers. They gave him every penny he asked for. Myers invited them all to church. The men shut up their business and went to hear him preach, secure in the knowledge that the sightless man could never point them out as donors of illicit gains.

Catholic families awaited the arrival of traveling priests, who visited several times a year. John and Ellen Hynes offered their home for Mass since the parishioners had land but no church building. Finally, in 1886, walls went up at Church and Cornwall streets. A modern Catholic church remains on the site in 1997.

When County Judge Paul Phelan Court settled into the new Aransas County courthouse in 1889, its elegance seemed to prove that Rockport was the equal of any little town in America. Designed by J. Riley Gordon, the courthouse was an imposing Moorish-style brick beauty three stories tall, with a teardrop dome topping that. Rising from a half-above-ground basement, the courthouse towered over the two-story jail next door.

Aransas County's imposing Moorish courthouse, with the jail to its right, and the high school in the background.

—Courtesy of James Frandolig Collection,
Aransas County Historical Society Archives

County officials rented out the first floor to J. I. Caruthers who ran a dry goods business there. On Saturday nights, workmen pushed aside the judge's bench on the second floor and the community dance began.

Four years later, the court ordered that "a good and substantial fence be put around the courthouse" since roaming livestock detracted from the building's dignity. A spiked wrought iron fence surrounding the whole block would take care of that. Four sets of iron steps or stiles, each opposite an entrance to the courthouse, provided access to the courthouse grounds. Later, the court found that "a necessity exists for the building of a brick foundation under the fence," so that was installed too.

W. M. Moore opened a small store on Austin Street. It would grow to be one of the largest pioneer general merchandising firms on the Coastal Bend, and Moore's son Ed would grow to be a significant local businessman and mayor of Rockport.

Presbyterians organized again in 1889 with T. H. Mathis and C. H. Butts elected as elders.

Col. John H. Traylor, a millionaire and former mayor of Dallas, saw much that he liked in Rockport—its main street was paved in shell, and although Charles Bailey's *Transcript* was gone, the *Rockport Enterprise* newspaper had replaced it. The town was progressing appropriately, but it had one problem—an obstacle that mattered to a man who was investing heavily. Rockport had a population over 1,000, but no bank. Traylor convened thirty-three leading businessmen to form one.

The men voted to apply for a charter with $50,000 in capital in one-hundred-dollar share lots, and Traylor sold them a block of land on Main Street between Austin and the bay shore, where the bank was built.

In response to Rockport's boom, F. C. Finney of Oklahoma City built houses south of town. He called his community the Finney Addition, although everyone else called it Oklahoma. Bates McFarland built homes there too, but transportation to town was difficult.

Since San Antonio had switched over to electric trolleys, a Rockport committee purchased two old mule-drawn vehicles from the inland city. They built county barns northwest of the Cove and laid tracks on Magnolia Street as far north as Orleans.

When the city of San Antonio replaced mule-drawn trolleys, Rockport bought some of them.

—Courtesy of Shirley Ratisseau Collection

Young boys from Rockport thought that riding the trolley was a lot of fun, but they never had money to pay for the treat. James Clark Herring later confessed: "We'd wait until the driver was in the barn, where he couldn't see us, and then we'd push the cars off [the track]. When he came back, we'd help him put them on again and he'd let us ride free. I don't think he ever did catch on."

Even with the trolley, Finney's Oklahoma development did not succeed. Some families ultimately moved their houses to Rockport.

The trolley continued four miles south of Oklahoma to Estes Flats. The first settlers there, Addison and Joyce William Barber from nearby Beeville, bought land from the John Phillips survey and raised cattle on it. Gradually, vegetable and hog farmers moved near them, and the settlement became known for its meat and produce.

THE RAILROAD AND THE TOURISTS

New York's Col. Uriah Lott finally achieved what George Fulton couldn't—he chartered the San Antonio and Aransas Pass Railroad. The *St. Louis Globe-Democrat* described how Lott did it:

"He moved up from Corpus Christi with all his possessions heaped on a two-wheeled cart. He got a Charter to build a railroad from San Antonio to Aransas Pass. He graded a mile of it, throwing a great deal more than one shovel full of dirt with his own hands." Lott purchased an engine that had been condemned six years before and he picked up two old cars at a bargain. On them, in bold lettering, he had printed in lamp black: S.A. & A.P. "With one mile of old track," the St. Louis story continued, "Lott started the Aransas Pass System. There has been some tall financing in the history of railroad building in this country, but there isn't anything which, for dazzling pluck, could approach this story."

Lott received no financial support from San Antonio, but used the city's name in an effort to attract San Antonio tourists. He got his money from Corpus Christi, Aransas Pass, Rockport, and private investors—all interests that would benefit from the San Antonio visitors.

By the time the rail's trestle spanned Nueces Bay in November 1886, the Coleman-Fulton Pasture Company had agreed to cede right of way for the tracks to continue on to Rockport.

The railroad provided Addison Barber's promising settlement (Estes Flats) with a siding and depot—as well as with the community's early identification as Barber Switch. For a while Barber Switch thrived; in 1905 the county passed a bond issue to build a school there. How or why the community came to be known as Estes Flats is now a mystery.

The first train arrived in Rockport in July 1888, with Charles Henry McLester as its engineer. Three-year-old Sid Freeborn, aboard the train with his parents, was completely caught up in the fanfare. But agents of the Morgan Steamship Line looked grimly seaward. Their last ship was sailing away, never to return. Rockport's water transport heyday ended.

The tourist era began. George Fulton gave a banquet at his mansion, honoring the people who came on that first train. Little Sid Freeborn was among them, and he slept that night in the Shell Hotel.

The hotel had been packery mogul William S. Hall's mansion south of Fulton. Lt. Gov. Barnett Gibbs had bought the grand house but lived there only a short time before turning it to commercial use. The Shell Hotel could accommodate one hundred guests.

From that time on, San Antonians boarded one of four trains to Rockport each day. They settled into elegant coaches, reclining chair cars and Pullman buffet sleepers. They enjoyed fine dining as the miles rolled by. Elegant buggies met them at the Rockport station; townspeople gathered to watch them alight. The Rockport Chamber of Commerce published a booklet:

BEAUTIFUL ROCKPORT
the Unrivalled Gulf Port of Texas
the coming City of 200,000 people

Soon the rail line extended to Ocean View—Live Oak Point. Promoters planned a townsite there, much as James Power did three-quarters of a century earlier.

Some men came for the game in Aransas fields and bays; elite sportsmen found that Rockport offered the most comfortable lodging when they angled for tarpon in the Gulf. A variety of private hunting and fishing clubs offered transportation from trains to the club properties. In all of them, sportsmen spoke of George Fulton as "the Prince of Southwest Texas." The *San Antonio Express* reported that when duck hunters gathered in Fulton's home, he liked to "mingle his basso profundo in their jolly choruses."

Less affluent Aransans—who found it odd that men might hunt for pleasure rather than for sustenance—shot game for Northern tables. Jim Bludworth was among them. One day, as his nephew Tom later told the story, Jim heard a rustling in the sort of bush "that quails like to be in." With one shot into the bush, he killed twenty-two quail.

Well-dressed ladies cluster excitedly as the latest train arrives from San Antonio.
—Courtesy of Gordon Stanley Collection

This mansion built by packery mogul William Hall became the Shell Hotel when the railroad reached Rockport. Old-timers claimed that Jean Lafitte built fires in the hollow of the oak tree. The window at upper right marks the room where James Sorenson, Jr. was born.
—Photographed circa 1900 by Rev. A. H. P. McCurdy
and given to Aransas County Historical Society
courtesy of his granddaughter Marian
(Mrs. Richard) Robertson

Jim and his brother Jed also hunted ducks, using a gunpowder formula they got from "Moore's Universal Assistant." One day they shot 200 ducks between them. An agent shipped their kills to New York by the barrelful.

The first conservation laws were still decades away and neither the Bludworth boys nor any other hunter could conceive of a time when their plentiful birds would be scarce.

The Conglon Hotel continued to attract guests and newcomers as it had from the beginning of the cattle boom, but after a while its name changed to Orleans.

Farther south on Water Street, the Bruhl Hotel had become Bayside Inn. A neighbor, Winifred Evans, wrote later that "the hotel was not large; its guests often were family groups or congenial friends." As a result, Bayside Inn became a sort of exclusive resort, frequented by society people like Miss Brackenridge from San Antonio.

The grandest hotel of all was the Aransas. Col. John H. Traylor bought all of Merchants Square to build it. It was the largest wooden structure of its time, standing three stories tall and covering almost the entire block bounded by Water, Wharf, Austin, and Main streets. A fourth floor tower had interior lighting and a flag pole, but the light caused such problems for ships that it was soon discontinued.

Opened in 1889, the Aransas Hotel boasted fifty rooms and wide verandas encircling the first and second floors. Most of the bedroom furniture was made by convicts at the Huntsville Prison. Professor Attwater displayed his extensive collection of mounted birds at the hotel, perhaps launching an appreciation of Aransas birds that continues to this day.

Colonel Traylor provided his personal yacht so that guests at the hotel could have bay and Gulf excursions. Surreys and hack carriages from Thompson's Livery Stables offered sightseeing trips across the peninsula. Other visitors rode the Estes trolley.

The Aransas Hotel dining room, with no visible support for its spacious ceiling, was a wonder to see. The food was a wonder too—turtle steaks on the menu every day, Taft Ranch beef, oyster cocktails. Guests sat in high-backed, ornately carved chairs to enjoy it all. The hotel's own bakery produced choice cakes and tasty pastries. Orchestras played nightly for dancing, with a Grand Ball every Saturday. Big bands came to town, including one made up entirely of women.

Soon "ragged-time" music was all the rage. It seemed to fit the mood and mode of Aransas—a county whose destiny, many believed, was to become a great tourist center and a great business center, the focal point of the entire Texas coast. The business community did everything in its power to make that happen.

SOCIETY PAGES

The Kennedy girls, Janie and Lizzie, took their triangular piece of land where the beach road met Austin Street and gave it to the city for a park. The King's Daughters, an interdenominational women's organization, built a large gazebo on the property, but then had to put up a fence to keep the cows out. A stile over the fence allowed human access to the park and gazebo.

Texas Governor James Stephen Hogg vacationed at the Aransas Hotel, and then the Bailey Pavilion opened. It was a marvelous thing, located at the end of a wharf in front of the hotel, and bathers splashed in its shade.

During the day, the Pavilion offered ice cold soda and mineral waters, lemonade, ginger ale, and sweet cider. In the evening, traveling troupes presented theatricals, minstrels, and medicine shows on the Pavilion's fine stage.

On June 9, 1891, the *Beacon* announced: "Dave Hertzfeld opened his fine new billiard parlor in the Aransas [Hotel] last Saturday night. The Mechanic's Band were in attendance and furnished some fine music on the occasion." Elsewhere, the paper mentioned that "the summer visitors are beginning to come in quite lively."

A rail line was completed as far as Waco. Professor Attwater, for whom the prairie chicken would later be named, used the train to advertise Aransas by exhibiting, in a specially decorated car, the fruits and vegetables raised by Aransas farmers. He also showed his collection of mounted birds.

HEADLINES

Too soon, the boomtown rush of instant gratification and the selfish, short-term goals of some businessmen resulted in economic collapse. Irene L. Norvell wrote in her memoir that the following winter was "very gloomy" and many buildings burned.

Several years earlier, in 1885, Sam Smith had given the city a fire wagon with a chemical tank and a large black horse to pull it. When a fire alarm came in, volunteers might hitch the horse to the wagon, or they might just tie a rope to it and pull it with their saddle horses. Fred Hoopes was the first fire chief and W. S. Doughty was the first to drive the rig to a fire.

A wedding photo of Irene Barton and Elisha Norvell. She introduced the game of Charades to the Bailey Pavilion crowd.
—Courtesy of Jackson family Collection

The arrangement was a good start, but hardly enough protection. People believed that the fires in 1891 had been started for the insurance. The first of them may have originated in a saloon in the middle of the business block facing west. It swept up the street destroying all in its path, including Sorenson's two-level brick store.

Irene Norvell wrote that fires continued "in different parts of the town, until it was rumored there was a combined effort to burn Rockport.... A watch patrol was organized. The men in their block took turns watching each night. Mama and I did not take off our clothing for five nights in succession, and kept our trunks packed and stationed by an outside door all winter."

Instability and ruin had resulted from the building boom. The *Beacon* ran a scathing anonymous article in June, summing up the situation and advocating planned growth:

Bayside Inn, an early tourist hotel on Walter Street, was popular with the San Antonio social set.
—Courtesy of Jackson family Collection

The Aransas Hotel, later renamed Del Mar, was the largest wooden hotel in the United States. Its dining room, with no central supports, was a wonder to all.
—Courtesy of Jackson family Collection

The elegant Bailey Pavilion at the end of its long pier was preceded by the Coleman-Fulton Pasture Company Building, left foreground, on the Rocky Point. This building was later moved to 708 N. Magnolia, where it still stands, with one room added. Postcard.

—Courtesy of Aransas County Historical Society Archives

The white house, center, is marked with an "X," and the postcard text reads: "This card will give you a view of the residence we rented while here." The weather tower is visible between that house and the next building. The Bailey Pavilion is in the background right, and the bank at left. Postcard.

—Courtesy of Gordon Stanley Collection

THE CITY

WHAT DO OUR CITY FATHERS INTEND TO DO

For several years, patiently waiting, the citizens of Rockport have elected men to administer the affairs of the city; they have begged, they have supplicated and entreated . . . but their supplications have been spurned, their entreaties disregarded. . . .

The sanitary condition of the city is in a deplorable plight, pet ordinances are passed, and recorded, and that is the last of that. . . . Smallpox is in our neighboring city Corpus Christi, yet no steps are taken to quarantine against that loathsome disease. . . . If the money that has been spent on our streets had been judiciously handled, there would have been enough to have an engine and a supply of water in case of fire—all this has been denied our people. . . . The crisis came, and then, oh! where was your fire department—none to be had. . . .

If you wish your city to grow, see that your laws are enforced . . . you will see a "boom what is a boom." Then the stranger will have to acknowledge that Aransas is really in earnest, and that real estate is real estate, and not for buncomb only.

— X.Y.Z.

In 1892 Aransas elected William Henry Baldwin as county judge. "The county was in bad shape," he wrote later, "and it was my misfortune, apparently, to have inherited the job of finding and correcting the trouble." He discovered that the Commissioners Court had passed an order to build a plank road from Rockport west along Market Street "to the prairie." Embroiled in political squabbling, Baldwin wrote that moving to Aransas was "a major mistake" from a financial standpoint and that accepting the judgeship was his second major mistake.

The passage seems poignantly reminiscent of James Byrne, but Aransas was feeling her way to greatness. She faltered sometimes, but business interests still had their eyes on the stars: Colonel Traylor removed his hotel's tower to make room for more accommodations and renamed the place Del Mar. James Hoopes converted his tall, turreted bayfront home to a luxury hotel. And it seemed that if a man wasn't working on a hotel or a house, he was building a boat.

THE *NOVICE*

Jim Bludworth, born on San José Island in 1869, had spent all his life around boats. He and his brother John worked with their father at the family shipyard behind Sorenson's store.

Roaming through the island dunes one day, the boys found a mahogany log. The plan they began to form started with a quick trip back to the mainland for dynamite. John and Jim returned to their treasure and set the dynamite in the log. Hiding behind some dunes for safety, they exploded the mahogany. There was no other way to get the huge trunk home.

That lumber became their framing for a special boat, one that Jim and John wouldn't talk about in any great detail. Those who saw the work of the Bludworth boys suspected they had their eyes on an upcoming sailboat race.

Such events often offered substantial prizes. Some boats had professional crews; most had tremendous sailspreads. Admirers followed the progress of favorite boats and skippers so avidly that fights were common. Enthusiasm over a close finish stirred the crowd to a frenzy.

When the Bludworths' mahogany-framed boat was complete to the last detail, the brothers held a christening. They introduced their creation as *The Novice of Rockport*. She was a thirty-foot sailing boat with a twelve-foot six-inch beam and a three-foot draft, finished just in time for the 1892 Fourth of July Rockport Regatta, sponsored by the San Antonio *Daily Express* newspaper.

People watched the thirty-mile race from all along the bayfront. Young Winifred Evans followed it from the upstairs gallery of a beach road home. Later, she wrote of the race: "Up to the turning point the victory was any boat's. After starting on the homeward lap, *The Novice* forged ahead . . . and, as the wind freshened and filled her cloud of canvas, the crowd became intent on the race in a quiet way, talking together in low tones."

The contest lasted only four hours, fifty-two minutes and two seconds. *The Novice* "came around the finishing stake with a flourish . . . greeted with a deafening roar from the crowd." Her nearest competitor arrived twenty-two minutes later.

At the banquet and ball that night, Jim and John Bludworth accepted an elegant trophy. For days, people speculated on their victory. *The Novice* had outdistanced good boats, handled by skilled seamen. "Was there some different angle about the prow," Winifred wrote, "or was the keel a little deeper to allow the carrying of more canvas? The Bludworths still were not talking." To the best of any-one's knowledge, *The Novice* was never defeated in any subsequent race.

Later, Jim Bludworth had business cards made and started to run a party boat:

The Yacht *Novice*
G. J. Bludworth, Capt.
Polite and Courteous Treatment
Your Patronage Solicited
Rockport

He returned, in a way, to his early days of hunting and fishing. And Jim Bludworth helped to establish the fine tradition of Aransas party boats still working the bays.

The Bludworth's sloop Novice *as she races toward the finish flag. Negative provided to the Texas Maritime Museum by James H. Sorenson, Jr.*

THE TOWN OF FULTON

Two hundred people lived in the town of Fulton by 1888. Their one-room school at Seventh and Cactus streets was two years old, and the citizens decided it was time to build a town hall. They voted to change the town's name, as well. It would be Aransas City, intending to honor George Fulton's earliest development activities on Live Oak Point. Few seemed to consider that it would honor, too, James Power, who started the *empresa*, and Escandón, who first chose the name.

TURTLES

So much attention to cattle had diminished an appreciation of the other great resource of Aransas—the life in its bays. By 1880 a federal government fisheries expert had become aware of that, writing that Massachusetts had less sealife than the "rich tribute of delicious fish and mollusks" blessing Aransas, but the northern state harvested five times as much of it as the entire Gulf Coast.

Local fishermen soon decided that if Aransas teemed with delights denied the harsh, cold north, the county surely had enough to share. They quickly discovered that northern markets were willing to pay any price for the magnificent fare of Aransas.

By 1890 the report of the Commissioner of Fish and Fisheries counted 311 sail craft and 536 skiffs—vessels propelled by oars—"employed regularly in the fisheries of Texas." Bay-seine fishing gave steady employment to 358 men. They generally worked on shares, and although the captain received no more than any of his men, the boat and seine, which he usually owned, counted as one share.

The bay fishermen caught redfish, sea trout, sand trout, sheepshead, croakers, jackfish, hogfish, drum, mullet, bluefish, Spanish mackerel, pompano, rockfish, jewfish, pigfish, and whiting. In lesser numbers, they also caught shoemaker, perch, pike, flat croaker, robalo, sawfish, catfish, calico-fish, needlefish, moonfish, gulf menhaden, and crabs—considered of no value and almost always thrown away.

These fish were not the only wealth the bays had to offer. In 1840 writer Benjamin Lundy had called Aransas turtle meat a great luxury. He considered it most savory when prepared as turtle soup, "a dish fit for London aldermen." Lundy expressed amazement that the delicacy was "cheap and ordinary food in the south and west of Texas." The romance of Aransas had begun to spread.

As early as 1870 beef packeries had begun small side-operations to process the plentiful turtles. One fisherman claimed to have caught eleven of the reptiles in one day at Shamrock Point, projecting westward from Mustang Island into Corpus Christi Bay.

At Aransas the months from June through September were most lucrative. The turtles came in, put on weight rapidly, and were soon in prime condition for slaughter.

In September 1877 Capt. Ned Mercer wrote in his log: "Commenced to build a turtle scull. Having a hell of a time to get the right shape." Two days later, Harry Douglas took two turtles to Fulton and brought back twine to make nets. After the completed nets were boiled and hung to dry, anchors secured them. Ned and John Mercer sold sea turtles to Charles Holden at the Fulton Canning Company for the next several years. Others did too.

On sloops, catboats, and schooner-rigged boats, turtlers worked the reefs of Aransas Bay and up into Matagorda with special fourteen-mesh nets. They brought in turtles as big as tables— the smallest of them weighing a hundred pounds and the largest a full 500—sometimes ten to a net. When the captain had a boat load, he returned to the canneries.

Netters usually earned from one to three cents per pound for their turtles, but Aransas Bay fishermen soon learned they could keep their catch alive and wait for better prices. They traded with Galveston markets; they trussed some of the turtles for live shipment by steamer to New York.

One French cowboy-turned-sailor (a Ratisseau) hoped to put old skills to new practice. An expert cattle roper, he was taken out in a boat, and asked to lasso turtles. Though it had seemed like a good idea, once a turtle had a noose around its neck, it dropped to great depths like a stone. The scheme failed.

In 1890 Texas landed more than half of the entire Gulf turtle catch by weight—250,000 pounds. Eighty-five percent of all Texas turtle nets deployed were in Aransas Bay, and the Fulton Canning Company produced 40,000 two-pound cans of turtle meat that year.

The cannery stood at the water's edge a little north of George Fulton's mansion. A wharf extended into the bay between Cactus and Chaparral streets, and the live turtles were kept in large pens on its south side. Sometimes there would be a hundred or more of the huge reptiles swimming around at once. Another pen was up in Copano Bay, just where Copano Creek flowed into it.

Turtle pens were twelve-foot-square constructions of wood stakes driven into soft sand beneath six feet of water. The stakes were placed a few inches apart to let water flow through, then roped together for strength.

Men at the cannery stripped off the turtle shells and threw them overboard; fish came in to feed. Local fishermen cast their lines on the north side of the wharf and got good catches of trout and redfish there.

After processing the turtle meat, the cannery gave away turtle broth by the bucketful, a boon for some families during lean seasons.

Young Henry Bailey managed the Fulton plant's ten employees. He hadn't much liked working in his father's Rockport print shop, though he was good at setting type. Before Henry was in his twenties, he'd had enough of ink and turned to turtles instead.

As he got to know his work, Henry found that he could get in the trap and grab free rides on the backs of the harmless giants. One particular evening, late, he stripped off his clothes and leaped into the turtle pen. He had just climbed onto a turtle's back when three young ladies strolled by for a look at the great reptiles. Henry couldn't hide himself and hang on to the turtle at the same time. He ended up under water, wishing he could drown. For days after, Henry imagined that people were staring at him and telling jokes behind his back.

The Fulton turtle pens, with processing plant in background. Worker, center right, gives size perspective.
—Courtesy Gayle Atwood, from the 1889-1891 *Report on the Coastal Fisheries of Texas,* from the Library of The University of Texas at Austin.

Too soon, turtlers began to complain that the resource was diminishing. By 1895 a law required turtle-fishing licenses and a minimum size of twelve pounds per turtle. Boats worked down the coast and into Mexico, casting out twine nets seven to ten feet wide and sixty to one hundred feet long.

Fishermen hoped especially for green turtles—so named because their fat was green—and they found them nesting in huge numbers on the deep sand shores of the Caribbean and Gulf of Mexico. The men anchored their nets in channels, snaring turtles by the head or flippers. Two or three animals a day seemed a satisfactory catch, though sometimes the men still got twenty.

By the turn of the century, most believed that setting a turtle net in Aransas was hardly worth the trouble. A few of the animals continued to turn up in seines for trout, redfish, and sheepshead, but that was all.

Fishermen began to learn that Mother Nature, however generous, has her limits.

GOLD AND ASHES

On March 12, 1890, Fulton's leading citizens staged the grandest social event that Aransas could imagine. George and Harriet Fulton invited a hundred or more friends to their golden wedding anniversary. Friends came from all parts of the state. Many arrived by special train from San Antonio and Corpus Christi, joining the Fultons' two sons, two daughters, and sixteen grandchildren for the gala celebration.

Friends from Maine to Central America sent letters, telegrams, and cards of congratulation. Packages for the Fultons covered several tables. In the midst of smaller gifts stood one from Mifflin Kenedy. It was a large, solid gold vase, engraved with the names of the honorees.

The *San Antonio Express* newspaper covered the anniversary celebration, describing George Fulton as "a man of most striking presence, very tall and so erect that it is hard to believe that he carries the weight of eighty years on his broad shoulders. His long beard is white, but his hair of youthful thickness is only iron gray. His eyes, voice, and manner are those of a man twenty years younger."

The paper reported that Harriet's dress was trimmed with "exquisite point lace . . . that she had herself made in the last year or two, proving that time had not trifled with her eyesight or energies." Harriet was sixty-eight, "a charming little dictator so small that she walked easily beneath his outstretched arm." The newspaper further described her as "quite fleshy, of fine social qualities, racy and interesting in conversation and not easily irritated."

The mansion's "grand halls and corridors were richly festooned with flowers" and the Fultons spread a beautiful and lavish supper. Their huge punch bowl "stayed full all the evening, though many healths were drunk . . . to the happiness of the bride and groom." Young people danced to the music of a good band.

"Everything," reported the *Baltimore Sun*, "was arranged as a sweet, delightful palace where wealth and love abide." After midnight, the guests "filed out of the house and proceeded to a long hall some twenty-five or thirty steps from the mansion." There a long table groaned under the weight of still more food. The festivities continued until two or three in the morning.

The *Express* concluded that the journalistic chestnut "Is marriage a failure?" could be easily answered by anyone who attended the Fultons' party: "Lovingly, hand in hand they have traveled along the pathway of life; and now celebrate their golden wedding in a palace. . . . No, marriage is not a failure, but is heaven born and a grand success."

Two years later, George Fulton was too ill to perform his duties as president of the Coleman-Fulton Pasture Company. The economic panic of 1893 robbed him even of his optimistic dream that the company could resume dividend payments.

It is likely that Fulton was not even able to respond to this letter from young Theodore Roosevelt, then a lowly civil service commissioner:

> I am greatly interested in our pioneer Western history and am preparing a work on the subject. Two volumes of it are published already and two volumes more are in the course of preparation. I shall then come to the period covering the Texas struggle against Mexico, and am most anxious to get any letters, journals, diaries, or any other contemporary memoranda of that eventful epoch. Would it be possible for you out of your own experience to furnish me with such, or to tell me where I could get them? . . . Trusting that you will excuse my writing to you in view of the great interest I take in the history of your State, and in thanking you in advance for answering me, I am, with great respect,
> Cordially yours,
>
> [sig.]THEODORE ROOSEVELT

George Fulton had been ill for a year. During the afternoon and evening of October 30, 1893, he suffered a series of violent seizures. When the end came at 7:45 P.M., however, it came "as peacefully as the setting of a summer sun." The body of Col. George Ware Fulton was laid to rest beside that of his little granddaughter Emma, at a funeral larger than any ever held in Rockport.

The funeral honored a man who had a dream equal to that of James Power. The two men seem as different as any can be, except that both intended to be empire builders. On a personal level, both might seem to have failed; at least the specifics of their dreams were never realized. Aransas has no grand port, no vast and wealthy ranch, no thriving industry. But James Power and George Fulton shaped the land and their spirits mark it still.

Power's influence now lives more in Refugio than in Aransas. George Fulton and others like him erased the Irishness. They made Aransas more heterogeneous, more vital.

The son, George William Fulton, died in 1895, leaving his widowed mother with no one to look after her interests in the financially-stricken ranch. Harriet Fulton closed her once grand home and moved away.

Over the next several years, her letters described the mansion's deterioration: "I am very, very sorry to have the old house so neglected, but I do not see how it is to be helped, as we cannot live there without the means to live on. . . . It is such a lovely house. . . . I wish some millionaire who is fond of hunting and fishing would come and buy it. It does seem too bad for the place to go to complete ruin for want of paint."

By then, the population of Fulton had fallen to twenty-five and the post office closed. But a few remaining citizens restored the name "Fulton" to their tiny community, and families kept their memories.

WOMEN ALONE

As Harriet Fulton was so painfully discovering, men and women were halves of a whole; they needed each other to make life work. Many a middle-aged widower married a young girl because he needed someone to make his home. Many a middle-aged widow found it less easy to attract a new mate.

The problem exacerbated if the single woman was working-class, not wealthy. Mary Ellen Wilkinson Close McHugh, widowed, remarried and divorced since 1873, was hard pressed to make a living for herself and two children. She purchased a lot from George Fulton in 1876 and opened up an "eating house." It was on the main road that paralleled the water, convenient to the packing plants. Every day she fed that rough crowd and raised her family.

Mary Elizabeth and Katherine Isabella Simpson came from a seafaring family. Their father was Capt. John Simpson, who moved from St. Mary's to Rockport in 1882; their grandfather Moses Simpson had first arrived at Aransas with Zachary Taylor. Their mother Catherine was the daughter of Capt. Joel Stinson, who ran a pilot service to the bay towns.

Captain Stinson met two- and three-masted sailboats at Ropesville, the developing town on Mustang Island, and because of the treacherous shoals in Copano Bay, he marked his route with stakes. It didn't take the ship captains long to figure that out, so they dispensed with Stinson's services and followed the markers themselves. Indignant, the canny pilot pulled up the stakes; by then he knew the way well enough. Less experienced captains ran aground and had to flag him in distress.

Katherine Simpson married ship pilot Frank Casterline, but he died while their four children were very young. Kate walked from Fulton to Rockport, where she did washing all day in private homes and then walked home. For all that labor, she earned a dollar a day. Her sister fared little better.

Mary Elizabeth Simpson met and fell in love with François Zephirin Rouquette, born at Campagnac, Aveyron, France. He was employed by the Quarantine Station on Shell Bank Island, where he inspected all incoming ships for disease. In August of 1888 he and his bride set up housekeeping at Ropesville.

The marriage certificate identified François Zephirin Rouquette as "Charlie Wilson," an Anglo name he liked to use. Sometimes people called him "Sundown" Wilson too.

After only a year or two, the Rouquettes moved to Fulton and by Christmas Eve 1898 they had four children to help them celebrate. Even so, François left home, telling his wife he had an errand to run.

No one knows exactly what happened after that, but it ended with Rouquette stabbed in the back. He managed to get home before he collapsed, but he died in the early hours of Christmas day.

Add Mary Elizabeth Simpson to the long list of women who survived *femme sole* in Aransas.

IN THE NAME OF PROGRESS

THE JETTIES

From the days of earliest voyages to Aransas, explorers and settlers had been baffled by the infamous Corpus Christi mud flats, just inside the Aransas pass. Ships could reach the mainland behind Mustang Island only by traveling north through Aransas Bay, then entering the cut between Quarantine and Shell Bank islands and looping south again. Still the water was shallow. As long as the mud flats remained intact, Aransas ports were easier to access than Corpus Christi could ever be.

Early in the life of the Republic of Texas, settlements all along the south-central Texas coastline—Matagorda, Lavaca, Indianola, Saluria, Copano, St. Mary's, and Corpus Christi—struggled for distinction as deep water ports. By 1853 the United States Corps of Engineers expressed an interest in establishing a harbor in the Coastal Bend.

Three years after that, Pryor Lea's Aransas Road Company received rights not only to construct and maintain a road or rail line, but also to improve navigation at the Aransas bar.

Henry Kinney, former resident of Aransas City and founder of Corpus Christi, twice received charters to improve the channels to his town, but he made little headway. In 1858 a company of English capitalists tried again, writing: "All that was necessary was to cut a navigable channel through the sand bar at Aransas pass to build up one of the world's greatest seaports."

A year later, local officials and businessmen published their

"First Annual Report of the Directors of the Corpus Christi Ship Channel Company." It proposed a channel nine feet deep, crossing the mud flats. The consortium boasted that their channel would make Corpus Christi a port second only to Galveston. They even claimed certainty that "less difficulty will be encountered on entering this port than is now experienced in running Galveston." The partners also proposed a rail line from Corpus Christi to Mazatlán, Mexico, on the Pacific coast, but no part of their dream ever materialized. The Civil War halted it.

Shortly after the war, Pryor Lea resumed his project. Since deepening the Aransas pass was crucial for Rockport-Fulton's cattle business, George Fulton assisted Lea with frequent letters to government officials and influential politicians.

In 1868 the citizens of Rockport subscribed $10,000 and built a 600-foot dike on San José Island. They might as well have dumped their money in the bay. Just two years later, army engineers surveying the pass found no trace of the brush and rock embankment.

Rockport *Transcript* editor Charles Bailey wrote of the urgency for deep water on February 12, 1870: "It is true that Aransas bar is in fine order, in fact, more depth of water than there has been in a long time. Yet it is liable to shoal again. The plan proposed by us was a dam across Corpus Christi Pass and Cedar Bayou, thereby compelling the waters of Corpus Christi Bay, San Antonio Bay and the smaller bays between San Antonio and Aransas Bays to find their sole outlet to the Gulf through the Aransas pass."

Augustus T. Morris and James Cummings completed an enduring "cut" in 1874, enhancing the future of Corpus Christi. Their channel, eight feet wide, crossed one hundred feet of mud flats between Corpus Christi Bay and the natural Lydia Ann Channel. A year later, the Texas-Mexican Railroad was chartered. Its directors had in mind, among other goals, the idea of shipping from its terminus, through the Aransas pass.

Next, the U.S. Congress resolved to deepen the Aransas pass, ordering a survey in 1878. The Corps of Engineers puzzled over the fluctuating shorelines of San José and Mustang islands where they abutted the pass. From 1880 until 1885, they had workmen planting trees on San José, building a retaining wall along the channel face of Mustang Island and installing sand fences at the heads of both islands—all attempts to halt erosion. And they built a south jetty 5,500 feet long.

Beginning at the Mustang shoreline, this Mansfield jetty—named for the engineer in charge of the project—ran out to the wreck of the *Mary*, then curved sharply north. But the structure, alternating layers of rock and brush "mattresses," just settled into the shifting sands.

In 1886 the Rockport post office changed its name to Aransas Pass, clearly a public relations move as new jetty work began under the direction of David Means Picton. A pioneer in the organization of the Aransas Pass Harbor Company, he had married Frances Ellen Hynes, daughter of Judge John Hynes. The *Herald* described Picton as "a very conservative businessman," who was "in no sense of the word a boomer, and has never owned a piece of real estate except for legitimate business purposes."

Professor Lewis M. Haupt and H. C. Ripley were consulting engineers with a new approach: Their jetty would be "detached from the shore and located on the bar to the 'windward' of the channel." It would curve in a gentle S "to produce reactions similar to those found in the concavities of streams."

The plan didn't work. The Haupt jetty intersected the old Mansfield at a forty-five-degree angle, blocking the natural water flow. Another organization took over.

Army engineer Col. Henry M. Robert inspected the situation. "The improvement of this pass," he wrote, "has been greatly complicated by the works of the Aransas Pass Harbor Company, and the pass will never be as good as it would have been had these works never been constructed."

By this time, Rockport had given up the name Aransas Pass, and the town of Aransas Harbor appropriated it.

Rockport had continued to focus on the rail transportation that would support its sea lanes. In 1891 the *Beacon* had reported "an important epoch in Texas railroad history. . . . We now have direct through communication from Chicago to Rockport. What more could we desire? All we want now is deep water to enable the great Rock Island Road [from Chicago] to become the successful

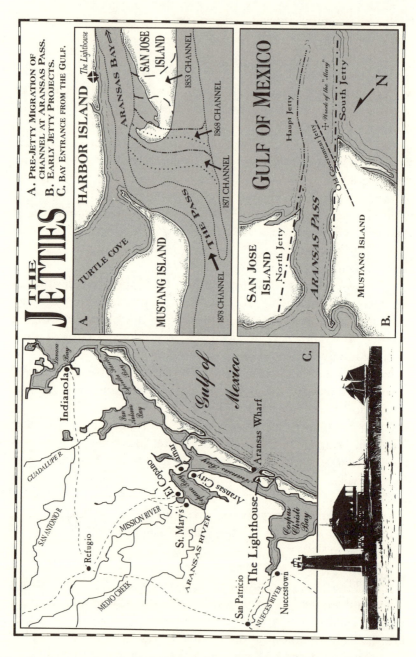

This drawing depicts several attempts to build effective jetties for the Aransas pass. Illustration by Chris Blum.

competitor of the Jay Gould system with its terminal at New Orleans. . . . The obstruction to navigation must be speedily removed."

The Corps of Engineers reassumed responsibility for the jetty work and soon understood that Haupt's jetty, unattached to either island, was a failed concept. The Corps received authority to connect that jetty to San José and to build a new south jetty on Mustang Island.

The struggle continued.

INTERFACE

With the coming of so much technology, Aransas at last became an integrated part of the world. The search for petroleum, underway in America for fifty years, had just reached Texas. In October 1900 mining engineer Anthony Lucas began to drill for oil in Beaumont.

His crew was changing the drill bit on the morning of January 10. Then, as Allen W. Hamill later described it, "the drilling mud commenced to boil up through the rotary, and it got higher and higher and higher up through the top of the derrick and with such pressure, why, the drill pipe commenced to move up. It moved up and started to going out through the top of the derrick."

A while later, Hamill "looked down the hole there. I heard— sorta heard something kinda bubbling . . . and here this frothy oil was starting up. But it was just breathing like, you know, coming up and sinking back with the gas pressure. And it kept coming up and over the rotary table and each flow a little higher. Finally it came up with such momentum that it just shot up clear through the top of the derrick." The name of the oilfield was Spindletop, and the event would change the entire Texas coast in ways few could then imagine.

In 1900 a commission including Dr. Walter Reed began the fight against yellow fever. Coastal communities would be safer than ever before.

In 1902 Wilbur and Orville Wright flew their airplane from a

North Carolina sand dune. Eminent scientists scoffed at the practicability of the craft, but by 1910, in San Antonio, Texas, the United States Army put together its first airplane—a sort of kit supplied by Wilbur Wright.

Later Harry Traylor and Ham Smith told of Aransas people who bent double laughing at the very idea that such a contraption could fly. But by the time the Army Air Corps had six planes, anyone who could get from Aransas to San Antonio went to see the flying machines. And sooner than anyone might have thought, planes landed at Aransas too.

A SPORTSMAN'S PARADISE

By this time, Andrew Sorenson had left the cattle business to become a sportsmen's guide. Sorenson first had a site on the west side of Port Bay, then in 1909 bought and relocated to a hunting center on the east side. He moved two buildings from the first site to his new Sorenson Club. One building would be the kitchen and the other a dining hall that became known as the Tall Tale Room.

Two years later, Sorenson incorporated as a private club—the Port Bay Hunting Club—and offered $150 shares to one hundred charter members. The shares were easy to sell because Sorenson already had an established following of satisfied customers. They

Port Bay Club hunters with a day's kill.
—Courtesy of the Port Bay Club papers

came not only from Texas but from great cities all over the United States and many of the men were notable: J. C. Cheeseborough of the company that made Vaseline; Max Fleischmann, the yeast company man; George Norman Pierce of Pierce-Arrow automobiles.

The hunters arrived, usually, on the San Antonio and Aransas Pass Railroad, but they did not ride all the way to Rockport. It was shorter to disembark at Gregory and continue by hired car to the club property. Most men stayed in four-bed dormitory-style rooms sixteen feet square; they shared a common bath. A few men, like oilman I. C. Thurmond, built private lodges.

Thurmond once claimed that "ducks would fly over the bay about 10,000 at a time, almost blackening the sky. You could shoot in any direction and hit them." At Swan Lake, two miles from the club, Thurmond wrote that he killed forty-two ducks with just five shots from his twelve-gauge automatic shotgun. "That was enough," he said. "I quit for the day." His birds, like those of other hunters, were sent home salted down in barrels.

Andrew Sorenson was hardly alone in the hunting business. The Oakshore Club offered similar services, and its prominent membership included Texas Governor James Ferguson. The old Fulton Mansion became the Texas Club, and E. H. R. Green built the Tarpon Club on San José Island.

A. J. "Moose" Adolphus started the first public hunting and fishing center in Aransas County.

By 1918 the whooping cranes of Aransas were almost gone; naturalists were able to account for only fifty of them worldwide. The birds found help when Congress passed the Migratory Bird Treaty Act.

Hunting and guiding continued to flourish. Jimmy Silberisen started out on Port Bay renting boats, selling bait, running a little restaurant called "Jimmy's." There he fished trot lines and netted. His children picked crabs and sold the meat. By the 1930s Jimmy was able to lease, and later buy, some land near Estes, on Redfish Bay. He called his place Jimmy's Duck Hunting Club and catered mainly to Houston, San Antonio, and Austin hunters. They all followed his rule not to kill female ducks.

Game birds blacken both the sky and a Copano Bay bluff in the 1930s.
—Courtesy of the Shirley Ratisseau Collection

FISH HOUSES

The Rockport newspaper *Beacon* wrote that in 1884 "the fish and oyster business was carried on upon a small scale." Four years later, twenty-year-old David Rockport Scrivner began operating Miller Brothers' Fish Company in Fulton, where Broadway met the water. A fleet of three or four fishing scows—sailboats—could easily bring in two or three thousand pounds of fish at a time.

Scrivner found he had to spend a lot of time on the road, trying to establish markets for the vast amounts of seafood that kept pouring into his fish house. He didn't like traveling from one town to another, Scrivner said. "Transportation was poor, and there were few hotels. A lot of those people didn't like the idea of fish. Some had never eaten any."

Soon two other fish houses joined Scrivner in Fulton, and he had a second location in Rockport. Nineteen years after he started, Scrivner had 170 men working on his thirty-two boats. All the fishermen were his friends; he knew their first names and he knew their children. And other fish houses lined the Rockport-Fulton shore.

Luis Cobilini and a Mr. Gentry opened the Union Fish Company in Rockport, behind a saloon north of Wharf Street. When Rockport citizens erected the first mast to fly weather warning flags, Cobilini manned it. The galvanized tower was located on the east side of Water Street, about where St. Mary's would be if it ran through.

Luis Cobilini sold his operation to Ernest Camehl and the metal tower rusted away. Simon Sorenson took over the job of weatherman and moved the mast to a spot between his store and the beach. The railroad agent received weather reports from Western Union and delivered them to Simon, who then placed the telegrams in his store window.

Winifred Evans Lowther later wrote that "fishermen and seamen . . . were grateful and appreciative of this gesture toward guarding their safety." They had another reason to be grateful: Sorenson's store allowed many of them to buy on credit during the dull nonfishing season.

Roy Jackson bought Scrivner's thriving business, renaming it Jackson Fish Company. Zeph Rouquette, son of widowed Mary Elizabeth Simpson Rouquette, ran it for him. Since Fulton had no ice house, Jackson had to get large blocks in Rockport, then bring them back and crush them.

At the end of each week, Roy cleared the floor of his fish house and held dances for the community. Local fiddlers provided the music and the ladies brought coffee and cake. Young couples put their children to bed atop the ice boxes.

Roy's brother, Stephen Ford Jackson, called Ford, was an executive in the business from the very beginning, and in 1905 Roy changed the company name to Jackson Brothers.

In 1912 Ernest Camehl moved his company just across the tracks from Jackson's Rockport location. W. F. Close, John Weber, and Wesley Atwood worked for him, and many nights they packed forty to fifty barrels of fish for shipment by railroad or express.

The caption on this 1907 postcard reads "81 crabs in 2 hrs., Rockport, Texas." Blue crabs have been a staple of Aransas waters since Karánkawa days. Postcard.
—Courtesy of Gordon Stanley Collection

Guy Hanks stands between the Hawes brothers. Although the fishing has always been good in Aransas, the postcard claim of "19 fish, 100 lbs." seems extravagant. And "caught with hands??" Postcard.
—Courtesy of Aransas County Historical Society Archives

THE OIL BUSINESS

During the 1870s, a landowner wanted a water well at St. Mary's. Workmen digging it brought a water sample to the surface and found it covered with a blackish oil scum. The landowner, worried that the well was spoiled, quickly had the hole covered up.

Hunters and fishermen, camping on nearby Power's Point some years later, claimed to hear loud explosions in the direction of Mission Bay. Early geologists interpreted the circular shape of that bay, and Mission Lake, as evidence of prehistoric explosions of natural gas.

After Spindletop set Beaumont reeling, landowners in Aransas began to dream of black gold. In 1909 Harry Hertzberg and Harry Traylor made the first effort to drill for oil at Aransas, but they never solicited enough funds to drill.

John E. Schell of Pennsylvania leased all of San José Island from T. D. Wood and Sam B. Allyn. He drilled to 3,000 feet, but then abandoned the well and released no information concerning it. H. E. Bahr had a large gas well at White Point, southwest of Aransas. He wrote that it produced "pure petroleum."

Drill derricks dotted Refugio and San Patricio counties. Storage tanks, necessary to hold all the production that was coming in, changed the landscape of Mustang and Harbor islands.

It was an exciting time, an optimistic time. Some wildcatters made promises to investors that would land a man in jail today. Speculators began again to promote Aransas land for homes and businesses. And deepwater issues came again to the fore.

POPULATIONS

WEBER'S STORE

For the few families remaining in Fulton, Fred Weber's small grocery store—at the northwest corner of Cactus and Beach Road—was the center of everything. He kept some supplies in a wire shed on the side of the little house and in the main store everything—even cheese—just sat out in the open. Weber weighed out beans and sugar from the sacks.

Boatmen were the only shoppers who purchased supplies for more than a day at a time; they bought for a week or so. No one considered anything more than the staples; extras came only at Christmas. Even then, a gift was usually little more than a handkerchief or a hand mirror, according to Fred Weber's niece Delphine.

The Fulton post office had been closed for some time before Weber reopened it in his store. Mail for Lamar arrived there, then went by horse and buggy to Live Oak Point and then by boat across to the far peninsula.

Other merchants made the rounds of Fulton homes, selling fresh meat or vegetables; Mr. Sparks delivered milk. People without ice boxes kept their ice in tubs, covered with blankets. On laundry day—almost always Monday—housewives slaved in their backyards, boiling the family clothes in large cast-iron pots over wood fires, poking and churning with wooden sticks. When the clothes were clean and rinsed, the housewives hung them on the clothesline. The next day, they ironed.

The only reliable road to Rockport was the beach road. Back roads were just sand; it was easy to get stuck there. But hogs often rooted up the beach. Since Fulton had no stock laws, cattle, hogs,

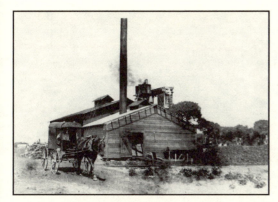

Rockport's first ice plant, with George Frandolig wagon; 1906.

—Courtesy of James Frandolig collection, Aransas County Historical Society Archives

donkeys roamed at will. At slaughter time, the hogs could be identified by their earmarks. The rest of the time, no one really cared.

For entertainment, the citizens of Fulton held dances in their own homes. Sometimes they took out the partitions between rooms to have more space. And at Christmas, people visited from house to house, drinking lots of eggnog and sometimes getting tipsy.

PROMOTERS

In May 1910 the Gulf Coast Immigration Company announced its plan to turn Rockport into a great city. This land promotion group envisioned a railroad running from town to Harbor Island. There an elaborate port facility would receive and dispense oceangoing freight, eliminating commercial clutter in Rockport itself. That way, the town could provide more attractive space for passenger-service ocean liners.

The brochure pointed out that Rockport was only 160 miles from "Uncle Sam's great military base in San Antonio." The promoters contended that "a great Naval base and dry docks must be established here by the Government before the completion of the Panama Canal." Rockport, they insisted, "can be more safely guarded than any other point; it is the nearest harbor to a foreign country. . . . All munitions of war can be more quickly delivered and dispatched to any point south and in only four hours run from . . . San Antonio."

View from the wharf, showing the telephone building and the First National Bank. The land company brochure claimed that Aransas Bay offered the finest fishing in the world. Gulf Coast Immigration brochure.
—Courtesy of Aransas County Historical Society
Archives, donated by Jimmy Sorenson, Jr.

"Homeseekers on the north shore of Rockport bidding adieu to a departing steamer which is taking a crowd of their friends across the bay to a surf bathing party on St. Joseph's Island," — the Gulf Coast Immigration Company brochure. Gulf Coast Immigration brochure.
—Courtesy of Aransas County Historical Society
Archives, donated by Jimmy Sorenson, Jr.

The brochure also touted magnificent vineyards and truck gardens netting over $600 per acre. Gulf Coast Immigration brochure.
—Courtesy of Aransas County Historical Society
Archives, donated by Jimmy Sorenson, Jr.

IMMIGRANTS

During this general period, a true immigration was occurring too. Silvestro Dominguez was part of this slow and quiet movement of people to Aransas. He came from Zatatecas, Mexico, to Soto la Marina before the turn of the century, then crossed the Rio Grande to Port Isabel. There the thirty-eight-year-old man married eighteen-year-old Maria Piña. The family came north along the Gulf beaches, along with other families named Piña and Reyes.

Silvestro Dominguez pulled a barge about twenty feet long, and he rigged up a sail to help him. All his possessions were on that barge as he hauled it through the water. Everyone else in his band walked on the beach. They walked, they rested, they fixed a lunch, and walked again.

At night Silvestro brought the barge to shore and tied it down. Men made a big fire so Maria and the other women could cook. The next morning everything went back on the barge and the people continued north.

They kept on like that until they came to Corpus Christi Pass. They circled Corpus Christi Bay and made their way to the town. Some families stayed there; Silvestro and Maria proceeded to Rockport.

In time they had children—Jesús, Willie, Josephine, Rosendo, Sobeida, Margaret—in a little house on First Street. They lived a simple life.

THE YOUTH OF ROCKPORT

Both the Mexicans and the Anglos attracted by promoters found that they had arrived at Main Street—a typical American town. Old settler families who had formed it and grown with it continued still.

Mary Pearl Herring, born to James Clark Herring and Marie Alice McRae in 1902, grew up in Rockport. Her school was two stories high and seemed elegant, but everyone—teachers and students alike—walked to attend it.

Drinking water was in buckets on a bench out under the trees and each bucket had a dipper in it. "When one wanted a drink," Mary Pearl remembered, "one might have to take the dipper and first push the woolly worms aside . . . but we didn't seem to mind and never heard of the woolly worms causing any ill effects." In 1907 the school graduated its first class to complete all eleven grades.

Often, in the evenings, Rockport families sat on their front porches to enjoy the cool breeze. Sometimes Mexican musicians came into their yards to serenade. "To us," Mary Pearl said, "this was the most beautiful music."

But in summer there was another music, as much a part of Aransas as anything could be. The air rang with a constant shrill treble: *EEEEEEEEEEEEEE*. It was the sound of cicadas and it seemed to come from everywhere at once. The locust-like insects sang throughout the season, and they shed their shells on porch rails, tree trunks, and fences.

Through all the days of cicada song, Mary Pearl enjoyed Sam Prophet's Confectionary and Ice Cream Parlor; she loved bathing parties at Bailey's Pavilion. Mary Pearl remembered that it was a special treat to pay fifteen cents and get to use one of the little rooms to don a bathing suit.

In the evening: "Anyone attending the dances held in the Pavilion would never forget this pleasure: the moonlight on the water, the gentle breeze, the dance music, all went to make it so romantic."

But hometown girls really suffered during the summer months in Rockport, as hometown boys turned all their attentions to the "summer girls."

One of these girls was Bessie Bell. "Rockport has been like a second home to me," she said. "Where I had my first date. . . . He had to go and ask Mother if I could go to the picture show with him."

Bessie's mother, Janie Kennedy Bell, liked to load young people into her big Overland car and drive them to watch the Rockport White Sox baseball team. Home games were played on the field southeast of the intersection of Pearl and the street that would become the highway, but Janie Bell drove to the out of town games too. The White Sox won fame by defeating teams as far away as San Antonio.

Janie had a special interest in the White Sox, since her sister Lizzie had married Ben Shelton, who organized the team. Like

M. J. Terry in front of his home, "probably near 209 North Austin," according to family members, circa 1900.
—Courtesy of Aransas County Historical Society Archives

In 1910 the Rockport school stood in lonely splendor on the prairie.
—Courtesy of Aransas County Historical Society Archives

Four Homes Still

The second S. F. Jackson home on Magnolia Street.
—Courtesy of Tommy A. Shults

The John Sorenson home on Water Street.
—Courtesy of Tommy A. Shults

Standing Today

The Simon Sorenson home on Water Street.
—Courtesy of Aransas County Historical Society
Archives, donated by Simon Sorenson

*The Leopold Bracht home as it was built in the Oklahoma subdivision,
and before remodeling on Concho Street.*
—Courtesy of Lola Bracht Woellert/ Winston Woellert

Albert Bruhl's Drug Store on Austin Street, 1919. To right is the building that became Marvin Davis' cafe; to left is the building that became Judy Collier's library; beyond it is the Sorenson store. The Aransas Hotel, renamed Del Mar, is in the background, left.
—Courtesy of Lola Bracht Woellert/ Winston Woellert

The Rockport White Sox baseball team. Someone named Jeff is at the left end of the front row, with Billy Stevenson next to him. Art Sheldon stands at the left end of the back row, and one of the two young men next to him is a Hertzfeld. Fred Bracht is fourth from left.
—Courtesy of Aransas County Historical Society Archives

everyone else who went to the games—and that was nearly everyone in town—Janie packed a picnic lunch for her crowd and arrived at the ball park early.

Most of the young men on the White Sox team, eighteen to twenty-five years old, played just for the fun of it. "Turkey" Jones was one and Ernest Silberisen was another. Ernest was good, but not particularly inclined to run after the ball. Fred Bracht, Leopold's son, was a good pitcher and he could hit the ball "a mile," as Fred, Jr. remembered it. Bracht always bounced a few balls over to his son during the game.

Not all team members were local boys; some came from Tivoli or other nearby towns. Liddy came from Bayside to catch for the White Sox. Fred Bracht said Liddy was the toughest man he ever met in his life—and Liddy never wore shoes during a game.

A team of professional ball players, not good enough to be in big leagues, called themselves the House of David. They often clowned around like the Harlem Globetrotters basketball team of later years, but the House of David got serious when they played the White Sox. They had a hard time winning in Rockport.

After a while, Beeville hired Fred Bracht away from the White Sox and paid him five dollars plus transportation and a helper when he pitched for them. Fred usually took along a black youngster that he liked very much, but he had to go through Aransas Pass to get to Beeville. And at both city limits of Aransas Pass a sign warned: "Nigger, don't let the sun go down under your nose." Fred put his friend down on the floorboards of the car and covered him up; it was like taking a criminal through, there was so much racial prejudice.

In 1908 Col. John Traylor, banker and entrepreneur, was elected mayor of Rockport and one year later William Howard Taft, half-brother of the manager of the Taft Ranch, became President of the United States. It wasn't long before President Taft paid a visit.

In a brief memoir, Judge Baldwin wrote: "Everything looked good again. We had arranged our finances . . . had made a tentative estimate and order for material to construct a causeway across Copano Bay at Lamar by 1914, when lo! the World War was declared.

. . . Again our prospect for a railroad and a port went up in smoke. I have not the slightest doubt, that had it not been for that War, Rockport would have had one of the finest railroads and ports in the State."

LARGE CAUSES, LOCAL EFFECTS

THE WAR TO END WAR

The war was hardly a surprise; much of the struggle to secure deep water had been built around military considerations. Congress got the Sixteenth Amendment passed on February 25, 1913, gaining the power to levy and collect income taxes, and eight months later, U.S. engineers blew up the Gamboa Dam, completing the Panama Canal. The Atlantic and Pacific oceans were linked and affairs in all parts of the world took on new importance.

On August 3, 1914, Germany declared war on France, and the next day Britain declared war on Germany. The United States proclaimed neutrality, but the Great War had begun.

It was a grand crusade, historian T. R. Fehrenbach wrote later, "blended of self-interest, self-defense, and an arrogant form of goodwill." Texas, he noted, "was ahead of the nation as a whole in belligerency."

In 1917 the United States entered the war. During a brief but nasty national persecution of families with Germanic names, the Brachts of Aransas found themselves in an uncomfortable position.

"During the war, we didn't want to be known as German," Lola Bracht Woellert said later. Of a neighbor, she remembered: "People said Klaeser was *Boche*, that they had a spy on him, because of how he spoke." That family changed their name to Glass, but the Brachts never had any trouble.

Lola's brother, Fred Bracht, volunteered for active duty. He was one of forty Aransans who did so, most enlisting in the Navy. Another forty-seven were drafted. Aransas provided two pilots and several commissioned and noncommissioned Army officers. It was the "war to end war" and "to make the world safe for democracy." But Lucille Lathrop had nightmares, imagining Germans at the window of her Church Street home.

Marvin Davis, World War I doughboy, home on leave.
—Courtesy of Marvine Davis Wix

She was glad, at least, to have the window, to have the house. Her parents had moved the family to Rockport in 1910 and settled them in a beach hotel. Lucille's father bought five acres on the dirt road that was then South Church Street. He had carpenters build a floor there and he pitched a tent for the family to live in until their house was built.

Five Brundrett brothers learned that the United States Army needed horses, so they contracted to deliver some to Fort Sam Houston in San Antonio. Shortly after they sold the horses, a recruiting sergeant rounded up the two middle boys, Fred and Oliver, and pressed them into service. Oliver, proud of delivering horses to the Army, was mortified to wind up handling mules in France.

Up in Beeville, lumberyard owners Fred and Carl Heldenfels were restless. The government had refused them for military service because they had large families. There were plenty of single men for the army, the enlistment officer maintained; family men should stay behind.

That was when Fred Heldenfels got his grand idea. His architectural degree, as well as his lumberyard, could go to war for him: Heldenfels could build wooden boats on the Texas coast, somewhere west of Houston. His discussions with the merchant marine (United States Shipping Board—Emergency Fleet Corporation) made clear that all he needed was a site.

Corpus Christi turned Fred Heldenfels down, as did Aransas Pass and towns along the Brazos River. But ambitious Rockport was eager for the opportunity. Its citizens offered Heldenfels a bonus of $7,500 on each of four planned ships—a total of $30,000—to offset the costs of transporting machinery from Houston. Additionally, Rockport donated thirteen acres to Heldenfels Brothers, on the condition that the shipyard remain a permanent fixture for at least five years.

The *Enterprise* newspaper, by then merged with the new Rockport *Pilot*, reported that the Shipping Bureau's Major Crowell described Rockport as an "ideal situation" for the shipyard. He considered it immune from submarines since the water was only ten feet deep. Rockport and Heldenfels won full and official approval.

The Emergency Fleet Corporation specified that each ship was to be 46 feet wide and 281 feet, 6 inches in length. Each would have a capacity of 35,000 tons and draw nine and a half feet of water. All four ships were to be completed by December 1, 1918, and delivered to Port Aransas.

It became clear then that Rockport's asset of submarine immunity was also a liability. Heldenfels' boats would need a channel twelve to fourteen feet deep in order to leave the bay. The struggle for deep water began in a new way.

Murry's Reef, just south of Lydia Ann Island, was the only shallow section of the passage. For more than six months, the Corps of Engineers at Galveston and the entire community of Rockport supported Heldenfels Brothers in a war of words over the cost of dredging out the snag. Ultimately, the Rockport Development Association was assured—but only verbally—that the United States government would share costs with local supporters. State senators got involved in the struggle, urging the Corps of Engineers to rush the dredge *Guadaloupe* to the reef area.

Meanwhile, shipyard construction began in October 1917 and Heldenfels laid its first keel in January 1918. Statistics were impressive: The four ships required 1.8 million feet of lumber. Wooden pegs—97,000 of them, pounded in by hand—would hold the timbers together. Compressed air would drive 600,000 pounds of steel nails.

The first ship hull was slated for delivery on May 1, 1918. The Emergency Fleet Corporation had finally agreed to pay one-half the dredging costs and deduct the rest from the money paid to

Heldenfels for "future contracts." But the dredge hit the rock ledge that gave Rockport its name. Arguments concerning cost overruns continued until the channel was completed.

Winifred Evans agonized over the changes in her beach. The shipyard "cut right through the white shell road, dividing it beyond repair, leaving two insignificant, ugly roads. . . . There was no possible recovery."

Fishermen like Coot Buffington weren't happy either, because of muddy water from the dredging operation. But a growing ridge of dredged sand produced the best shell collecting anyone had seen. And for many men, the shipyard was a blessing.

José Angél Covarrúbias was among them. He had been a woodcutter in the days when, according his son Fidél, one could "just go anywhere and cut trees with an ax. No one minded, then, and you could go cut trees anywhere. There were no fences." José chopped his wood in twenty-inch lengths, "the way people used it in the cooking stove."

As a boy, Joe Covarrúbias had learned to speak good English— "better than mine," his son observed later. "He used to visit the Anglos, used to sleep with them at their houses." And Joe's facility with language earned him a good job at the new shipyard. He made "a fortune—twelve dollars a week."

Joe's son Fidél, known to the Anglos as Frank, took lunch to his father at noon. "I used to leave here at ten o'clock to walk over to the shipyards and I had to fight cows to go through," he said. At the shipyard, men on lunch break sat under "a big roof out of palm trees and stuff, for shade. And underneath it they put benches. . . . There was enough room for about two or three hundred people to eat there."

Other workmen walked to the Lathrop house on Church Street. They begged Mattie Lou to fix them a meal; town was too far away for them to walk.

Ham Smith, who had operated a water transport service for years, started a car service and transfer business. In addition to hauling freight, he transported workers to and from the Heldenfels Shipyard each day.

Joe Covarrúbias worked as a diver, a job too complicated for his young son to comprehend. As a grown man, Frank could still only describe what the child had understood: "He did some work on the boats on the bottom. They had a big suit with a solid bronze head and lattice over the face where you could see, and hoses running. The suit was made of something waterproof and the shoes were made out of lead. Each weighed about twenty pounds. The whole thing—suit and shoes—was all together, so the water wouldn't get in there. They had a hand pump at the top. It wasn't dangerous. One man died because of something wrong with the pressure. My daddy died in 1924, of a kind of a thing in his chest. They didn't say . . . it wasn't cancer, but I didn't know what it was."

At the peak of construction, over nine hundred men worked at Heldenfels Shipyard. Roy Court was there, along with Galvino Garza, and Robert McHugh. The hotels, except for old Del Mar, completely derelict, were full of newcomers to town. The First National Bank converted its top floors to lodging. Citizens were encouraged to board workers in extra rooms.

Heldenfels Shipyard, with Baychester *decked out for launching.*
—Courtesy of Aransas County Historical Society Archives

But the town canceled its annual free-to-all-comers barbecue on July 4 that year; there were just too many men to provide for.

Irene Norvell had more applicants for music lessons than she could manage. And she had other responsibilities. "Every woman," she wrote, "was working for the Red Cross or doing her bit in some way. I gave several costume recitals, donating the proceeds." Other volunteers were busy knitting and rolling bandages. Blacks had a separate Red Cross branch.

On August 22, 1918, the Emergency Fleet Corporation canceled its original contract with Heldenfels, insisting that the four hulls be completed on a cost plus basis. That looked impossible to the businessmen, and gloom settled in.

Then Travis Bailey, grandson of the newspaper and pavilion man, flew his Curtiss "Jenny" airplane to Rockport and gave the town a lift. He was a second lieutenant in San Antonio's Kelly Field Army Signal Corps, and on the weekend of September 28, 1918, he landed his plane on the flats south of town. All the citizens gathered there and gave Lieutenant Bailey a silver cup. Its inscription lauded him as the "first Rockport boy to visit us in aeroplane."

The Sneed girls, Edith and Ruth Linda, visited in California during the war, then came home to scandalize Rockport. They smoked; they wore pants (jodphurs, so they could ride astride while hunting). Worst of all, Edith and Ruth Linda wore no stockings beneath their knee-length wool bathing skirts. The Sneed girls lived in a modern age and they lived it to the hilt.

Then the worldwide flu epidemic of 1917 reached Rockport. There were so many deaths, Irene Norvell wrote, that she would be sent "to conduct the music at funerals . . . for utter strangers." People went to the hospital and never returned; survivors stacked up coffins for removal at night.

The good news of Armistice (November 11, 1918) was bad news for the shipyard. The Emergency Fleet Corporation agreed that the first two hulls could be completed as planned, but the others would become only barges. By March 1919 the contract for a second four hulls was canceled absolutely.

Not long after, some Rockport boys still in the service saw a small news item in a Paris paper: "The largest building in Texas burned." It was the Del Mar Hotel, and according to Lola Bracht, the fire lasted "for a solid week." Nina Diederich and her family could see the flames in Fulton. The winds were light when the blaze started, and the walls of the hotel collapsed inward, so there was little damage to other buildings. But as the winds increased, a ten-foot-square section of roof took flight, crossed all of Live Oak Peninsula, and came to rest in Copano Bay.

On July 31, 1919, Heldenfels launched its first ship, Hull #643, the *Baychester*. The wife of President Woodrow Wilson chose the name. Governor William P. Hobby, along with the Lieutenant Governor, the entire Cabinet and scores of celebrities, came to the christening. Special trains brought people from San Antonio for the gala event.

That excitement had scarcely died down when Heldenfels launched the *Zuniga* on September 9. People convinced themselves that the future of Aransas still looked bright.

PROHIBITION

Wets and Drys had been at each other's throats for years. The American Temperance Society, founded in 1826, grew until the Civil War interrupted it. After the war, a Prohibition party and the Woman's Christian Temperance Union formed. The Anti-Saloon League reached national scale by 1895. Carry Nation stormed saloons with hatchet in hand.

Most Texans considered prohibitionists to be reformers and "liberals;" they preferred the old conservative Establishment. South Texas, with its German-Mexican influence, was particularly averse to banning liquor. T. R. Fehrenbach wrote that "prohibition was another Anglo-American frenzy utterly incomprehensible to the Latin Catholic mind."

Rockport attitudes were generous. A saloon keeper named Hanks was "known as a law-abiding citizen and highly regarded," wrote Winifred Evans Lowther. "He knew no other way of taking care of his family and he had pride in his occupation. When a customer had had enough to drink Mr. Hanks sent him home. Many women whose husbands had 'the weakness' gave Mr. Hanks friendship and gratitude. Others said if there had to be saloons it was a pity that there were not more men like Mr. Hanks to run them."

Not everyone agreed, as Winifred was well aware. She wrote that "Mrs. [Irene] Norvell . . . whose family traditions went deep into the English aristocracy, brought her inherited code of living . . . to this small remotely-situated Texas town. Among things that came naturally to Mrs. Norvell was the knowledge that one did not visit nor meet socially saloon keepers' wives and families, though their houses might be side by side."

But Irene Norvell knew that there were times to break the code. When Mrs. Hanks' sister, who lived with the family, died of consumption, Irene went next door to offer help and sympathy. She was rebuffed.

"For years now," Mrs. Hanks said, "we have managed without knowing our next door neighbor; there is no need of knowing her now." Irene had to acknowledge that her inbred exclusiveness required alteration. Winifred Lowther concluded that the "change in this Virginia family made them more admirable and likable than before."

Families like the Norvells surely were disappointed, nonetheless, when a statewide referendum defeated prohibition by six thousand votes. Then, strangely, the Great War abetted prohibition efforts—first with pleas for conservation of grain, then through a call to patriotism that closed saloons to soldiers. In a flush of wartime fervor, Texas voted out liquor in 1918.

Saloons that had profited from the shipbuilding crews had to close their doors, or alter their methods of operation. All along the coast—both then and after ratification of the Eighteenth Amendment to the U.S. Constitution—bootlegging, speakeasies, and rum-running flourished.

Small boats, loaded with whiskey, champagne, brandy, and rum, slipped through Aransas Bay under cover of darkness, headed for the Lamar peninsula. There trucks would take the illicit cargo to Houston.

On one memorable night a Federal revenuer spotted the smugglers and bore down in hot pursuit. The first bright spotlight caught the surprised smugglers just off Nine Mile Point. Frantically, they threw hundreds of bottles overboard, down to the soft sand and mud bottom of the bay.

Time and tide worked on the bottles, moving them gradually closer to shore. The north winds of winter pushed water from the bay, exposing the shallows. There lay the bottles, apparently in perfect condition. Citizens of Rockport and Fulton tasted the contents, "to see if they were still good." Then, because the wind was sharp, they drank more "to keep warm."

But the good old days of Rockport gambling houses and saloons were over. Prohibition was the second harsh blow to the city in a decade—both human decisions beyond the control of local interests. Still, these defeats would pale by comparison to the blow that Nature had in store.

"THE WORST HURRICANE IN HISTORY"

—Weather Bureau Report
Washington, D.C.
September 12, 1919

Throughout the history of Aransas, storms had beset it. The one in 1919 became forever a marker for measuring time in Aransas. It began this way:

On the last day of August in 1919, gentle, easterly winds rippled the tropical Atlantic. Despite the steady breeze, radiation from summer sun kept the ocean warm. South and east of the Windward Islands, massive quantities of water evaporated into the atmosphere.

Warm air carried the vapors aloft, cooling them, condensing them to cloud and then to rain. Sealevel heat pushed intermediate clouds still higher; they compressed into a thunderstorm one hundred miles in diameter. Air in the cloud mass—cold, dense, and heavy—tried to sink, but the pumping action of warm air convection prevented that. Instead, the cold air moved to the sides of the upwell, strengthening its wall.

Air flowing up the center of the weather system, and out its top, produced lower air pressure at the surface of the sea. There, warm air rushed in. Snaking its way to the center of the storm, the air created a rotation. Surface winds reached twenty miles per hour, then twenty-five.

The morning's events were not unusual. That convergence was one of many moving west across the tropics, separated from others by clear-weather regions of high pressure. There was nothing unusual in the afternoon either—just intensified evaporation and con-

238

densation that trapped warm air and spread it out in all directions. Someone high in the crow's nest of a ship saw the rain bands and yearned for a cooling shower.

Rotation within the storm increased; winds rose. The lookout clambered from the crow's nest to estimate wind speed. He dropped an inflated paper bag from the bow, marked how long it took to reach the stern, then calculated the minutes against the length of the boat. Comparing that to the wave caps and to the flutter of the flags, he estimated the wind at thirty-nine miles per hour. The lookout reported this news to his captain; the purser signaled it to other ships by light and flag. The captain of a docking vessel relayed the word to telegraphers: tropical storm.

Aransas County received the warning.

If more air had entered lower levels of the convergence than could exit at its top, the system would have died. That was not the case. Everything fell into place just right—or all wrong. Each ingredient necessary for hurricane development appeared with extraordinary efficiency.

The tropical storm continued westward, encountering an upper level disturbance. The top of the cloud mass blew off; convective flow accelerated. In just one day, the storm reached hurricane force—seventy-four miles per hour. Every minute, it released as much energy as 400 twenty-megaton hydrogen bombs.

The storm's forward speed was slow. Often it covered only four miles an hour, and it never topped seven as it sidled northwest. The storm slipped between Puerto Rico and Hispañola, raked Grand Turk Island and the southern Bahamas, then turned west.

A week and a day after its spawning, the hurricane slammed into the Florida Keys. It dallied there September 8th and 9th and 10th, then finally passed Key West forty miles to its south.

Still that island took the full force of the storm. Winds of 110 miles an hour whipped and shredded palm trees. Waves slammed into buildings, smashing walls. Three people lay dead in the wreckage.

On Thursday, September 11, headlines in the *Corpus Christi Caller* declared: "South Florida Prostrated by Gale; Property Loss Appalling." Texans shook their heads at Florida's misfortune, but figured the end of the storm was in sight. Most hurricanes, after all, live only nine days.

Tourists were making merry on Coastal Bend beaches as the storm kept moving. Clear of the Keys, nothing impeded its way across the warm, open water of the Gulf of Mexico. Ships found safe harbor. Bereft of eyewitness reports from sailors, no one on land knew precisely what the hurricane was doing. Some speculated it would blow ashore in Louisiana.

At the far western edge of the Gulf, Aransas County tried to track the storm, listening to weather bureau reports relayed from Washington and New Orleans. On September 12 the Weather Bureau in Washington, D.C. issued a clear warning: "This is the worst hurricane in history."

That seemed a lot to say, only nineteen years after the disastrous storm in Galveston. Most Aransans shrugged it off; weather warnings were a dime a dozen each September. A little rain would be good for the crops and for personal comfort, some said. Most believed the storm had gone ashore in Florida, anyway.

Still people thought of the 1916 storm, the one that took dead aim on the lighthouse. Frank Stevenson was the keeper then, and his whole family huddled together in the tower for sixteen hours of horror.

In Rockport, that storm destroyed the beautiful Kennedy house and its pier. The Kennedy girls and a hundred people from the La Playa hotel had taken refuge in the jail. Thinking about that storm, people hoped it wasn't a drill for greater disaster.

Capt. Roy Court brought his inspection boat, the *Mildred Collins*, from Quarantine Island to the Sorenson wharf at Rockport. He knew hurricanes. One had zeroed in on the Fulton Mansion the year he was born. In the thirty-eight years since then, Roy Court had seen eighteen hurricanes hit the Texas coast. He was too young to have known much about the destruction of Indianola in 1875 and 1886, but he was a man, twenty-eight years old, when the awful storm hit Galveston. Roy Court prepared for the worst.

The situation seemed grim for the ranch on San José. It was wholly a Wood family enterprise, since Samuel B. Allyn had sold his interest in 1912. Richard Wood, and his sons Will and Tobias, had 6,400 head of purebred Hereford cattle penned up for shipment on Monday and no way to get them all to the mainland sooner. Loading the cattle onto barges was a slow process. Crossing the bay with batches of them took still more time.

A fine new hotel on the Rocky Point. Postcard.
—Courtesy of Gordon Stanley Collection

The ranch hands and their families—thirty-eight souls—were a more serious concern, if the hurricane should come. Will Wood took power boats and barges across the bay and brought the families to the relative safety of Rockport.

Plowing across five miles of bay, the ranching families looked to the sky. They saw nothing out of the ordinary, just bright blue and white-hot glow. And seemingly typical summer clouds on the far southeast horizon.

Out there, unseen, the hurricane filled the Gulf, its whirling arms touching Louisiana and the Yucatán, reaching for Aransas. Low pressure at the storm's center sucked up a mound of water one foot high and fifty miles wide, creating a growing storm surge. Ahead of the hurricane, the level of the sea rose as much as fifteen feet.

September 3 started out calm—not eerily calm, just one of those flat summer mornings with a bay sleek as satin, the view of the island erased by humidity. There was not a breath of air. High above the town a frigate bird circled. Some people said that frigate birds over land meant that a storm was coming.

But as the town woke up, most people were thinking baseball. Fred Bracht and his White Sox teammates were ready. Cuero's team had spent the night at the La Playa and was flexing to play. By game time, the temperature rose to ninety-two degrees.

Then, the game was important; now, no one even remembers the score. But some remember that when the game was over, everyone was more agitated than they had been before. School teachers recognized that; children always get wild when the pressure drops. It wasn't just children that Saturday—everyone seemed keyed up.

Lucille Lathrop had not gone to the baseball game. She played in her yard that Saturday, but somehow nothing felt right. Before noon, the wind was blowing.

It could mean a storm, some thought. It could be that the hurricane was coming, after all. Then John Sorenson put the storm flags up. There was nothing anyone could do about it. No one was fool enough to try to run away, to risk a frail buggy or a balky motor car on open, flat land. No transportation could get far enough, fast enough, for safety. The people of Aransas County would meet the hurricane, if it came, head on. Some people knocked on the Lathrop front door, asking to use the telephone.

The boys from the Cuero baseball team ended their post-game party at the La Playa hotel and headed for home. Only one young man, caught up in his pleasures, elected to remain in the hotel.

Everyone in the Bracht household was so keyed up that Clara Bracht hated the thought of keeping them calm at home. She told Leo she wanted to have a picnic supper on Nine Mile Point. Oysters were back in season; they could take a sackful—and a goat to barbecue.

Leopold said they had to take precautions first. He and his brother Roland were no longer partners; each had to secure his own store against the possibility of storm. Leopold hustled his family to Bracht Mercantile on Austin Street at North. He directed them to pile everything of value into the elevator.

Eighteen-year-old Lola grabbed fancy cookies; Clara got the sugar. The boys decided that canned goods could stay where they were. Leopold ran the elevator up to the second floor and then, confident that his wares were protected from rising water, walked down.

The family loaded up their picnic supplies, laughing at neigh-

Inside the Bracht store.
—Courtesy of Fred Bracht, Jr. Collection

bors who said, "Don't you know we're going to have a storm tonight?" The Brachts heard that every year. And Clara liked the idea of keeping her family's minds off impending disaster. By midnight, however, rain started to pour down, ending her picnic.

On Sunday morning, September 14, a stiff wind blew.

"It's a norther," some visitors said. "Hurricanes come from the south." Locals knew better. They tried to tell the visitors about whirling winds and how they first came just west of north, then from the north, east, south and west again, in slow, harrowing sequence.

Mariners quoted hurricane warnings in the Corpus Christi paper; they pointed out that water was up over the first road. When John Sorenson hoisted the flag signifying "tropical storm," Clara Bracht told her family to prepare to leave their home.

Down on Water Street, Irene Norvell lay in bed, listening to the wind. She realized there would be no Sunday School or church; no one would brave that storm to go into town. Irene decided not

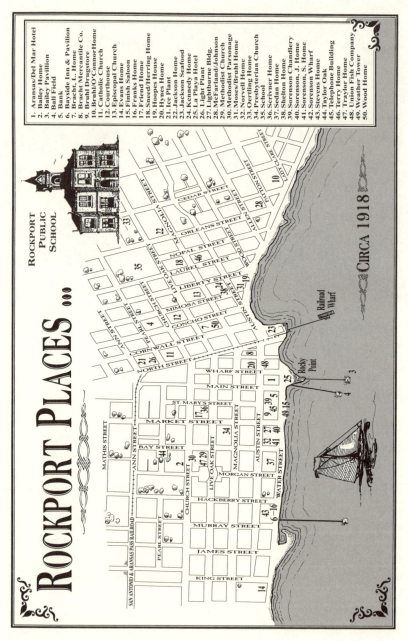

ROCKPORT PLACES ...

ROCKPORT PUBLIC SCHOOL

CIRCA 1918

1. Aransas/Del Mar Hotel
2. Bailey Home
3. Bailey Pavillion
4. Ball Field
5. Bank
6. Bayside Inn & Pavilion
7. Bracht, L. Home
8. Bracht Mercantile Co.
9. Bruhl Drugstore
10. Bruhl/O'Connor Home
11. Catholic Church
12. Courthouse
13. Episcopal Church
14. Evans Home
15. Finish Saloon
16. Franks Home
17. Friend Home
18. Sneed/Herring Home
19. Hoopes House
20. Hynes Home
21. Ice Plant
22. Jackson Home
23. Jackson Seafood
24. Kennedy Home
25. La Playa Hotel
26. Light Plant
27. Lightburne Bldg.
28. McFarland/Johnson
29. Methodist Church
30. Methodist Parsonage
31. Moses/Bruhl Home
32. Norvell Home
33. Oertling Home
34. Presbyterian Church
35. School
36. Scrivner Home
37. Sedan Home
38. Shelton Home
39. Sorenson Chandlery
40. Sorenson, J. Home
41. Sorenson, S. Home
42. Sorenson Wharf
43. Stevens Home
44. Taylor Oak
45. Telephone Building
46. Terry Home
47. Traylor Home
48. Union Fish Company
49. Weather Tower
50. Wood Home

Rockport, Texas, 1918. Illustration by Chris Blum.

to hurry and dress, but lingered in the bed's comfort. She and her husband Elisha lived alone, their children grown and gone, her parents passed away.

Elisha was up like a shot. As soon as he had his pants on, Elisha went out to look at the water. He came back with an excited expression on his face and said he was appalled at the bay. Irene decided to see for herself.

She returned to the house and studied each wall, as though memorizing it. "I am not going to stay here a minute," she said. "Oh, go on," Elisha chided. "Don't be a quitter."

They would be safer, Irene responded, at their daughter's house. The girl, also Irene, was married to Ford Jackson and lived away from the water, on Magnolia at Orleans Street. The senior Irene suggested to her husband that they could help out with the grandchildren there: four-year-old Norvell Jackson, little Jim Bart, and baby Isabel.

Elisha saw the wisdom of that. "Get breakfast first, though," he said. Of course, Irene went to the stove. The wind and the waves, though strong, were something she and Elisha had dealt with before. They found reassurance in the ordinary. But in the Gulf, unrecognized, chaos churned toward them.

When he had eaten, Elisha said he'd leave Irene to tidy up her kitchen while he found a car. He was still gone when a blind blew open on the northeast window of the living room. Irene struggled to pull it in, then found that the catch had broken. Just within her reach, a calendar hung on the wall, held by a heavy silk cord. With her free hand and her teeth, Irene managed to loose that cord and use it to tie the blinds together. Then she covered up the piano and got together some silver and other valuables.

By that time, Elisha had returned. He had been unable to find a car; no owner would risk making the trip. And there was no use to think of walking, Elisha said. He'd had to bend almost double.

"We can go on Dick," Irene answered, so in a few minutes they were mounted on the horse, heading north on Water Street.

The Hanks' house next door had become Morris Hotel. There one of Irene's music pupils looked out the window. The girl could not believe her eyes: Irene Norvell was not sitting properly on the horse, but man-fashion behind her husband. The student put her hand over her mouth, laughing, and motioned to her mother to look too.

The mother did not laugh. That sight made clear to her, as nothing else had, the gravity that Aransas was facing. Fine Mrs. Norvell could stay on her horse no other way in the growing storm. If the Norvells considered the situation so dangerous that they must evacuate, the mother realized she should get her family out as well.

She took a rope and tied her children into a line. They struggled over to Austin Street, but could make it no farther. They took refuge above a business and moments later they watched a wave smash Morris House to kindling wood.

The water was not yet high on inland roads, but as Elisha and Irene fought their way toward Magnolia Street, the wind was strong. Sometimes it struck the horse broadside with such force that he skidded across the road. Then again it would strike him in the face and he spun around like a top.

The rain stung like needles. Irene kept her head down and Elisha did too. As they rode near the railroad station, something lashed them like a whip . . . like wire. Irene's heart stopped; she feared they would be electrocuted. Later she could not have said what wires had frightened her so, but she remembered the terror of that moment.

Six more blocks and they were at their daughter's home. Elisha Norvell deposited his wife there and retraced nearly all the long, arduous journey, to the block behind his own house. Elisha had to see about his responsibility to the Lightburne spinsters.

He implored the two old ladies to leave their house; they must go immediately, he said. The Misses Lightburne argued against it, showing him wide substantial shelves that reached almost to the ceiling of their kitchen. They could climb up, they argued, if the water got high.

Elisha tried again to persuade them and at last the ladies agreed to look at the breakers showing above the Ridge. They contemplated the fury of the waves and agreed to leave—provided that Elisha would read some Scripture first and pray.

The prayer was a short one, and the Scripture disregarded altogether, as Elisha hastily revised his plan. He had wanted to put one of the sisters behind him on the horse, take her up Bay Street to the Traylor place on Live Oak, then come back for the other woman.

Now he was too late; too much time had been wasted. Elisha put both old ladies on Dick and walked beside the horse to lead him.

When the Lightburne sisters were safely ensconced, Elisha rode south along Live Oak to Hackberry, then turned again east to Water Street. He wanted to check on Judge and Mrs. Stevens. The wife was indeed relieved to see Elisha coming, because the Judge had refused to leave home. Elisha was able to persuade him and escorted the couple as far as the little bridge over a low spot.

There faithful Dick balked. Elisha couldn't see the bridge at all, and he thought it better not to force his horse. Judge Stevens agreed. As much as Mrs. Stevens would have preferred to ride out the storm in the company of friends, they seemed in no great danger. Elisha left them in their strong home and went on to the Jackson house to join his family.

Other evacuees crowded the Lathrop house. None of them brought any clothes or groceries. Mattie Lou had food on hand for a week—but only enough for her family. She counted her jelly jars and the big cans of peanut butter, worrying about how to feed the uninvited guests.

By ten Sunday morning, when Capt. Roy Court and his brother Kinney went out to check the *Mildred Collins*, the atmospheric pressure had dropped. The wind was so high that Roy and Kinney could not stand upright against it, nor walk directly. In effect, they had to sail themselves, tacking at an angle to the gale, trying to stay in the center of the Sorenson wharf.

They pumped out their ship and secured her with extra lines, so intent on their work that they hardly felt the wharf shudder.

A fishing boat, broken from its moorings, had smashed against the wharf and cut it in two. The brothers were stranded.

When Roy and Kinney headed back to shore and saw the breach, they stood a moment, surveying it, then sailed themselves back out the wharf to the *Mildred Collins*. Roy boarded her, located life preservers, put one on and handed another to Kinney. Down the wharf they sailed again, as far as possible. The Courts looked at each other solemnly, then shrugged and grinned like boys. With a whoop, they jumped into the water.

The brothers made their way safely ashore, though the wind

and tide carried them a little south of James Street. There they saw that H. R. Franks was still in his small cottage in the 900 block of Water Street. With him were his wife Minnie, his twelve-year-old son and daughter, and his younger son, just nine. Roy and Kinney begged the family to leave, arguing that they were not safe in that little house, but the Frankses refused to go.

Four or five blocks away, in a house just north of the one the Norvells had vacated, eleven-year-old Paul Clark Sorenson stood at his front window. It was from that vantage point, earlier, that he had watched fishermen fighting to pull their nets in. By the time Paul went out to help, there was no beach left; they had to haul the nets all the way up to the street. Paul's mother (the former Lola Herring) wouldn't let any of her children out of the house after that. Paul's father checked to see that his warning flags were still secure on their tall pole, then got his brother to help him board up the house.

Since they couldn't board the upstairs windows from the outside, John took bed slats and nailed them across the windows on the inside. Lola jammed pillows between the windows and slats, protecting the glass from wind gusts, while still allowing the family to look outside.

At eleven o'clock, the first really hard wind from the northwest swept over the bay. The tide was higher than anyone in the Sorenson house could remember. By noon, water met and covered the high ground upon which their home was built. Soon, two or three inches of water covered the Ridge and stood seven feet deep in the backyard.

Ford Jackson had stayed at his fish company office until water covered the floor. He was home by the time John Sorenson had hoisted the red flags indicating hurricane force winds and Ford feared that their big front window would blow in. As he and his father-in-law Elisha Norvell nailed bed slats across it, Irene Jackson noticed that water covered the road.

"Ford," she said, "is that the bay?"

"Oh, no, I think not." But he made some excuse and left the

room. When Ford returned, his face was grim and his words terse. "It is the bay."

Then came the frantic work of trying to make possessions as safe as possible. A tree went down in the backyard and only young Norvell Jackson saw good news: "The switch tree is gone," he chanted in childish glee. "The switch tree is gone!"

Ham Smith kept his transport company vehicles busy, rescuing people marooned all over town, but the Brachts never did leave their home at Cornwall and Live Oak. Clara put a candle in an upstairs window. "Somebody might see the light," she said. In time, 250 people would make her home their refuge.

Clara's daughter Louisa and her husband, Travis Johnson, were with them, of course. Somehow, the tall Bracht house seemed safer—and it felt good to be with family.

Travis was concerned about the Franks family, as the Court brothers had been. He kept going down to check on them, but they wouldn't leave. Minnie Franks said that God would take care of them. Travis made his last trip in a boat and warned H. R. that it was his final chance. Still, the family would not come.

At about one in the afternoon, just before the Franks' home went down, the five of them finally clambered into an open boat. Their goal was to cross over the flats, to the safety of live oaks on the west side of town. The Merkinses watched them get caught in an eddy, right in the middle of Austin Street.

Mr. Merkins saw a gust of wind capsize the Franks' boat and he turned his family's eyes away. Alone, he witnessed the flailing arms, the grabbing hands, the bobbing heads. He saw someone hold on to the boat's keel for a moment or two, but a wave ripped him away. Mr. Merkins closed his eyes as every one in the Franks family drowned.

The middle of Austin Street—the middle of town. Just the day before, he had strolled there; now people died there. And there was nothing to do but watch, nothing to do but stare as blankly as the impassive store windows stared.

David Little, a restaurant owner, died the same way, in an Austin Street eddy, along with his wife and ten-year-old son, Dave, Jr. Capt.

Roy Court had begged them to go back, not to brave the waters in their small, open skiff.

The horror seemed worse than drowning at sea. No one should die surrounded by buildings, watched by neighbors in relative safety. The people who drowned were the kind who could not adjust or act quickly enough, who failed to see when the lines blurred and the rules shifted, who thought that life would go on as it always had, no matter what. But life is change; only death is immutable.

At four o'clock, eighteen inches of water covered Ford Jackson's yard on Magnolia Street, and the family was ready to flee. The women loaded themselves with provisions and dry clothing. Elisha Norvell put his grandsons on the tired horse Dick, but Jim Bart screamed that the rain was stinging his face. Ford, carrying baby Isabel, held the big milk bucket over her head, so she stayed in "the best of good humor."

They plodded through the water on Orleans Street, heading for the school a block away. Then Frank Sparks came riding up. "Don't go to the school house," he said. "The walls are falling." Some who had been at the school headed for the jail; others went to the courthouse.

Ford directed his family toward the Oertlings' house instead. They found men from the shipyard already there, and in time, fifty people crowded the house.

Many families made their way to brush and live oak groves on high ground. Hundreds of them—black families and whites together—rode out the storm there. Surely, they were surprised when a house came to meet them. It was the Kertell house, from the corner of Water and Corpus Christi streets, carried across the flats to the edge of the brush.

Captain Kertell hadn't been living there at the time; he'd rented the house to Captain and Mrs. Jones and they had made their escape in a rowboat before the storm got too bad. Someone joked that the Joneses could have stayed in the house, had a good ride, and enjoyed plenty of room when the place came to rest. People made foolish remarks like that and everybody laughed; it was a way to break the tension.

Paul Sorenson, still on Water Street, stood at the boarded-up window, his cheek pressed against the bed slat buttressing it, his skin scratched by the roughness. The wet stench of feathers filled his nostrils and his fingers gripped the pillow ticking. There was just one hole where he could see out.

What Paul saw was a world turned to water gone mad. There was water everywhere, and the always bawling wind. Paul watched the Bailey Pavilion come ashore, watched its timbers stack up in front of his house, joining the destroyed boats and wharves that formed a barricade there.

Thirty people found refuge in the Lightburne Building, at the northwest corner of Market and Austin. Great waves swept into the second story. One Mexican woman there watched "whole big buildings picked up by the wind and moved several blocks. Then they were beat to pieces by the waves." Miraculously, no one in the Lightburne Building was injured.

The young men at Leopold Bracht's house crossed the street for Oscar Dye and his mother, a nurse who had taken in a sick lady. Mrs. Dye said she couldn't leave her patient, but the boys said she couldn't stay in that little house; she'd be washed away. They floated the patient across the street on a mattress, and Mrs. Dye stayed with that sick lady in the Bracht parlor all night.

Lola Bracht closed her eyes against the hurricane, but she could not close her ears. She could not help but hear the horror of the storm. The sound was incessant and its message was clear: everything in Aransas would be destroyed. Lola heard the breaking of trees and buildings, even over the roar and the howl of the wind.

At about midnight, thunder crashed. Lightning brightened the room where Lola cowered; lightning flickered on the waste outside. Then, suddenly—silence. As though the demon winds had granted everyone's wish to hear no more. Cautiously, all listened to the hush.

No one was breathing. In the silence at the center of the storm, each soul held within its lungs whatever air remained, as though it were the only air that ever would be. Each face looked as though the wind had pulled at it, erasing the laugh lines, contorting the features.

Then someone expelled a large gust of relief and despair. And someone tittered. It was not a laugh, it was nothing like a laugh, but a nervousness. "The eye," someone said. "This is the eye."

Each person in that room, without intending to, looked around, as though expecting to make out and measure the walls of the hurricane's eye encompassing them. It encompassed each of them separately, isolating them, not gathering them together.

"How long will this last?" No one answered for a heartbeat or two. Then: "Not long enough." All the men rose and went to see what they could shore up before the wind came back.

It did come back—and too soon—for only the edge of the eye crossed Rockport. The storm's center, a wall of silence surrounding mayhem, moved inland near Baffin Bay. Aransas County was in the storm's northeast quadrant, the most vicious side of any hurricane.

From the opposite direction the wind came, trying the opposite side of the house. This time the gale did not build slowly, as it had on the morning that seemed a thousand years ago. The wind came like a hurricane still at its full height, which indeed it was.

Listeners covered their ears again and endured.

Out on Rockport's rocky point, out at the cutting edge of land meeting water, eleven people were trapped in the La Playa Hotel. Early on, debris had piled around the doors and imprisoned them there. Water rose in the lobby, forcing them to the second floor of the hotel. They had looked out at desperate families in open boats, watched the city's destruction, shuddered as portions of their own building slid beneath the waves.

One of those trapped, an Episcopal priest, tried to minister to the rest—and to himself at the same time. The Cuero ballplayer regretted his Saturday night party. Oil-wealthy Mr. and Mrs. I. C. Thurmond wished they'd cut their vacation short. Cyrus Heard, a prominent rancher from Refugio, wondered why he'd ever left home.

When water reached the second-story window, the boy from Cuero decided to jump and make a swim for safety. As he began stripping off his clothes, Cyrus Heard nodded that he would go too. Cyrus was the grandson of Lydia Ann and James Wells and a relative of Mary Ann Heard McRae; he had the blood of families who had always stood up to challenge.

I. C. Thurmond, eyes wide and anxious, came over to Cyrus. "I can't swim," he said, "but I want my wife out of this building. I'll pay you half a million dollars if you will carry her to a less dangerous place."

Half a million dollars was a lot of money in 1919. The oil man had bought his way out of more than one scrape and always got pretty much whatever he wanted.

But not this time. Other resources are required for a bargain with nature. Cyrus Heard looked I. C. straight in the eye. He said that he feared he could not be of assistance. He promised that he would return with help, when he was able.

At about eleven o'clock, Cyrus and the ballplayer finally jumped out of the hotel window. They began their swim toward the light that Clara Bracht had left shining as a beacon.

It was past midnight when the eye of the storm clipped Aransas. Winds were estimated at 125 miles per hour; tides were ten to fifteen feet above normal. The boy from Cuero and Cyrus Heard swam through that.

Cyrus Heard reached the Bracht home before dawn on Monday. The Cuero ballplayer fell exhausted on the steps soon after. Lola saw him first and hardly noticed he was naked.

The storm was over, but the travail was not. At first light Cyrus found a little boat, took it back to the hotel and ferried the Thurmonds and others to safety at the Bracht house. Some refugees stayed there several days.

Throughout Monday, people sloshed through mud and slime, taking pictures. They saw fishing boats and pleasure boats, blown ashore and wrecked. They saw that all the wharves were gone and whole blocks were swept clean. Three out of every four buildings in town showed damage and some were such complete wrecks that they would have to be torn down. There was so much broken glass in the streets that it was hardly safe to travel.

Charles Gibson's Rockport Fish and Oyster Company was gone, along with Camehl Fish Company, Jackson Brothers, and Miller Brothers. The fishing industry would be paralyzed for some time. Few boats were intact; nets and seines were gone.

All over town the stench was terrible—slime, mud, dead ani-

1916

From the SAAP tracks, south along Water Street.
—Courtesy of Gordon Stanley Collection

The bank, and south along Water Street.
—Courtesy of Gordon Stanley Collection

1916

Front of LaPlaya Hotel.
　　　　　—Courtesy of Gordon Stanley Collection

Bayside Inn.
　　　　　—Courtesy of Gordon Stanley Collection

1919

The school.
—Courtesy of Aransas County Historical Society
Archives, donated by Mrs. Fred Bracht

The LaPlaya Hotel.
—Courtesy of Aransas County Historical Society
Archives, donated by Iris Sorenson

1919

Downtown.
—Courtesy of Lola Bracht Woellert/ Winston Woellert

Looking South on Austin Street.
—Courtesy of Lola Bracht Woellert/ Winston Woellert

1919

The bank (on left) and telephone building.
—Courtesy of Lola Bracht Woellert/ Winston Woellert

mals, decayed fruits and vegetables, burst septic tanks, wet lumber, moldy dry goods.

Pharmacist Albert Bruhl knew that he had to get back to work. Unsanitary conditions posed a risk of fever; everyone in town would need disinfectants and medicine. His drugstore in the Lightburne Building looked all right from the front, but when Albert stepped through the door, he saw that the floor sloped sharply upward. He stumbled through debris toward the back of the building, stooping more and more as floor and ceiling came ever closer together.

The town was under martial law. Property owners wore identification badges while trying to pick out their ruined possessions.

In Leopold Bracht's store, the family selected some foods that might be salvaged, but government inspectors condemned it all. Canned foods were safe, but none had labels; meals were made of strange combinations. Other than that, the Brachts had only the fancy things that they'd placed on the elevator and taken upstairs.

Across the street, Adolph Bracht's store had the only undamaged flour and sugar in town, since he'd moved it all to the second floor. Federal authorities took charge of it all and parceled it out to families that needed it. At Hooper Brothers' grocery, on Austin near St. Mary's, the second floor had dropped down where the first should have been. All the grocery stores sold their unlabeled cans at three cents each. School boys recognized the distinctive Eagle Brand Condensed Milk containers and ate the sweet stuff with spoons.

Judge Baldwin's extensive law library was washed away. His large iron safe had moved clear across the room and over onto its face. The contents were water-soaked.

The entire dance floor from Bailey's Pavilion floated up on the vacant lot between David Rockport Scrivner's house and Miss Ethel Friend's, at the northwest corner of Live Oak and Market. If the dance floor had drifted just a little either way, it would have knocked one of those houses off its foundation.

At the west corner of Pearl and North, the city light plant was out of commission. The ice plant on Ann Street was severely damaged, but repairs were made so quickly that the town was never out of ice. People were grateful for that. Without ice, a lot more food would have spoiled.

Ben Shelton had a crew of men removing debris from around his house on Austin, just north of Mimosa. That close to the water, all sorts of things had washed in—including snakes. Ben kicked several dead ones out of his way, then grabbed a tree limb lying where his front porch should have been. He hardly heard the rattle, it was so weak, so lost in the clamor of men working—but the snake had enough energy to coil and strike him.

Down the way, the bodies of the Franks and Little family members were found, then buried, along with an unidentified Mexican man.

That evening Todd and Jim Tuttle, along with a Mr. Burris, arrived by raft, using a blanket as a sail. They had been drilling an oil well at the north end of San José Island, in the employ of the Rockport-Corpus Drilling Company, when the storm came.

For eight hours the three men struggled to reach the ranch on Matagorda, only a few miles away. Sheltered in the attic of a house, they built the raft, then launched it through a hole in the roof. Todd

Tuttle, who had not enjoyed France as a soldier during the Great War, nonetheless stated that he would take another trip to France rather than go through the Aransas hurricane again.

Monday was a long day.

On Tuesday, Paul Sorenson found an old skiff that had somehow retained its sails. He bailed her out and sailed up and down Austin Street until his father caught him and sent him back to work. The family store had four feet of water in it and two inches of mud and slime all over.

Just down the street, Paul's uncle, Bob Sorenson, had discovered a curious thing. The family, hurrying to close up their house in preparation for the hurricane, had lowered one window only so far as a coffee cup on the sill. After the storm, there was a small live crab in that cup.

Wednesday, workers found a body washed up on the beach. It was old Coot Buffington, who had lived alone on Traylor Island. People speculated that he was simply swept away by the storm.

That same day someone found a body floating in the middle of Aransas Bay. It turned out to be John Griggs, a fisherman from Port O'Connor, who had evidently been at sea when the storm hit.

The snake that got Ben Shelton on Monday was just one among many. By Wednesday, people found snakes everywhere— water snakes and marsh snakes, garter snakes and ribbon snakes. Rough green snakes, dying, turned turquoise blue. There were king snakes and rat snakes, coachwhips and racers. Harmless hog-nosed snakes lay tangled with venomous vipers and deadly rattlers.

Men waded waist-deep in the water, picked up the snakes on the tines of rakes and carried them ashore. Patrols shot the snakes, raked them up in piles, then doused them with oil and set the mess afire. Other flames cremated dead chickens, pigs, and pets.

On Thursday, Irene and Elisha Norvell finally got a look at their Water Street home. The fences were down and the yard was a sight to behold—six boats, a piano, big timbers from the Pavilion, and one tremendous trunk of a tree. Some chickens had saved themselves by coming up on the back porch.

The house, by some miracle, was not damaged a great deal. The chimneys were uneven with the roof. One side of the porch lattice had blown in, the other out, but the front lattice remained. Still the Norvells could not get in that way because of logs and rubbish. The northeast window in the living room—the one Irene had worked so hard to secure—had blown in; the curtains and rug were ruined. Irene and Elisha knew at once that they would not be able to stay in the house until repairs were made.

But the place could be saved. Of the entire waterfront, only their house and others in their block, on that ridge, survived the storm.

The Norvells walked south along the Ridge, stunned at the wrecked homes and devastation everywhere. They walked carefully, stepping over dead snakes every few yards. One block down, the whole south wall of Captain Sedan's home was gone, displaying beds and dressers for all to see. Salt seeped into every crevice of every home, ruining furniture and clothing.

That day, too, the cattle floated in. Most of them were dead and already bloated; the smell was terrible. The only thing that could be done, officials said, was to drag the carcasses off and burn them. Some cattle were still alive; Lola Bracht heard them lowing, lowing all night long.

Somebody decided to butcher the cows for their meat. Women kept coffee boiling and bread baking; they freely shared anything remaining in their pantries, feeding all who came to their doors. Still about ten days went by before anyone ate enough to feel full.

Mr. Bonner, of the Bonner Oil Company in Houston, sent a trainload of food and provisions, but the rail was impassible beyond Aransas Pass. San Antonio sent supplies, too, but it took four horses to pull the wagons through wet sand and mud. David Means Picton brought in supplies at his own expense. Clara Bracht wouldn't let Lola go for any of the donated food, though in truth, the family didn't have much that was good to eat.

Merchants sold dry goods at any price to prevent it from mildewing on the shelves. Shopkeepers went without sleep for two or three days at a time, trying to meet the demands of needy consumers.

Every home halfway fit to live in welcomed all who sought it. The Leopold Bracht house, refuge for many, was so badly wrecked that Clara didn't want her family to stay in it. They lived over the store for several months, Lola said, "till Mama got over her nervousness." Even when they went back home, the house was so badly damaged that Clara didn't want to live there. Leopold arranged with Emma Craig to operate the place as a hotel for those who needed somewhere to stay.

The bank issued its own emergency currency—produced by a government-approved printer, signed as prescribed by law and mailed to Rockport in sheets. Before the sheets were cut, Bank President A. C. Glass co-signed each bill.

Reports began to come in from towns all along the coast. The Herring ranch house on Matagorda was destroyed, and the motor boat sank right in front of it. The cattle were drowned and swept all the way to Seadrift, but the cowhands all held to cattle pens and saved themselves from being washed away.

The Aransas Light Station had problems too. Improvements that had begun there in May of 1918 still weren't completed when the hurricane struck. The assistant's house was swept away, but a new house, at a greater elevation than the old ones, remained standing. The new oil house went down, so for several nights the beacon was dark. The raised walkway was gone, of course, along with the water closets and the foundations of the cisterns.

The ten feet of water that washed over San José swept away the Wood family fortune. Only 350 head of cattle were saved; one Hereford bull carcass even washed into the lobby of Corpus Christi's Nueces Hotel.

Oil storage tanks on Mustang Island burst. Thousands of barrels of crude oil coated Aransas County's south beaches and the flats behind them. Some scientists, however, speculated that the oil came from a seep on the Gulf floor, opened during the storm.

Several hundred people had taken shelter in Captain Sims' home on Mustang Island. When the house overflowed, other refugees raced to the highest point of land, Money Hill, and sat out the storm there. Harry Corkill was among the men and boys who held the edges of tarpaulins while women and children huddled in the center. They had no food for three days.

People had been warned to leave the Corpus Christi lowlands by ten o'clock Sunday morning before the storm hit. Even though automobiles were commandeered for a great evacuation, most people refused to go. Later, tourists at the hotels on North Beach tried but failed to get across Hall's Bayou to the town; the water-level causeway over a normally shallow natural channel was impassible. Some few lucky souls made it across the SAAP railroad trestle before tidewaters became too deep and too swift to cross.

North Beach, only five feet above sea level on a normal day, was wiped clean. Two hundred and twenty-nine elegant summer homes were just gone. Only the Beach Hotel, a part of the Spohn Sanatorium, and one other building remained. Most people who lived in that area were swept into Nueces Bay and across to White Point.

In Corpus Christi itself, huge combers pounded into homes and businesses below the bluff. Two blocks inland, buildings were crushed under bales of cotton, pilings, and timbers. The official death count was 280, but some estimates ranged as high as 600.

People in Aransas County shook their heads. It was frightening to think that devastation so much worse than their own had happened that close to home. Aransans knew then that they had surely been spared. The ridge, the brush, and the live oaks had saved them from a North Beach fate.

Some days after the storm, Irene Norvell finally found time to see about her music room at the school. It was more than a room, really; it was a small house behind the main school building. Irene took a "Negro girl" along to clean up.

They had to run most of the way because of big mosquitoes that settled on them in quantities. "They were a new variety, sluggish," Irene wrote. "You could brush them off but they had a sting."

When Irene got inside her room, she promptly slipped on the wet, slimy floor and fell down. Salt water was still standing on the Steinway piano. Throughout Rockport, twenty-five pianos had been destroyed and Irene felt certain no one would return to her class, considering how many worldly goods people had lost.

Throughout the area, the mosquitoes got so bad that Aransans covered their horses with tarpaulins; they wrapped their own arms and legs with newspaper to keep the insects from biting. People lacking window screens or mosquito bars were hardly able to sleep.

Irene and Elisha Norvell stayed with their daughter through-out the long period of restoring the house on Water Street. Irene loved the children and grandchildren, but she yearned to be back home, away from the noise of little ones. When she most needed peace, Irene walked back to her damaged Water Street home. She found somewhere to sit and write.

The beach—what little remained of it—was still covered with debris. Men had made a narrow, rough path through the rubble; their horses almost brushed Irene's porch when she sat by her front door. It was five months before Elisha got all the trash moved so he could put up the fence.

Captain McHugh found the wreckage of his fishing boat *Josie*, built in 1881 by Murdoch McRae.

Someone found the fan of the windmill from George Fulton's old mansion, lodged in the top of an oak tree. Farther north, the high, sloping bluff of Live Oak Point had been carried away by wind and water.

Strollers everywhere outside of town discovered one curious gain: artifacts of the Cópane tribe. Not only did people find arrow and spear heads, scrapers and knives, but also fifty-five complete skeletons, some with beads and hair.

Mr. Korges, at Bayside, found a fine knife shaped like a lance and double pointed. Someone found a round stone pipe for smok-ing. It had a bowl protruding from the upper surface; the drilling passed straight through the bowl and the sphere that formed the body of the pipe.

Nothing at all was left of the Cópane middens on Frandolig Point; that land was bare. Modern buildings were gone too; Fran-dolig's orchards and gardens had been washed away. Snakes, how-ever, safe from the town's patrollers, made the island their haven.

At Heldenfels shipyard, every building and all the machinery was destroyed. All but two ships under construction were washed away, and damage estimates ranged to hundreds of thousands of dollars. The Emergency Fleet Corporation assumed responsibility for the loss and bought the two barge hulls, but Heldenfels paid for most of the cleanup and restoration with no compensation.

Although the conclusion of the Great War had slowed the need for ships, it was the hurricane that finished the Heldenfels shipyard.

The Hurricane of 1919 turned out not to be the "worst hurricane in history" after all—merely the worst in the history of Aransas County and its neighbors.

BOOK THREE

AFTER THE STORM

A Safe and Adequate Deepwater Harbor

By 1920 Rockport was rebuilding, but it was scarcely larger than it had been a decade earlier. The population stood at 1,545, outstripped even by Aransas Pass, which had 1,569 citizens. And Corpus Christi had 10,522.

The numbers were particularly significant since Congress decided that year to provide funds "with a view to the establishment of a safe and adequate deepwater harbor" in the vicinity of the Aransas pass. The town that got the port would prosper; the others would remain second-rate.

Small as Rockport was, the citizens felt confident. They had worked hard to earn the port. And they believed their town was the best place for it.

Robert J. Kleberg and his King Ranch favored Corpus Christi as the port site. Kleberg called bankers, merchants, railroad executives, owners of other vast ranches, professional men from all over Texas. He invited them to a meeting at Kingsville, where they organized the Deep Water Harbor Association. The men sent Roy Miller to Washington to lobby in favor of Corpus Christi, and in May of 1922 Congress issued its report:

TOWN	COST TO U.S.	COST TO LOCAL INTERESTS
Aransas Pass	$1,005,000	$632,000
Rockport	$1,038,000	$994,000
Corpus Christi	$1,967,000	$3,084,900

Rockport and Aransas Pass were jubilant. One of them, surely, would win the port, since Corpus Christi's expenses were so much greater. But Roy Miller, speaking for Kleberg's Deep Water Harbor Association, had convinced Congress that Corpus Christi was destined for growth. Although locating the harbor there would require the longest ship channel from the pass, Corpus Christi was served by four railroads and three banks. Natural gas had been discovered nearby, complementing a diversity of agricultural efforts in the area. The town had already begun building a breakwater to protect its shore from a repeat of the 1919 storm disaster.

These persuasive arguments from Kleberg's organization won the day. President Warren G. Harding signed the Corpus Christi deepwater harbor bill into law in September 1922, and work began almost at once. The Port of Corpus Christi opened to ocean-going vessels on September 14, 1926—seven years to the day after the devastating hurricane.

COPING

Times of change are often times of great conflict, and Aransas had experienced all the change it could stand. Dreams of a bustling seaport had vanished. Hurricane debris still littered parts of town. Gambling halls and proper saloons were gone. Some boys had never returned or fully recovered from the war.

And that was not all. In the blink of an eye, it seemed, the world had changed. Automobiles had replaced horses. The telephone had connected every place on the planet. Modest schoolgirls had become flappers. Radio and motion pictures seemed more entertaining to a new generation than did family stories told beside a fire. Alone, each change modified the county no more than one ripple reshaped the shore. But in the aggregate, new ways washed away the daily life that old-timers had understood.

Step by step, and perhaps not even consciously, the citizens of Aransas felt their way to a changed world. Alpha Kennedy Wood, who lived through those times, wrote: "The rebuilding process came slowly. There was no rush to be the biggest and the best. . . . Growth came naturally."

Growth was natural because it came from the assets that Aransas had always enjoyed: a fine bay teeming with sealife, sturdy oaks, good people, frequent and faithful visitors. Aransas delighted the eye and fed the soul. That was a strong base from which to start.

Ford Jackson bought out his brother's interest in their fish house, then changed the name to Jackson Seafood Company. Over the ensuing years, he restructured and expanded until the organization became widely recognized throughout the seafood industry.

Ernest Camehl's Union Fish Company was so wrecked after the hurricane that he had to hire a surveyor to locate his property lines. Even Camehl's huge safe had disappeared, but he did find one small typewriter. Without delay, Camehl rebuilt. He assembled a good crew—W. F. Close, John Weber, Wesley Atwood—and soon had a flourishing business again.

Wesley Atwood's father Joseph, and his French mother Victoria DuPont, had come to Aransas County around 1870. Wesley married Fannie Mae Rice. By the time their sons—Burton, Hayes, and Ted—were teenagers, fishing was a way of life for them all.

The Atwood boys virtually grew up living in a boat. They worked off a sailboat, using it as both living quarters and transportation for their fishing skiffs. Behind them, the Atwoods towed a "live barge." Since they had no refrigeration or ice and generally stayed on the water for days at a time, the slatted barge served as a mobil fish trap to keep their catch alive.

If bad weather beset them, the Atwoods just holed up some place and let it blow over; they just kept going, but young Ted got tired of that. He wanted to get back to town and prowl around a little bit.

Johnny Atwood told his father's story later: "One of the ways he could get himself back home after four or five days was either to dispose of the old man's chewing tobacco or get rid of the bread. When the sailboat was underway, he would chute the bread or tobacco out the centerboard case so that it would go under the boat and out with the wake so nobody would see it come up."

Fred Bracht had been managing Rockport Mercantile since 1910, except for his stint in the Great War. After the 1919 storm, his father Leopold and uncle Roland Bracht established a furniture store behind the Mercantile. They called the second floor Bracht Hall and opened it to the public for dances and meetings. Clara Bracht, who had felt shaky in her tall house ever since the hurricane, moved to a one-story beach cottage in 1920.

That year, Fred Bracht married Inez Campbell, and the Fire Department gave the couple a party in Bracht Hall. "Everybody in town was there," Inez said later, then added that "there wasn't too many people in town then." Lola Herring Sorenson played piano for the guests to dance by.

Baptists didn't believe in dancing, so Nina Diederich, Lucille Lathrop, Earl Bowles, and Marion Johnson enjoyed another kind of entertainment with their friends. They called it "Shoo-la-lay." The young people formed circles and went through steps similar to square dance movements. They didn't dance in couples, close to one another, and they didn't have musical instruments. Someone might sing or just call out the moves.

Marvin Davis—whose family had come to Texas with the Tennessee Volunteers at the time of the Revolution—started a coffee shop on Austin Street, just north of Market. He had some success selling sandwiches there in the late 1920s and early 1930s, but when beer licenses became available Marvin bought one. He moved to a larger building some doors north, not far from Sorenson's old chandlery, and started a cafe. Family members believe that he had the only beer license in the county for several years—though there were still some bootleggers around.

Cyrus B. Lucas had bought Samuel B. Allyn's half interest in San José Island just months before the great hurricane. In May 1922 the Woods conveyed to him their interest in the ruined ranch. Lucas also bought out small owners on the Blackjack Peninsula, consolidating their holdings into one large ranch. There he ran several thousand head of Hereford and Durham cattle.

Lucas never lived on his ranch, nor did he lavish money on his resident employees. The women, yearning for window screens, resented his parsimony. On one of Lucas' visits, a foreman invited him to supper and his wife cooked up her best. Lucas thought the food was good, but rather spoiled by acrid smoke that billowed from beneath the sturdy table.

"I smolder cow chips in a dish pan there," the housewife explained, "to keep mosquitoes away." The next day she got her window screens.

But Lucas had reason to scrimp; his financial problems ran deep. Between 1911 and 1922 he had negotiated large mortgages, then failed to make payment on his notes. He lost his interest in San José Island to Mr. Gieseke of San Antonio, and then the San Antonio Loan and Trust Company foreclosed on Blackjacks ranch. One of its principals, Leroy G. Denman, took over. In 1924 Denman sealed off the head of the peninsula with an eight-foot-tall game-proof fence.

He brought in wild turkeys, which had not been seen in the Blackjacks for years, and native white-tailed deer, almost as rare. Denman also introduced five foreign species—California quail, mule deer from Utah, Asian ringnecked pheasants, European fallow deers, and European boar.

With both the Blackjacks and San José under private ownership, Aransas County seemed much smaller to the average citizen.

But people in Rockport felt safer too: Aransas County had formed a Navigation District in 1925, with J. S. Peters, A. L. Bruhl, and A. C. Glass as commissioners. Within a year, a breakwater and dragline dredging created the general shape of a harbor, but there were no concrete bulkheads, only wooden ones. The harbor opened to the bay at right angles to the shore, not paralleling it as the channel does now, and there was an island in the center. Some years later, additional dredging circled "Jackson's Island" near the end of the railroad pier.

A brochure for the new Kool Koast Kamp began to circulate in 1924. It featured a double-page drawing of the bay, with all the amenities of a first-class resort. One had to look closely to see that individual rooms beneath a palm-roofed cabana were really just tents. The eye moved at once to the dining room, nestled near leaning oaks, and to the tall cross that towered there.

"Many of our people are not privileged to enjoy an outing such as this will afford," the brochure bragged, "because of the great cost usually attached thereto." The Kool Koast Kamp provided "real family recreation under high-class moral conditions."

It offered "boating excursions to strange islands, covered with historical relics of the deep." A swimming instructor was constantly available on a beach that was shaded "for complexion protection." There were "shades over water, over pier. Shades everywhere." And, of course, there was fishing for "babies, for refined ladies, for rough and tumble men," with all the tackle anyone could need.

One section of the brochure, headlined "The Family," made a special promise: "Wonderful Mothers: This Kamp is deeded to you. No drudgery. No worry. The Fiery Cross guards you at night and an officer of the law, with the same Christian sentiment, guards carefully all portals."

The Kamp was run by the Ku Klux Klan. "Boost our Encampment," the brochure urged. "Get fifty Klansmen from your town to bring fifty non-Klansmen and let them see and hear and know what we are. If any trip ever opened a non-Klansman's eyes this one will."

From the Kool Koast Kamp brochure.
—Courtesy of Gayle Atwood Collection; Jackson family Collection

Such writing may be a shocking eye-opener for modern Aransans, but it did not surprise anyone in 1924. Two years earlier, the *Rockport Pilot* had run an article headlined: *"Pilot* Editor Witnesses Klan Ceremonies; Barbecue Staged."

Emory Spencer, a relatively new arrival from East Texas at the time, later explained that "newcomers, so to speak, probably exceeded the number of old settlers and the situation was just ripe for such an organization as the Ku Klux Klan." Across the South, the Klan's prejudice included Catholics, Jews, and "Negroes," but there were very few of the latter two categories in Aransas. Spencer said that the Klan's bigotry "really amounted to an exclusion of the Catholics only." In Aransas that meant most of the families with long roots at Lamar and nearly every Mexican.

Spencer said that his father was among the many people who reacted against the Klansmen's intolerance and sided with the Catholics. "In 1923 it cost him his job as County Agent of San Patricio," Spencer added.

Much more savory—and more enduring than the Kool Koast Kamp—was the St. Charles Bay Hunt Club. When it opened in 1925 with J. Howard Mills as the manager, it was just "a few buildings and an old ranch house," Mrs. Edith Mills recalled. The club still stands on the east shore of Lamar Peninsula, facing narrow St. Charles Bay and the Blackjacks beyond it.

Frank Johnson ran a hunt boat at the club. He lived in Fulton and traveled by barge from Live Oak Peninsula to Lamar. Most of the hunters—"sports," the guides called them—came overland from Refugio.

Guides usually took their parties north into St. Charles Bay, but some of the best hunting could be found in Dunham Bay. Traveling there, boats passed Teal Reef, then turned east around Blackjack Point and north into Dunham Bay. The total trip took a little over an hour. Hunters filled a string of fourteen-foot wooden skiffs, towed by a slow, shallow-draft boat called the *Gray Goose*. When the towboat reached a blind, the captain sounded a foghorn, and the guide in the next-to-last skiff untied the boat behind him. Guides quickly learned to tie a knot that could be released under strain, because the towing boat never slowed down. A guide could expect a lot of razzing if he impeded the train's progress while untying a hard knot.

The guide in the released skiff rowed to a hunting blind made of leafy, aromatic branches of sweet bay. While his "sports" waited in the boat, the guide waded through the shallow water, setting out ninety or more decoys. Then he pushed the boat into the blind, which was conformed to fit it. The guide looked for ducks, sometimes whistling for sprigs, or giving a soft "*brrrrt-brrrrt*" for redheads. He told his hunters when to shoot and served as "bird dog" to retrieve their kill. He even picked the feathers from the ducks and geese.

One memorable day, Henry Ballou, whose family had been at Lamar since the 1830s, performed the familiar guiding ritual with two colleagues. The weather was cool and the hunting a great success, but just before the towboat was due to pick up the hunters, a wet blue norther roared in. The temperature dropped to freezing. And the towboat did not come.

After a while, Henry and the other guides came to the grim conclusion that their tow had broken down; they started to row back to the club. The job wasn't too difficult heading south, but when the guides rounded Dunham Point, they were aimed almost into the teeth of the wind. They had to get out of their skiffs and push.

Henry Ballou landed in water over his boot tops and his slicker leaked. He began to get very cold. Conditions worsened as the guides rounded Blackjack Point at East Pocket and headed almost due north. They had a hard time wading across Teal Reef; it was slow, wet, frigid work. Henry was turning blue and shaking uncontrollably. The other guides and the hunters worried about him.

Finally, someone came up with an idea. The guides got Henry to lie down in a skiff and covered him with the ducks the sports had shot. No matter that the birds were wet and bloody—they were good insulation.

The two remaining guides continued to push and haul. Finally, the unhappy party made landfall near the intersection of Main and Bay streets in Lamar. A truck picked up the hunters and took them to the Club House to get warm. The guides got gizzard stew—a pungent but warming supper—and Henry survived to guide again.

Thirteen-year-old Roy Hinson moved to Rockport with his family in 1926. They rented a large, two-story house on the beach, one block south of the Sorenson home. "It was really a good place to grow up," Roy said later, remembering the last days of the old ways. "During the summer, we spent a good part of our time swimming in the bay or rowing a scull, just monkeying around. It was really a nice, peaceful environment. My best friend got me involved in roaming the woods, the brush around Rockport, picking huckleberries in the fall. And we had a Boy Scout troop that went on Saturday night camping trips out to the back bays—the present Copano Village area."

Roy remembered an old community house where graduation exercises were held, along with community entertainment. "There was a movie projector," he said, "and seats for any local people who wanted to see movies, and the school programs and high school plays were put on there. I think the building was left over from the old days when they had all the hotels before the 1919 storm."

A. C. Glass, who had become associated with Rockport's First National Bank shortly after the hurricane, purchased Travis Johnson's insurance business in 1928. The next year, Johnson joined Charles Picton to establish the Charles T. Picton Lumber Company. Fred M. Percival purchased the *Rockport Pilot* in 1929—just months before the beginning of the Great Depression.

Since most of Texas had no industry, the state was not laced with long lines of unemployed workers, but money was woefully scarce. Although no one was considered rich, the Brachts, the Pictons, and Travis Johnson seemed to do better than most. Everyone got enough to eat; the bays provided, as they always had.

"It was sparse living," Jim Furlong said, "but there wasn't degradation like there was in the cities."

Roy Lassiter rarely wore shoes, even to school. But when he arrived at Sacred Heart Church to serve as altar boy, Father Kelly made him—and the others like him—wash their feet before they went inside.

The Coleman-Fulton Pasture Company, known for some years as the Taft Ranch, finally dissolved. The Davidson family, who had owned the Fulton Mansion off and on since 1907, was hard pressed to maintain the grand structure. They decided that tourists might help and charged twenty-five cents to any who would come in and look around.

In 1930 Aransas County's population hit a high point—2,219. Of the 522 tallied, exactly half were homeowners and the rest were tenants. Rockport had a population of 1,545 in 1920, but by 1933, as the Depression did its worst, the census dropped to 1,140. More than twice that number lived in Aransas Pass, and Corpus Christi boasted 27,741 citizens.

Aransas seemed a pathetic place, but interesting bits of bravado burst through. J. F. Bullard, who had moved to Rockport from Missouri in 1923, wanted pine trees. He refused to listen to anyone who said they could not prosper. Working with the extension service of Texas A&M University, Bullard learned that slash pine is the best choice for Aransas. He set out 5,000 seedlings, and a grove began to grow between Rockport and Fulton.

PESCADORES AND "COLORED" COOKS

The Mexican-Americans of Aransas were almost all fishermen. Hillis Dominguez remembered "old Rodriguez" from the early days. He recalled "Alfredo Covarrúbias in a big house. They had a piano that I guess was the only one in Rockport belonging to a Mexican-American." Hillis also mentioned two Solís families, the Pulido brothers, Steve and Chano Garcia.

As more Mexican-American families came to Rockport, they settled close to one another in the west part of town. Frank Covarrúbias said that they were "kinda separated" from the Anglos. "Sometimes you'd find the Mexicans scattered, living along with Anglos, but not too close to them, you know." Frank's people realized that living close to Anglos inevitably brought on misunderstandings, "so we stayed away from them. And mainly they stayed away from us too," he said with a sort of chuckle.

Frank Covarrúbias had been one of the early arrivals among Mexican-American families. He had gone to a Mexican public primary-grades school, segregated from the one for Anglos. It was "up in the brush," Frank said, "close to the city barn." That was near the Heldenfels shipyard.

In 1926 Frank started to Catholic school, but even there the

Mexicans and Anglos were in separate rooms. Only families who could afford tuition were required to pay.

Hillis Dominguez attended the Mexican public school in 1934. Then it was "a little wooden school in the playgrounds of the Rockport Elementary." At recess, children from both buildings filled the yard, but even there they were segregated—"maybe a hundred feet separate," Hillis said.

By the time Hillis was in the fourth or fifth grade, school officials transferred the Mexican-American students. "I don't know what happened, but they put us in the Rockport Elementary school," Hillis said. He could not remember any Mexican-American who graduated while he was there. (Costáncio Solís was the first, in 1941.)

Avelina Falcón began her education in Rockport in 1938: "I didn't start when I was six; I started when I was seven because I had to walk to school. I went to first and second grade in the elementary school and then in the third grade they separated me and put me with the Mexican children. I don't know for what reason."

Avelina's mother "didn't let us go out too much, but when she did we went to the movies. Of course, they had us separated. They had a section for Mexicans only and a section for the white people and a section for the Negro people. It was like that several places. We couldn't go in because they didn't allow Mexicans."

No sign proclaimed it; everyone just knew. Hillis Dominguez understood that there was only one restaurant he could enter. "We couldn't go to barbershops—they wouldn't cut our hair. An old man who worked for the Highway Department would cut our hair over there in the barrio."

The things Hillis remembered mostly were "the everyday things that we did. We bought food at Kelly's Food Store. We didn't buy the *Rockport Pilot*, because my parents didn't know how to read. And they didn't have time to buy it. Mother worked. She walked everywhere there was work in those days."

The youngsters had their own ways of making money. "We'd walk all the way to Frandolig Point," Hillis said. The objective was oysters. "We'd take a bench, we'd take a bucket and there was usually two of us." One would pick oysters while the other sat on the bench, opening shells and putting the meat in the bucket. From time to time, the friends swapped jobs. "When we filled that buck-

Typical Mexican road crew with ox-cart.
—Courtesy of Shirley Ratisseau Collection

et of oysters—which was a couple of hours, I guess—we would start back."

The boys walked one behind the other, shouldering a stick, and the oyster bucket hung between them. "We'd walk all the way back to Jackson's Fish Company. And he would give us a dollar for that gallon of oysters. Which was pretty good. We got fifty cents apiece. You went to the movies and you bought popcorn and a Coke and you still had twenty-five cents left."

The grown men worked at harder jobs, and Frank Covarrúbias had quit school to join them. "We fished with a scow sail boat," he said. "It didn't have points; it was a flat boat at both ends with big sails." Boats like that were sturdy, but quick and inexpensive to build.

Frank remembered: "We used to go across to St. Joseph. And we went to Port O'Connor. We had nets maybe a thousand feet long that had a big bag in the center, so that we could make a circle and scare the fish into the bag. The boat pulled one end of the net and three or four of us would pull the other end." The men and boys walked at the edge of the water—"in the dry," Frank said, or maybe wet up to their hips—while the boat moved away from them, toward deeper water.

"After we'd walked about two or three hours, we came together and made the circle and gathered the fish—mostly trout and redfish. Sometimes we'd pick up two or three hundred pounds. There was a place where we caught about twenty or thirty thousand pounds of fish. We sold them for five cents a pound. Three cents for a flounder and things like that. They had a big fish house over here and they shipped it out. Charlie Gibson's used to be the main fish house then."

Charlie Gibson's Fish House. Postcard.
—Courtesy of Gordon Stanley Collection

Frank Covarrúbias said he "made good money at that time. We got by with three dollars of groceries, all week. You buy a nickel there, a nickel that, nickel everything. And they give you a lot of lard, a lot of sugar, lot of coffee, potatoes, beans, everything. You don't buy no more than a nickel and at most a dime. So you get two or three big bags of groceries for a dollar-fifty or two dollars. So if you made four or five dollars a week, you'd get by."

Frank remembered Charlie Gibson's wife, Gladys Bruhl, from

the time that they were children together, but her Fulton family heritage may have meant less to him than to some.

What Frank Covarúbbias remembered was that Gladys Bruhl Gibson "had a good-looking husband. Very good-looking man, well dressed all the time. Although he was the owner of the fish house, he dressed in white all the time—white shoes, white pants and a white shirt. Everything. That guy was neat all the time. His complexion was kinda rosy, not quite a red. I always admired that man. He was neat all the time.

"Travis Johnson was his bookkeeper. And then Mr. Gibson left and Travis built his fish house, so we went on and worked for Travis Johnson. Most of the Mexican people knew him pretty well, so he was good to them."

A few years later, Hillis Dominguez was catching fish in Copano Bay; Johnson's Fish Company truck came to meet his band of fishermen. "We came to shore with the fish and put it in barrels there—sometimes as many as ten barrels. We'd bring it that way because it was too long to come by water all the way around Live Oak Point and down to Rockport."

The fish were not cleaned. "The fishermen who caught the fish didn't have time to gut them," Hillis explained. "They put them in a barrel with guts and they'd bring them to the floor of the fish house. Then other boys would be there ready to gut them. You'd get a dollar for a hundred pounds of gutted fish."

Frank Covarrúbias recalled that the Mexican-American community, like the Anglos, enjoyed Bracht Hall. "We used to make dances there, big dances, you know, high society dances. We had a lot of Mexican dances—just about every Saturday. And when we had marriages, people would go to one of two big halls and everybody would dress in the best they could."

Marvin Davis built a place right across the street from Bracht Hall and sold the dancers beer to go. It was a simple establishment—just a wood floor and the wall frame covered with cold drink and beer advertisement signs.

Frank Covarrúbias described a Mexican lodge called the Blue

Cross. "The man that formed it came from the Valley," he said. "Most every Mexican belonged to the lodge. The head of the family would pay a fee and then whenever someone got sick, the lodge would help out with medicine and doctors and things like that. Once in a while, they made dances and fiestas to support the lodge."

Throughout South Texas, organizations formed to improve the circumstances of Mexican-Americans. In 1927 representatives of these groups convened in Harlingen and out of their meeting eventually came a new organization—the League of United Latin American Citizens, LULAC.

The National Association for the Advancement of Colored People (NAACP) had been founded in 1909, but there weren't many blacks in Aransas, so no one thought much about that organization.

Like the Mexican-Americans, the "Negro knew where he went," Baby Ruth Stubblefield Dunman said. Walter Dickey started school in 1911, when all the black children were in one room. He bought his books from Mr. Glazer, since none were furnished by the school.

Most of the blacks lived in a little row of houses fronting on Market Street, just west of Church Street. At one time, the St. Charles Hunting Club employed twelve black cooks, who lived on the place and worked shifts.

Walter Dickey delivered ice when Henry Bailey ran the ice house in 1926. He remembered that Cap Lassiter took ice in twenty-pound blocks for his meat market.

John and Baby Ruth Dunman moved in from Salt Creek. There the Dunman home had one bedroom in Aransas County and the other—along with the kitchen and living room—in Refugio County. The Dunmans

An unidentified child, posed in her finest.

—Courtesy of Walter Dickey collection Aransas County Historical Society Archives

registered to vote in Aransas, but if they had other matters with the court, they went to Refugio.

Baby Ruth remembered that the black children in the lower grades then went to school in Aransas Pass. Older ones had to go all the way to Corpus Christi. A turn-around bus—not a school bus—carried them, some as far as Lamar. Each child had a visa that paid his fare.

There was little work for the parents. John and Baby Ruth Dunman said that blacks could be cooks, houseworkers, fishermen, janitors, or cafe help. One cafe had a place behind it where the blacks could play music—guitars, mostly. Someone would hand them beer or a soda out the window. If they wanted a meal, they did not go in the cafe's dining room, of course, but ate in the kitchen behind it.

For a while, there was a cafe on the beach, at 911 Navigation Circle—a building that later became the Navigation District office. Blacks went in the water there to baptize newcomers to the faith.

Blacks were allowed in the second show at the movies. The first show started at six or seven each evening. Then the blacks would stand in line and wait for it to end so that they could go in.

Restrooms carried three signs: White Men, White Women, and Colored. With black men and women sharing one restroom like that, a person never knew who might come in. "It was embarrassing," Baby Ruth said.

GIFTS FROM THE SEA

Every shade of human skin was equally affected by one small event in the mid-1920s: Jim Tuttle threw out a hand net in Aransas Bay and hauled in shrimp. Some men were already catching the crustaceans near Corpus Christi, but no one realized the wealth of them at Aransas. Soon shrimpers worked two sailboats side by side, dragging large nets between them.

"They brought in huge loads of shrimp," Roy Hinson remembered. "Small bay boats could go out and in just one day get five or six thousand pounds of shrimp." There weren't many boats and there weren't many people to head the shrimp that they brought in. "Jackson's was there," Hinson said, "an old wooden building right

BIRD'S EYE VIEW LOOKING EAST FROM COURT HOUSE, ROCKPORT, TEX.

Still plenty of room for development in downtown Rockport. Postcard.
—Courtesy of Gordon Stanley Collection

alongside the railroad track, out on the railroad pier, as we called it, at that time. And Scrivner's."

Boats tied up to the railroad pier. "They would unload the shrimp into barrels and then put them on a little rail handcar and truck them in," Hinson remembered. "This was the end of the line for the railroad. We had a turnaround for the locomotive, just down about where the Bracht lumberyard is now [at Ann, west of North street]. When the train came in was the high point of the day."

The company Roy Hinson worked for "was equipped to process the shrimp by having them peeled," he said. "We headed the shrimp and shipped them out by rail. And then they would cook them and can them and ship them that way, too, in gallon cans. They shipped redfish, trout, and flounders too."

For each pound of shrimp Roy headed, he made three-fourths of a penny. He and other fast workers could each head about a hundred pounds in an hour and make seventy-five cents. But the barbs at each shrimp's head and tail—and the rough shells—soon took their toll on even the toughest skin, Hinson said. "By the time you worked an hour or so, your hands would be so miserably sore you could hardly pick up a shrimp. Sometimes we'd work from about four in the afternoon till ten o'clock."

Soon Cecil Casterline began a seafood operation in Fulton. Bunker Wendell and Zeph Rouquette were in business there too. In 1935 Travis Johnson and Charles Picton founded the Johnson Fish Company in Rockport. No matter that "Fish" was part of the company names, shrimp was the focus of business.

There are a number of varieties of commercial shrimp in the Gulf of Mexico, all with somewhat different habits, but all prolific breeders. A female of one variety can release 500,000 to 1,000,000 eggs that hatch within twenty-four hours and swim shoreward. By the time the infant shrimp arrive at the Aransas pass, they are one-fourth of an inch long. These post-larval shrimp continue across the great bay to the salt marshes, to the small back bays and the shallow bayous. They grow rapidly, casting off their shells and forming new ones. If the bay water temperature falls below sixty degrees, growth is interrupted and many shrimp die. Of course, they must also avoid predators—trout, redfish, and others. When the surviving shrimp reach two inches in length, they start a long swim back to the Gulf and the reproductive cycle begins again.

Johnny and Steve Atwood often shrimped with their father, Ted, employing a process little changed from the earliest days. Remembering that time, Johnny said, "Shrimping was totally unlike anything that exists now. We didn't just go throw the net in the water and drag it up and down the bays all day long. We hunted the shrimp, looked for shrimp in bunches. In the 1940s it wasn't anything for one of these small boats to bring in three or four thousand pounds of shrimp in a day. That's all they could put on the boat, but they could have caught more, lots of times." He didn't recall ever catching a turtle.

There were two ways to look for shrimp, Johnny said. The primary way was with a "try" net. It was a small net, usually six or seven feet across, and in the top of that net the shrimper tied a linen thread. He always used linen, because it wouldn't stretch. It was a very stiff string, the same kind he used to patch his fish nets. Johnny explained: "You put it across your finger, pull it taut and when the shrimp went in that net it was kicking; it would telegraph that feel up the string and you knew when a shrimp went in that little net."

Johnny and his father used the try net all the time they had the big net in the water; it was their search net. They criss-crossed a section of bay, found a few shrimp here and there, and then they might run into the mother lode.

Sometimes they saw the birds working and used that as an indicator. When the shrimp "really got thick," particularly in the shallows they made the water muddy. In shallow bays, Johnny watched the prop wash; he could see shrimp jumping out of the water. But in places like Mesquite Bay, the little try net wouldn't work. Loose bottom grass so fouled it that the net couldn't catch a shrimp. The Atwoods often threw a cast net instead.

Once, as they returned from shrimping unsuccessfully near Mission Bay, the Atwoods reached a spot near Lenoir's Landing at Copano Village, where they kept their boat. They saw a muddy spot in eight feet of water and decided to give it a try. The net had not even reached bottom "when the bottom just rose up to us," Johnny said. What he saw was "just white, all big white shrimp, jumping in the skiff with us. I was sitting on the bow with a dip net and catching the shrimp with that."

The Atwoods had pulled their net only ten or fifteen minutes when Ted decided he'd better stop; he didn't want to exceed his limit—about 300 pounds. Johnny said, "We picked that net up and we had eight hundred pounds of shrimp—absolutely gorgeous big, old shrimp, not a fish among them. When you catch shrimp like that, it's a thrill, much better than catching any fish on a line."

Men who follow the shrimp have a jargon all their own. Today most of them catch table shrimp in trawls—cone-shaped nets that taper to a narrow end, called the cod-end, cod-sack, or simply "the sack." The two "wings" of a trawl are attached to wooden "doors" weighted with metal "shoes," or runners. Lines run from the shrimp boat to each door. As the shrimp boat tows the trawl over the sea floor, the spreading doors hold the trawl's mouth open, producing a kite-like action.

Shrimp scooped into the open trawl pile up in the sack—along with a bycatch of "trash fish." When a previous drag has been processed, shrimpers pull the trawl on board the boat. One man grabs the line that holds the cod-end closed. He tugs at it and the catch falls to the deck. Shrimpers separate their treasure from the "trash," throwing overboard croakers, ribbon fish, mullet, crabs, and jelly fish—along with some fingerling snapper, trout, redfish, and turtles. Many of them are dead from the ordeal.

Most Gulf shrimpers stay out for weeks. To preserve their catch, they snap the heads off the shrimp, then wash and ice them down. At the dock, the shrimp are sucked off the boat through a pipe, washed again, and packed in 100-pound wooden boxes. Many are delivered to freezing plants where they are unloaded, washed one more time, sized, and packed in five-pound pasteboard boxes. They are shipped in refrigerated trucks.

Smaller operations work mainly for bait shrimp. They make ten to twenty short tows a day using small trawls, ten to twenty-five feet wide. Bait sellers hold their live shrimp in watertight pens made of plywood or concrete. Seawater, pumped in continuously, supplies necessary oxygen to the pens.

Twelve million pounds of Texas shrimp were landed in 1936. The supply of them seemed endless.

HUGGING THE COAST

Roy Hinson left the fish houses in 1929 and went to work for Archie Knox, agent at the train depot. Still Roy didn't get away from seafood.

"Fish, shrimp and anything else would be shipped from here," he said. "I transported it to the depot and loaded it on the express cars or box cars."

Since there were a number of small farms in Aransas County, the railroad shipped crops too. "I don't recall that there was any truck traffic at that time," Roy said. "Carroll Moore operated a freight service to Corpus Christi, using a truck that he owned. That was the only thing I know of."

By this time, the SAAP had sold its franchise to the Southern Pacific line. There was still at least one passenger train a day, but there were few passengers, Roy said. It seemed to him that the main focus was on the crops and seafood shipped out.

People were talking about the new Hug-the-Coast Road—Highway 35, that would link Aransas to Houston. Ham Smith, who was still operating his transport business, purchased land on the highway's proposed route. There he opened a combination home, filling station, and grocery store.

Marion Johnson worked on a dredge boat, digging mudshell for the road's foundation. Later, Johnny Atwood commented on that sort of enterprise: "These bays all radically changed because of the extensive shell dredging. Copano, particularly, was completely wiped out of live oysters as an indirect result of dredging the so-called dead ones. It became a very muddy bay, where it used to be a very clean, clear bay."

Johnny said that mudshell made a "wonderful road base—probably the best road base ever found. Most all Rockport streets were covered with mudshell. The shape of that old shell interlocks and makes a pad and it doesn't work itself down into the sand.

"In a muddy area, like the old Blacklands [around Taft], it's the same thing. The shell doesn't get worked down in to the mud. It makes a pretty firm base. There is enough mud on it—a good mud shell had a blue clay material on it—and it would dry hard as a rock . . . . Drilling rigs used it as a base too."

Johnny Atwood estimated that, over time, dredgers took "millions and millions of cubic yards of mudshell out of these bays. They dredged the north end of Aransas Bay, Copano, Mesquite, San Antonio—all of those bays.

"Legally, they couldn't dredge a live reef, but unfortunately what happened was that the dredging of the dead reef, the taking of the shell, was an operation that involved washing a lot of sand and stuff out of the shell and that would drift down-current and silt over the live reef. So what was alive this year would be one [reef] that they could dredge the year or two hence, because it would kill it. It left big mud holes. Around Hopper's Landing [on the shore of the Aransas Wildlife Refuge] there are some big mud holes twenty to thirty feet deep. The shell was that thick."

With the roads well underway, engineers turned to the biggest job in constructing the Hug-the-Coast Highway: They had to build a one-and-one-half-mile causeway from Lamar to Live Oak Point. Twenty feet wide, it was constructed of timber spans that supported concrete six inches thick. To allow boat passage from Aransas Bay to

The Bascule Bridge in the Copano Causeway, 1930. Centennial booklet.
—Courtesy of Aransas County Historical Society Archives

Copano, the causeway would feature a bascule bridge, counterbalanced so that when one end was lowered, the other rose.

The Hug-the-Coast Highway ran, and runs now, just east of the site of James Wells' house, isolating it from the McRae property and Stella Maris. On the Live Oak Peninsula shore, the highway created a final division between the almost-forgotten homesites of James Power and Henry Smith.

On Thursday, April 24, 1930, the *Rockport Pilot* heralded the news:

2000 ATTEND CAUSEWAY CELEBRATION
Throngs Come to Help Rockport Make Merry
Big Dredge Digs In as People Celebrate Event

Then this:
HUGGINS IN WRECK RETURNING HOME FROM CELEBRATION

Judge W. O. Huggins was editor of the *Houston Chronicle* and principal speaker at the causeway celebration. His injuries were not serious, but the accident pointed up the fact that Aransas County's new link to a driving world would hold risk as well as promise.

H. E. Dickinson, a San Antonian who represented Texas on the National Board of Realtors, was also a speaker at the dedication ceremony:

"The first time I ever visited this town, I thought it was the jumping-off place. There was a nice hotel that you haven't now, and a nice bathing and dance pavilion you haven't now, but there was only one way out of the town and that was by train . . . and if you missed the train, it was all off until the next day. The dirt road was impassable."

Dickinson was speaking to a tiny community, a poor community. Even so, he saw much that attracted him. "I was very much surprised . . . to find that Live Oak Peninsula has an altitude twice as high as Houston. . . . I predict the day is coming when the land here will be devoted to grape culture and covered with vineyards. . . . The Hug-the-Coast Highway will bring many thousands of people . . . to and through Rockport, and I predict that many people buying seaside homes will cause land values to mount rapidly. . . . One thousand dollars a front foot is not too high and will some day be considered quite cheap. . . .

"Rockport will wake up; the citizens will come out of . . . their long sleep and become active. People of wealth in Houston and San Antonio will be coming to Rockport . . . and building beautiful homes. . . . If the Rockport people do not do something themselves, they will find soon that others will do it for them."

Locals disagreed with Dickinson. Aransas was not inactive—just taking a much-needed breather from its ambitious past, taking time to reassess its values and cope with the aftermath of disaster. But Dickinson's words offered a wake-up call, alerting Aransans to the views and values of outsiders.

Howard "Harry" Mills, who had been managing the St. Charles Bay Hunt Club, heard the message. He decided to start his own hunting and fishing camp at the edge of the new highway. In 1932 he bought a piece of Lamar property that looked straight across to Live Oak Peninsula, and there he built Mills Wharf.

Which early settler, which thriving business, might once have occupied the site is a fact lost in time, but Mills Wharf became history itself.

Harry had a museum of sorts, filled with oddities that intrigued a succession of regular tourists. At one time he displayed a redhead duck that had been captured by an oyster in Copano Bay. It made "Ripley's Believe It or Not" in all the newspapers. Harry also had an octopus retrieved from Copano Bay; two alligators from the Guadalupe River; twenty-eight unborn snakes, taken from the belly of a large rattler and pickled in a jar; other poisonous snakes, mounted; a live Gila monster from Phoenix, Arizona; and a mounted collection of the many ducks and geese seasonally seen at Aransas. But there were pictures, too, of proud hunter/fishermen with mammal dolphins, mother and child, strung up as trophies.

Another businessman, Skeet McHugh, followed an old family tradition of food service. He opened an oyster stand, and then a sandwich shop, on the new highway where it intersected Broadway in Fulton. Later, he had a Texaco station too.

Delo H. Caspary had a Gulf Service Station at the corner of Austin and Main streets. There he entertained customers with a stack of shoreline maps and a running account of sportsmen's records. Already Rockport was a far cry from the town Caspary had first visited in 1925. Then, he had driven into Rockport from Wichita Falls and saw not a single car. Caspary saw only one man—John Sorenson, who was standing on the corner by his store. But Caspary had a very successful hunting trip and the coastal climate appealed to him. He had decided then that he would make Aransas his home.

As times improved, Travis Johnson, A. C. Glass, Charles Picton, and Fred Johnson decided that Rockport needed a movie theater. They opened the Rio in 1936 and it was a first-class show house. The businessmen claimed they never intended to make money from the venture and were just feeling civic-minded.

Ancel Brundrett had moved to Port Aransas, where he ran a party boat and served as a guide for fishermen and hunters. He started a taxidermy business with Alfred Roberts, and in 1937 he mounted two tarpon for President Franklin Delano Roosevelt.

That same year, Oliver and Horace Brundrett opened a gas station on the triangle of land south of town, where Business Route 35

Mills Wharf, Lamar.
—Courtesy of Mills collection, Aransas County Historical Society Archives

Man dangles duck nabbed by oyster. Oyster has duck by most tenuous of toe-holds. (Man identified as Capt. John Howard Mills.)
—Courtesy of Mills collection, Aransas
County Historical Society Archives

slanted to meet the main highway. Appropriately, the brothers named their enterprise Triangle Service Station. They advertised that they "threw away the key" and stayed open for business twenty-four hours a day. They sold not only gasoline and oil, but sandwiches, beer, and cold drinks in the Triangle's cafe annex. Patrons were encouraged to "come as you are" to dine and dance.

The Triangle was probably the most popular dance hall/beer joint in the county during the 1940s. It was the site of many romances—and about as many fights. When Oliver Brundrett saw a sailor getting a little too-well lubricated, he'd feed the boy a "greasy pig." That pork sandwich was almost guaranteed to make the sailor toss his cookies, whereupon he would sober up enough to start all over again.

South of the Triangle, the community of Estes Flats had continued through thick and thin. Walter Stryker, who still lived there in 1997, told the story: "The 1919 storm blew away everything, took everything my folks had worked for since 1888. I think they were so mad at the storm that they moved away and had me. But then I turned out to be so mean that the storm didn't seem so bad after all and they came back!"

The Strykers rebuilt on their original thirty acres, and Walter grew up there. From 1928 to 1934, he and other children trudged a seldom-traveled shell road to attend school in Rockport. "We might walk the whole way without anybody driving by. Sometimes Guy Barber would come along and give us a ride. He was our best hope because he had a meat market in Rockport."

In 1935 Estes Flats got its second one-room school house. Miss Katie Lee Clarke taught seven grades of children there at one time. "There was no electricity," Walter said. "We had kerosene lamps and a wood-burning stove. I graduated salutatorian from the seventh grade—out of a class of four." As time passed and Estes Flats failed to regain its former population, the schoolhouse was moved to Rockport where it could be better utilized.

Perhaps the most widely held memory of Estes is more recent and not of the community at all, but of a tree there. John Wendell said that early motorists felt compelled to honk at the large oak and that they called it "the hanging tree." Shirley Ratisseau remembered it as later being called "the leprechaun tree." She wrote: "County passersby always honked when they passed the tree, to insure good luck and a safe return. There was hardly a soul from Rockport-Fulton who did not honk under that tree when passing."

Few seem to remember such things in this modern age. Not many in Aransas know the history of Estes at all. Motorists see only a road sign, a few small businesses, a scattering of up-to-date homes and modern bayfront developments on canal lots. Then Estes is gone, a fading image in the rearview mirror.

When the highway through Estes was new, natural gas sold at a low rate—just pennies for one thousand cubic feet. The price had been that low since the earliest oilfield days in Texas. Residue gas, a by-product of oil production, was so valueless that it was simply blown into the air, flared and wasted. It seemed good for nothing but lighting the night sky "bright as noon" in the little oil camp towns springing up across the state.

Then the Texas Railroad Commission ruled that residue gas could be used to produce carbon black, and Loland Grisso developed a new process for making it. He built two pilot plants in Borger, Texas, using them as a model for an Aransas plant completed by United Carbon in 1939.

The plant had a 2,300-degree furnace where channel iron (an iron "C"-beam) hung above a row of gas jets producing fires about the size of a standard candle flame. A reduced supply of oxygen to the jets prevented the gas from burning completely, so it produced a soot on the channel iron. The soot was collected by electronic precipitation, resulting in a smoke that was sent through an electronic charge. This caused the particles of carbon black to drop into a collection system.

Almost immediately, local merchants began to complain. They were appalled at the fat plume of black soot that towered above the United Carbon building. It coated the trees, the grass, the marshland. The company closed down under the pressure of protests. Then merchants grumbled that without the plant's employees, their business was falling off. United Carbon reopened.

Sportsmen in the bays came to depend on the dark coil of smoke as a convenient landmark and navigation point.

Ella McRae Clay, still living in the old family homestead at Lamar, had not welcomed the highway. In 1939, she wrote a history of her town, published in a special edition of the *Rockport Pilot*. It contained this passage:

"The dauntless men and women who braved the terrors of the wilderness to find a new home are no longer here. . . . A new generation is springing up, liberally educated and imbued with progressive ideas. . . . Dear, drowsy, old-time Lamar! . . . In the forced marches of our nearer towns, she seems to halt and lag behind. . . .

"Railways, and gas, and stucco, and automobiles will slowly win the day. Searchers for the town's ancient landmarks . . . will feel impatient of the wide new streets . . . and almost angry at the modern dwellings that will elbow in those cherished but lonely broken walls. . . .

"Lamar is destined to be one of the county's big towns. Then in fancy I can see 'put-your-nickle-in-the-slot' machines occupying every available place. . . . Farewell from one who still hears the whispering of the waves and the mocking birds' sweet song."

Marvin Davis had slot machines, and marble tables, too, in his Austin Street cafe. H. E. Stumberg, formerly of San Antonio, owned them, along with more legitimate businesses. Stumberg had come to Aransas along with a flood of new people—many of them the sort who wanted to return Aransas to the high-life gambling days that had characterized the county before its storms.

When H. E. Stumburg came into Marvin Davis' cafe to collect coins from his machines and make them into rolls, he gave leftover change to Marvin's daughter Charlene and son Dave. He asked them to put it back in the machines for him, so the children got an early experience with that kind of gambling.

Dave Davis remembered those as the good days. "Dad was probably making more money than anybody in the thirties," he said. Dave had his first sailboat when he was only three years old and "I had the run of the main street [Austin Street]."

His father had a bakery next door to the cafe and was selling bread. Dave remembered a fifty-foot lot between the bakery and the restaurant, where the pool hall went in. "That was my lot to play in. Next to it was Sparks Dry Goods, Sparks Meat Market, Cleveland's garage and filling station, the post office, then the yellow building where Dad's original coffee shop was. Then they put the picture show in next to that. . . . I rode my stick horse up and down."

When a man once wanted to put in a shoeshine stand on the lot where Dave played, Marvin told him that was the boy's lot and he would have to give permission. Dave remembered: "I cut him a deal about how he would have to shine my boots every time they needed it."

Dave had less influence with Justine Mixon, whose dad, Pat Mixon, was with the bank. "Every morning about ten o'clock Justine would come flippin' down the street goin' to the bank to take her dad a sandwich and I would be standing in front of the bakery with sugar cookies to entice her, to impress her. She would just ease past and pick up my sugar cookies and keep on skippin'."

Some older boys told Dave that he couldn't impress Justine because he had so many freckles, but that just as soon as he started shaving, the freckles would go away. Dave went to Fred Hunt's barbershop across the street, between Market and St. Mary's and Fred gave him a shave.

"I started drinking long before I went to school," Dave said. "The CCC boys would come into the cafe and leave a glass of beer at the edge of the table where I could reach it. I'd drink that beer and cut 'em a few monkey shines before the evening was over."

Things changed when Emory M. Spencer took office as County Attorney in 1939. He later recalled: "One of the worst situations in Aransas County at that time was the operation of slot machines, marble tables, punch boards and kindred gambling devices. . . . The talk got around pretty quickly that I intended to do something about the slot machines. I think that I am safe in saying that I didn't have a friend in the courthouse when I took office."

H. E. Stumberg offered Marvin Davis the machines in his cafe, for only $100. Dave Davis said later, "I can remember him saying that you might get by with them for a week, you might get by with them for six months." And the weekly take on those machines was $100—just what Marvin paid for them. It wasn't long before the law came in and took the slot machines, but they left the marble tables alone for some time.

Emory Spencer said, "Having once convinced them [the citizens of Aransas] that I intended to enforce the law and intended to be fair and impartial about it,—and having convinced them that I really didn't care what they thought—I got along better with them."

Aransas had affirmed its value system and found men who were prepared to support it. The economic answer for Aransas was, again, its use of the bays—the rich harvest of seafood, tourism, and hunting. Families who could not afford the fine hunting clubs camped on the shore north of Fulton.

Shirley Ratisseau wrote this story about the time during the Depression when she and her parents camped on Copano Bay:

THE BIGGEST (TRUE) FISH STORY EVER TOLD

In the 1930s, when I was very young, my parents and I took a vacation and camped at Live Oak Point on Copano Bay. We lived in a tent all summer while they decided on whether to move to Aransas County.

One morning, my dad George Ratisseau rented a rowboat at Barrow's campground over on the Aransas Bay side of the causeway. Dad left my mother Thelma on shore to talk to the ladies, and put me on the back seat of the rowboat; I was to sit quietly with my perch pole and tiny hook. He rowed out some distance, lowered the anchor, and started to fish with the medium to heavy gear he always used to handle large fish.

Suddenly, a great black monster glided by us near the surface, basking in the sun. It was a huge manta or devil ray. Banking into a U-turn, the giant lazily struck my dad's bait. The top of its back broke through the water. Everyone who saw it that day later estimated its size to be about eighteen to twenty feet from wing tip to wing tip.

Then it began pulling our *boat*, the *anchor*, and *us*, out to the middle of Aransas Bay, toward Lamar. Dad was very strong, but it was all he could do to hold on to the rod and reel. To reach his knife to cut the line was impossible. He yelled for me to sit on the bottom of the boat, which I did, but I could still peer over the side.

Dad tried to turn the fish back to land, which made it

moody. It shrugged one wing, slapping our boat so that it almost overturned. "Throw the fishing pole away!" my mother screamed from shore. People all along the beach were shouting at us and at each other.

Then the fish settled down and slowly pulled us beneath the causeway to the Copano Bay side. Thereafter it moved at great speed until there was a mile between land on either side.

With the little boat bouncing wildly over the water, we crossed back under the causeway, and again swooped into Aransas Bay. We were going to the Lamar side again, toward Mills Wharf.

Close to the Lamar docks, with fishermen shouting and people running to watch, the manta suddenly leaped completely into the air. I still remember the *unbelievable* sight of that leap. The manta was the biggest thing besides an elephant that I had ever seen. Its underside was cream colored. Splashing down, it wheeled to return us to the beach and my mother on the other side.

Halfway across the bay, it soared in the air once more. After that jump, the manta came up close to the rowboat and just rolled over on its back—like an old dog back-porching in the sun who wants its belly scratched. Finally it rolled right side up and headed back toward shore and my mother. At closer range, I could hear her yelling at my dad: "Throw the rod and reel away!" In the Depression? Fat chance. He caught our food with that gear during the whole camping trip.

Almost to land, I saw that my mother was wading out into the water. Her fists were clenched. Dad hollered: "Stay ashore! You're in harm's way!"

"I want the baby!" she yelled back. Mother was coming to save me! My mama, such a gentle person, was going to sock this fish—or maybe, I thought with interest—sock my dad.

She was already up to her waist and still moving out to deeper water when the manta came up to boatside again. (I later told my brother that it looked up and winked at me.)

And then the line snapped. The biggest fish in Copano and Aransas Bays had caught us all right, but by some miracle we got away.

Still watching the creature, we saw it pick up speed and soar into the air for a final time. *The beauty of it!* Such a silence followed—both from us and all the people on both shores. Then it was gone.

Dad looked down at me and grinned. Then he looked toward

my brave, wet mother and, still grinning, shouted: "Sweetheart! We're moving to Aransas County!"

COTTAGES

From the advent of the automobile, public lodging for travelers had begun to change. The same year that construction began on the highway that would run through Aransas, the first motel opened in San Luis Obispo, California. The owners called it Motel Inn. After that, rows of tourist cabins grew along the roadsides of America, then evolved into tourist courts, where cottages grouped around a central courtyard. Once Aransas was on the highway, unpretentious accommodations popped up all along its shore.

The Cedars cottages, built by the S. B. Daggett on property where Winifred Evans once lived, formed a broad U that opened to the bay. The Cottage Haven Motel stood a little farther north. Fred Hunt and his father Frank, from Beeville, bought the place and changed its name to theirs. Then on additional land they developed Hunt's Courts all in one line, for a perfect view of the water. "Strictly modern," the Hunts advertised. "Write or wire for reservations where the sun shines all winter."

George and Thelma Ratisseau built the Jolly Roger Hunting and Fishing Camp close to Redfish Point, the farthest northwest reach of Live Oak Peninsula, where Major Burton had tricked the Mexicans with his Horse Marines.

In 1934 on the beach road between Laurel and Mesquite streets, Mr. and Mrs. C. L. Harris opened the first seven units of their Fulton Family Cottages. Two years later, on the main road four blocks from the center of Rockport, Violet Percival opened cottages bearing her name. In 1939 H. E. Stumberg opened the two-story Oak Shore Apartments north of Fulton, and then Palm Courts just north of Frandolig Point. Stumberg's advertisements carried a gambler's promise: "Each day the thermometer registers below thirty-two degrees, you receive two days free rent."

Sid Freeborn remembered another Oak Shore at another location—the one that had been Oak Shore Inn, run by Andrew Sorenson before the storm, and that had been called Shell Hotel before that, when Sid had come to Rockport on the first train. Even earli-

The great marsh that lay behind Stumberg's Palm Courts has since become Harbor Oaks. In the background rose Carbon Black's exhaust plume that stained homes, waterways, and vegetation.

—Courtesy of Sue Hastings Taylor Collection

Hunt's Courts, Water Street. Postcard.

—Courtesy of Genevieve Hunt

er, he knew, the place had been William Hall's mansion. Sid had rarely stayed anywhere else; he certainly couldn't be content in some of the crude tourist lodgings that were going up. Sid said that one had a bath that "was just a long room, slots in the floor where the water could roll through, and you'd go in and take a shower with no hot water. So when we wanted a bath, we generally went out into the bay."

Sid Freeborn discussed the situation with his boyhood friend, Jimmy Sorenson. Jimmy had learned from his father Andrew and was running some tourist cottages at the time. When Sid said he was thinking of buying a piece of land north of Fulton, Jimmy replied, "Get a little bigger place and put some cottages on it for me; I'll run them for you." The land Sid bought was the land he had always loved, on Fulton Beach Road, just north of Traylor Street.

Where wealthy packer William Hall had built his mansion and entertained the gentry, where romantic couples had strolled among oak trees on spacious grounds, Sid Freeborn built Forest Park Cottages. "You couldn't see through those trees," he said, and he described scratchberry vines running through the branches like a curtain. He assumed that the Hall mansion had fallen in ruins. Sid completed a house for himself and another for the Sorensons. Then he directed a crew to start clearing more brush. "Seventeen men worked seventeen days," Sid said.

Then Jimmy Sorenson exclaimed: "Look there, look there! You can see the big house!" Hall's old mansion was revealed at last.

Jack Davis and his wife Pearl took over brother Marvin's small beer establishment on Austin Street. They put in a grill and started making hamburgers, then sold to another brother, Charlie, and his wife Molly. Charlie and Molly converted the place to a drive-in cafe with car-hop service and they called it the Cap Davis Drive-in.

MARINERS

There was progress on the water as well as on land. In 1925 the U. S. government had appropriated $9 million for a ship canal from the Mississippi River to Galveston. Two years later, Congress approved the canal's extension to Corpus Christi and envisioned the day their waterway would reach Brownsville.

The idea had been a long time coming; it had its roots in the Republic of Texas. From that time on, men who dreamed of railroads had also dreamed of ship canals as important aspects of a total transportation system. For centuries, waterways had protected maritime travel from the treacheries of the open Gulf. They had carried commerce where marsh made road construction difficult.

In June 1938 the Commissioners Court of Aransas County conferred with the Intracoastal Canal Association. They decided that natural channels, already in use by ships, could reduce construction costs for extending the canal through Aransas. Only the area of Bludworth Island required right-of-way permits.

When this was accomplished and dredging completed, channel markers went up—white signs with the word "Intracoastal" in black and a red arrow indicating the route. Judge B. S. Fox wrote in the *Pilot* that "there is no doubt the Intracoastal Canal will mark a new era in the upbuilding of Rockport."

In 1936 the Navigation District obtained a state patent for submerged land near the harbor. Three years later, work on a $110,000 seawall and improved small boat harbor began. The railroad pier was cut in half to improve access; the breakwater was extended and capped. Baby Ruth Dunman was visiting Rockport for the first time then, and she didn't have a very good impression of the town: the work of the Bauer-Smith Dredging Company made Rockport almost as smelly as it had been during the packery days.

As fine concrete bulkheads went in and the odor dissipated, locals began to call their new harbor the Fish Bowl. Fishermen stood shoulder-to-shoulder on the edge of that bowl and pulled out trout as fast as they could bait hooks and throw them in again.

The basin was perfectly round, with no piers except on the west side, where later Morrison's Boathouses would accommodate yachts forty to fifty feet long. Just seaward of the boathouses were a few shrimp boats and Jackson's Seafood Company.

On the Fourth of July weekend, 1940, Rockport held a "Million Dollar Boat Parade." The *Pilot* declared: "Due to the number of entries now listed, the celebration promises to be one of the major events of the year." There were speed boat races, sailboat races, aquaplane races. The president of the Intracoastal Canal Associa-

The "Fish Bowl," Rockport's new small boat harbor.
—Courtesy of Jackson family Collection

tion spoke at the breakwater dedication, and the waterway was officially opened through Aransas County.

It was a glorious day, but a day that marked radical change in Rockport's shoreline. The old railroad pier, owned then by S. F. Jackson, had been cut off short. Even part of the Rocky Point—focal spot from cattle days, source of the town's name, base of the La Playa hotel—had been blasted away to make the harbor's entry. No new generation can visualize Rockport the way it was before.

Undoubtedly, Rockport needed that harbor; boats were proliferating. A. M. Westergard, native of Norway, had started building pleasure craft in the late 1920s. As he wrote later, his thirty-six-foot marconi-rigged ketch, the first of its kind in the area, "caused quite a few arguments and also a renewal of interest among local sailboat men." Soon, according to the *Pilot*, Westergard had boats "scattered all the way from Beaumont to Port Isabel."

Many mariners considered (and still consider) Aransas the best sailing bay in Texas. Since it is long and narrow, waves do not build up as high as do those in Corpus Christi and San Antonio bays. There is almost always a good sailing breeze, and Aransas offers numerous good anchorages and cruising areas.

When Raymond "Chick" Roberts built the *Diablo*, sailboat racing as a sport was back to stay. Daggett had the first snipe-designed boat in the area. A. C. Glass, Bev Sorenson, Travis Johnson, Bill Frandolig, Travis Bailey, Paul Clark Sorenson, Ernest Silberisen, and others were actively racing.

Chick's father George had been born on San José in the mid-1800s—son of an Englishman and one of the Brundrett girls. When he was grown, George delivered goods to the island in his sixty-foot sailboat.

Chick was out on his own by the time he was seventeen—working charter boats, rowing people from Port Aransas to the jetties to fish. He worked on a tugboat during the Great War. When he returned to Rockport in 1937, Chick started building cargo ships in Rockport.

Oilman T. Noah Smith bought the tall, old Hoopes house at Austin and Highway 35 and made it his vacation home. Smith dedicated the next several years and thousands of dollars to restoring the house to its former grandeur. He started a small boathouse and repair business too—the Rockport Yacht and Supply Company. Later, it would become big business.

In 1932 Ernest Camehl's Union Fish Company had quit selling fish; it became a ship chandlery instead. News of boat races filled the *Pilot*. Travis Bailey won the Farnsworth trophy in 1935, sailing the *Aeneid*, a boat designed and built by Westergard. Anything Westergard built was a masterpiece, and Bailey was undefeated that entire season. In the Labor Day race of 1938, Travis and the *Aeneid* won again, but by only twenty-five seconds, on a 100-mile course.

Roy Hinson took a new job at the Aransas Pass Light Station in 1936. W. G. Browder was lighthouse keeper then, and Hinson was his third furnace assistant keeper. It took three assistants and the keeper to handle new responsibilities added to the lighthouse regimen, so four families lived in quarters that had been built for two.

Rain was the only source of drinking water, and four families taxed the supply severely. As a means of rationing water, Browder ordered the indoor plumbing removed; families had to carry their water in a bucket filled at the tap beneath the house. They heated bath water on the two-burner kerosene stove in their rooms, emptying it into a tin tub one bucket at a time. There was no indoor toilet, only a "two-holer" outhouse on the back porch.

But Roy said his life was wonderful: "I had a job, shelter, clothing and food while lots of other folks had nothing. Our crew was like a family. Sometimes we argued, but we all respected each other and had a good time; and besides that, I was a newlywed."

His main duty was the traditional one—standing watch on the light. The old kerosene beacon had been replaced by electricity—a 500-watt lamp in the old, reliable lens.

Local fishermen celebrating the day's catch for a fish fry, raising money to build the Fulton Community Church. Top, left to right: John Weber, Rev. Frank Walker, Zeph Rouquette, Bill Johnson. Bottom, left to right: Burk Johnson, Cecil Casterline, Ray Wendell, Frank Casterline.
—Courtesy of Casterline Collection

Keepers stood two watches—one from dusk until midnight and the second from midnight until dawn. The first shift began with a climb up the tower to open curtains that protected the lens from damage by strong sun light. The rest of the light system was mechanized. A switching device turned the light on at sundown and off at sunrise. All night long, a cam revolved, turning the light on for five seconds, darkening it for five seconds. At dawn, a keeper climbed the tower again and closed the curtains.

Even with modern conveniences, the Aransas Light was obsolete, an anomaly. The jetties, built in accordance with one of the pass' many shifts, bordered a channel almost a mile out of line with the lighthouse.

To solve the problem, the Light Station maintained a small radio house that broadcast a direction-finding signal to ships at sea. The Galveston Light Station and the one at Port Isabel, broadcast identifying signals too. A ship could pick up the lines of these signals, and their intersection showed the ship its position.

Like his co-workers, Roy Hinson also took his turn at maintaining the channel-marker lights from Rockport to Corpus Christi. To do so, he traveled in a thirty-foot motor launch with a standard three-cylinder gasoline engine. He checked the channel lights to see that they were burning. When the batteries were exhausted, he replaced them.

On off-hours, Roy and his wife Bertha rowed across the channel to San José Island. There they collected shells; during nesting season they watched the birds.

Too soon, that idyllic life ended. The Coast Guard at Port Aransas assumed responsibility for the radio signal and the channel markers. Those would be only parts of the Guard's broader focus on a militarily strategic coastline, as the world geared up for another war.

CONFLICT AND INDUSTRY

WORLD WAR II

Historian T. R. Fehrenbach wrote that Texans almost instinctively sensed Nazi Germany as an enemy. For Aransans, the threat seemed very close to home.

On September 3, 1939, a German U-boat sank a Canadian liner bound for Montreal. The next month, a U-boat penetrated defenses of a British naval base off the northeastern coast of Scotland. What if those boats entered the Aransas pass? What if they came through Lydia Ann Channel?

Aransans had no intention of seeing their bays violated again, as *Veracruzana* had defiled them in 1836, as Kittredge had ravaged them in 1862. "My grandmother," Jackie Shaw said, "used to sit on her porch at Lamar, shake her fist toward the island and curse the Yankees." Her grandmother, Ida Mae Johnson Loman, was Capt. Peter Johnson's daughter. The family knew how seafaring enemies could uproot homes.

Little of the Great War had touched Aransas waters—just the Heldenfels ships going out and then the stranding of the steam tug *Baddacock* as she towed a wooden ship, *Utina*, out to sea. But the world had changed since then. Aransas understood her vulnerability.

Perry Bass operated a shipyard—the Bass Boat Works—for the Coast Guard in Fulton, just south of Broadway. Six fireboats were built there, and boats that patrolled the Gulf—mostly confiscated private yachts—hauled out there. Over time more than one hundred "Bass Fire Boats" were built by the Coast Guard and used in the war in the Pacific.

Early in 1941, Rob Roy Rice, Jr., assumed control of the Wester-

307

gard Shipyard, and Jimmy Sorenson, Jr., set up the new company's accounting system. Rice-Westergard's 250 employees began turning out wooden submarine chasers.

PC-498 on a trial run off Rockport, 1941. Second of twenty-four 100-foot subchasers built as Westergard-Rice Boat Works. Negative provided to the Texas Maritime Museum courtesy of Jack DuBose, Jr.

According to an article in the *Rockport Pilot*, Lt. Cmdr. Eugene F. McDaniel told men who had been on ships "sunk by the Japs" that they would have the avenger they had prayed for—the PC boat. McDaniel said the time was coming "when men need no longer lift despairing hands as they sank beneath dark waters; need no longer scream as flaming oil cooked their eyes, their lungs, their flesh."

McDaniel was an evangelist of "the Patrol Craft religion." He told the sailors of "a craft fast enough to catch the quarry, able to wheel about on its heels to follow the squirmings of the U-boats below the surface and to drop depth charges that would burst the enemy's steel-laced seams. Here was a craft with marvelously acute detection devices and mechanical ears capable of tracing the under-sea boat's course, no matter how devious."

The *Pilot* article concluded: "Rice Brothers and Company can feel justly proud of their record in building and sending to sea near-ly a score of these fast, sub-seeking little war boats. Of course the full story of the boats built here will not be known until after the war, but unofficial reports bring a feeling of pride to everyone who helped build them, and an inspiration to carry on to their fullest abil-ity in a vital war job." Ultimately, Rice-Westergard built twenty-four wooden submarine chasers, each 110 feet long, and a few sixty-five-foot rescue boats. Skilled boatbuilders nailed a sign over a shed door: TIME IS SHORT.

On December 7, 1941, an undetected Japanese force arrived off the Hawaiian islands. Two successive waves of bombers, torpedo planes, and fighters sank or disabled eighteen U.S. ships, crippling U.S. naval power in the Pacific.

In Aransas, news of it flashed on the radio just as hunters were coming in from the duck blinds. One young navy flyer lay his guns and string of ducks carefully on the ground, then burst into tears. Soon the rest of the men stood with him, weeping silently. They knew their lives had changed. Those already in the military hurried back to their bases.

President Roosevelt told a joint session of Congress that De-cember 7 was "a date which will live in infamy," and Congress voted to declare war on Japan. The European and Pacific fronts merged in global conflict.

Again, young Aransans went off to fight halfway around the world. Those mentioned here represent many. James Frandolig was drafted away from his shipyard job; he and Jimmy Hunt went in the army together. Jimmy Sorenson, Jr. left Rice-Westergard and joined the Air Force. He was commissioned a second lieutenant in the first class to attend the Army Air Corps' first Officer Candi-date School at Miami Beach. Herbert Stewart became a Navy Seal.

Kyle Ratisseau was in the navy, and his sister Jean Elizabeth was one of the first women in the nation to join the WACs. She served in the South Pacific. All female branches of the military were served by other Aransas women including Janice Ingersoll, a mem-ber of the WAFs, and "Corky" Robb, a WAVE.

As the government encouraged civilians to eat more seafood, and meat rationing cut homemakers' choices, the shrimping business boomed. Texas harvested 18,000,000 pounds of shrimp in 1942, up by a third in only six years.

The war was good for Aransas in another way too. Gas rationing kept tourists close to home, and the motels filled with Texans who might otherwise have made longer trips. But food rationing presented problems; there simply wasn't enough to go around. Grocers, butchers, and bakers often turned newcomers away in order to fill the needs of their long-time customers.

Since naval air training bases were located in Corpus Christi and the surrounding area, the entire coastal region was considered vulnerable to attack; civilians were banned from Gulf beaches. That also kept more tourists at Aransas. It didn't bother people that everyone who took a boat out on the water—not just tourists, but even bay fishermen working there—was required to have an identification card with a photo on it. That was just how things would be, for the duration.

Boys and girls worked on paper drives at the school. They scavenged scrap metal for bombs to smash Tojo. And some of them were familiar with the *Recognition Guide to Operational War Planes*. That spotters' handbook warned that Japs might attack in a last-ditch suicide attempt, so the youngsters watched for enemy aircraft in the skies above their bays.

Thelma Ratisseau, who was a plane spotter for the Naval Air Station, took an early morning walk from Redfish Point to the eastern tip of Live Oak and then back again. Once she passed the site of James Power's home, Thelma called fancifully out: "Mr. Power! Have you seen any enemy?"

On Thursday, January 28, 1942, the *Rockport Pilot* put out an Extra edition. Its headline proclaimed everyone's worst fear:

ALL-NIGHT BLACKOUT ORDERED: SUB SIGHTED IN GULF NEARBY

Aransas County Ordered to Black Out All Night in First Wartime Safety Precaution Against Enemy Raiders

One story began:

Rockport's complacency and feeling of security from enemy attacks changed today! The stark realization that war may come to these peaceful shores came with official reports that enemy submarines were lurking offshore not over fifteen miles away.

The 'practice' blackout set for tonight turns out to be an ironic gesture of fate, the one-hour . . . set for the practice blackout was suddenly changed to an all-night wartime precautionary measure.

According to Lieutenant McCauley of the U.S. Naval Air Station at Corpus Christi, one enemy submarine was sighted. A smoke bomb, used as a danger signal by submarines, was seen four miles from it, suggesting that at least a second submarine was in the area.

The *Pilot* itemized blackout precautions: All lights that might be visible from the outside had to remain off all night. Windows and doors were to be covered with "quilts, oilcloth, heavy drapes or other opaque material." But Aransans should not "crowd or stampede stores to get it. . . . Be ingenious—improvise." All this because "the light that can't be seen will never guide enemy bombs and shells. Remember a candle light may be seen for miles from the air."

The *Pilot* suggested that Aransans "prepare one room, the one with the fewest windows, in the strongest part of your house, for a refuge and blackout room. Put food and drinking water in it if there are children. Put a sturdy table in it. Put mattresses and chairs in it. Take a magazine or two, and a deck of cards if you like. If you have a portable radio take that, too."

Everyone was to stay inside; no one should drive a car, except wardens with special equipment. No one was allowed to smoke out of doors: "If you must smoke, go inside a covered place to do it."

Floyd Huffman and Norvell Jackson were named as observers atop the courthouse. Alice Thomerson, Emory Spencer, and John Williams would be in the Chief Air Raid Warden's office. Twenty air raid stations and their wardens were listed.

One wonders if a reader, taking all this in, was able to pay much attention to one line of one story, in capital letters: "KEEP CALM."

Not long after, submariners off the Yucatan Peninsula torpedoed the *Worthington*, a 400-foot Liberty cargo ship. It was towed through the Aransas pass but sank at the west shoreline of San José, just opposite the lighthouse. There it was salvaged, and the remains lay as a silent caution. But some confusion about the *Worthington* started a local legend that a U-boat had come in through the jetties.

Civilians and government officials alike pondered where the U-boats' land base might be. According to Tom Townsend, author, researcher, and shipwreck diver, no proof has ever been found to show that U-boats were re-supplied in Mexico. Evidence is suggestive at best. "The primitive nature of the coast," Townsend wrote, "is such that it would be hard for the [Mexican] Government to know what was going on in many of its provinces."

It is a known fact that German spies operated out of Juarez, Mexico, and the Nuremberg trials confirm at least one attempt to land agents at Galveston. Artillery bunkers still line the Gulf shore there.

On June 17, 1942, the *Moira*, flying a Norwegian flag, was torpedoed off the northern Gulf coast of Mexico. Townsend believed her attacker was probably the German submarine *U-166*.

Just over one month later, a Mexican freighter, the *Oaxaca*, headed east through Pass Cavallo, past the Naval Air Station at Decros Point. Ten to twelve miles outside the Matagorda jetties, the *Oaxaca* was torpedoed and sunk. Personnel at Decros Point heard the explosion, but the raider vanished without a trace. Townsend credited *U-166* with the kill.

On August 1 Henry White piloted a Coast Guard patrol plane working sixty miles off the Louisiana coast. There he spotted a German U-boat, bobbing on the waves. As White turned to attack, the boat began to submerge. He released his bomb at 250 feet and saw it explode the sinking conning tower of *U-166*. Black oil stained the surface of the bay.

At their Jolly Roger camp on the tip of Live Oak Peninsula, George Ratisseau and his wife Thelma listened to the radio. On August 29, 1942, it was not enemy invasion that worried them—they had heard disturbing weather reports of a hurricane. The center of the storm was to make landfall near Port Lavaca. The Ratisseaus never heard any indication that the hurricane's course might change, but by midnight they knew it had.

"Every window in the house, and later the boards that covered them, blew out," Shirley Ratisseau wrote later. "When the roof began to go, my parents decided to try to run for the high, protective hill some distance behind our home. As my father lowered me out a window, I found myself in water almost to my shoulders. My mother and father crawled out after me. . . . The rain was so heavy we could hardly breathe."

The family had struggled only fifteen feet or so when a tourist cabin next to their home literally exploded. A moment later, George Ratisseau had a heart attack. He sank to the ground, unable to move. Shirley struggled to help him, wondering why her mother was not helping her hold her father's head above water. Thelma Ratisseau was stunned, bleeding, hit in the head by a flying board from the cabin.

George rallied enough to tell his wife and daughter to leave him and go on toward the hill. Shirley and Thelma answered in one voice: "No, we'll stay with you." Later, Shirley could not remember how long they stayed. Lightning was constant, illuminating the nightmare around them.

Finally, Thelma led her family to some gnarled and twisted mesquite and huisache brush. Shirley described what happened after that: "Exhausted, we hung onto those thorny branches all the endless hours of the time before the dawn. I remember thinking of all my friends, recalling each face, and reciting the alphabet over and over. I don't know why."

When the still eye of the hurricane passed over the huddled family, Shirley wanted to run, but George Ratisseau cautioned against it. As he had expected, the storm came back. And it was worse. "The water washed around us," Shirley wrote. "The wind shrieked as though it felt cheated, and the rain was so hard it felt like needles and nails.

"My father reached over to me and pulled something off of my neck and shoulders. It didn't even bother me when I saw that it was a rattlesnake about four feet long, cold and unable to move, and clinging to me in order to be saved."

Day came. The Ratisseaus followed the fence line to the hill. Each strand of the barbed wire served as an eerie clothesline of personal belongings mixed with sea weed, land weed, assorted debris.

When they reached the hilltop, the Ratisseaus saw that its

height would have put them in even greater danger during the storm; giant oaks there had been "snapped like toothpicks."

George and Thelma and Shirley looked down on the remains of their Jolly Roger camp. The cabins and boats were all gone, along with part of the pier. A section of the large beach pavilion was in fine shape—but floating three miles out in the bay. The livestock were dead or scattered, and "an old gray goose hen swam to and fro, calling forlornly for her lifelong mate."

The Ratisseaus "wandered around doing some of the sad things that had to be done." Three days later, they heard the goose honk in excitement, saw her take off running up the hill. George joked that "it had taken three days of missing her gander for her to lose her mind." But that was not the case.

"The goosey gander had found his way home," Shirley wrote. "It took many minutes for those two to reach each other, and they ran, honking their glad cries. When they met they rubbed necks and were still gabbling when we walked to meet them."

Thelma Ratisseau bent down and picked up a piece of water-soaked paper—her and George's marriage license. "Now we can go home and start building over," she said. Thelma and George began walking, holding hands. The two geese and Shirley followed. "Aren't we lucky," Thelma said. "We're all here together."

Sid Freeborn rode out the storm, too, at his Forest Park Cottages, but he sent his wife and children to San Antonio. Although he had tried to persuade his renters to leave, those who worked at the shipyards could not go. And there were others. Sid said that when he tried to send one fellow away, the man responded. "I've been following these storms all my life, and I've always been too late to see one of them. I think I'm going to see this one."

When Sid took a walk around the grounds, checking on his boats, he saw his skiff lying crossways under two big limbs of a tree. On impulse Sid "picked the nose of the skiff up, turned it around so it was in the center of those two big limbs and went on. It didn't take ten seconds." People do intuitive things like that in preparation for crisis.

All the renters gathered in Sid's office—except for the man who chased hurricanes. "Along about midnight," Sid remembered, "here he come in. He was in the second house down from the bay and he come across there, limbs flying out of the trees in all directions. And the lightning—it was just bright as day outside. He come in and stayed in the room with us for a half hour or more, and then he went out on the porch and went on.

"He was gone for five or ten minutes, and he come back in and sat around there for a little while, and in a little while he got up again and went out, and he come back in again. And about the third or fourth time he went out, I went to see what he was doing. There he was going across the yard over to his house. And when he come back in I got up close to him and, sure enough, he had whiskey on his breath.

"He didn't have enough whiskey to go around a whole bunch, so he'd go over and get a drink and come back. This guy, he was so scared. When it would wear off a little bit, he'd go get another nip and come back."

After the storm, Harry Traylor, who had stayed at Forest Park for years, said, "Sid, come look where your boats are!"

Sid saw trees blown over the boat, the big limbs missing his skiff by only inches on either side. Sid said, "There wasn't a bit of paint scratched on that boat. Not a thing! I claim that's a miracle—because what made me ever move that boat around in front of those two limbs, nobody'll ever know. I didn't like the looks of that boat crossways underneath those two limbs. It wouldn't have been kindle wood left if I hadn't moved it."

Aransas rebuilt and went on with its contributions to the war effort. Even before the storm hit, a decision had been made to tear down the wrought iron picket fence surrounding the courthouse. It was to be donated to the defense plants. On August 27, 1942, a newspaper article summed up the situation: "War is never a nice business, and sentimental sacrifices must be made. For Rockport, the donation of the fence is such a sacrifice."

On December 10, 1942, T. Noah Smith, founder of RYSCO, made a personal sacrifice. He delivered his two private yachts to the U.S. Navy—both his 104-foot *Adroit* and the forty-five-foot *Lady Cora*, named for his wife. The vessels served as submarine patrol boats.

All was not sacrifice, however. The Civil Aeronautics Administration built an airstrip on land furnished by the county. Heldenfels Brothers got the contract for leveling and grading and for building three 4,500-foot runways. The navy would use the strip for the duration, but at the close of the war Aransas County would have a civilian field.

On May 18, 1943, the first airplane landed and took off from the new Aransas County Airfield. It was a small trainer, and right after the unidentified naval officer landed, he had a heated discussion with officials. He wanted a telephone line taken down, but he made a successful takeoff in his little yellow plane.

In the summer of 1943, Orian (Dick) Stewart, an army private, was killed in the North African campaign—the first Rockport man to die in the war. T. J. Johnson, Jr., of the 509th Parachute Battalion was called back from leave in Paris to fight the Battle of the Bulge. He was seriously wounded on December 29, 1944.

Jimmy Sorenson, Jr., was wounded in North Africa, and Fred Bracht, Jr., with the U.S. Army 37th Division, was seriously wounded in the battle for Manila on February 16, 1945. Ralph C. Wendell, a twenty-eight-year-old Seabee, died in the invasion of Rendova. His body was returned home for burial.

"Mostly all the Mexican-Americans from Rockport were in the War," Frank Covarrúbias said. He went in the service in 1943, a carpenter with a squadron in the Air Corps. "We started in Negres Island, south of Leyte. We fought all the way from Leyte to Okinawa. I saw MacArthur in person. He was a good man, very serious man, but he was friendly. He wasn't stuck-up. A handsome man, and he always walked with his cane all the time, smoking that pipe. He was in front all the time."

Marion Johnson was in the first wave of troops that landed at Okinawa.

John Henry Kroeger, Jr., grandson of Lamar settler Henry L. Kroeger and Indian-captured Eve Thommen, was a captain with Pan American Airways and commander of the First National Air Maneuvers. He was flying as an air transport pilot when his plane crashed in Africa on January 25, 1944. Kroeger was killed. He received full honors at a military burial overseas.

That same year, Ham Smith's son Francis drowned near Goose Island. His death did not carry the transcendant meaning that war casualties did, but every death is immediate, personal. Francis Earl Smith's bore irony. He was the third generation of his family to carry the name Francis and end in a watery grave. His grandfather, Francis McKenzie Smith, was lost off Pass Cavallo in 1877; his uncle, Francis, Jr., was aboard a ship that sank near Galveston in 1908. Records do not show any subsequent family members bearing that name.

By year's end, Aransas students had formed a Victory Corps. They already wore dog tags like those of military personnel—except that the youngsters' tags carried their parents' names as well as their own. Soon they had uniforms, too, and a Navy lieutenant trained them while he waited for his PT boat.

Marine Corp. Bruce Davis served at Guam, Guadalcanal, and Iwo Jima. Naval officer O. C. "Buck" Bailey, grandson of the Rockport newspaper man and pavilion developer, was aboard the U.S.S *Monterrey* near Guam. He participated in the Marianas "Turkey Shoot" which downed hundreds of Japanese aircraft.

Buck was flying a combat air patrol at 14,000 feet when the engine of his Hellcat quit, and the plane caught fire. He parachuted to the sea, suffering a broken nose and "an overload of salt water." For that and other feats, Buck Bailey earned the Silver Star, Distinguished Flying Cross, and five Air Medals.

Lt. "Port" Little, a much-decorated Navy pilot, also did his share in downing Japanese aircraft.

In 1944 the *Rockport Pilot* reported that Aransas tourist reservations were stacking up: "For the most part Rockport's guests this summer will be men and women who have been busy for a year or more in defense plants and on essential war work, and who are planning needed respite from their labors. There will be hundreds of vacationers here this summer, a survey of cottage groups reveals."

By April 12, 1945, U.S. forces were within sixty miles of Berlin. Gen. Dwight D. Eisenhower informed Joseph Stalin that he was leaving the city to the Soviets. By the end of the month, the

Russians penetrated its center. German soldiers and civilians, fearful of revenge from the Soviets, hastened to surrender to the Americans and the British. Allied troops liberated one concentration camp after another, and victory in Europe became official on May 8, 1945.

The August 23 issue of the *Pilot* ran a small feature story on Rockport Pfc. Candelario P. Torres. He was a member of the 351st Engineer General Service Regiment who helped build the Supreme Headquarters for General Eisenhower—and he had to use some of its air raid shelters before they were completed. Candelario helped build hospitals and repair roads, bridges, and rail lines in Brittany. He said that he ate well from captured German cold storage warehouses.

T. Sgt. Alfred J. Court, son of Capt. and Mrs. Roy Court, was awarded the bronze service star for participation in the crossing of the Rhine and battles in Germany. Alfred's brother Milton was a warrant officer at Port O'Connor. Roy Court, Jr., was in the Philippines.

Throughout the Pacific, U.S. bombings had intensified in 1945. As Allies captured air bases in Japan's home islands, that empire was on the verge of collapse.

Henry Travis Bailey III, Buck's brother, was stationed in Sian, China. He flew Lockheed P-38 "Lightnings," fitted only with cameras for the purpose of aerial recording.

On July 26 United States President Harry S. Truman, Britain's Prime Minister Winston Churchill, and Chinese Republic President Chiang Kai-shek issued an ultimatum demanding Japan's unconditional surrender. On August 6 and 9, the U.S. dropped atomic bombs on Hiroshima and Nagasaki.

Frank Covarrúbias was at Ieshima, getting ready for the invasion of Tokyo. "We were pretty close when the bomb dropped. You could see the light where we were, but we didn't know what it was until the next day."

Japan signed a formal document of surrender on September 2, aboard the U.S. battleship *Missouri* in Tokyo Bay. Frank Covarrubias remembered:

"We got word that Japan surrendered right after the Allies dropped that bomb. On the way to sign the Treaty, they stopped on Ieshima to gas up, for the airplanes. Some of the Americans wanted to jump the Japanese officers who were going to sign the treaty. So the MPs got pretty scared and roped the whole thing off."

THE RETURN

The family of John Henry Kroeger, Jr., wanted their loved one home; they wanted to bury him in the old Lamar cemetery. That had been John Henry's wish—to lie where so much Kroeger history lay—even though he knew the old burial ground had been lost for years.

The last person interred at Lamar had been Leonard Roberts, who died in 1912. Since then, oaks had grown; yaupon, baybrush, and tall grasses crowded them. The population of Lamar was down to twenty-five; state maps no longer marked the town. Rockport realtor, oilman, and historian Harry Traylor decided to make the cemetery, and John Kroeger's burial there, his cause.

Traylor found the succession of titles to the site; he found oil leases, he negotiated. "The land owner and the oil firm were greatly cooperative," Traylor said. "They gave quitclaim deeds to the cemetery." But how to clear the land?

Mae DeLisle Kroeger, sister of the war hero, formed the Lamar Cemetery Association. The group raised funds, and county commissioners got a road built. Slowly, the Association uncovered a ruin.

Headstones were toppled and broken. Tree roots had heaved graves, buckled tombs and fences. Wood markers had become earth, or were so rotted that their inscriptions were indecipherable. Here and there, workers found small stakes to which wooden crosses or markers had once been nailed.

But John Henry Kroeger, Jr., was returned to his home ground. And, ironically, that was the beginning of Lamar's resurrection.

When Hillis Dominguez headed back to Aransas after the war, he was not at all sure what to expect. He and his friends who had served overseas—or even just on the West Coast—"saw the difference in the way Mexican-Americans were living in California and the way they were living here," Hillis said later. "In 1940 in California, there was no discrimination against the blacks or the Mexican-Americans."

Hillis had been shocked before, when he came home on leave. That was when he went to Kane's Cafe and found that it had a new name. Still, he recognized the waitress, the mother of a shrimping buddy, Johnny Wright. She recognized him too. They talked a while. Then, as Hillis told it, "I wanted a glass of milk and a piece of pie. And the owner of the place came in and told Mrs. Wright, 'You can't serve him in here. He's gotta go in the back.' Mrs. Wright told the owner, 'He's in the service.'" The owner just said "Oh."

Hillis decided not to go to that cafe again. "That's the philosophy of the Mexican-American. If he's not wanted one place, he won't show up." Later, Hillis pondered the appropriateness of that response and said, "I just don't know."

Hillis continued: "When we came back over here, our life was hard to accept." Nothing had changed—except the Mexican-Americans. They had been treated like equals during the war; when they returned to Aransas they saw discrimination more clearly than ever before. The Anglos of Aransas were still oblivious to the issue. "We couldn't go to the pool hall," Hillis said. "We couldn't go but to one restaurant. In the theater, we had to sit in the front.

"We knew that if we didn't like it, we couldn't do anything. No jobs were good. Any good job went. . . ." Hillis' voice trailed off, leaving the thought incomplete. He continued in a different vein. "You went back to shrimping. That's the only thing you could do then, here. There was nothing for anybody. Any young people would have to leave and get a better job. And that's about it."

L. C. Huff had joined the army in 1945, when the war was almost over. His job was to get things ready to ship back to the United States. When L. C. got out of the service and went home to Austwell, he found no good way to make a living.

L. C. and his wife, Elsie Mae Dukes, are descended from the Huff, Dukes, and Williams slave families who were freed and given Blackjacks land before the close of the Civil War. "Old man Dukes had the most land," L. C. said. Mr. Dukes farmed; he had watermelon and cotton. Elsie Mae's parents worked for Sid Richardson on San José.

In 1947 L. E. Casterline went to Austwell and met L. C. Huff. He said that the Casterline Fish Company had more work than workers. L. E. told L. C. that he had a row of houses for his employees, right at the edge of the water. L. C. took the job; he was accustomed to moving around and was constantly amazed at how many people had "hardly been to Corpus Christi."

L. C. and Elsie Huff stayed in one of those little Casterline houses, saved their money, and got a boat of their own from L. E. Casterline. They bought a home in 1951.

Jimmy Sorenson, Jr., got his release from the Air Force in July 1945. He was spending a terminal leave at Rockport when an August hurricane came through. Jimmy went to Victoria and visited friends there until the storm had passed. When he came home, A. C. Glass was waiting for him in the front yard.

Jimmy remembered: "He was looking for someone to help him with the terrific volume of claims that were being presented to his insurance agency and asked if I would just please come help him. I went down to work still in uniform. And from that association came my association with the First National Bank. Mr. Glass told me he hoped to retire within the next three years and asked if I would be interested in becoming a banker."

James Sorenson, Jr., started with the bank as a teller in October of 1945, and by the end of the year he was assistant cashier and a member of the Board of Directors. He remained with the bank until his retirement, ultimately serving as President and Chairman of the Board. He is married to Marie O'Connor, direct descendant of the original Tom O'Connor.

A WAVE, Cora Robb, received her discharge at the Corpus Christi Naval Base. As soon as her recently discharged fiancé Denver Agler could join her, they were married and moved to Rockport. They opened a small cafe and called it by Cora's nickname—Corky.

Denver and Corky moved from one Rockport location to an-

Corpus Christi auto salesman nicknamed "Jiggs" (left) and the Casterline Brothers (l. to r. Cecil, Frank, L.E.) with first Kaiser-Frasers available after World War II. The license plates read "1947."
—Courtesy of Casterline Collection

Fulton Harbor before completion. A shell island inside the breakwater has yet to be removed.
—Courtesy of Casterline Collection

other, building bigger and better. Finally, they had a large restaurant on the west side of Austin Street, a little north of Market. Corky's Restaurant was an Aransas institution for years.

Fulton needed a harbor as much as Rockport did. There were a few piers, but no protection from the bay. For a while there was talk of locating the Fulton Harbor in Little Bay, so the Navigation District catalogued the plans as "Little Bay Project." By January 1946, the site was changed to Fulton proper, and county commissioners called for a bond issue.

The first stage, completed in late 1949 or early 1950, was just a breakwater that ran out from a nub of land north of Chapparal Street and continued south to private land near Broadway. Behind the bulkhead lay a channel ninety feet long. Boats tied up on the west shore, to the lee of a small island in the middle of the harbor.

In 1955 dredge was pumped from the bayside of the bulkhead and the fill used to stabilize the western shore and create a land area north of the harbor. The shoreline was bulkheaded to private property—Wendell and Rouquette, Bill Johnson, Casterline Seafood—and landowners completed the bulkhead beyond that point, ending ultimately even with Palmetto Street, where the breakwater terminated.

By then, the Rockport Sailing Club had formed. The group had no clubhouse, but the broad, paved area east of the Rockport harbor seemed fine to them. On race days, the sailors' wives parked their cars wagon-train style and sat down to await their husbands' arrivals on the sailboats. They came from Corpus Christi, Port Isabel, Port Lavaca, San Antonio, and other towns. Some of them laughingly called the meeting place their "Pierhead Yacht Club."

Each sailing club decided on a particular holiday for its regatta. Corpus Christi selected Buccaneer Days, in May. Port Isabel had June. Rockport, following an old tradition, held its regatta on the 4th of July. Two generations of Baileys and the Bludworth boys were hot contenders.

The Rockport races were always *to* the town, never the other way—mostly because of the course. An experienced sailor, Chris Wenger, described it this way:

"From Corpus Christi, you had a tight beat to Port Aransas, then a spinnaker-run for Port Aransas to Rockport. If you reversed the course, you would have had a dead beat to Port Aransas and likely a foul current until you turned at Port Aransas to go to Corpus Christi, and then a quartering course to Ingleside and maybe a spinnaker-run to Corpus Christi. And Corpus Christi Bay in the afternoon is always very rough in the summertime."

During the forties and fifties, children experienced Aransas as "a very, very laid-back and easy place to grow up," Johnny Atwood said. "We had free rein of the place; we could do anything. We spent our summers either up in the top of a grape-vine-covered oak tree, smoking grape stems, or we would go out in Little Bay and chase crabs, chase fish, maybe catch a few crabs. When I was in junior high or high school, we'd go out and get two or three dozen crabs and sell them.

"Of course I was totin' a BB gun from the time I was five years of age. Connie Hagar—and some others around here—didn't particularly care for me because our targets were mostly flying species. But I learned an appreciation for birds and how to identify them through that.

"Life was very comfortable. We were poor, but we didn't know that. We basically took our shoes off when the weather got warm enough to take them off, and we put them back when it got so cold we had to put them on. I still recall going to school on occasion barefoot, just for the hell of it. It was that sort of a place, and we had it pretty nice. The shrimp were everywhere and my family were shrimpers and fishermen and boat-builders amongst other things."

When Johnny was about thirteen or fourteen years old, his father taught him how to make and repair shrimp nets. "Doing that, I had a pretty good flow of income when I was in the eighth grade through high school," he said. "In 1950, it wasn't unusual for me to make seventy-five to one hundred dollars in a day. I didn't do it every day, because it wasn't available, but we were capable of doing it. In those days one hundred dollars was a lot of money—you could buy a J. C. Penney sport shirt for thirty-five cents.

"We had a skiff we used to play with. As we got older, we used to take the fish nets and go fish. We served as deckhands when shrimping season opened, but normally school interfered with that activity.

"We had duck hunting. It was fabulous, but we didn't get to go often because it was quite a chore. We usually hunted on the Saint Joe shoreline somewhere. It was load the boat—the old shrimp boat. Get the duck skiff out, put it on the deck, load it all up, take an hour and somethin' to get over there and anchor the boat. And we poled or rowed to shore. We hunted—usually in the afternoons—get home eight or nine o'clock, then start picking ducks.

"Even during the war, we were fortunate enough to have some ammunition for the shotguns. My dad bought a trailer-load of personal goods from a guy, and it happened to have a case or so of shotgun shells, so we were fixed. Sometimes we killed more ducks than we should, legally. The limit was about ten per person when I started hunting with my dad. That declined as time went on, but it wasn't unusual for us to kill thirty or forty ducks in a three-hour period. And they were all good ducks. We wouldn't shoot anything but pintails or maybe an occasional redhead. But they're too hard to pick so we preferred not to.

"On occassion we'd give somebody some, but essentially anything we killed we had to eat. Anything we crippled we chased— miles and miles, we chased—with no shoes. And when we would run across a live, growing oyster reef, it was murder on your feet. But we would still chase the ducks. It was part of the thing we were taught—the ethic—to take what you could handle."

The fire department, inactive during the Depression days, reactivated in June 1938, right after a fire at the Natalie Apartments on Water Street near Bay Street. Rockport's equipment was no match for the fire; only a change of wind saved the town. Then the Aransas Pass Fire Department came in to extinguish the blaze.

Dr. Albert Collier called on a group of citizens to form an Aransas County Emergency Corps. Its mission would be to protect lives and property in emergencies such as hurricanes, tornadoes, and fires. They would also patrol Rockport and Fulton beaches and run an emergency ambulance service. P. C. Sorenson served as president, with Ernest Silberisen vice-president, Iris Sorenson secretary-treasurer. The City Council appointed Albert Collier fire chief, with Francis Smith and Norvell Jackson as his assistants.

Many of the teen-aged boys were among the Corps' members; they loved getting out of school whenever the Rockport Fire De-

Rockport volunteer firefighters pose around their old firetruck on the day that a new one arrived. Left to right: Chief Albert Collier, Herman Caraway, Francis Smith, asst. chief (later chief) Ed Barnard, asst. chief (later chief) Norvell Jackson. Courthouse is visible in background, left.
—Courtesy of Jackson family Collection

partment siren went off. But fighting the hot, dirty brush fires was hard work. And handling a drowning was almost too sad to bear.

In 1947 the Fulton Fire Department joined the Corps. That was a drought year. Two tropical storms and one hurricane struck the Texas coast too far away for its rains to help Aransas.

One Saturday in the fall, wildfire hit Live Oak Peninsula. It began when a landowner wanted to burn off a pasture or two, according to Jim Furlong. "A couple of his neighbors got on bended knee to ask him not to set the fire, but he paid them no mind and set the fire, and it developed into a holocaust."

By midmorning, the fire threatened homes in Copano Village; by noon it had swept almost to the airport. It leaped the full width of the highway and caught grass and brush on the east side. As the fire began its march on Fulton beach, only a half-dozen spectators were present to confront it.

"We were fighting a losing battle," Jim Furlong said, "because none of us knew anything about fighting brush fires. And it just so happened that a car full of men was coming up from the Valley, and they were professional brush fire fighters." The tourists told the locals how to set backfires. "If it hadn't been for our setting the backfires, Fulton would have burned to the ground—and a lot of Rockport would have gone too."

Fire equipment from Fulton, Rockport, Aransas Pass, Ingleside, Portland, and Corpus Christi battled the blaze. Trucks from Mathis, Odem, and Port Lavaca joined them. Businesses closed as employees entered the battle. Boats pulled out of the harbor to the safety of the bay. Fire trucks siphoned saltwater to fight the blaze.

By seven that evening, the fire appeared to be under control—but the wind shifted to the east, igniting grass and brush close to Sparks Colony. At midnight, the blaze was so huge that people in Portland—twenty miles to the south—could see it.

By nine the next morning, everyone believed that the fire was out. Then the wind came from the north again. Volunteers continued their battle until five o'clock Sunday evening. The fire was finally under control, but small outbreaks continued until Monday afternoon.

The time had come to assess damage. More than fifteen square miles of Live Oak Peninsula—from Copano Bay, through Fulton, west almost to Sparks Colony and south to the outskirts of Rockport—had burned. Nine houses were gone, along with buildings at two tourist cottage complexes.

The *Pilot* mourned other losses as well: "Less tangible, but probably more costly, was damage to the widely-advertised live oak groves and thickets which are a considerable tourist attraction." In those thickets rabbits, squirrels, racoons, and wildcats had perished. The fire also destroyed wood markers in the old Fulton Cemetery; some historic graves still have not been identified.

MAKING A BUCK

Most people, remembering Aransas in the 1930s and 1940s, focus on important people who dedicated their lives to Aransas. These people are spoken of less for their accomplishments than for their humanity:

Judge Bernard S. Fox was "a kind, thoughtful and exceptional man." Once, when a young man of a good family got himself arrested, Judge Fox heard the boy weeping in his cell. He learned that it was the boy's birthday and ordered a birthday cake. Nine women responded, so everyone in the courthouse celebrated along with the prisoner.

James Clark Herring ("Mr. Clark") was the county district clerk for ten years, following his father who had served in that position for forty-two years. Clark was around the courthouse all his life. He had his first paying job (as janitor) there when he was only eleven; he served under his father as a deputy, from time to time, for fifteen years. Clark's knowledge of the town and its people resulted in his nickname: "Mr. Encyclopedia." When Clark resigned at age eighty, his wife Edith Sneed Herring completed his unexpired term. Mr. Clark was considered one of the kindest, fairest, and most caring men in the county.

Joe L. Johnson, Sr., and his wife Helen Miller owned for many years a popular drugstore on the corner of Austin at St. Mary's Street. The soda fountain was *the* gathering place for young people and also a favorite coffee spot for many in the days before most places had their own coffee pots. Joe was a fine person, outgoing, honest, and courteous—a good friend and a good druggist. Helen, who worked side by side with her husband, was a woman of great beauty, dignity, and poise.

Shirley Ratisseau remembered Lynn Wendell, the youngest brother of many siblings, including Jerry Wendell and Judge John Wendell. She said that he "often looked as if he was contemplating with amusement something the rest of us didn't quite understand. Which is why his nickname was Possum."

Of Zeph Rouquette, she said: "He rode a horse straight-backed and proud, and he was cowboy-hatted and western-booted to a T." Shirley thought that for looks alone "the Western movie makers in Hollywood could have taken Zeph Rouquette . . . as the perfect patriarchal cowboy figure. . . . He was a wonderful man, he was kind, looked the world right straight in the eye and was so highly regarded, many men removed their hats around him."

Many Aransans believed that Neva Porter Jackson, Norvell Jackson's wife, had the most beautiful singing voice ever in Aransas County. She sat patiently through hours of juvenile singing rehearsals at the schools, always smiling and always encouraging.

The period following World War II was a great time for entrepreneurs. In Aransas, that meant, for starters, the seafood industry and new ways of promoting tourism.

Jack Blackwell had followed his father as owner of the *Rockport Pilot*. He brought in groups of reporters and travel writers and saw that they were well-entertained. Jack was an art photographer as well, so he sent beautiful pictures of Aransas to the newspapers in many cities. Since he foresaw tourists flying to Aransas in private planes, and business benefitting from aviation, he worked to equip the airport with the latest technology.

As across most of Texas, other Aransas entrepreneurs were intent on developing the oil business and related enterprises. Although only a few large landowners benefited directly from the oil business, everyone did in one way or another.

As early as 1923, an expert in oil geology had reported that prospects were good for developing production on several thousand acres on and around Live Oak Peninsula. As with earlier and often inexpert exploration, test wells produced little result. The first commercial production was brought in on the McCampbell Ranch by the Buckingham Oil Company in 1936.

In 1947 George W. Graham and the William Herbert Hunt Trust Estate drilled just north of the airport and brought in the No. 1 Spencer-Kent-Crane well. Many wells and many oilmen followed.

"When I think of the oil industry in Aransas County," James Sorenson, Jr., said, "I think of Emory M. Spencer in particular."

Spencer himself explained: "The discovery well was drilled on my land. Beginning in 1948 I became an operator, drilling wells principally in the west Rockport area." He saw himself as one of an exceptional few, but noted that the benefits of oil production came from more than the wells themselves.

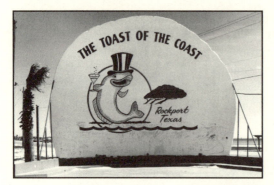

Rockport Beach Band Shell with well-known logo, now replaced.
—Courtesy of Tommy A. Shults

Locals and tourists set off for a day of fishing aboard a typical party boat.
—Courtesy of Shirley Ratisseau Collection

The crab later became a landmark in the area now known as Veterans' Memorial Park. Postcard.
—Courtesy of Gordon Stanley Collection

Other jobs were jobs created by the production. Jerry Wendell and Delo Caspary, friends since high school, learned that a drilling rig had moved into Copano Bay and needed boats to service it. The recent college grads put their small bay boats to the task.

Soon they were supplying crew boats and had a few built for the purpose. In 1957 Delo and Jerry bought a government surplus air-sea rescue boat and restructured it for use in servicing offshore drilling platforms. Their ninety-five-foot offshore crewboat, one of the first, soon followed.

A contract to service drilling rigs required more boats, and Caspary-Wendell continued to grow. They were pioneers in the industry, developing supply vessels, equipment for offshore and seismic work, and the first 100-foot crew boat. A relationship with Burton Shipyard in Port Arthur, builder of most of the boats, was "a big boost," Jerry Wendell said.

Ultimately, Delo and Jerry sold out to Santa Fe International, a global operation. With American Offshore, they built another international business. By 1972, Caspary-Wendell was preparing fleets for the North Sea and worldwide.

Ted Little—apparently no relation to Murdoch McRae's stepson, but seeming to follow in his footsteps, nonetheless—started leasing boats to the oil industry in about 1945. Robert and James T. Little joined their father to form Ted R. Little and Sons in 1953.

Atlantic Richfield requested that they develop a method for laying pipe underwater, and that technique became the main focus of their business. It involved a plow pulled behind a boat, digging a trench that the pipe just naturally fell into; sand automatically settled over the pipe, burying it.

By 1969, the Littles formed State Services to build bay and offshore platforms. Their facility between Rockport and Aransas Pass has been so successful that the company recently added another site. A third generation of Littles works there.

The Rice Shipyard turned to building fine yachts. Bob Keys was the general manager and a talented man with wood. Rice built a boat for himself out of all the finest materials—bronze, stainless steel—and named it *Rusty*.

Rockport Yacht and Supply grew. In about 1950, Smith used his oilfield equipment to build and install one of the first vertical lifts, turntable and trackage mechanisms. With this modern facility,

RYSCO could handle vessels up to one hundred feet in length and one hundred tons in burden. The United States Navy contracted with the Rockport Yacht and Supply Company to repair and maintain vessels in the one-hundred-foot class.

By 1960, RYSCO began building seventy-two-foot wood-hulled fishing vessels. Francis "Monty" Rouquette was a carpenter who crafted the wheel houses, and did other work too. Within two years, the design was a clear success. From the plans of the wooden seventy-two-footers, Albert Silchenstedt developed a sixty-seven-foot steel hull design for RYSCO. The first four ships went to Nippon Reizo Kabushidi Daisa of Tokyo, Japan. Over the next twenty years, RYSCO built more than 500 seventy-foot trawlers—200 of them for the Japanese market.

RYSCO's success created a problem for Rob Roy and Winnie Rice—one that had nothing to do with competition. The Rices lived at their shipyard in a garage apartment of sorts—above a boathouse stuck out over the harbor. They couldn't stand the noise from RYSCO—hammering and banging around the clock. The dust was

More than five hundred fishing trawlers were constructed and launched from RYSCO Shipyard for use around the world.
—Courtesy of Jackson family Collection

incessant too. Rob Roy sold out to Tiny Smith (T. Noah, Jr.), making RYSCO even bigger.

Smith put in a "ways" (a cable lift) that could handle one hundred tons, and it ended at a turntable. But when the oil industry suffered its great slump in the 1980s, the world fisheries business went down with it. RYSCO's era in Rockport came to an end.

In 1979 David Pilgrim started Coastal Production Services, joining other operators in similar businesses. In the beginning, he ran the enterprise from his Lamar home. His operators, gaugers, and roustabouts travel by crew boat or helicopter, servicing oil and gas wells in the gulf and bays. Pilgrim's second company, Production Services Group, uses advanced technology for continuous production monitoring. A third company designs, manufactures, and installs production platform safety systems, performs inspections, and provides life-saving equipment and aids to navigation.

Aransans might well wish such services were more prevalent in oil lands to the south. On June 3, 1979, an oil well just off the Yucatán Peninsula, in Mexico, blew out. Thirty thousand barrels of oil a day spewed from it, and currents carred the mess toward the Coastal Bend.

At the time, it was the largest oil spill in history. The slick reached San José, Matagorda, and Mustang islands. Man-made booms stretched across narrow entrances to bays, estuaries, and marshes to protect wildlife there.

Modern Aransans, like others around the globe, are left with a dilemma—wanting to preserve its rich and unique wildlife, but also wanting modern conveniences and enterprise. Finding an equitable solution remains the greatest challenge.

Oil enterprises and others paid taxes that enriched Aransas County coffers. In 1949 the area's various schools consolidated as the Aransas County Independent School District, and soon the county built a fine high school.

When the commissioners wanted to use some of the increased tax base to build a new courthouse, however, taxpayers defeated the proposition 308 to 15. The citizens were unwilling to tear down their antique Moorish structure.

A *Corpus Christi Caller-Times* reporter wrote that "the courthouse today is listed along with the Fulton Mansion, the sites of the turtle and meat-packing plants, the foundation of the old black-smith shop at Lamar where Colt is presumed to have perfected his revolver, the Hall home and the sites of old Copano and St. Mary's as points of historic interest for local tours." Terming the court-house "Aransas County's most famous landmark," the reporter added that it would "remain a tourist attraction—for a time at least."

A significant portion of Aransas tax revenues came from the seafood industry. Boats belonging to several branches of the Cast-erline family worked out of L. E.'s fishhouse. Most men shrimped at night. They received from one to three cents per pound for the shrimp, with a limit of three thousand pounds a day.

By 1950, Texas was processing 51 million pounds of shrimp, and a significant percentage of them were processed in Aransas County. During shrimping season, as many as 700 boats might be tied up at the huge Conn Brown Harbor shrimp processing plant, just in the edge of Aransas Pass. Some shrimp were frozen and sent out with the shells still on; others were processed even to include breading.

Aransan Willie Close, Jr., died that year, having set a record for catching more fish during his lifetime than any fisherman on the Texas coast.

Johnny Atwood described commercial fishing as he had known it: "It was quite a thrill to me when we caught fish with nets. You somewhat look for your fish, but other times, you just strike blind. We call it strike—that's when you run your nets out, and you make a bunch of racket in there and drive the fish to them. It was quite a thing to see four or five big old redfish hit that net in water two feet deep."

The Atwoods used trammel nets, not to be confused with seines or gill nets. The nets were twelve- to thirteen-hundred-feet long and made of three layers of webbing. The inner layer was linen, a very deep section of webbing, and its mesh had a stretch of ap-proximately three inches. On either side of that was the braille, made of cotton. The mesh had an eight-inch stretch, and it was about four-and-a-half meshes tall. In effect, the nets were put together in walls, with a braille on either side of the inner net.

The nets were hung on a lead [weighted] line and a float line. When in the water, they stood three-and-a-half to four feet tall. The inner webbing, about eight or nine feet tall, was very slack. Its mesh size was such that undersize trout would not often stick in it. That created a sort of culling mechanism, and the small fish usually were not hurt. A fish ran into the net, went through the big mesh and hit the slack, smaller mesh. He carried that surface material through the other side and hung in the pouch.

"It was hard work," Johnny said, "but it was quite fun." He didn't recall ever catching a turtle—and he started fishing in about 1945. He remembered seeing turtles, though, in the tall grass at the mouth of St. Charles Bay, but "you couldn't set a net or anything."

Most of the boats were powered with old automobile engines. A man just took off the gear and clutch and made a stub shaft. Then he installed a saltwater pump to cool the engine. No marine engines were available until after World War II, so fishing was "still fairly primitive," Johnny said.

There was a common occurence each year near the first of September—the beginning of bay-shrimping season. "You would hear this *ka-whump*, and that meant another boat was blown up. You looked in the sky to see a black ring of smoke going up and figure which way it was—whether it was Rockport or Fulton or where. It was all a matter of whose boat was it? Was anybody hurt?"

Gasoline power in a boat was dangerous in itself, but the problem was exacerbated by the fact that most fishermen used old, thin-walled fifty-five-gallon drums as fuel tanks. Many of these tanks were under the boat decks, and sooner or later, unnoticed, they began to leak. "It doesn't take but about half a teacupful of gasoline to blow the side of a boat all to pieces," Johnny said.

Until diesel engines became common, one or more boats blew up every year. According to Dave Davis, the last one that blew up, the *Texas Twelve*, was on butane. The fuel wasn't for the main engine, but for the cookstove. "It blowed pieces all the way from Jackson's Fishhouse all the way over to where Corky's Cafe was [on the west side of Austin Street, just north of Market]."

Johnny Atwood added: "And of course nobody had insurance at that time. You didn't have insurance on yourself, you didn't have health insurance, you didn't have any insurance for your home, automobile, anything. You just took care of yourself, and if you didn't you were in trouble."

Following World War II, many navy surplus marine engines became available. Boats began to get bigger, and off-shore shrimping became increasingly significant. Elva Mullinax—who was married to "Teet" Casterline—said, "Somebody's going to get drowned in the Gulf, trying to get those expensive shrimp." At that time, the price for the small crustaceans had just gone up to nine cents.

"The whole industry just blossomed," Johnny Atwood said. "The engines went from gasoline engines to diesel engines, and the boats went from wood to steel. But the prettiest things to see were some of these wood boats being built; they were works of art."

By 1946, when Ed Beasley took over as Rockport's Southern Pacific Railroad Agent and Telegrapher, the rail line was a far cry from the grand old SAAP. The passenger car had been discontinued; train service consisted of only a freighter that ran to Gregory each afternoon and Sunday, then returned to Rockport to await the next day's run. Ed supervised a Western Union messenger who delivered telegrams and a station laborer who helped handle loading and unloading freight.

During the early fifties, the layover point for the crew was changed to Gregory. The train came to Rockport only when there was business—road and street material, building supplies, oil well cementing products, maybe gasoline or cattle feed coming in. Sometimes the engine came just to move empty cars out. Southern Pacific transport trucks carried express loads going out—cattle from Sid Richardson's island ranch or fish, oysters, and shrimp. With better roads, rail lines everywhere were losing business to trucks, which sometimes offered faster service.

The depot closed in about 1967, and the tracks to Rockport were removed after that.

In 1952 J. C. and Evelyn May, of El Campo, purchased the Fulton Mansion. They had big plans: a restaurant in the basement, hotel rooms on the second and third floors, a cluster of period guest cottages on the grounds. Most of the grand design never materialized.

The Mays made essential repairs to the old mansion, but also damaged its historic substance. In order to make space for the restaurant, they tore out the cooling trough and the drying racks in the basement; they stuccoed the wood walls there. They planted an arc of palm trees at the entrance to the mansion and painted its exterior walls a "perky pink."

In 1960 Mr. and Mrs. J. Felix Boldin, of Lubbock, purchased the Fulton Mansion and developed the Mays' beginnings of a trailer park on the grounds. A Mansion staff member later defined this turn of events: "The house was not inhabited. It rather served as an increasingly decaying monument to the past, open to tourists, with the basement serving as a recreation center. Perhaps the most positive aspect of the last two ownerships [the Boldins and then Mr. and Mrs. Robert Edwin Copeland] is that very basic attempts were made to shield the house from the elements and vandalism."

The era of "Winter Texans" came into its own in the 1950s. It had begun earlier than that, with the first men who came to the hunting clubs. It grew as the use of the automobile grew, and as the roads improved. Praise for the climate of Aransas spread even during the Depression and through the War. Then many retirees from the cold north began to enjoy warm winters in Aransas.

Toddie Lee Wynne built the Sea-Gun resort, enveloping Mills Wharf. It was a complete complex, offering boat trips to the whooping cranes' winter home, goose leases in the Tivoli area, daily fishing trips, swimming pools, activities for children and families.

Soon, a more revolutionary change in the Aransas landscape was underway.

THE CANALS OF KEY ALLEGRO

The hurricane of 1919 had swept Frandolig Point clean. From that time on, more than thirty-five years, the island served as an ideal habitat for wildlife. A few people crossed a rickety bridge, or waded through the shallow pass, to reach it—anglers headed for favorite fishing spots, birders and shell collectors, young couples seeking a bit of privacy.

By 1953, the Aransas County Navigation District had become aware that the Texas General Land Office was required, by law, to sell submerged land to any navigation district that asked for it —at the bargain rate of $1 an acre. The Aransas County Navigation District bought 604 acres in Little Bay.

Frandolig Point had passed from Franz Josef to J. D. Guinn and others, then to the family of Harry Hertzberg and then to the family of Dabney and Ona Petty. The Pettys filed suit against the Navigation District. They claimed that 165 acres of the District's purchase was not in fact submerged, but had risen above mean high tide and was a part of their island. When Rockport's district court ruled in the Pettys' favor, the Navigation District bought Frandolig Point from them for $55,000, then put up a sign:

NOTICE:
Please!
Do not pet or annoy our RATTLESNAKES

In 1958 the Navigation District decided to make a profit on its investment. While retaining some acreage for the expansion of recreational and pleasure boat facilities, they offered Frandolig Point for private development.

San Antonian Carl Krueger, Jr., and his wife Pat had vacationed in Florida and fallen in love with Fort Lauderdale's canals. When they returned to Texas, the Kruegers spent months searching for a place on the coast where they could replicate that Florida lifestyle.

"One day we happened to drive out across that little bridge onto Frandolig Island, and I immediately knew this was it," Carl said. He realized that Aransas was within an easy drive of Houston and San Antonio, and already noted for its wildlife and rich history. Carl C. Krueger, Jr., and Associates was the only bidder when the Navigation District put Frandolig Point up for sale. Once the deed was in his hands, Carl began dredging canals for the development he called Key Allegro.

He was not the first who had that idea in the Coastal Bend. *Bahia Azul*—Blue Bay—had begun at Ingleside in 1952, following

Carl Krueger crossed this bridge and envisioned a new community.
—Courtesy of Gordon Stanley

Florida's "Venetian Canal" concept. By 1957, the idea was in Aransas: George Strickhausen began digging canals for Copano Cove.

In 1960 Raulie Irwin, Sr., and Doyle Brashear were at work on Palm Harbor. Their vision was modest—something better than fishing shacks, but still just weekend places. They gave no thought to the possibility of full-time residents, so the first houses were no larger than 900 square feet. They had no heat or air-conditioning.

The Irwins moved to Palm Harbor in 1961 and opened a sales office. In September, Hurricane Carla struck. North, at Lamar, water was twenty-six inches deep in Sea Gun's main office. Palm Harbor sales were slow for a year after that.

Undaunted, Carl Krueger started Key Allegro in 1962. Dave Davis remembered: "Most of the natives didn't think that Key Allegro would ever work. . . . I was doing some carpentering and boat building, and I had a friend out in Midland, Texas, that wanted to buy three lots on Key Allegro. He could get those lots for $1,250 and wanted me to build three houses. . . . I took him around and showed him all the marinas that had started over in Ingleside and what have you, and how they were all fallen into the bay and bulkheads were all falling down, and they'd been there maybe seven or eight years and never went well. I talked him out of doing it."

Dave chuckled. "It's come to look like another error. Key Allegro never did slow down. Once it got going, it just kept on." But even then, most of the natives thought the newcomers were crazy to invest there. "They thought the first hurricane would wipe it out. And someplace down along the line they gotta be right, but so far it's been a long time, and it hasn't happened yet."

As Carl Krueger shaped his canals, he used the dredged sand to raise the level of the land. His streets would be higher than the mainland road leading into Rockport; his lots would be two feet higher than Corpus Christi's North Beach had been at the time of the 1919 storm. Soon Carl had a marina, a motel, a restaurant, a private club, and some condominiums.

The first homes were simple—mostly little weekend getaway stilt houses for people from San Antonio and Houston—but that changed. Key Allegro's success was phenomenal. By the time the land was stable for the final section to develop, the price of lots was so high that people felt they had to build mansions. Some did.

But the people on Key Allegro gave parties that were warm and welcoming; if you lived on Key Allegro, you got invited. Most of those parties were held at Allegro House, the island's community building.

Families on Key Allegro worshipped in Rockport churches. People worked in the schools and area businesses and began to assimilate into the larger community.

Carl Krueger entered a "Porpoise Period" in 1965 and wrote about it later:

"It was about eleven o'clock New Year's Eve morning in 1964 when a vintage Chevrolet station wagon pulled up in front of the sales office, oddly leaving a path of water drops on Bayshore Drive. A dapper, moustached man entered the office and introduced himself as John Walls. He said, with some agitation, that his two dolphins were in danger of dehydration and badly in need of a temporary home.

"This was not a request we were used to hearing, but we followed him to his car. Walls lifted the lid from one of two caskets, and inside lay a five-foot-long porpoise in about two inches of water. It was obvious the porpoises needed help." It was equally obvi-

ous that John Walls had a traveling dolphin show—one that Carl
Krueger might have use for in advertising Key Allegro.

As Krueger explained, "Our sales manager, Ed Harper, brightly
suggested we fence off a spot at the end of Albacore Canal as a temporary home for the dolphins. A quick trip to Picton's Lumber Yard
produced a roll of goat fence and a couple of cedar posts. With Walls
working in the water, we soon had a fenced-in area about sixty feet
square at the end of the canal. The dolphins were gently lifted from
their caskets and eased into the water. After exploring and defining
the limits of their new habitat, they settled down and began cavort-
ing as dolphins are given to do.

"John the Porpoise Man proceeded to give his dolphins a snack
of mullet that he'd kept iced down in the station wagon. Then he
had a suggestion for us. If we could offer free room and board to
him and the dolphins, they might stay over indefinitely.

"Harry Cole offered to put John up at his motel and feed him
too; we agreed to provide sustenance for the porpoises. Shortly, we
built a new pen at the Marina gas dock and a platform from which
John would conduct his act.

"What a show it was. Corpus, San Antonio, Houston, and Dallas papers carried news of it, and folks crowded the dock area—some
times as many as one hundred of them at a show. We couldn't charge
admission in such an open arena, so the enterprise was an aesthetic
success, but not a financial one.

"John Walls had an idea: We could catch porpoises in Aransas
Bay and sell them to businesses like Sea-Arama for a handsome
profit. As wild as the idea seems now, we had a boat built, and with
the help of Buddy McLester, a local fishing guide, John was ready
to catch porpoises."

The men herded dolphins into shallow water along San José Island, then trapped two of them in a net stretched between two
boats. Sea World in Galveston bought the dolphins, but that one
sale seemed to flood the market, and no additional prospects were
found.

"After six months," Carl continued, "we were painfully aware
of the economic need to get out of the dolphin business. We transferred the whole operation to a man at Port Aransas and were glad
to see the last of it."

Still, a dolphin makes its way through Little Bay sometimes. It seems to tarry at the entry to Albacore Canal, as though returning to an old haunt.

Hurricane Celia, in 1970, was a rough storm for Aransas. No one had expected that; Celia was predicted to be a minor hurricane, with winds no more than eighty miles per hour. One hundred and eighty was more like it.

John Jackson remembered: "Celia was a summertime storm, August 3, and a daytime storm. I was off at college, but I came home, as did my younger brother, to help our dad with our fleet of boats. About midafternoon the

Key Allegro residents enjoy an enviable lifestyle.

—Photo by Thom Evans

wind got so fierce that we got out of there. I was driving the old red panelled truck, heading for the sheriff's office, and tin from the Morrison Boat Houses was flying around us. My dad was fearful that we'd get a flat tire from driving over tin with nails in it, so he got out in front of the truck, to clear the tin away. If a piece had caught him, it could have beheaded him. My brother and I were pretty scared about that, but we all got out."

People in the fledgling community of Key Allegro felt particularly vulnerable. A crowd of them huddled in a cooler at the marina. Homeowners rebuilt, and Key Allegro grew after that storm, as all of Aransas did.

Jackson Seafood decided to diversify by building a fleet of boats to work the East Coast, harvesting sea scallops. They had an eye toward South America as well.

But the good days were almost at an end. The scallop resource disappeared almost overnight, and only 1981 and 1986 brought good catches of shrimp. All shrimpers tightened their belts.

MODERN TIMES

BOUNDARIES

By the early 1960s, the fine Copano Causeway had turned into a bottleneck. Heavy truck traffic couldn't use it at all, and boat traffic had problems with the fifty-foot clearance.

A sturdier LBJ Causeway, replacing the original one, has an elevated bridge section that eliminates the land traffic delays connected with a drawbridge. For marine traffic, it provides 320 feet of horizontal clearance and seventy-five feet of vertical clearance. The cantilever lift section of the old causeway was removed, and its two remaining sections became the longest fishing pier in the world.

John Wendell was County Judge then, as he had been since 1951. When assumed the position of County Judge in 1951, he was the youngest man holding that office in Texas. He retired thirty-nine years later, with the longest tenure of any sitting county judge.

The intervening years were anything but easy. John Wendell took the helm of a county heavily in the red and paralyzed by outstanding debts. Aransas had a weak tax base; the little revenue that did come in was needed to meet daily expenses. Wendell's focus had to be on the bottom line.

Wendell laid off employees; he made needed repairs himself. He instituted a cash-only operation for anything other than major capital improvement. He developed a system of rotating road repair equipment among his four precinct commissioners long before state lawmakers came up with the unit-road system. During Wendell's administration, numerous improvements in the County Airport secured a viable facility.

For more than thirteen years, abutting counties argued over boundaries. "Most people thought we were fighting over just a little piece of land," Judge Wendell said, "but that was not the case. Of course, anyone would have liked to have Harbor Island. When you look at the oil tank field over there, you'll see all the valuation sitting around." (No one remembered the island as French explorer Béranger had seen it; no one knew that oak trees had grown there.)

The contention between counties had started when the Aransas County Navigation District leased land near Harbor Island, believing it to be in Aransas County; Nueces County claimed the land too. Judge Wendell, reviewing the matter, saw a greater concern: The dividing line between Aransas and Nueces counties had never been extended into the Gulf of Mexico. No one really knew which county could claim revenues from Gulf oil production there.

Aransas wasn't particularly interested in taking Port Aransas from Nueces County "because of the hardship of maintaining the roads over there," Wendell said. "We'd have to go back and forth on the ferry." Aransas County had owned Conn Brown Harbor in Aransas Pass all along, and the huge shrimping fleet there was a significant source of revenue for the Aransas Navigational District.

As the issue escalated, all coastal county judges met in Austin, hoping to come to agreement on boundaries and angles of projection. Nearly every judge had a different idea, and none could come up with an answer that suited the rest.

Aransas County hired Hobart Huson, the Refugio historian, as attorney and settled the issue of county lines abutting Nueces. Wendell said, "We moved their boundary back off our shore to the middle of the Intracoastal Canal between here and Aransas Pass. Our shorelines are all in Aransas County now, and they weren't before, according to Nueces County's contention."

Aransas County also got the lighthouse, Talley Island, and Shell Bank Island, where the Civil War fort once stood. A line was drawn from the jetties, nine miles out into the Gulf, and all the coordinates were defined. "It wasn't a matter of fighting over some marsh land," Judge Wendell said. "We didn't have a boundary, but we do now. We know who to tax."

As oil and gas depleted, the schools had to increase the tax rate on property, counting especially on the better subdivisions in Aransas County. "We're depending on that type of development," Judge Wendell said in 1971. "But oil is the major economy. I don't know what the people of Aransas County would have done without the oil activity."

In 1986 Aransas found out. An oil glut created by international cartels slowed Texas industry. Tourism dropped off; home sales slowed. Recovery took ten years.

RIGHTS

Just as Mexican-Americans and blacks felt more acutely their places in Texas' cultural-political systems after World War II, so did women. Active as they had been in the war effort, women were still far from enjoying full political rights. Most accepted the role of housewife once more. But some found voice in public life through clubs, civic organizations, and political parties.

For many years, the Democratic party had been virtually the only party in Texas. In most counties, the Democrat who won a primary was the person who took office. The Republicans didn't count for much, in most minds, but when an Aransas woman, Shirley Ratisseau, became the first female Republican county chairperson in all of Texas, she created an uproar.

Shirley was unable to find a public facility for her primary in 1962, so she held it under an oak tree in her own front yard. She awoke on election morning to find five dead rattlesnakes tied to her fence and a sign that read: "NO TWO PARTY."

Race relations came to a crossroads when the Civil Rights Act passed in 1964. Aransas County Attorney Emory Spencer visited L. C. Huff to tell him that segregation had ended, but Huff was not pleased. Neither were his neighbors. "We told Mr. Spencer that we didn't want to integrate," Huff said. "He said he was sorry but the law was that we had to go to school together." The Huffs and their friends didn't think it would work out at the time; they feared negative reactions, even overt action, from the whites. Later, however, L. C. said "We never had a bit of trouble."

Mexican-Americans quickly grasped the importance of the new sentiments of equality. They were eager to apply the new laws to a variety of old irritations. One of these was usage of the Rockport Cemetery. Its east side—the side with most of the old graves, the side with the best view—had water for its lawn, but the west side, the Mexican-American side, did not. According to Hillis Dominguez, the Rockport Cemetery Association cleaned the east side, but expected Mexican-Americans to clean the west. Hillis and his friends complained to the Chamber of Commerce about that, but nothing much came of it.

Then an Anglo veteran died. His Mexican-American wife bought a plot for him on the Anglo side of the cemetery and claimed the right to an adjoining plot for herself. The Cemetery Association denied her request, citing a policy written in 1899. It defined three discrete sections for Anglos, blacks and Mexican-Americans.

Hillis Dominguez went to the city, to the county, to the Justice Department in Washington D.C. When he learned that the Civil Rights Acts of 1964 included cemeteries that had received tax funds, Hillis went to the State Human Rights Commission. And the woman he had championed got the grave beside her husband.

For a while, LULAC (the League of United Latin American Citizens) was "pretty active," Frank Covarrúbias said, "but we got tired of fighting all the time." The last case Mexican-Americans fought for had to do with hair, in an era when teens everywhere were shocking their parents with long, stringy locks.

Frank said "a Mexican couldn't grow no long hair, or they put them out of school. But the Anglo could. They all had an excuse for it, you know? So we got lawyers from Corpus, and then you could use hair as long as you want to.

"I tell my boy, the only way to fight the odds is education. How can you fight for that job if you can't do it? You gotta be educated. You have to be pretty good, so you won't have so much trouble in life like we had. The only thing we could do was fish."

Many Mexicans were unemployed, and Anglos often considered them lazy. "Looking back," one said, "it is obvious that there were just not any jobs around, and what there were usually went to the unemployed Anglos first."

Speaking in 1989, Frank Covarrúbias said that some nearby coastal towns had no distinction between races. "But over here in Rockport, it still is—in jobs. I hope we can live better. We used to be better than now in Rockport. This generation we got in City Hall, or the County—nothing but young boys. They make it hard for us Latins; I don't know why. They make it harder and harder for the black people, too, to make it over here. I hope we don't have to fight them in court for that. Because all we have to do is call Corpus, and they send a lawyer right away." The tone of Frank's voice carried just the hint of a threat.

One person who grew up in Rockport and returned to Aransas County at the close of his business career said: "We white kids were really oblivious to the shameful treatment of the minority population. I didn't know any black children, and although we went to school with the Hispanics, we did not know how they were treated in general."

He added that during the years he was growing up in Aransas, people "had an affection for the black adults we knew—Aunt Ida, Uncle Lee—and did not even know that those terms were patronizing. We were all conditioned by our parents and peers that the blacks 'should know their place and not be uppity.' Looking back, it's really a shame to see how these people were treated."

In 1973 Perry Bass worked with the Texas legislature to restore the Hispanic name "San José" to the barrier island fronting Aransas. He pointed out that it was the only one not retaining an Hispanic name, but families with long histories at Saint Joseph resented that. They, and many other Anglos, still use the affectionate term "Saint Joe." Bass, who owns the island, admonished: "Don't do that; it isn't right."

REFUGEES

"I still don't understand why I came to Aransas County," Hue Nguyen said. He had left his home in the horror of 1975, when Communists from North Vietnam invaded Saigon. "We didn't want to live under communist rule, so we had to get out of there as fast as we could. We didn't know where we were going to go. We thought maybe we'd get out of there just for a certain time and come back again, but it did not turn out like that."

Hue, who was in the military, escaped eight days after his parents and sister. They went on an American merchant ship to Guam; he left by fishing boat to Thailand. "Whatever we had, we left behind," Hue said. "I had just a couple of pairs of clothes. My parents had a few personal bags. We didn't have any money or valuables. We were just glad to get out of there alive."

The family was finally reunited three months later at Fort Chaffee, Arkansas. There the Catholic agency suggested that the family might relocate in Rockport. "They showed me this little town by the water," Hue said. "I love water, so I said I'd go." He knew it would suit his father, Nguyen Van Ban too; Van Ban was a fisherman and a carpenter. None of the Nguyens spoke any English, but two Aransas families agreed to sponsor them.

The Nguyens arrived in Aransas in October 1975—seventy-five-year-old Van Ban, his sixty-one-year-old wife, two sons, a daughter, son-in-law, and three grandchildren. Van Ban was too old to work, but his sons were skilled in heavy-machinery operation and mechanics. Hue found a job in just two days.

"We were here alone for quite some time," Hue said. Other Vietnamese families—and Hue's sister—joined them in 1979-80. Many of the refugees were city people, military people, with no background in fishing. They learned it in Aransas. Although everything was strange to them, they learned quickly. Hue said Vietnamese are proud that what they see, they can do.

"There wasn't anybody too happy to see them come," Dave Davis said. "Everybody was really opposed to moving in more people and putting pressure on our seafood. We could see it was just a matter of so many more boats in the area cutting down the amount of shrimp any individual boat was going to catch. We tried to get a moratorium on the number of boats and licenses allowed on the

Texas coast to keep from over-fishing. We were probably right, but I can see now there wasn't any way to stop it. We were already to the point of probably overfishing ourselves."

Local shrimpers were not the only ones who complained. Environmentalists criticized the Vietnamese for harvesting eggs from rookery islands, the sites where water birds nested. In 1921 Texas had given the National Audubon Society a long-term free lease for some of those rookeries, but now the Vietnamese were scrambling next year's roseate spoonbills, reddish egrets, and gulls.

Farther up the Texas coast, protests were more vehement. The Ku Klux Klan took on the new cause, burning crosses and bombing shrimping boats. The confrontations became the basis for a Hollywood movie filmed largely in Fulton; local citizens played bit parts.

Thanks to Fulton's Vietnamese population, the general growth of Aransas and increases of tourism, the town incorporated in 1978 and elected L. E. Casterline as mayor.

In 1980, when Hurricane Allen threatened, Vietnamese and old settlers faced it together. Although the storm filled the Gulf and appeared awesome on television radar, it caused little damage. Two years later, the town of Fulton built a lighted fishing pier 1,200 feet long.

Some resentments may linger, but now the Vietnamese are a real part of Aransas. All shrimpers chafe under the restrictions of turtle exclusion devices. Dat Nguyen (no relation to Hue) was a starting player for the Texas A&M University football team in the 1995 and 1996 seasons. The family displayed his jersey in their popular Fulton restaurant, just blocks from the site of Mary Ellen McHugh's old packery "Eating House."

It was in 1979, the year that many Vietnamese arrived, that Fulton instituted its Oysterfest. Tents fill the area between Fulton Harbor and the Highway. There are the standard craft booths, entertainment and dancing, but Oysterfest is known for its contests. Oyster decorating is the most benign.

When men and women sit down for separate oyster-eating contests, some stomachs turn. Men are given five minutes, and women two minutes, to swallow as many oysters as they can, by

A new generation of Americans. Emily Nguyen wears a traditional Vietnamese dress; Phi-Long Do, beside her, appears to evoke early seafaring days. Andrew Le, to the right of Phi-Long, wears purely American garb, as do Duy Le and Hieu Nguyen, left and right, in the back row.
—Courtesy of Sam Nguyen

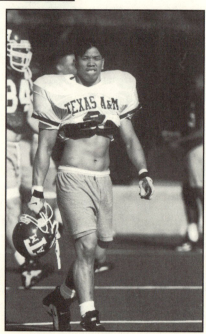

Dat Nguyen, all conference linebacker Texas A&M University, 1996.
—Courtesy of 12th Man Magazine, Texas A&M University

any means. All must must keep the slimy mollusks down for an additional five minutes. Some do.

Contestants in the oyster-shucking contest are given a sack of whole oysters to shuck and clean as fast as possible. In 1997 L. E. Casterline celebrated his seventy-eighth birthday by winning the contest for the fifteenth time. He started shucking when he was seven years old, and as an adult entered every Oysterfest contest. He lost only once and missed one year while recovering from surgery. L. E. announced his retirement from future competition.

ACTIVISTS

Key Allegro became more than a weekend getaway for the wealthy; it became home. And the people who lived there wanted a part in the larger community. Although their big-city brand of activism was not in the local style and not always welcomed, it began to make a difference. When the town and the island worked together, great things happened.

One significant community activity started with a simple rummage sale. Dorothea Montgomery and Pat Picton suggested the project to Catholic and Episcopal women, who operated for a time under the name "Concerned Women." Their work developed through the Ministerial Alliance as it grew to include other churches. Within a few years, someone came up with a new name—Castaways. It is an enterprise that has grown beyond all expectations, operating from its own building five days a week.

Other philanthropic efforts followed. Religious and secular groups, cooperating as "Good Samaritans," give low-income families short-term help with food and other necessities.

Self-described "little old ladies in tennis shoes" worked to establish an Emergency Medical Service for Aransas County. Their baking, canning, and craftwork resulted in a full-time emergency staff, three ambulances, and all sorts of advanced equipment.

One group of activists developed the idea of tidying up Aransas. This Clean Team wants to get the picturesque boats out of side yards, clean the brambles, mow the weeds. They instituted curbside recycling and now stage regular trash-offs and beach clean-ups. But even their best efforts draw criticism. It just isn't the old way.

"People come here because it is a nice, quiet, sleepy little fishing village," Dave Davis said, "and then as soon as they get here, they want to change it so it operates like it did in Houston or wherever they came from. And the growth gets more complicated, and pretty soon they might as well be back in San Antone. This country doesn't have a pollution problem, it doesn't have a water shortage problem, it doesn't have any of those things we worry about. What we have is an over-population problem, and without the population, we wouldn't need chemicals to pollute."

Johnny Atwood agreed. "Our greatest problem is too much growth, too many people. That all leads to overuse of the resource that we have and we enjoy—fishing, shrimping, that sort of thing. That is accompanied, of course, by pollution—either by sewage or automobiles or commercial activities. It is on the land as well as in the water. The biggest problem is the channelization of the bays—which began a long time ago—and the damming of our water supplies. I would suspect that pollution in the way of pesticides are probably contributing to the demise of our bays."

A raised consciousness regarding the environment is at work everywhere. United Carbon, now DeGussa, has cleaned up its output of soot and all the sullied surroundings. Scars remain; as recently as June 1996, an earth-mover turned up old, stained soil.

Something else turned up on the east side of Austin Street, south of St. Mary's. The old Rio Theater—renamed the Surf in the fifties—was torn down, revealing an advertisement painted on the wall of the business next door: It was a drawing of a giant sawfish, on display at the Cool Coast Camp, and it raised spectres of the KKK's Kool Koast Kamp. Most peope speculate that the advertisement had been painted by someone at the Cool Coast Cottages which took over the location on Fulton Beach Road, a little south of Bahama Drive.

Other activity changed the downtown landscape even more drastically. A combination of dire economic factors forced Jackson Seafood to close. The company sold its land in 1990, and its fleet in 1991.

John Jackson felt the pain of it. For generations, his family's company had been a stable place of employment for fifty to one hundred Aransans. His father and his grandfather had spent long hours, grueling hours there; the work was their life. And it was over.

Jackson Seafood's next door neighbor, Rockport Yacht and Supply Company, had closed some years earlier, victim of the Texas Oil Depression of the eighties. Thirty-two hundred lineal feet of waterfront stood vacant—a unique property in a unique town. John dreamed of a fine waterfront development, one that would evoke the town and the time that his great-grandmother Irene Norvell had known.

John Jackson took his ideas to Perry Bass. John said later that "we struck a deal on a napkin," but many formal papers followed. After a year of negotiation, the final result was Rockport Harborfront, Limited Partnership, with Bass as General Partner. "If it hadn't been for Perry Bass' personal interest in Rockport," John Jackson said, "it wouldn't have worked."

After the partnership razed the derelict metal buildings, gossip summoned all the worst specters of Atlantic City-style development. But the land is just there. Perry Bass said that green space was all he intended; John Jackson and others still dream that something wonderful might arise.

Aransas snubs most industry, bringer of noise and air pollution, but high-tech offers new possibilities. A local company operates by computer, telephone, and other electronic devices to provide doctors for hospital emergency rooms across the state. Its waterfront building looks more like a gracious Southern home than a business, and it carries no commercial sign to detract from the scenery.

Activists, who might choose up sides on some issues, have worked together on one grave problem. Aransas County waited for years for a new bypass highway to keep trucks from rumbling through a growing town. What they got was insufficient—a road that claimed five lives and caused forty-five accidents in less than one year. County Commissioner Glenn Guillory led twenty Aransans to the state capital to fight for something better. The county is still waiting for a resolution of the issue.

Other concerns and changes loom. The Texas Parks and Wildlife Department offered to buy back licenses for bay-shrimping in an attempt to curb escalating activity that may have resulted in overfishing. The idea was part of a long-term management program, certainly needed—but it's hard for most people to imagine Aransas harbors without shrimp boats.

Shortages of another reserve—even more significant because more basic—could bring about still greater changes. Officials are debating ownership of one of Texas' most precious natural resources—fresh water. Aransas County does not produce enough drinking water for its increased population and is dependent on supplies outside its jurisdiction; the county lies vulnerable to rationing and price increases. And Aransas isn't alone. Some experts predict that all of Texas may experience a new kind of range war—with sections of the state pitted against one another, not for land, but for water.

THE GIFT

"Today is a gift," someone wrote; "that's why we call it the Present." But the Present can be a difficult thing to see. It is easier, in some ways, to look at the past, where everything is settled. Sometimes we are inclined to consider the Present simply in the bald terms of its facts.

The facts concerning Aransas County in 1997 are these: a population of 18,545 is sixty-five percent white, twenty percent Hispanic, three percent Asian, less than two percent black, and just over one-half percent American Indian. Almost nine percent are unidentified in any of these categories. Close to seven percent of Aransans are unable to find work.

From 1990 to 1997, Aransas County experienced a growth rate of twenty-one percent—most by far in the Coastal Bend, and twenty-seventh in all of Texas. The San Patricio growth rate was slightly over sixteen percent, and Nueces was about eight-and-a-half. Refugio County lost population—down almost one percent. Ninety-seven percent of Aransas' growth came from people moving into the county. Rockport Mayor Glenda Burdick said that military personnel from Naval Station Ingleside accounted for some of the growth, but she and County Judge Tony Harden also credited the active Chamber of Commerce, attractive coastal atmosphere, reasonable taxes and a strong spirit of volunteerism.

Rockport and Fulton are the only towns in the county. Rockport holds 6,300 citizens, while Fulton has only 763. In many respects the two are one town, although residents of Fulton work to preserve their separate identity. "Rockport is more of the go-getter for industry and enterprises," a Fulton condominium manager said. "Fulton tries to capture and stay what it is. We aren't out for a lot of glitz and glamor."

The famous Fulton Mansion is now, ironically, within the boundaries of the town of Rockport. The two towns' water and sewer systems are tied together. Students attend combined Rockport-Fulton schools for most grades. The Early Childhood Center accepts kindergarteners and first graders from all over the county, but grades two, three, and four have two locations—one in Fulton and another far west on Market Street, where the thoroughfare is called Farm-to-Market Road 188. A middle school (beginning with fifth grade), junior high, and senior high provide great flexibility whereby any one facility may be used for more or fewer grades, depending on need.

Rockport's old downtown area carries little of the city's commerce. It is an arty strip of galleries, souvenir shops, stores displaying resort wear and adornments. More prosaic business fills modern buildings along Highway 35, between Rockport and Fulton.

Five bed-and-breakfast homes cater to a new kind of tourist. The first to open was in Bates McFarland's bayfront house, better known to locals recently as the Picton place. The second occupies a 1950s ranch-style home with a special claim to fame: It is shaded by the wide-spreading oak that sheltered Zachary Taylor's troops in 1845. Another, owned and operated by a former Peat-Marwick accounting firm secretary and a British attorney, stands high on the ridge north of Fulton. A descendant of one of Jean Lafitte's pirates operates a lodge that faces the marshy shoreline of Copano Bay. He caters to birders. Most recently—yet returning to an old practice—Colonel Hoopes' tall, yellow house has opened its door to visitors.

Some tourists, thinking about hurricanes, ask why anyone would choose to live in Aransas County. Residents typically respond that big storms are an occasional thing—years can pass between even small ones—and now radar reports their spawning off the coast of Africa. Such advance warning gives residents time to board their windows, pack cherished possessions, and leave town.

In other parts of the country, people live under threat of disasters that strike more suddenly—earthquakes, tornadoes, flash floods. Wherever people are, nature is. When it deals its worst, people either move out or rebuild.

How Aransas rebuilds may be the issue. Johnny Atwood said "I guess one of the greatest fears I have is the ultimate hurricane. We're going to get it one of these days, and it's going to alter this town severely. It has in the past, and it's going to do it again."

After Hurricane Gilbert hit the charming Mexican fishing village on Cozumel, the historic place was rebuilt with new money. It became a caricature of itself, both faux-antique and severely modern. Cozumel lost its charm. Something similar could happen in Aransas County.

Johnny Atwood said, "We have an opportunity to try to slow all this down, to try to do something about it. I hope we take the opportunity *not* to make this a 'glitzy' place. We have people, I think, who would like to have it resemble a Florida resort with the palm trees and plastic pink flamingoes. But I think the very thing that attracted people here in the first place is the style of life which is pretty laid-back.

"I see a trend away from that at this point, and I hope that it doesn't continue." Johnny spoke for many who shared their feelings while this book was in progress. "As we lose the people who knew the town as it was—not primitive, but the charm of the old town—as we get more and more people in here who are short-timers and they have a new idea of what they think the place ought to be, it's going to be a hard problem to keep this thing from changing too radically. Now there's a generation of people who have to have their comforts—air-conditioning, sheets changed every night, pampered. Me, I'd prefer to have something away from that. Clean, but not sterile."

Nature and a rich history are the great gifts that Aransans have received. The county offers them, in return, to travelers from around the world.

NATURE AND HERITAGE

ECOLOGY

Throughout the 1930s, Aransas had a growing sense of the need to protect her native wealth, and as early as 1932 President Franklin Roosevelt had seen preservation work as part of the solution to the nation's economic depression. His Civilian Conservation Corps, designed to employ idle youth in the husbandry of wasted resources, finally reached Aransas in 1938.

The Aransas CCC boys had 47,215 acres to work on. The Aransas Migratory Waterfowl Refuge, precursor of Aransas National Wildlife Refuge, had been established on the last day of 1937.

The boys built shell roads, cleared brush to reduce the possibility of fires, built dams at Barkentine Creek and Bill Mott Bayou. They built residences, a boathouse, the Lookout Tower, baths. They made signs to mark the Refuge boundary and constructed brick walks. The boys helped Refuge Manager James O. Stevenson collect plant specimens for a research project; they counted deer for him as they drove across the range.

Those crews were not the only ones on Blackjack Peninsula; Continental Oil Company was drilling. When a well on Little Devil Bayou "went wild," the CCC and Continental worked together to prevent damage. Then Continental offered help with road building. A long and amicable relationship began between interests often assumed to be at odds.

In 1931 private owners deeded portions of the Lamar peninsula for the Goose Island State Recreation Area. The park's entrance ran beside Neptune Mound, created when Murdoch McRae left an old ship in the bayou between Goose Island and the peninsula. The

357

CCC boys built fine, broad shelters on the shoreline and campsites back in the oak trees.

World War II ended all the CCC projects, but its lasting effects have enhanced Aransas County.

Old-timers, watching work at the Refuge, remembered flocks of birds. They remembered stories of ancestors who had lived off seemingly inexhaustible supplies of them. All that had changed. CCC boys never saw the rich avian life enjoyed by the first settlers.

When James Power's colony was new, stout-winged whooping cranes by the thousands had risen annually from their native marshes in Saskatchewan, Canada, and made their awesome migratory flight to Aransas. In less than one hundred years—in 1922—only thirty-five of the migrant birds could be accounted for. Two years after that, the Rio Grande Valley recorded its last. The whoopers were all gone from the upper Texas coast in 1936. By 1937, the King Ranch migrant whooper population was gone, and all the marshland of Louisiana held just twelve of the great cranes. Eighteen remained in the Blackjacks.

James Stevenson, Refuge manager at that time, said: "One of the saddest tragedies of natural history has befallen the whooping crane. For some reason, they seem doomed to extinction. We are trying to afford them every possible protection. . . ."

If modern Refuge managers are more hopeful, it may be because they have better information to aid them in combatting the problems. Resident Refuge naturalists Wayne and Martha McAlister summarized the obstacles in their guidebook to the Refuge. Their explanation included these points:

Whooping cranes don't produce enough young to offset the risks of their lifestyle and secure the propagation of their species. A pair of adult cranes broods only two eggs each season, but the chicks' competition for food and attention is so fierce that usually only the older one survives. That chick is vulnerable to predators and severe weather.

There are the problems of migration, as well. Some birds simply are not strong enough to make the trip; others run afoul of power lines or are shot by careless hunters.

During Stevenson's time, other birds were disappearing too. In

1935 only 1000 brown pelicans remained in all of Texas. The Attwa-ter prairie chicken—named for the old professor who displayed his stuffed birds in the Aransas Hotel and in a car of the SAAP rail-road—was nearly extinct. A mere 8,700 of them scrabbled through prairies where once clouds had risen as horsemen rode by. Hunting the delicious hen-like coastal bird was forbidden in 1937.

At Lamar officials sought to protect the Big Tree by building a fence around it in 1936. John Dunman, who worked as a wood cutter nearby, said that the fence was made from the great oak's own limbs.

That same year, Dr. Albert Collier established a biological lab. Ten years later, the *Pilot* reported that Rockport was to have a $25,000 marine laboratory. Located at the south end of the seawall, the laboratory was home to Doctors Joel Hedgpeth and Gordon Gunter, who would study the problems of commercial fishermen on the Texas coast. Later, the facility added a small aquarium.

Just a week after the lab opened, the Game, Fish and Oyster Commission began levying fines on oil-transporting vessels and tankers that pumped oil into Coastal Bend waters. Aransas, at last, was ecologically aware, although then, as now, not everyone agreed with preservation tactics.

In 1987 the City of Rockport, aware that development threat-ened its landmark oak trees, passed an ordinance to protect them. Any builder was required to obtain a permit to cut down or remove any tree with a circumference of sixty inches or more (a diameter of fourteen inches). A committee of city officials—two city staff members and the directors of Public Works, Parks, Planning and Zoning, and Building—worked with builders to determine if con-struction might somehow avoid a given tree; they gave permission to cut it down only where absolutely necessary. In such cases, mit-igating action was required.

In 1996 a new ordinance upgraded the original. Its stated pur-pose was "for preservation and enhancement of the natural seaside forest of Rockport." The ordinance guards the rights of individuals while protecting all varieties of trees six inches in diameter and four-and-one-half feet tall. The committee of decision-makers was

George Nava, Earl Slocum and Capt. M. B. "Pug" Mullinax (left to right, aboard the Game and Fish Commission boat) visit Harbor Island in the early 1950's. The place bears no resemblance to the tree-covered island described by explorer Béranger.
—Courtesy of Shirley Ratisseau Collection

altered to include three citizens at large (at least one a horticulturist or other expert) and members of the Parks and the Planning and Zoning boards. Citizens have enthusiastically accepted the ordinance and are often eager to move trees at their own expense, rather than cut them down.

ANTHROPOLOGY

Had any of the Cópanes survived in Aransas, they might have been heartened by the attempts to protect their environment; indigenes often value their land more than newcomers do.

The 1919 hurricane had uncovered some artifacts of Cópane life, stirring the curiosity of George C. Martin and Wendell H. Potter. During the 1930s, the men marked Cópane campsites along the shores of Aransas and Copano bays, then presented their *Preliminary Archaeological Survey of a Portion of the Texas Coast*. In 1961 William W. Newcomb, Jr., published his illuminating book, *The In-*

dians of Texas From Prehistoric to Modern Times. Thoughtful readers began to understand indigene life in a more complete way.

When Aransas began making plans for a highway bypass route, Al McGraw, archaeologist with the Texas Highway Design Division, opened an investigation into a shell midden extending more than sixty-five yards along the water's edge, just behind the airport. Like the nearby oilfield, the dig took on the name Kent-Crane.

The midden contained remains from two distinct cultural periods between 2000 B.C. and 1250 A.D., and McGraw considered it one of the top three sites in coastal archaeology. But the shoreline was eroding. "In another ten years," McGraw said, "the site won't be there." And indeed by the spring of 1997 much of the old shoreline had fallen into the bay.

Local citizens pressed for a decision on their highway in the early 1980s, and the site was placed on the National Register of Historic Places. It was thus provided some protection from souvenir-hunters as well as from highway construction.

Artifactors—primarily amateur arrow-head hunters—were excited by the site. They began to look for Cópane potsherds and flint points all along the Aransas coast.

In 1996 Robert A. Ricklis published *The Karánkawa Indians*, a scholarly work. Dr. Thomas R. Hester, who had collaborated with Herman Smith on other Karánkawa investigations, edited the book and wrote its Foreword. Hester described Karánkawas as "the most maligned and misunderstood Native American peoples who once inhabited Texas." He said that Ricklis allows us "to see the Karánkawas as a native population responding to normal human patterns of adaptation."

Ricklis detailed the manner of Karánkawa adjustment to European newcomers, then expanded the thesis in his book's final pages: "The Karánkawas' case, though only a single study, appears to offer support from a long-term historical perspective for the view that viable change can occur only within the framework of ecological tradition." He went on to say, in effect, that we have become a global village, wherein the humane approach to intercultural relations might be based on real needs, and where awareness of tradition might affect the manner in which we introduce change.

ENDANGERED SPECIES

Today, as in the past, cultures and species collide. Still, we have no easy answers as to which ones shall prevail.

On a hot June day in 1991, the Hawes family gathered on Matagorda Island. All were descendants of Col. Hugh Walker Hawes, who settled on Matagorda and started ranching in 1839; some were direct descendants of James Power. The reunited family members were not celebrating heritage nor the approaching Independence Day; they were giving up. The Hawes family faced a July 7 deadline to vacate their land.

Brent Gietzentanner, Aransas Refuge manager with the United States Fish and Wildlife Service, had ruled cattle grazing incompatible with the island's plant and animal life. The cattle trampled sand dunes, he said; they dried up ponds where invertebrate species might thrive; they destroyed native grasses.

Seventy-year-old Joe Hawes looked at waist-high grass. "After all this time, to say that cattle or sheep are not compatible with wildlife is a silly, stupid thing," he said. Joe had spent fifty years— his entire married life—fighting the inevitable. He called that day "the end of an era."

The problem began in 1943, when the United States government took over Matagorda Island for military use, paying the Hawes family seven dollars an acre—a dollar and a half above the current market rate. According to Joe Hawes, his father Lloyd felt he had no choice but to accept the money. There was no written contract, and the land was never returned to Hawes, who received a 9,000-acre grazing permit annually.

While the Hawes family's land on the north end of the island was condemned, the south end, owned by Toddie Lee Wynne, Jr., was not. The Wynne family built an airstrip large enough for multi-engine airplane use during the war, and later sold the ranch to the Texas Nature Conservancy.

Matagorda became a federal wildlife refuge in the late 1970s, and Gietzentanner issued his ruling regarding the Hawes cattle ten years later. "I've lost a lot of sleep over this," he said. "It's so unfortunate that my job is creating so much pain for one family."

In the Hawes ranch house, women dipped up glasses of iced tea and lemonade, pared potatoes for salad, deveined shrimp, and prepared brisket for barbecue. Men drank beer in the shade outside. Tiny Victor David Huber slumbered. His mother, Lydia Ann Hawes Huber, promised to tell him about that day, and all the Hawes island days before.

"This is . . . a bad, bad day," said Evelyn Hawes Carroll, age seventy-three. "If I could have just one little acre, I'd come back and spend my last days here."

Today nesting terns enjoy the air force runway. Tourists, brought to Matagorda Island by ferry, are shuttled past them on the way to the Gulf beach. Along the way, they might see rattlesnakes, raccoons, deer, coyotes, feral hogs, horned toads, and alligators. A federal official called Matagorda a paradise for endangered species.

ORNITHOLOGIST CONNIE HAGAR

On June 14, 1886, two years before the railroad arrived in Rockport, Martha Conger Neblett was born in Corsicana, Texas. In time, Connie would create a stir of equal proportion.

By 1935 Connie had convinced her husband Jack Hagar to move to Aransas so that she could enjoy the birds. Jack bought the Rockport Cottages on Church Street and remodeled them. Soon his eight small cabins were filled, spring and fall, with birders eager to join Connie in watching the migrations.

Birds were almost the only thing Connie Hagar cared about— just her birds, her husband, her dog Fuzzy. The diminutive woman gave nature talks. She wrote birding articles for the *Rockport Pilot* and then for the *San Antonio Express*. In May 1936 the *Express* gave her a five-column headline: "Texas Gulf Coast is Haven for Bird Life."

Before long, Connie had a protegé—Annie Ruth Jackson of the seafood family, granddaughter of Irene Norvell. They worked at the sometimes-difficult skill of identifying birds. Once Connie said to Annie Ruth, "People are always saying how smart I am. Well, the truth is, I'm not really smart, I'm just a sticker. I stick on a problem until things unfold." It was a trait that would win Connie Hagar international acclaim.

The great men of the birding world responded skeptically to Connie's claims of sightings in Aransas, but her detailed notes on observations and her careful research convinced them, one by one, of the rich bird life in Aransas.

In 1945 the Texas Legislature designated Little Bay as the Connie Hagar Wildlife Sanctuary. Subsequently, the sanctuary was expanded. Its boundary line runs along the Aransas Bay shoreline to the southern Rockport city limit. There it turns east, stretches one mile into the bay, and heads north. At a point even with Fulton Harbor, the line turns west, then follows the shore south, back to Little Bay.

Awareness of Aransas' avian wealth increased through the 1950s, while the Continental Oil Company was again active in the Blackjacks. Some called it the "whooping cranes' oilfield." Field superintendent Austin B. Taylor, Jr., quipped: "My drilling program was based on the mating habits of the whooping cranes."

When the Navigation District put Frandolig Island up for sale in 1961, Emory Spencer, Thomas Picton, and James Sorenson, Jr., had spoken in favor of the action, but Attorney General Will Wilson, State Land Commissioner Jerry Sadler, and the Welder Wildlife Foundation opposed it. They asked that the island be kept for public use. Wildlife conservationists worried that the nesting grounds of native birds might be endandered by Carl Krueger's resort project. Development won.

The irony Connie Hagar saw in that was personal. Her husband Jack believed—as Chambers of Commerce members often do—that bigger is better, and growth is the goal.

Connie was grim when she saw a sign erected at the entrance to the new canal community project: *KEY ALLEGRO: A Birdwatcher's Paradise*. "But it was a birdwatcher's paradise when it was Frandolig Island," she mourned. Connie remembered grass and brush, a few small trees. She remembered the island at nesting time, home to herons, egrets, ibises, least bitterns, and willets. She remembered it in winter, haven for shorebirds and waders. "I learned so much on that island," she said.

The Aransas County Navigation District approved a developer's application for yet another subdivision in March 1971. Abutting Little Bay, it would cover a broad marshland that ran behind Palm Village and almost up to Forest Park Cottages. Woodstorks had gathered there in summer, rails arrived in winter. Again, environmentalists and proponents of progress angrily confronted each other. The protesters lost, and work began on Harbor Oaks.

"It was too valuable a piece of property," Judge John Wendell said. "I mean, I don't think a bird knows the difference between a $16,000 lot and a $160 lot. To me, it's a lot of damn foolishness. I don't believe in killing birds and destroying their nests, but I think they can be put in

Connie Hagar and Fuzzy depart on a birding mission.
—Photo by Edwin Teale/ Aransas County Public Library

places where they will thrive as well as in a spot that holds maybe a third of the valuation of the county. You know you've got to have tax dollars to perform."

Wendell said that the Navigation District played a very important part in Aransas County's development. "We have Cove Harbor, the Fulton Harbor, the Rockport Harbor, the Ski Basin, and adjacent Key Allegro, on a waterway partially man-made by the Navigation District."

Connie Hagar's body gave up in 1973, but her spirit lives. Perhaps her influence is best summed up by a scroll that the National Audubon Society presented to her in 1962:
>"You opened our eyes to that great miracle of the natural world, the migration of birds;
>
>You enriched our knowledge by patient, open-minded and courageous observation and reporting of facts—so many of them unbelievable;
>
>In your selfless devotion to the truths of Nature, you have literally discovered the link between heaven and earth;
>
>You stood so straight among the wind-bent trees of your coast that you saw what others before you failed to see."

In 1963 the coast harbored only fifty brown pelicans. Four years later, the count of Attwater prairie chickens had fallen to 1,000. But that same year, the Aransas Refuge added 7,568 acres to its territory, and in 1969 the owners of San José Island barred commercial beach seiners.

Only one brown pelican was raised on the entire Texas coast in

1972. The following year—the year that Connie Hagar died—Congress passed an Endangered Species Act and placed the pelicans on the list. Attwater's prairie chicken was also designated as endangered.

By 1983, the Aransas Refuge, enlarged yet again, reported two healthy nesting colonies of brown pelicans in San Antonio and Corpus Christi bays; banning the insecticide DDT had helped pelican eggshells grow strong. The next year, pelicans fledged 230 young, and fifteen whooping cranes made a winter home at the Refuge.

But the prairie chicken was reported closer to extinction—only forty-two birds in the wild, down from one million in Texas and Louisiana a century before.

Today, the numbers generally are much better. One hundred and forty-five whooping cranes arrived at the Aransas Refuge for their 1996-1997 season. Recent data suggests that expenditures to protect them in their summer and winter habitats amount to $330,000 per bird. It is unquestionably a hefty sum. Perhaps we pay such money as a token apology for all the ecological damage we've done. In any case, visitors come away with some hope that humankind really can save the creatures it has put in jeopardy, even some of the most fragile ones. And Aransas? It takes great pride in being the winter home of the whooper—and pride in taking part in the creatures' sheer existence.

In 1988 Jesse Grantham, National Audubon's Texas Sanctuary Manager, proposed a novel idea for Aransas—a Hummer/Bird Celebration. Betty Baker took the suggestion to the Rockport-Fulton Area Chamber of Commerce, which eagerly embraced the idea.

Two hundred birders attended the first festival in September and their numbers rapidly climbed—topping 5,000 in 1996. Visitors come from many parts of the United States and Canada. Some are expert birders; others are simply people who want to know more about nature in general. The Hummer/Bird Celebration boosts Aransas economy during a slack time in the tourist year. School lets out for a day so its auditorium and cafeteria can provide lecture and display space for the crowds.

School involvement shows up in other ways too. For years, high-schoolers held a homecoming bonfire at the north end of the

Rockport Beach Park, constructed in 1988. But when black skimmers roosted late in the season, the students were glad to give up their tradition rather than risk injury to the nesting birds.

Near the former bonfire site rises a tall pole—the one the Sorensons used to fly hurricane flags. Now it is the base for a Christmas Tree of Lights. On either side of it, four pavilions stand, their shape reminiscent of the one Henry Bailey had built almost a century before.

Throughout the 1990s, captains of fishing boats learned a new use for their knowledge of the bays. In the off-season, some become tour guides, ferrying birders to the wildlife refuge and the rookery islands.

Connie Hagar's Rockport Cottages are no more. The site on South Church Street is bare, only a tangle of brush and grass. An organization called Friends of Connie Hagar owns the lot and maintains it as a sort of motel to transient birds, and a wandering spot for nature lovers.

On September 7, 1995, Roger Tory Peterson—ultimate authority on birding, twice nominated for the Nobel Prize and holder of twenty-two honorary doctorates—came to the Connie Hagar Cottage Sanctuary. There he dedicated the first stop on the Great Texas Coastal Birding Trail, designed to link birding sites along a 500-mile stretch of Texas coast.

Peterson acknowledged that the trail should have a formidable economic impact on Texas, but beyond that, he said, "it is clearly and unequivocally the right thing to do." Peterson described birding as an exceptional means of communicating with nature. "It can be a science, an art, a recreation, an ethic or a sport," he said. "It can even be a religious experience."

Connie Hagar knew that. She was a sticker—and she made a difference in Aransas.

NO NEW THING UNDER THE SUN

Aransas had existed long enough to have a history and for that history to repeat itself. A newspaper sportswriter described his experience at the Port Bay Club as "hunting in a time warp."

Hometown boys continued to seek summer girls, and the girls

welcomed their attention. One young man gave his name simply as "Coon," and when San Antonio girls went home they addressed mail to him that way—just "Coon, Rockport, Texas." He always got their letters.

Many boys found the curving road through Palm Village a perfect cruising lane. Lola Bracht's son, Winston Woellert, met Sallye Trautschold there, vacationing from Dallas, and he married her in 1949. Some years later Pat Smith, the Harbormaster's son, met Carol Proll of San Antonio on that same road; they married in 1956.

According to "Coon," most hometown girls of that era would have preferred to wither on the vine rather than chase after boys. But some girls met navy boys or tourists and married them. A few of the couples, like the Woellerts and the Smiths, live in Rockport today.

The Schoenstatt Sisters of Mary had acquired the Lamar property James Byrne gave to his church so long before. Their movement sought "to dare a step further into the world and to serve the Church in places and occupations which the former orders and congregations could not reach." Stella Maris—the tiny chapel proposed by James Byrne, contracted by Murdoch McRae, built of shellcrete by white settlers and at least one slave—was restored in 1931, as the shellcrete homes of Lamar crumbled around it.

Later, when the Sisters of House Schoenstatt built a new chapel, they gave the Lamar Women's Club permission to use Stella Maris for interdenominational worship. The old church returned, in a way, to its beginning.

In 1972 Dennis O'Connor sent a $10,000 check from the Kathryn O'Connor Foundation to make additional repairs on the chapel. By then another church had organized at Lamar, so Stella Maris was little visited, other than as a tourist attraction. House Schoenstatt wanted the church's land to enlarge their retreat center.

The Aransas County Historical Society assumed the brave task of moving 128-year-old Stella Maris—twenty feet wide and thirty-six feet long, with shellcrete walls fourteen inches thick—to a new home.

The chapel made the trip intact. People of the community, as long before, shared in the labor of making it beautiful. Since 1986,

Stella Maris has overlooked the Lamar Cemetery graves of many who worshipped within its walls.

Some things are past redemption, however, and the county courthouse seemed to be one of them. Judge John Wendell called it a "real picturesque architectural monstrosity" that wasn't doing its job. Every time a jet airplane came in from the Gulf and broke the sound barrier, Wendell's desk was littered with plaster, as was every other desk in the courthouse.

Further, Wendell was concerned because the district courtroom was on the second floor, inaccessible to elderly people or those in wheelchairs. According to Wendell, architects and engineers surveyed the building but found no way to remedy its many problems.

But Jim Furlong got San Antonio architects Richard Colley and O'Neil Ford to take a look. They reported nothing wrong with the courthouse structurally—other than a lack of maintenance. "Someone had deliberately removed a cover over an access hole into the attic so that the weather could come in," Jim claimed.

He represented a sizeable group of people who loved and wanted to preserve the courthouse, but in the end, a majority of citizens agreed with Judge Wendell. The landmark, and the jail beside it, would be razed. Sentimental or avaricious Aransans bought the courthouse furnishings at auction in 1955, and then the old building came down. Its stone went for riprap to protect an eroding shore.

The next year Aransas County's healthy tax base paid for a new building, pale brick and one story tall, sprawled in place of the outdated Moorish design. "It's plain vanilla," Jim Furlong said. "It would be all right someplace else."

During an interview in 1971, Judge Wendell repeated history more than he might have realized. Keenly aware that the Intracoastal Canal played a major role in offshore drilling activities and in the shrimping industry of Aransas County, he said: "If it wasn't for the Intracoastal Canal, large boats could not come into Cove

Harbor or into the Rockport area. It's the hope of the Navigation District that this channel will be deepened."

If Aransas County failed to get deep water, Wendell worried, Port Aransas might become the stronger shrimping port. "It is a must that Aransas County get twelve to fourteen feet of water in order to compete," he said.

"There is an attempt now to deepen water from Port Aransas to Aransas Pass to Conn Brown harbor. There's no reason why we can't get ships—or the smaller ships—up the Intracoastal Canal toward Rockport within the next fifteen or twenty years. This could develop as a large port for foreign shipping.

"Because there is a causeway from Aransas Pass to Port Aransas, and the Intracoastal Canal is on the Rockport/Aransas County side, all the deep development will come into the area that is Aransas County. . . . We feel that the area from the lighthouse on into Cove Harbor will develop, will be a tremendous port.

"San José Island . . . will [probably] be a private development, and I hope it stays that way. Padre Island and Mustang Island will be a national seashore, and I feel that's enough mileage. Maybe it's selfish, but I like to see private enterprise develop properly. Naturally, private enterprise will put tax money into Aransas County."

John Wendell's dream echoed Pryor Lea's in the 1850s. Rockport citizens invested in such a hope after the Civil War. The Corps of Engineers was involved by 1880, and Rockport's David Picton took on the jetty job. In 1910 the Gulf Coast Immigration Company envisioned tourists boarding ocean liners in Rockport. Heldenfels shipbuilders dredged across Murray Shoal.

Others, too, will carry that dream. In the spring of 1997, a newspaper headlined Corpus Christi's interest in the cruise-line industry.

For one day—September 9, 1982—residents of Aransas became part of the Space Age. They were already accustomed to grandiose activity on San José and Matagorda; they had been party to barging building supplies to the islands and barging fattened cattle back. They had observed the comings and goings of the rich and famous—which has now included presidents from Franklin Roosevelt to George Bush—at the island retreats of Clint Murchison and Sid Richardson. But even the Aransans involved in that would never have imagined the 1982 turn of events.

They watched from boats and rooftops as the world's first private-sector space rocket—*Conestoga I*—hurtled with a roar and great plume of smoke up from Matagorda Island. It broke the boundary of outer space, then travelled down-range some two hundred and seventy miles. Mission director and astronaut "Deke" Slayton deemed the launch a complete success and the beginning of a new industry.

Funded primarily by Toddie Lee Wynne, it was a reprise of every dreamer-speculator project launched throughout the history of Aransas. After the rocket blast, the islands lay silent again. Guarded by both state and private preservationists, Matagorda and San José remain special sanctuaries—as natural and unchanged as they are unpredictable.

In 1973 Charles C. Butt had purchased the 116-year-old lighthouse on Lydia Ann Channel and began its restoration. By 1988, Rick Pratt was the keeper, and the light shines again each night. Invited guests enjoy the lighthouse lodge as a base for hunting and fishing expeditions.

On the Columbus Day weekend of 1975, Rockport instituted a new celebration of the bay—SeaFair. Bill Christian, a Key Allegro builder and Chamber of Commerce director, said that he conceived it as a "fun party for everyone, but primarily as a means of showing off to tourists the wonders of the seaside resort town." SeaFair featured—and features still—seafood, a craft sale, entertainment, and a big parade. Gordon Stanley and others exhibited antique outboard motors and fishing equipment.

Each year the marine exhibits became a bigger and more popular attraction, leading Christian and a group of hard-working volunteers to dream of a maritime museum. They worked for several years to raise money; they leased Navigation District land near the harbor; they won state designation as The Texas Maritime Museum. Ultimately, though, it was the fund-raising ability of local banker

James Sorenson, Jr., that built the museum's impressive Sorenson Building, transforming dream into reality.

Ten years later, Texas Maritime Museum curator Andrew W. Hall had an interesting proposition for the members. He had been approached by Rick Pratt, the Aransas Lighthouse keeper, who hoped that volunteers at the museum might build and display an old-fashioned scow fishing sloop. There were none left to buy, since the fishermen's long gill nets had been outlawed in 1952.

From the Museum's membership and the Rockport Sailing Club, from Aransas Pass, Houston and San Antonio as well as Rockport, Andy gathered thirty volunteers. And he solicited funds to pay for materials.

Rick Pratt had already found Miguél "Mike" Garza, Jr., a master boatbuilder in Corpus Christi who agreed to supervise the work. "I started to make these boats when I was very small," said fifty-seven-year-old Miguél. He remembered working on the boats in Port Isabel with both his father and grandfather. From the early 1920s, his family would build a boat, fish from it for a while, then sell it and build another.

Miguél did not need plans to build the museum's sloop. "This is from my memory. We used to make it, and I know how to make it." He only asked "How long do you want the boat?" When Andy answered, "thirty feet," Miguél rattled off a series of dimensions and set to work. Throughout the project, he made few measurements and never used drawings of any kind.

The volunteers, who agreed to use only the hand tools that had been available to an earlier generation, started to work on April 1. They made the frame and rudder of fir; the tiller came from a tree that had fallen in Miguél's yard after a freeze. Planks, sides, and decking were cypress. When a fir beam purchased for the mast split too badly to be used, Miguél suggested using a thirty-foot telephone pole. Miguél said a mast should always be as tall as a boat was long.

A professional sailmaker made the eighteen-gauge canvas mainsail and jib, but volunteers did all the lacing by hand, sewing rings at the reef points and edges of each sail. Although the project did not include making nets, the Garza family had made theirs by hand, as well. The scows were used only for fish, not shrimp, because a boat needed power to open the doors on the shrimp nets, Miguél said.

School children submitted names for the boat, and the winner was Rode Roberts, who suggested *La Tortuga* to honor his pet turtle.

After seven months of weekend work, Miguél and his volunteers launched the scow sloop on November 15, 1990. *La Tortuga* drew sixteen inches of water and could make fifteen knots with a good wind of twenty to thirty-five miles per hour. After just one voyage—to the lighthouse and back—she was dry-docked on the museum grounds.

The Texas Maritime Museum preserves other memories in a quiet side room of the Sorenson Building. There volunteers for the William A. Mann Library and Center for Oral History enable old-timers to record their invaluable tales.

Key Allegro has no further room for growth. Builders have begun tearing down or radically renovating some early, modest beach cottages. Wealthy people from Houston and San Antonio want palaces, just as Realtor Dickinson predicted in 1930.

All around town, people are buying the old houses and altering them, sometimes so severely that the original styles are difficult to recognize. The character that the homes once had is lost. Certainly, people want convenient, modern kitchens and such, but—traditionalists argue—it should be feasible to retain the facades. It should be possible for new owners to honor the treasures they have bought.

Newcomers have purchased business properties too. They bought cheap during the Oil Depression, speculating on future growth. When a listener demurs, "I see Aransas the way it used to be," the newcomers respond: "We see it the way it is *going* to be."

Some old-timers see these entrepreneurs as freebooters, come to town again—freebooters who know the price of everything and the value of nothing.

In 1976 the Texas Department of Parks and Wildlife purchased the Fulton Mansion, answering Harriet Fulton's dream: A millionaire who loved hunting and fishing would restore the house. One year later, TPW purchased an additional parcel of land at the southeast corner of the Mansion property. It includes the original approach to the mansion and the "Old Surveyor's Oak." The tree was marked with an X in the 1830s and served as a frame of reference for mapping that part of Live Oak Peninsula.

Once the Mansion was beautifully restored and furnished, the TPW staff trained volunteer docents to lead tours. The house seems lived in. Fresh flowers highlight a table one day, a bureau the day after, in a tall vase or a round bowl. One imagines that Harriet Fulton may have placed them there on a whim, just a moment ago. Sometimes the dining table is set one way, sometimes another. Who is coming to dinner?

One anonymous docent got the "scare of my life," she said. It was her second tour of the day. She'd already noted the changes—Harriet's brush left out on the vanity table, George's slippers by the bed.

The Holden bedroom looked tidy; apparently neither Fulton daughter was in residence. As the docent approached that room again, she was already into her routine comments. She faltered when she saw a coat and hat and parasol flung carelessly across the table. How did they get there? "Those girls," the docent finally stammered. "They never put their things away."

The docent left it at that, even after she saw the handler of the mysterious items. It was the curator, working in a corner out of the tourists' sight.

Each Christmas, the house sparkles with new vitality. Docents and staff bustle about, moving furniture, lugging boxes from storage. As the decorations take shape, someone steps back, looks at the scene, and utters the traditional phrase: "This is the prettiest our tree has ever been." Surely, Harriet nods, smiling.

But by the late 1990s, some of the gleam was gone. The State's oil-revenue-depleted coffers could not afford intensive maintenance for the grand old Mansion. Citizens echoed Harriet Fulton's cry: "It does seem too bad for the place to go to complete ruin for want of paint." Docents and others formed "Friends of the Fulton Mansion" to address the problem.

In the spring of 1992, two sailing ships hovered just outside the Aransas pass. They were waiting for another, habitually the slowest. When she arrived, the *Niña, Pinta,* and *Santa Maria* sailed between San José and Mustang Islands and past Harbor Island, no longer covered with trees. On March 7, the *Corpus Christi Caller-Times* reported:

"The U.S. Coast Guard issued strict controls on boaters and others who plan to view three replicas of Christopher Columbus' ships scheduled to arrive in Corpus Christi Bay next week. The safety and security zones established are needed to safeguard the vessels against sabotage. Members of the American Indian Movement have vowed to try and stop the ships. They say Columbus should not be celebrated as a hero."

Columbus, of course, is only a symbol of exploration. Even without him, the European instinct for conquest and expansion would have reached this shore. There would have been people like de Vaca, Béranger, LaSalle, Lafitte and all the settlers who made Aransas what it is today.

THE ARTS
IN VARIED FORMS

As Aransas progressed, there was time for richness to feed the soul. By the mid-1930s, Judy Sorenson Collier had started a private library in the building immediately south of the Sorenson Chandlery. Local children "rented" Big Little Books for a few cents a day and loved to flip the pages to produce a moving picture story.

In 1956 the Woman's Club of Aransas County decided the library should go public. Arthur Bracht had just built a new store in Fulton, so he donated his old one to the cause, and a community drive brought in 2,000 books. Bracht supplied orange and apple crates to shelve them. In six months, the library had 3,500 books. As the need for a permanent home for the library became increasingly evident, the Woman's Club addressed the Aransas County Commissioners and got a small room in the courthouse. The Club purchased lumber for shelves, and Julia West served as first librarian. She was replaced by the first full-time paid librarian, Mrs. C. C. Atchley. In 1988 the library moved again, to a freestanding modern facility. It contains Aransas County's official law library, donated by Mrs. Emory Spencer.

That same year, two Rockport couples, interested in the folk art of square-dancing, signed up for a class in Aransas Pass. They were so excited by what they experienced that they invited all their friends to a square dance party in their garage. Almost everyone there wanted lessons, so Blackie Hardy came from Corpus Christi to teach.

The group rapidly grew from six squares to twelve and ran out of space, so the determined square dancers raised a barn-like structure of natural-finished wood. It stood on the Fulton bayfront between Fulton and Palmetto streets, and the dancers called it Paws and Taws.

The meaning of the term is obscure. Locals say that the words refer to men and their women partners. One old Webster's confirms "taw" as a square dance partner, and another defines "paw" as a quick or clever movement— "grab your partner," perhaps.

The couples who danced at Paws and Taws paid for their building in just two years by taking turns manning a filling station. Since then, the building has been moved several blocks north and changed ownership. Winter visitors meet there; local groups rent the hall for private functions. But the original purpose continues. Up to 240 people visit Fulton for fourteen big square-dancing weekends each year, a significant boost to the Aransas economy.

Among the men and women who come from miles around to enjoy line dancing are Lucile Fagan, direct descendant of Nicholas Fagan, and her husband Tommy Snider. They drive down from their ranch on the San Antonio River every Thursday night. Couples dance the old steps, straight-faced, so solemn that one would think they weren't enjoying themselves. The look is part of the art.

Square-dancing has roots in old Irish dances, and some of the tunes at Paws and Taws could make James Power feel right at home. But if Aransas was to have a renaissance of the culture Jane O'Connor had created with her academy, citizens needed to look to other art forms as well. The natural beauty of Aransas dictated what those forms would be.

SIMON MICHAEL

When Simon Michael moved down the coast from Port Lavaca in 1948, he was a strange fit for Aransas. Born of a Phonecian-Syrian-Lebanese line, son of a priest, twice married and twice divorced, Michael was a world traveler, a painter of nude women. But he purchased a fifteen-room house on Fulton beach and established the Fulton School of Painting. Michael patterned it after a Cape Cod colony that had produced some of America's top artists.

Painters were avid to study with him. From that Fulton base, Simon Michael held weekly classes at Palacios, Bay City, Victoria, Goliad, Yoakum, and Rockport. He also traveled intermittently to teach at Corpus Christi, Beeville, Cuero, Schulenburg, Fredricksburg, Brazosport, Freeport, Lake Jackson, and Clute.

In 1950 Michael purchased five acres on King Street in Rockport. He cleared brush around old oaks and built a home. When hordes of pretty young women arrived for workshops with the handsome and self-assured newcomer, gossip ran rampant. Some Aransans threatened Michael, damaged his property, urged the "artist fellow" to move on.

Michael stayed. He bought a thirty-five-foot cabin cruiser, named it *Rambler*, and took students aboard a floating art school. "Don't paint pictures," he told them. "Paint experiences!"

When Michael deemed his students' work ready for an exhibition, he offered the townspeople free barbecue along with an opportunity to view the art. Two thousand citizens could not overcome their curiosity. Afterward, leaving Simon Michael's studio, some may have been a little confused by his wild, bright canvasses, but others were stirred by feelings of youth and vigor.

Simon Michael's studio grew. He added wings to the house and filled them with an energetic hodgepodge of wood furniture, copper buckets, iron tools, clay jugs. Michael treasured things made by hand, but what he started in Aransas goes far beyond the tangible.

ESTELLE STAIR AND THE ART ASSOCIATION

Her first name means "star," and her country pronounciation of her last name sounded like "star" as well. One might say that Estelle Stair was the lucky star of the growing art colony in Aransas.

Arriving in Rockport close on Simon Michael's heels, she was both his student and his employee. Like Michael, she was an en-

Simon Michael, grand old man of the Rockport art community.

—Courtesy of Simon Michael

courager, a confidence-builder. Like Connie Hagar, she was persistent.

In 1967 Estelle joined Jan Wendell and other local artists to organize the Rockport Art Association. A few years later, the members decided they needed a gallery, so banker James Sorenson, Jr., allowed them to use the old Thompson's Spa restaurant. The gallery operated there for several years. The Thompson's Spa building was sold. The Art Association negotiated with Tom Rogers and Fred Bracht and found a new home in the old Bracht Store on Austin Street at North. Again artists restored an old building with their own hands. "Blood, guts and perseverence led to the art colony in Rockport," Estelle Stair said.

Soon many galleries were opening around town, and members

of the Art Association decided not to compete. Estelle assumed the organization's financial debt and took over its gallery. She assured the Art Association it would always have a home with her.

In 1978 Estelle moved her business into Simon Sorenson's old ship chandlery and grocery. She kept the antique ceiling beams as well as the wood planks that were Simon's first improvement over a dirt floor. The Rockport Art Association moved with her and operated out of that gallery until May 19, 1984.

What happened next was one of those happy events when history comes full circle. The tale turns on Tom O'Connor, grandson and namesake of the young man to whom Nicholas Fagan so unwillingly gave his daughter's hand. This Tom O'Connor was a prominent rancher, oilman, and banker with a home in Victoria, but he loved the coast. In 1943 he had bought Albert Bruhl's old beachfront home between Sabinal, Cedar and Lady Clare streets. His family spent vacations there, adding onto the house from time to time, but retaining its facade.

In the spring of 1983, Tom O'Connor met with members of the Rockport Art Association. He would donate his house to them, he said, if they would move it. Providentially, the association had already purchased property on Navigation Circle, between the harbor and the seawall; they were happy to accept O'Connor's offer.

Fred Wright, an architect and member of the Art Association, volunteered to draw plans which would both preserve the old home's traditional lines and more effectively utilize the interior space. Wright would also oversee the moving and remodeling of the house. Volunteers and professionals worked for months.

The new Rockport Center for the Arts opened its doors with 5,000 square feet of gallery and classroom space. Its first show—eighty-one pieces of art—included painters Jack Cowan, Leon Hale, and Harold Phoenix, and art scholar Michael Frary. The first art class started the next day.

But an old treasure like the Bruhl/O'Connor house is a costly thing to maintain. The Rockport Art Association faced continuing expense, and a celebration of art—a festival—seemed a happy way to raise funds.

CELEBRATION

Rockport had a long tradition of regattas on the Fourth of July. The Art Association, building on the idea of those festivities at the height of the tourist season, put up tents in Navigation Park. Artists sweltered there, but their paintings sold. As the Rockport Art Festival grew, competition for its 125 booths became fierce. The result is an exciting range of styles and media. There are toys and jewelry as well as canvasses in oil and watercolor. There is artistry in pottery, sculpture, fabric, glass, and wood.

The finest Aransas artists, whose reputations reach far beyond Texas, do not sit in hot tents on the Festival grounds. Each year one of them is chosen to provide the Festival poster and that artist has a special showing in the Art Center.

Many noted artists are represented at a reserved-seat Patron Auction that launches the Festival. The bidders know the artists' names and styles as well as they know their own: Evelyn

The Rockport Center for the Arts in the Bruhl/O'Connor house, now located between the harbor and the seawall.
—Photo by Thom Evans

Atkinson and architectural precision; Al Barnes and dramatic moments of sportfishing; Herb Booth and hunting scenes. Art connoisseurs consider granites, massive or playful, from Jesús Bautista Moroles, and light-filled waterfronts from Steve Russell.

On the festival grounds, and in the town's galleries, shoppers find paintings, pottery, glasswork and weaving by more exceptional artists than most of them could name.

Other organizations also contribute activities to the Independence Weekend celebration. On the morning of the Fourth of July, the Rockport Yacht Club sponsors a decorated boat parade; at noon, acrobatic airplanes circle above the Beach Park. In the evening, boats fill Little Bay, and cars crowd the shoreline, to watch the Wendell family's fireworks display.

Rockets light the night sky, celebrating America, celebrating Aransas.

THE PAST AND PRESENT MEET

Near Pass Cavallo, marine archaeologist J. Barto Arnold searched for history. The pass, one of two main entries to the Aransas bay system, was once the border of James Power's colony. For seventeen years, Barto Arnold had crisscrossed bay waters there.

By the summer of 1995, he had reason to hope that his sophisticated electronic equipment had located the oldest vessel ever found in the New World. One hot July day, the first scuba divers went down to find out.

The bottom was only twelve feet below them, but the divers were in "black water"—murky bay water where they could hardly see. They explored with their hands and identified portions of a ship's hull; they picked up musket balls, pottery, a brass buckle, small bronze bells. The divers' breath came faster as they began to think that they might be touching the wreck Barto Arnold had hoped to find.

On the third dive, Chuck Meide and Sarah Keyes went down together. Chuck's hand just happened to fall upon a cylinder with a curved projection, and he could hardly believe what sensation told him. The discovery came too soon; it was too lucky. If he were touching the grip on a cannon, he should find a second handle . . . and there it was. Chuck put his face close and tried to see. He touched lightly with his fingers, as though reading braille. And Chuck concluded that the twin raised loops were in the form of arched, leaping dolphins.

He grasped Sarah's hands and put them on the dolphins, then

patted, to indicate that she should stay put. Chuck groped along the cylinder to its wide end. It cut inward sharply, then it billowed into a ball bigger than Chuck's hands; that was the cannon's cascabel. He felt along the cannon, back to Sarah and past her to the cylinder's narrow end. Chuck's fingers curved over and into the bore. He and Sarah swam together to the surface.

Chuck Meide broke the news. Sarah Keyes, when her turn came, said she had heard him screaming through his scuba regulator, all the time that he explored.

The crew cheered, and when their cheering stopped they settled down to serious planning. Over the next several days, divers excavated around the cannon and rehearsed their moves for lifting it.

On July 13, they brought the treasure to the surface. What Chuck Meide's hands had first explored, eight archaeologists then examined. The dolphin handles were distinctively French. A crest on the cannon identified it almost beyond doubt. Barto Arnold had discovered his dream: the flagship *La Belle*, a gift from the King of France to the great René Robert Cavelier, Sieur de LaSalle, seventeenth century fur trader and explorer of the Mississippi.

It seemed a long time before any of the archaeologists saw much more—there was all that black water. Arnold and his experts decided to build a cofferdam around *La Belle*, pump out the water and recover the artifacts by dry land methods. Their cofferdam is the only one built thus far in saltwater for archaeological purposes. Inside its steel walls, trained men and women began to uncover the past. . . .

AUTHORS' ENDNOTE

. . . It is the summer of 1996. You are a "participating scholar" aboard the archaeologists' crewboat Anomaly, *enroute to the* La Belle *excavation site where you will work. It is an exciting and unexpected part of your research in writing the story of Aransas. You are elated by the book project, but you find it daunting too. How can one tell a story at once so small and so vast?*

Probably, you can't. But you put such abstractions aside for the moment, choosing to live in the miraculous present. As the Anomaly *motors east, you half-believe that the quiet bay and bleak Matagorda*

Island have not changed in three hundred years. It is easy to imagine LaSalle sailing there.

At the cofferdam surrounding La Belle, you videotape the discovery of a copper pot and the cleaning of a hawk's bell. You sift through wet sand and find small beads. You touch history as you never have before. It is an experience so personal that it forever alters your sense of time and place.

Back home, you tap new information about LaSalle into your computer, then pause to look out across the bay. At first glance, a shrimp boat seems to be a barkentine. You drive through town and sense the shadow of buildings no longer standing. By a cemetery stone, or under the branches of an old oak, the constant wind whispers to you like a voice through time.

You imagine a parade out of Aransas' past—ancient hunter-gatherers, early explorers, sturdy pioneers, brave troops in battle, builders of towns, struggling fishermen, survivors of storms, painters of beauty, protectors of nature—residents, all, of a special, charmed place.

Such magic exists in a few other sites, but not many. Each of them, you think, should be preserved.

But is it possible? Is it realistic to hope that expanses of land might never be developed at all? Can we find a resolution to our conflicting needs for conservation and progress?

Long ago, a Basque shepherd saw a vision of the Virgin, supporting her Babe and the globe. Today, in a very real sense, we have taken the world into our own hands, and we hold an awesome responsi-

Windswept oaks.

bility for shaping its future. Before us is a vision of Aransas, sitting in the stickers.

NOTES AND SOURCES

Early in our work on this book, someone asked how we would distinguish between the history of Refugio County and that of Aransas, which was carved from it. The process has seemed simple to us: All relevant Texas history was covered in the early sections, with little regard to county lines at all. Then, as the focus became more distinct, we continued to address those parts of Refugio County that border the bays. They have had, and continue to have, the greatest impact on Aransas. In fact, we found it irresistible to consider Copano Bay and its shore as an entity, unencumbered by county lines. When it was appropriate, that is what we did.

Another problem was place names. How do we handle telling of a Spanish explorer on what is now Harbor Island? When do we refer to our barrier island as San José and when as Saint Joseph? Our decision was an arbitrary one, in favor of the reader. In all cases, we used current place names for their value in orientation and for consistency. Still, it must be noted that most current residents of Aransas County refer to the barrier island not by its politically correct name, but familiarly as "Saint Joe."

The works of Will Durant, Joe B. Frantz, T. R. Fehrenbach, and Hobart Huson regularly provided guidelines, resources, specifics, and wisdom for our work.

Aransas County is the fifth smallest county in the state. It encompasses a total area more than 326 miles square, but much of this is under water. No two agencies come up with the same figure for the land area, probably because of tidal variations, but most suggest something close to 250 square miles.

BOOK ONE
PROLOGUE

Father Cyril Matthew Kuehne provided a definition of the word Aransas in his book *Hurricane Junction*. We use his story of the shepherd's vision. It was confirmed by *Historia de la Virgen y del Santuario de Aranzazu* by R.P. Adrian de Lizanalde.

The Very Reverend Thomas L. Meany also presented origins of the word in his paper "ARANSAS—What is in a Name?" Meany stated that most names in the New World are "traced to the Indian language and its phonetic equivalent in a European tongue. . . . Some say the word Aransas belonged to the Karánkawa Indian dialect. If it did, most likely the Indians were saying something that sounded like a word already familiar to European ears. . . . The settlers of the New World . . . had the habit of naming places after the homes they left behind in Europe."

Father Meany held that Balzátegui did not see a vision; he found a statuette and with it a large cow bell attached to the side of a tree branch. The miraculous discovery is said to have led to a cessation of Basque civil war.

The fourteen-inch stone statue and cow bell that exist in Spain today are of Gothic style, suggesting they date from 500-700 A.D. In her arms, Mary holds her Son and a globe of the world, topped by a cross.

Basques, living in northern Spain and southwestern France, historically have been ardent Roman Catholics, but their speech bears no relation to Romance languages. It may be linked to ancient Iberian, basic Celtic, the Hamito-Semitic group, or Caucasian tongues; no one knows for certain. Of the many languages used in southwestern Europe before the Roman conquest, only Basque continues to be spoken today.

THE BEGINNING

Three highly readable books gave us a scientific orientation to the Coastal Bend. These are: *Shells and Shores of Texas*, Jean Andrews; *Shore Ecology of the Gulf of Mexico*, Joseph C. Britton and Brian Morton; and *Guidebook to the Aransas National Wildlife Refuge*, Wayne H. and Martha K. McAlister. A Knight-Ridder news service article published in the *Corpus Christi Caller-Times* provided information on the value of wildfire.

Although "Blackjack" is now the preferred usage for both tree and peninsula, there is within the Aransas community a dissenting opinion. In 1981 county surveyor and engineer Jerald L. Brundrett wrote to the Geographic Names Coordinator of the Texas General Land Office regarding "Black Jack Peninsula": "The correct usage, as far as I'm concerned is . . . two words. I have . . . seen it as one word, which according to 'Webster' is not a correct usage for the black jack tree for which the peninsula was named. . . . Hobart Huson's usage is also two words." Brundrett noted that he had strong feelings about the correct name because members of his family were early settlers who "purchased a considerable amount of land" in the "Black Jacks."

The *Karánkawa Indians of Texas* by Robert A. Ricklis, and *Karánkaway Country* by Roy Bedichek, supported our thinking that the early tribes were less grisly than some reports maintain. *Archaeological Resources of the Coastal Bend* by Herman Smith and Dr. Thomas R. Hester, and their "Archaeological Investigation at the Allison Site, Nueces County" provided helpful information too.

No one is sure what the name *Karánkawa* means. Often, groups were named by their neighbors, which may explain some unflattering appellations. The

Karánkawas, however, used that name for themselves, according to sources quoted by Huson. It's unlikely, therefore, that the word meant, as some have suggested, "Carrion-Crows" or "Buzzards."

Some have said that *Karánkawa* comes from *comecrudo*, meaning a Coahuiltecan, a "dog lover." It's not clear whether the idea was that the people of Coahuila loved dogs as pets or as food, since no one documented an observance of either practice. Some people called the Karánkawas "Wrestlers," "Barefooted Men," or "People Who Walked in the Water (*ndah keen dah-day-hay*)." Since early explorers and settlers saw the Karánkawas striding across the shallows, and believed that *Karánkawa* meant "Water-walkers," we consider this the most likely choice.

We have found no definition at all for the Karánkawa band named *Cópane*. It was Spaniards, later, who wrote the tribe's name phonetically; in English, we might render it *COE-pah-nay*. George C. Martin and Wendell H. Potter's report, *Preliminary Archaeological Survey of a Portion of the Texas Coast*, provided rich detail on Cópane skills and habits. We gleaned other information from: the Corpus Christi Museum of Science and History; *History of Refugio Mission*, William Oberste; *National Geographic*, "Buffalo: Back Home on the Range;" and *Corpus Christi* and *El Rincón*, Bill Walraven.

The information on turtles, from Robin W. Doughty's article, "Sea Turtles in Texas: A Forgotten Commerce," was published in *Southwestern Historical Quarterly*. The piece quoted John K. Strecker, a naturalist in 1915: "If all the green turtles shipped from the coast country are captured in Texas waters, the animal must be quite abundant." But by then thirty years of exploitation had stripped Texas of the resource.

VOYAGERS
"DISCOVERY": SPANISH EYES

Some sources already cited continued to be of value in this section. We obtained other information from: *The Atlantic Monthly; Exploration in Texas*, John L. Davis; *The New Grolier Multimedia Encyclopedia*, Grolier Electronic Publishing, Inc.; and *Smithsonian* magazine.

We found details of Columbus' voyages in issues of *National Geographic*, November 1975, November 1986, June 1990, January 1992; in a Public Broadcasting System special, *Columbus*; and in a *Corpus Christi Caller-Times* report, June 3, 1991.

According to the Corpus Christi Museum of Science and History, pre-Columbian skeletons in the Americas carry evidence of syphilis, but there is no such evidence in Europeans prior to 1492.

Following Columbus, other Europeans wasted no time in getting to the New World—John Cabot, Amérigo Vespucci and many more.

Cortés' first landing in Mexico may have been at Cozumél. A commemorative plaque there proclaimed that his arrival did not bring the mastery of one people by another, but the birth of a new race.

Historians still argue as to which island might have been Cabeza de Vaca's landing place. Some think Galveston; others believe Matagorda. Hobart Huson, citing Judge Coopwood, made a strong case for San José. The greatest force of the littoral current strikes the north end of San José Island, so it makes sense that boats would drift there. Cabeza's description of Malhado's size and its distance from the mainland suit San José and, Huson wrote, "cannot be adjusted to any of the others from Pass Caballo to the mouth of the Bravo [Rio Grande]." Huson fully described other points of topography, equally relevant. Recently, a group of highly qualified researchers have focused on Dagger Point (now part of the Aransas National Wildlife Refuge) as Cabeza's first mainland locale.

In Spanish, *nueces* means "pecan."

The complex history of the world from the 1500s through the early 1800s had a great impact on Aransas, but including an account of it in our text seemed tedious and ultimately, off the point. For those who enjoy chronology and context, however, we offer some of the story in this and following sections of our Notes.

Not long after Cabeza de Vaca, other nations challenged Spain's monopoly in the New World. When England's Henry VIII broke with Rome, vast properties returned to the English crown and Henry began to build a powerful navy. Philip II of Spain faced strong anti-Spanish and anti-Catholic opposition in the Netherlands. His action to suppress the Dutch revolt threatened England, and a long war began.

Similar religious and political civil wars consumed France, where Calvinists, or Huguenots, formed a strong and often aggressive minority. When those Huguenots attempted to colonize Florida in 1562, Spain countered with a settlement at St. Augustine.

Seven years later, Mercator created his navigational map of the world. Francis Drake toured the West Indies, then set out on a round-the-world voyage. When he reached San Francisco, Drake claimed the surrounding region for England.

Spanish King Philip, believing that nothing short of conquest could stop English depredations in the New World or halt English aid to the Netherlands, assembled his Armada to invade England. British naval power was equal to Spain's, however, and defeated Philip's fleet. As English confidence increased, the crown proceeded to claim New World islands right and left. On the mainland, Spain established Santa Fe, now in the state of New Mexico.

Frenchmen settled Acadia, in Eastern Canada. Just south of there, the Netherlands acquired New World territories with the help of the Dutch West India Company. Jamestown, Virginia, was founded in 1607; the first black slaves arrived twelve years later. By 1620, Pilgrims landed at Plymouth Rock. In 1625 Peter Minuit founded the Dutch colony of New Amsterdam, only to have it seized by the English in 1664 and renamed New York.

French King Louis XIV claimed the Spanish Netherlands in 1667; England, Sweden, and the Dutch formed a Triple Alliance against him. Then France and

Britain declared war on the Dutch. Later that year the Dutch, French, and Spanish interests made peace.

"DISCOVERY": FRENCH ACCENTS

After LaSalle navigated the Mississippi River, Spain feared he would head south, intruding farther into Spanish territory. Spain even interpreted as encroachment LaSalle's extraordinary claims regarding the river. Spaniards insisted Hernán de Soto had discovered and claimed the watershed in 1541—forty-one years earlier. The lands were Spanish and the river was not Colbert—the name LaSalle gave it—but Espíritu Santo. No one paid any attention to the natives, who long before had named it *Miscipipi*, meaning Big River.

The dimensions given for LaSalle's flagship, *La Belle*, are the most recent estimates of on-going archaeological investigation. The ship ran aground approximately twelve miles northeast of the present town of Port O'Connor. Jim Bruseth directed the excavation project, removing the ship's contents and then carefully taking apart the hull—400 pieces of wood carefully numbered for reassembly. Interestingly, similar identification numbers appear on the wood from its original construction.

Six castiron cannons were unearthed on the shore of Garcitas Creek in the summer of 1996, firmly establishing the site of Fort St. Louis on the Victoria County side of the creek.

After the demise of Fort St. Louis, Spaniards made a third salvage attempt on LaSalle's *La Belle*.

In addition to other sources already cited, we found helpful information in *Eyes of Texas Travel Guide*, Ray Miller; and *LaSalle, the Mississippi and the Gulf: Three Primary Documents*, Robert S. Weddle, editor. Béranger's *Discovery of Aransas Pass*, translated by William M. Carroll, included not only the stories summarized here, but a tale of Simars de Bellisle as well. The Béranger translation also explained, in a footnote, our understanding of the Karánkawas' cannibalism as it relates to the Christian doctrine of transubstantiation.

LAS MISIONES

The Spanish word *presídio* comes from the Latin *praesidium*, meaning a garrisoned place.

THE ANGLO-SAXON TAPESTRY

The clash of European cultures in America came about largely as a result of wars elsewhere. The French were more successful with Indians than were other colonizers, primarily because they did not enslave the natives or move them from ancestral lands. This cooperative approach proved particularly beneficial to France in its Canadian struggles against England. Nonetheless, by 1713 the British forced France to relinquish Acadia, then renamed it Nova Scotia.

In 1755 the British forcibly deported Nova Scotia's French peasant population. Thus, were born romantic stories of the Acadians—the Cajuns of today. Some of these people ultimately settled in Aransas.

The expulsion of the French also marked the beginning of the multinational Seven Years' War as an extension of the more regional French and Indian Wars. Early victories in the American battles were all French, but gradually, the British gained control of the seas. With France less and less able to support its colonies, the tide of battle turned. A decisive British victory at Quebec in 1760 marked the beginning of the end for French power in North America.

As a result of the French and Indian War, France ceded Louisiana to Spain. Britain gained all of North America east of the Mississippi River, including Canada and Florida, in 1763. A short thirteen years later, however, thirteen American colonies declared their independence.

The resulting United States of America was a tiny country, and beyond its borders European nations still struggled for possessions. In 1800 Napoleon Buonaparte forced Spain to return Louisiana by secret treaty.

Napoleon had visions of a vast French domain in the New World. The island of Hispañola was to be the heart of an empire including all the lands bordering the Gulf of Mexico; the Mississippi Valley would be its food and trade center. A Haitian rebellion ended Napoleon's grand design, and we can only imagine what Aransas might have become had that dream been realized.

After Napoleon lost Haiti, he had little use for Louisiana, much less Aransas. Facing new conflicts with Britain, Napoleon needed cash. Precipitously, he offered the United States all of Louisiana—800,000 square miles—at about four cents an acre. President Thomas Jefferson jumped at the bargain.

Many historians believe Jean Lafitte to have been born in Bayonne, France, but others give Haiti or the east coast of the Yucatán as his birthplace. *Under the Black Flag: The Romance and the Reality of Life Among the Pirates* by Dr. David Cordingly confirmed the concept that pirate spoils often were divvied up democratically.

T. R. Fehrenbach wrote that ". . . the Scotch-Irish . . . did great damage to this land." They were not careless, he maintained, just untrained "to see or dwell on beauty." Further, the frontiersmen considered killing Indians as "hardly more meaningful than killing catamounts or bears." What the early settlers did to the land and its life was their means to an end—a land developed according to their own ideas of perfection.

Fifteen thousand Spanish-speaking people lived in Nuevo Santandér by the year 1800, and New Spain appeared to be a success. Beneath the surface, however, problems simmered like hidden hot springs: on *diéz y seis de Septiembre*—September 16—in 1810 mestizo priest Miguél Hidalgo issued his famous *grito*, starting a peón revolution for self-government. Fifty years of chaos followed.

During this period, Aransas gained an intriguing legend that explains the name of San José Island landmark, Vincent (or Vinson) slough. As the story goes, a nameless church padre took all the treasure from his parish and sailed for New Orleans. When something went wrong on the voyage, the captain decided to put in at St. Mary's, but he wrecked the ship in Cedar Bayou. All hands were lost except the *padre* and a man named Vincent. They buried the treasure near a slough and continued on foot toward St. Mary's.

Only Vincent ever returned. He found that the sand dunes had shifted, erasing his landmarks and hiding the treasure even deeper. For years Vincent wandered the island in rags, his hair matted and his eyes wild. From time to time he stopped to dig and he harrassed the men on the mail route when they came by, but Vincent never found his treasure. Some like to think that he walks the island still, carrying a lantern, staring insanely.

FREEBOOTERS

Among Lafitte's petitioners was James Bowie, whom Bill and Marjorie Walraven described in *The Magnificent Barbarians* as "a slave smuggler and an Indian fighter who worked with . . . Lafitte to circumvent the law. He and many others were land speculators."

Another who sought Lafitte's assistance was Dr. James Long. He had marched from Natchez to Nacogdoches. From there, he planned to invade Texas and establish a Republic. Long was canny enough to realize that winning a battle against the Spanish was only half the job; Lafitte was the real power of the region. Long, as self-proclaimed President of the free and independent Republic of Texas, needed that support, but Lafitte rebuffed him.

Doctor Long returned home to find that the Spanish had defeated his men, but by then Long loved the freebooting life. He formed a partnership with *empresário*/slaver Ben Milam and a Mexican Republican exile, Don Felix Trespalacios, then led an expedition by sea along the Texas coast. In the process, it would seem, Trespalacios gave his name to a bay just north of the Coastal Bend. He later became the Governor of the state of Coahuila and Texas.

Doctor Long established a small fort at Point Bolivar, on the north side of the Galveston pass. Leaving a few troops to guard his family, Long sailed for Copano Bay, intending to take Goliad and then San Antonio. After a short-lived victory at Goliad, Royalists defeated Long's men. They marched the doctor to Mexico City, but no one was sure what to do with him. When Long's Patriots at Bolivar heard the news, they sailed back to New Orleans, ending the freebooting era for Aransas.

Long's twenty-year-old wife Jane Wilkinson Long found herself deserted at the tiny Bolivar fort. She was a niece of the old conniver James Wilkinson, with all the gumption required to survive her situation.

We found valuable information in "Bolivar! Gulf Coast Peninsula," A. Pat Daniels; and "They Made Their Own Law," Melanie Wiggins.

Needless to say, other counties have their own legends about Lafitte and the location of his buried treasure. The story we tell belongs to Aransas, where many old-timers remembered "Grandma" Frank. A Captain Frank, presumably her husband, has been verified as one of Lafitte's men.

THE *EMPRESA*

JAMES POWER AND FRIENDS

The Spanish caste system was a complicated one. Spaniards born in the old country held highest rank. *Criollos* came next; their blood was pure, but they had unfortunately been born on the wrong side of the Atlantic. Below the two elite classes came *mestizos*, or Hispanicized Mexican Indians, and then *culebras*, the mulattoes. The word *culebra*, meaning "snake," would seem to be the bottom of the hierarchy, but *índios*, the pure-blooded natives, were at a lower level yet. In many cases, however, the only real difference between an *índio* and a *mestizo* was the latter's use of Spanish and his decision to wear Spanish clothing.

Throughout the colonial period, many northern European men married women from wealthy and influential Mexican families. Certainly it cemented their relationship to the established communities and gave them greater power. James Bowie and James Hewetson both appear to have chosen this route, and when James Power's first Mexican wife died, he married her sister. It is possible, of course, that these men just fell in love with Spanish eyes. Stephen Austin, the most noted *empresário* of them all, remained a bachelor all his life.

Felipe Roque De La Portilla was born in Carriazo, Santandér, Spain, in 1766 and came to North America as a captain in the Spanish Army. At least one report suggested that he was a partner with Power and Hewetson in forming their colony, and it is clear that the Portilla family settled in what is now San Patricio County as members of that colony.

Irish *empresários* John McMullen and Patrick McGloin established their colony later than Power established his. It was west of his, with a capital on the bank of the Nueces River, about five miles north of the Lipantitlán mud fort. McMullen and McGloin named it San Patricio, in honor of Ireland's patron saint, but the site clearly encroached on Power and Hewetson's concession and that engendered hard feelings.

FAGAN'S SETTLEMENT

According to Lucile Fagan Snider, great-granddaughter of Nicholas Fagan, her forebears were not Power colonists, but came earlier, on their own. Later they negotiated with James Power for their land holdings within his *empresa*. It was Mrs. Snider also who pointed out the ultimate Fagan ownership of the original mission site.

The Copano landing area was much less brushy then, much more of a plain. As settlers prevented natural wildfires, mesquite and other brush crowded out the prairie grasses.

In *Some Texas Stream and Place Names*, George C. Martin wrote that the body of water now known as St. Charles Bay was called *Laguna del Bergantín* by the Spanish. "The name," he explained, "has been corrupted into Brigantine, and so it appears on some government maps, although late issues bear the spelling changed to "Burgentine." *Bergantin* is Spanish for *barkentine*, and Martin held that the wrecked ship utilized by Nicholas Fagan gave rise to the place name. He continued: "Spanish records mention the *Costa del Bergantín* (Shores of the Barkentine), *Isla de Bergantín* (Goose Island) and *El Bergantín* (the watershed or bay)."

A barkentine is a square-rigged ship with a forward mast; the similar term *brigantine* carries more piratical connotations.

According to Annie Fagan Teal, three Refugio mission bells—other than the one the Mexican *rancheros* gave Nicholas Fagan—"were left on the road near the river, where they lay undisturbed. One day a horseman tied his horse to one which bore the date 1722; the animal becoming frightened, ran away dragging the bell several miles, where it was left with the rim broken off."

Another version of the story suggested that Fagan did not get his bell until the Revolution. The Texians needed money and planned to sell all the bells as scrap. One bell was said to have been traded for fifty head of cattle. The other three were loaded on an ox-cart bound for Victoria when a wheel stuck and broke in the sand of the San Antonio River. There the bells were abandoned and one was broken. Later, Nicholas Fagan recovered a bell that had been hauled to Victoria.

Fagan subsequently gave—or willed—his bell to his grandson Dennis O'Connor, who may have installed it in the chapel of his San Antonio River ranch. That chapel was destroyed in the hurricane of 1942. Mrs. O'Connor gave the bell to the church, and Father Oberste gave it to the Refugio Historical Society.

A story in Lucile Fagan Snider's *Refugio County History* reported that blacks who "entered the neighborhood and built Mt. Zion church" took possession of the 1722 bell.

POWER COUNTRY

Cera means wax, or a wax candle. George Martin's booklet on place names stated that early Spaniards used the phrase *Rincón de Cera* to describe the black, waxy soil of an area at the southern end of Copano Bay and between Port Bay and the wide estuary where Aransas River joins Chiltipin Creek and flows into the bay. Lookout Hill, south of the Copano Bay shore, was known to the Spaniards as Wax Hill.

Modern Spanish dictionaries define *rincón* as a nook, a hideaway, a corner—a usage inconsistent with the large areas so designated on Spanish colonial maps. It seems likely that early cattlemen were using *rincón* as the Franks used *rink*, meaning a ranch or range.

Lipantitlán is an interesting blended word. *Lipan* refers to the Indian tribe;

titlán is a Nahuatl (Aztec) suffix denoting place. In other words, *Lipantitlán* means "place of the Lipans."

THE HARTS' CROSSING

Most of the Spanish-surnamed Power and Hewetson colonists were families already on the land when the Irish arrived. They and the other original settlers bore these family names:

Aldrete	Daly	Holden	McMasters
Allison	Davis	Holly	Navarro
Anderson	Day	Howth	Nira
Austa	Devereaux	Huizar	Nuñez
Banuelos	Dietrich	Hynes	O'Brien
Bartlett	Dolan	James	O'Boyle
Bartels	Douglas	Keating	O'Connor
Baumacker	Downey	Kehoe	O'Donnell
Beauhan	Doyle	Kelly	O'Driscoll
Bennett	Dugan	Lambert	O'Leary
Blanco	Dunn	Langenheim	O'Reilly
Blair	Eyles	Lavery	de la Peña
Bowen	Fagan	Lawlor	Perkins
Bray	Fernet	Linn	Pobedando
Brown	Fitzsimmons	Lopez	Pollan
Brush	Flores	Loupy	Portilla
Burke	Fox	Macias	Power
Byrne	Galan	Malone	Quick
Cameron	Gallardo	Manchola	Quinn
Carbajal	de la Garza	Marchand	Quirk
Carlisle	Garza	Martin	Ramon
Carroll	Gates	Menchaca	Redmond
Cash	Gillam	Morris	Reilley
Cassidy	Gomez	Moya	Reiner
Castillo	Gonzales	Mullen	Reojas
Castro	Goseacochea	Murphy	Reyes
Clark	Gould	Musquiz	Reynolds
Cobarrubias	Hall	McAuly	Rios
Cobian	Hart	McCafferty	Roach
Coffin	Hays	McCamley	Robertson
Collyer	Hearn	McCown	Rodriguez
Corason	Hermans	McCune	Ryan
Coughlin	Hernandez	McDonough	St.John
Crane	Hewetson	McGeehan	de los Santos
Cunningham	Hews	McGuill	Sarates
Dale	Holbrook	McKnight	Scott

Serna	Smith	Townsend	de la Viña
Shearn	Suarto	Traviezo	Walmsley
Shelly	Sumner	Vairin	Ward
Sherry	Teal	Valdez	Westover
Sidick	Tobin	Vidaurri	Williams
Sinnot	Toole	Villa	Winchester
Smiley	Torres	Villareal	

The cholera that decimated Power's Irish immigrants took its toll all across Texas. San Antonio was badly hit; Úrsula María de Veramendi, daughter of the San Antonio commissioner and bride of James Bowie, was among the victims.

REFUGE

The small red pepper that Irish settlers learned to enjoy is the wild one widely known today as *chile petine*. Archaeologist/ethnologist Albert S. Gatschet considered the name a Mexican derivation of the Aztec/Tlascaltec word *chiltipin*. Jean Andrews, however, called that plant *chiltecpin* in *Peppers, the Domesticated Capiscums*, and didn't mention either *chiltipin* or *chile pitin*.

REVOLUTION

In addition to sources previously cited, we found helpful information in: *Why Stop? A Guide to Texas Historical Roadside Markers*, Claude Dooley and Betty Dooley; *Discovery Channel Monthly*, March 1996; *The Irish Texans*, John Brendan Flannery; *A Texas Coastal Bend Trilogy*, Hobart Huson; *The Irish Empresarios and Their Colonies*, William H. Oberste; and *Texas Treasure Coast*, Tom Townsend.

Our conversations with Lucile Fagan Snider added a special dimension to the information provided by her books *Refugio County History* and *Pictorial History of Refugio County*.

We found other quotations from early settlers and visitors in Huson's books and in the Byrne family memoirs, a part of Doris Ruttiger's compilation of data regarding the Lamar Cemetery. Quotations from the Mexican commanders came from *The Mexican Side of the Texas Revolution* by Carlos Castañeda, who was Latin-American Librarian at The University of Texas in 1928.

AUTUMN

According to a family biography, Walter Lambert, age thirty-two, was one of Power's first immigrants. He served in the municipal militia, was elected a Third Lieutenant of Artillery, saw action at the Battle of San Jacinto. After that victory, he voted for the Constitution of the Republic of Texas and the Act of Annexation to the United States. Lambert served as Sheriff of Refugio County and became a leading merchant of the town of Copano. He married James Power's daughter and raised a family of five, then became Chief Justice before his death at age sixty-three. Walter Lambert was buried at Copano.

A photostat of Henry Smith's letter to his nephew was supplied to the *Corpus Christi Caller-Times* by former Aransas County Attorney Emory Spencer and published April 16, 1965.

Fehrenbach cited Rives' remark about Texians considering Mexicans inferior; we have rendered it less general.

The freedman Sam McCullough recovered from his Goliad injury and participated in other campaigns. Congress exempted him from the law prohibiting residence of "Negro freedmen" in the Republic, and Texas granted him a league of land.

T. R. Fehrenbach wrote that "no competent Texas historian really believes that Travis actually drew his line on the ground." Bill Walraven stated that Ben Milam, not William Barrett Travis, made that dramatic flourish. Walraven's source was Stephen Franklin Sparks, of Rockport, who saw and described the event. Walraven speculated that another of the last surviving battle veterans heard the tale from Sparks and associated it with Travis. The Walravens' book provided other colorful items for our account of the Revolutionary period.

The Goliad flag probably had its origin in the legend of The Bloody Hand of Ulster: A flotilla was invading ancient Ireland from Spain and several chieftains in the group agreed that the first to touch Irish land would have first choice of territory. When one ship lagged behind, its chief drew his sword, slashed off his own left hand and hurled it to shore. The other chieftains acknowledged his claim.

Through the years, a bloody *right arm* came to denote firm intention in battle and was used on the shield design of an Irish king. Dimmitt borrowed the idea to express the Texians' determination at Goliad.

According to Hobart Huson, "practically every able-bodied man in the Refugio colony" served at one time or another in Dimmitt's company at Goliad.

Huson cited, but did not name, "eminent authorities" who claimed the General Council "saved Texas" by overriding Governor Smith's veto and allowing Mexican Federalists to vote at Washington-on-the-Brazos.

Henry Smith couldn't have been all bad. Three sisters in succession were pleased to marry him. Smith's second wife bore Harriet, who would grow up to marry her father's friend, George Fulton.

In a biography of Smith commissioned by his family, John Henry Brown noted that Gen. Sam Houston ultimately agreed with Smith regarding Edward Gritton and asked that he be tried as a traitor and spy.

Sam Houston had linked his success to that of President Andrew Jackson, and he clearly desired to bring Texas into the United States.

In his memoir, Walter Ehrenberg reported that strong winds blew down the flag, and that among mutterings of "evil omen," someone raised it again.

"Horse Marines" was a soubriquet too good to die. It came to life again during the Civil War, used then derogatorily. There were several versions of a song about Captain Jinks and his Horse Marines. Perhaps some Texas historians had those songs in mind when they wrote that Maj. Isaac Burton's Revolutionary Horse Marines became "famous in song and story."

Some sources spell Gideon Jaques' name *Jacques*, but the former appears most commonly.

WINTER

Some details around the Fannin battlefield, near the small town of Fannin, lead one to ponder. The battlefield is a fenced-in shrine—with a sign at the gate that reads "Firearms prohibited." Coleto Creek is now best known as the name of an electric power station not far away. The Spanish word *coleto*, which means a close-fitting jacket or vest, is used in an idiom that suggests saying, or admitting, something to oneself. In the little time he had left, did Fannin admit harsh truths to himself, for leading his men into such a predicament?

Manehuila may be a word of Karánkawan origin, though no definition has been found, according to George C. Martin's book of place names.

A State Historic Site Marker commemorating the Yucatán Soldiers described the aftermath of Ward and King's stand at Refugio and the colonists' stacking of the dead soldiers. It cited Sabrina Brown as the eyewitness who described that sad duty.

SPRING

Marjorie and Bill Walraven noted that the Texas Revolution was a joint effort of Anglos and Mexicans and that most *rancheros* served with the Texas Federalist armies. The Walravens commented: "If the Tejanos had joined forces with the Centralists, it is very likely that Santa Anna would have been victorious at San Jacinto, and dreams of a free Texas would have been long delayed."

Fehrenbach stated that "it became almost articles of faith that United States intervention won the war. . . . Mexican propaganda, completely submerged during the war . . . almost won the point: the world came to believe that even in 1836 the 'powerful' United States wrenched Texas from 'poor, bleeding Mexico.'"

THE LONE STAR
A Cast of Characters

Under the word "speculation" in Hobart Huson's index, he made this note: "See Joseph F. Smith, Henry Smith."

Richard Taylor Byrne, James Byrne's nephew, was also active at Lamar. His direct descendant, Caroline Williams, lives in Rockport. After years away from the area, her husband Odell "brought her home" in 1996.

John Howland Wood was born at Hyde Park, New York, descendant of a royal Dutch family there when the place was called New Amsterdam. His forebears had married families of the first practicing medical physician and first treasurer of New Amsterdam, and the founder of Hyde Park. Later, they included the seafaring Howland and Wood families of Massachusetts.

Ultimately, the crowning jewel of Wood's holdings would be Bonnie View Ranch, just where Amos King and the Refugio refugees had met Urrea's army. Not far away, the town of Woodsboro would grow.

Wood also built the fine home still standing in Bayside and acquired San José Island to run cattle there. He participated in every Indian fight of his time; he served in the Confederate army. Wood died at Rockport, the new town on Live Oak Peninsula, that he helped to develop.

Virginia G. Meynard's "The Scottish Clan Macrae and Some American Branches" provided valuable information augmenting Ruttiger's compilation.

James Wells' middle name is also given as "Babbage." The description of his good looks came from a family memoir written by William T. Radeker, quoting John McOscary Brundrett, Wells' son-in-law. Radeker also gave this:

"Lydia Ann came from a very influential family and her attachment to a mere sea captain was discouraged, their marriage forbidden. However, she was permitted to accept the proposal of his best friend, Mister Paye. It seems the two men, who owned a boat together, were competing with each other for her hand and had an agreement: the one who lost the girl would completely own the boat."

Lydia Ann Dana Hastings Hull Paye was the niece of Richard Pearse, a wealthy exporter from Matamoros and New York. She was also the cousin of George R. Hull, one of Byrne's partners in establishing Lamar, and she was related to the D. M and E. D. Hastings families.

Paye soon died. Lydia Ann married James Wells and often provided the only medical treatment available to settlers at Saint Joseph and Lamar. Where doctors were in the towns, their services ran approximately according to this schedule: day visit, twenty-five cents; night visit, thirty-eight cents; emergency, fifty cents; consultation, one dollar; and twenty cents per mile.

The Stage is Set: Aransas City

The Fulton Mansion's information book for docents, and some mansion brochures, contradict both Huson and Oberste, stating that George Fulton, not James Power, was Henry Smith's partner in developing Aransas City. An *Aransas Harbor Herald* article written by Fulton on March 17, 1892, provided quotes and other information that we used. Fulton did not identify the man he met in the

General Land Office, but only wrote that he was "accompanied by a lawyer of the city and a translator." Aransas County Historical Commission records located the site of Henry Smith's home.

Smith's description of the land, and his predictions for it, were included in the April 16, 1965, *Corpus Christi Caller-Times* article already mentioned. The article also described an old cistern about a mile east of the present causeway, believed by Emory Spencer to have been on Smith's property. The cistern was built of imported limestone and handmade bricks. Even in that late day, a trickle of fresh water ran across the bottom of the structure and down through the canebrake to the bay. Although some photos show the cistern clearly, no sign of it remains today.

Power had no reason to be surprised at Texas' laws regarding unsettled land. According to Brown's *Life of Henry Smith*, a draft declaration of independence, November 7, 1835, clause eight, stated that Texas would reward military volunteers with land and accept them as citizens. Although no one from Power country signed the document, James Power had further warning in Article XVIII of the Plan of the Provisional Government: "All grants, sales and conveyances of lands illegally and fraudulently made by the State of Coahuila and Texas, located or to be located within the limits of Texas, are hereby solemnly declared null and void, and of no effect." Power and John Malone signed that document November 11.

The same paper, in Article X, also stated that the oath of office should include these words: "I . . . do solemnly swear (or affirm) that I will support the Republican principles of the Constitution of Mexico of 1824, and obey the declaration and ordinances of the 'consultation of the chosen delegates of all Texas in general convention assembled,' and the decrees and ordinances of the Provisional Government."

According to Hobart Huson, residents of Aransas City at one time or another included:

John Armstrong	Geo. M. Collinsworth	Lewis H. Gibbs
William P. Aubrey	Jas. B. Collinsworth	Parsons Griswold
James C. Allen	Henry Crooke	Samuel Hewes
Bartlett Annibal	William Davis	William Henry Hunter
John R. Baker	Philip Dimmitt	Benjamin C. Jackson
Edwin Belden	Edmund Drew	R. C. Jackson
Joseph Callaghan	Duncan Drummond	Gideon R. Jaques
Ewen Cameron	Cyrus W. Egery	John Henry Johns
Israel Canfield, Jr.	John Ely	Daniel Kean
Joel T. Case	Jeremiah Findlay	A. H. Kinney
John Cassidy	Edward Fitzgerald	Henry L. Kinney
Jonas Casterline	Moreau Forest	Patrick Lambert
John Chain	Michael Fox	Walter Lambert
John Clark	Richard A. Foster	Martin Lawlor
Matthew Cody	George W. Fulton	Joshua W. Littig

Arnaud Victor Loupe
John McDaniel
William McDaniel
John W.B. McFarlane
John McSherry
William Mann
David Morris
James H. Morris
Benjamin F. Neal
Thomas Newcomb
Stewart Newell
Edward O'Boyle
Edw. Joseph O'Boyle
John O'Brien
Edward O'Connor
Peter O'Dowd
John C. Pearce
Richard Pearce

Stuart Perry
Alex. H. Phillips
Leonard Pickens
Francis W. Plummer
Jos. E. Plummer, Sr.
Jos. E. Plummer, Jr.
Samuel A. Plummer
James Power
Martin Power
Richard Power
Thomas Ransom
Henry Redmond
James Reynolds
Willard Richardson
Reuben H. Roberts
Willis Roberts
Richard Roman
James W. Robinson

Henry Ryals
Gov. Henry Smith
John W. Smith
Joseph F. Smith
Alexander Stevenson
John Sutherland
John R. Talley
Thomas Thatcher
John Toole
John Trapnell
William Trapnell
Francis (Franz) Welder
John Welder
Thomas Welder
Alvin E. White
Samuel Addison White
Samuel W. Wybrants

THE STAGE IS SET: LAMAR

The Ballou family and the Gunderman/Ratisseau family both protest the McRae family claim as the first to live in Lamar.

Anna Catherine Braun's name was misspelled in Irish records, making her Brien. But Anna Catherine's family owned the American-Hamburg Ship Line in Germany. Frederick Gunderman was considered radical as a university student believing in democracy. When they married, they immigrated to Galveston. Only three women (or six by some accounts) lived on the island to keep Anna company. There Frederick practiced the craft of brickmaking—a skill that came in handy again at Aransas.

The old Lamar shoreline streets, Water and Bay, have now washed away; the current Bay street is in a different location. Tomahawk Drive was named in 1950, by Charlie Johnson's heirs, who developed his land as Indian Cove. Charlie had let peaceful Indians camp there.

Origins of the salt operations at Lamar remain in doubt. Both the Byrne and McRae families claim construction of the first salt mill. Virginia Meynard wrote that McRae ground his salt in "crude mills operated by man, horse, windpower, or perhaps oxen."

Joan H. McCreary, published in the Lamar Cemetery volume, described Byrne's 1862 salt mill as "wind-powered, having giant Johnny Armstrong arms on the grinders." Keith Guthrie (*Texas Forgotten Ports*) wrote that there were two mills on the peninsula, run by Byrne and McRae. He was referring to Civil War salt works, however, while other sources said the Confederate government itself established an elaborate salt works then.

We have not been able to determine which member of the Power family lay in the coffin built by Murdoch McRae in 1867.

By the time of the Civil War, families in and around Lamar and in outlying settlements on St. Charles Bay, the Blackjacks, Salt Creek, and Copano Creek included, or had included at one time or another:

Sam Allyn
George Armstrong
_____ Atkinsons
Lugenio Ballou
Seth T. ("Jim") Ballou
John Bartels
A. Bass
Mrs. Benet
_____ Bickford
Lyman Brightman
William Brightman
_____ Bruchmiller
George Brundrett
John M. Brundrett
Capt. James W. Byrne
Thomas King Byrne
Charles R. Byrne
Richard T. Byrne
William Byrne
Israel Canfield, Jr.
John Chain
_____ Charlesworth
J. M. Crandall
_____ Deaderich
Capt. Charles Dean
_____ DeForest
_____ Dubois
Dr. W. H. Dulaney
John Fagan
_____ Faulkner
Patrick Finnegan
James Fox
_____ Garcia
_____ Garza
James Gourlay, Jr.
August Graf
Jacob Graf
H. S. Gregory
Frederick Gunderman
E. D. Hastings
William F. Hawes, Sr.

William J. Hay
Joel Heard
William Hill
John Hope
_____ Howard
William Huff
J. G. Hughes
George Hull
Elizabeth Huntington
William James
Capt. Peter Johnson
Capt. Theodore Johnson
William H. Jones
Richard Jordan
Tully Kemp
John King
Henry Kroeger
J. Labadie
_____ Lamardo
Mrs. Nicholas Lambert
_____ Ledesma
William Lewis
George R. Little
John Little
S. L. Lynch
Joseph Margaratt
Archibald McRae
Capt. Murdoch McRae
Joseph Meekers
James Murray
Capt. Philip D. Newcomb
Capt. William Nichols
Mrs. Jane P. O'Connor
John Henry O'Connor
Edward O'Meara
James S. Patterson
Capt. Philip Paul
Simon Paul
Augustus M. Peaks
Edward Perry
Frank Peterson

Leonard Pickens
Mrs. Mary A. Plummer
_____ Ramires
Capt. George M. Roberts
Leonard B. Roberts
Isaac E. Robertson
James Ryan
Capt. Henry Scott
_____ Sideck
Moses Simpson
M. Findley Simpson
John Smith
Antoine Strauch
_____ Stubblefield
Judge John R. Talley
Sidney A. Taylor
Charles H. Teal
John Teal
Walter Teal
William Teal
John Thomas
John Jacob Thomas
James Upton
Samuel E. Upton
_____ Villareal
Samuel C. Vineyard
S. P. Walker
Dr. R. W. Wellington
Capt. James B. Wells
Judge James B. Wells
Mrs. Bridget Whelan
Alvin E. White
_____ Wigginton
W. Williams
Richard H. Wood
J. Woods
John Young
F. W. Young
H. W. Young

The Stage is Set: Saint Joseph

Jackie Shaw, great-granddaughter of Capt. Peter Johnson and current Rockport resident, agreed with Hobart Huson that the old town was near the southern tip of the island, where Lafitte had his fort. However, a U.S. Coast Guard Survey map, 1851, marked both a warehouse and a village some distance north of the island's tip. A rough map from 1862 showed Mercer's Wharf projecting into the ship channel, toward Lydia Ann Island. North of Lydia Ann, this map outlined a large block of land that may denote the village. Within the block is a small square that might be the warehouse; another wharf extends into the channel there.

Saint Joseph residents included:

Paul Anderson	Alex Dorsey	Frank Peterson
Capt. Frederick Augustine	Charles Gardiner	Joseph E. Plummer
Capt. John R. Baker	Jack Harding	Henry Redmond
D. Ballou	Evan J. Henry	Jacob Roberts
Seth T. Ballou	Parry Humphreys, Jr.	George Rogers
Catherine P. Benoit	James F. Irvin	Capt. Henry Seward
A. Benson	Thomas Jenkins	Capt. Marion Seward
Capt. L. Bludworth	Capt. Peter Johnson	Moses Simpson
Isaac W. Boone, Sr.	Capt. Theodore Johnson	John Smith
Isaac W. Boone, Jr.	William H. Jones	Robert Smith
George Brundrett	George Little	Capt. William Smith
John M. Brundrett	John Little	Capt. Spears
J. W. Brundrett	William Little	James Sullivan
Thomas Brundrett	Capt. John Low	John Thomas
James W. Byrne	Capt. James Mainlan	C. Thompson
William Cabban	William Mann	F. Thompson
J. A. Casterline	John McGinnis	George Wadsworth
John Chain	Archibald McRae	Robert J. Walker
Mary Ann Chain	Robert A. Mercer	Capt. James B. Wells
H. L. Clark	Charles Hays Miller	Lt. David Williams
William P. Clark	_____ Myers	H. N. Williamson
Thomas Clubb	Jack Paleka	J. Woods
Capt. Geo. M. Collinsworth	James Paul	
J. M. Crandall	Capt. Philip C. Paul	

Almost all the men titled "captain" were commanders of seagoing vessels and many of them served in the Texian navy. Most of the other island settlers were engaged in ranching.

The Holinworth family name is alternately given as Hollingsworth and Hillingsworth.

The description of fresh water on San José came from Capt. W. S. Henry of Gen. Zachary Taylor's army, as quoted in Huson.

Jackie Shaw supplied a reminiscence regarding Johnson, Moses Simpson, and others, written by Lyman B. Russell.

The question of how George Brundrett met his death was addressed in a paper written by his descendant Bill Radeker. The swinging boom story remained the same, but it took place on Lake Erie. Radeker added the story of the missing money and possible mutiny.

The many Brundretts married into just about all the other early families in the area, some not mentioned in the text. They include these bloodlines: Sparks, Hawes, Smith, Johnson, McRae, Paul, Rowe, Hanks, Hastings, Court, Roberts, Wells, Bludworth, and many others.

CRITICAL EPISODES

We found useful information in *Republic of Texas*, Stephen B. Oates, editor; *Fire and Blood*, T.R. Fehrenbach; and *Mexico: A History*, Robert Ryal Miller.

CRITICAL EPISODES: THE INDIAN PROBLEM

Huson's two-volume *Refugio* indicated that the Lipan who made the treaty with Power was Chief Cuelgas de Castro, but in *A Coastal Bend Trilogy* Huson wrote that Power negotiated with two chiefs, Castro and Culegasde. If the man's name was Cuelgas de Castro, it is an interesting one. *Cuelgas* means bunches of grapes cut from the vine, or gifts; castro comes from the verb "to castrate."

Anthropologist William W. Newcomb's statement regarding the prevalent negative view of indigenes came from his work *The Indians of Texas*.

Nicholas Fagan had some misgivings when Power's nephew, Thomas O'Connor, began to call on his daughter Mary. Thomas didn't seem much concerned with farming, but preferred hunting or serving in the Texas army. He had also learned, from a Mexican craftsman, how to make saddletrees, and he used the proceeds of that work to buy his first horse. Even though O'Connor's army service had added to his original 4,400-acre grant, Fagan feared the young man wouldn't amount to much. When, reluctantly, Fagan gave his consent to the marriage, he also gave O'Connor some of his cattle. His own herd, after all, had started from the generosity of a neighbor—Carlos de la Garza. In time, those cattle grew to one of the largest herds in Texas and O'Connor became one of the state's largest landowners.

CRITICAL EPISODES: THE MIER EXPEDITION

Mier is a village 120 miles upriver from Matamoros; its name rhymes with *fear*.

Mexican President Santa Anna never stopped believing that Texas belonged to Mexico. He had hopes—so long as Texas was not a part of the United States—that he might move his border north of the Rio Grande. Texas President Sam Houston was determined not to allow that, but he did not favor the plans of firebrands to attack across the Rio Grande.

Regarding the Aransas River as the boundary between Texas and Mexico,

Oberste cited General Altamonte, minister from Mexico to the United States: "The true line should commence at the mouth of the River Aransaso, and to follow it to its source [not far west of the present State Highway 181, between Skidmore and Beeville}; thence, it should continue by a straight line until it strikes the junction of the Rivers Medina and San Antonio, and then, pursuing the east bank of the Medina to its headwaters, it should terminate on the confines of Chihuahua."

The bodies of the men who drew black beans remained where they fell until the Mexican War. They were then placed in Gen. Zachary Taylor's headquarters and carried across Mexico. The remains were finally taken to La Grange, Texas, and placed in a vault at Monument Hill.

In 1848 a new county was formed at the southern tip of Texas, bordering the Rio Grande. It was named in honor of Ewen Cameron.

Gen. Alexander Somervell was a key player in the Mier Expedition. Later, when the Texas government moved its Custom House from Aransas City to Port Lavaca, Sommervell was appointed Custom Collector. Archibald McRae dealt with him when collecting his merchandise at the port, and they became friends.

Somervell had a pair of Kentucky rifles made by Dixon, the most famous gun maker of the day, but they were flintlocks and Somervell wanted them changed to percussion. Archibald did the work, pleasing Somervell so greatly that he gave Archibald one of them. That rifle, one of his most prized possessions, is said to have been on display at the Alamo.

TO PLEDGE ALLEGIANCE
THE AMERICAN FLAG

In *Taylor's Trial in Texas*, author Robert H. Thornhoff cited old diaries indicating that Zachary Taylor's men camped on Live Oak Peninsula. The large oak tree is near the present intersection of Pearl and Bay streets. The *Rockport Pilot*, August 31, 1939, stated that some men camped in the area that would one day be Fulton.

The chain of events leading from the Mexican War to the Civil War was succinctly described by David Saville Muzzy in *The United States of America, Volume I*. Historian Lynn Montross provided a helpful perspective, and we gleaned some information from *Smithsonian Magazine*, April 1996.

Gen. Thomas Jefferson Jackson earned the nickname "Stonewall" at the First Battle of Bull Run, where he stood firm "like a stone wall" according to Gen. Bernard Bee, for whom Beeville and Bee County, north of Aransas, were named. Both Jackson and Lee were at the Menger Hotel in San Antonio, Texas, when U.S. President Abraham Lincoln issued the Emancipation Proclamation. They went north to resign their commissions.

Casterline may have been a French Huguenot name. Some sources define it as Dutch for "brewery tester" or "bartender"—or perhaps for "keeper of the castle."

According to Bubba Casterline (Leslie Eugene, Jr.), members of his family were in New York in the 1700s and served in the Revolutionary War.

Jonas Casterline lived for a while on the point of land that became Key Allegro, but he had a legal battle with the Welders concerning its ownership. He served as Justice of the Peace for Refugio County at one time.

CULTURE AT THE END OF THE ROAD

Viktor Bracht's description of Texas came from his book, *Texas in 1848.* His wife was Sybil Shaefer.

Murdoch McRae's brother died before his father did, leaving Murdoch the sole heir. Archibald McRae was buried in Victoria's Evergreen Cemetery. A memorial erected by the Daughters of the Republic of Texas now marks it. The old oak tree still graces his Lamar homesite, and the salt cedars still line the shore.

As a homebuilder, Murdoch rented, by the day, Dr. Seth Ballou's old slave Moses, who was a skilled carpenter. In 1854 Murdoch completed a home for the Wells family—James, Lydia Ann, infant son Jim. The house sat in the oak grove now south of Park Road 13 and just west of Highway 35.

James B. Wells, Jr., received his early education at Jane O'Connor's Lamar Academy, then graduated from the University of Virginia Law School in just one year. Wells supplemented his school funds by playing poker, but he always quit at midnight on Saturday because he had promised his mother he would not play cards on Sunday. In later years, he became a renowned South Texas judge. Jim Wells County was named for him in his lifetime, a rare honor.

John Henry Kroeger's name is pronounced "*CRAY-gur*," with a "g" as in "girl."

Anton Strauch has been credited with growing the first tobacco in Aransas, but many Karánkawa clay pipes turn up amid other artifacts of their culture. Huson suggested that Mexicans were growing tobacco on Live Oak Peninsula in colonial times, and there are references to tobacco in Revolutionary warehouses.

The Colt brothers, Samuel and James, also became interested in Lamar. The Colts had partners who helped them purchase 14,000 acres of land, including all of Lamar Peninsula and Goose Island, excepting some townsite properties and the salt works. Since they were the founders of the Colt Patent Fire Arms Company, all sorts of rumors spread. It may be true that they had intended to build a munitions factory; several Colt partners were military men who might have had particular interest in that. But it's also possible the businessmen in the partnership planned to develop the port, or that all those Easterners simply wanted a Texas ranch. In any case, the Colts sold out within fifteen years and had never improved their property in any way.

Captain and Mrs. James Byrne donated outlots seventeen and eighteen for the Stella Maris chapel. It was completed in 1857, measuring twenty feet wide and thirty-six feet long, with walls fourteen inches thick. Windows went all the way to a floor of butted cypress on cedar beams. Twelve feet overhead, a ceiling of yellow pine planking also rested on cedar beams. Harriet Odin Byrne died a year later, and officials of the Lamar Cemetery "are sure" she is buried there, although the marker for her grave is gone.

Jane O'Connor's Lamar Academy was not the first school on that peninsula. Archibald McRae built one in 1840, and Murdoch McRae replaced it with another thirteen years later.

Jane O'Connor, James Byrne's niece, had been a school teacher in New Orleans. There she had married Patrick O'Connor, the bookkeeper at Byrne and Sloo Iron Foundry; there she had given birth to a son.

Though Patrick O'Connor was a young man, his health was failing, and in 1854 the doctor suggested that he should travel to a rustic area and rest there. Patrick chose Lamar, sailed to Galveston, then took a packet ship on to his destination. He had scarcely reached Lamar and settled comfortably on a sofa, when he fell back dead. The date was August 8, and Patrick O'Connor's body was the first interred in the Lamar cemetery.

Despite Patrick's death, his widow Jane kept to her original plan and arrived at Lamar the next year. The family settled into a cottage while Murdoch McRae built them a shellcrete home. When they moved into it, the cottage became the first school, but its great success caused classes to spill over into the larger house.

Students Sarah and Carrie Little remembered the Gregory/O'Connor house as "a beautiful place." They described "galleries twelve feet deep and forty feet long at the front and back, with square columns."

In the 1950s, the skeletons of several shellcrete homes still marked Old Lamar. By 1996, only a portion of one—the Bunker home—remained, its bricks still stacked to the shape of steep-sloped gables. The home appeared to consist of two buildings, very close together. One was probably the main living area and the other a separate kitchen—a design often used for safety from fires. Family records affirmed that the McRae home was built in this style.

Mary Ann Heard McRae wrote a brief autobiography. We have often corrected her spelling and punctuation errors for clarity in the narrative. Otherwise, we have retained the essence and appeal of her words.

Mary Ann never had a home of her own. Her mother-in-law Vincey was always in control. And that was only part of the problem: Mary Ann wrote that Murdoch "was the idol of his old mother and his mother was his idol. How could they give each other up for a sixteen-year-old girl? It was hard for the poor old mother to give her son up. She never could understand why he should love the girl the best."

Mary Ann learned the habit of holding her tongue. Both she and Vincey "thought too much of him [Murdoch] to give him any trouble," she wrote her autobiography. But Mary Ann made a point of confessing: "I did step on the cat's tail and it hollered for dear life."

Vincey McRae and Murdoch loved their house cats, Mary Ann explained, but "I was not very fond of them. At least I never had the time to give them so much attention." Treading the cat's tail may have been negligence born of hurry, or it could represent Mary Ann's one subtle retaliation.

But Mary Ann wrote that Murdoch "did take good care of me. He was the best man that ever lived in Texas and I am not the only one that said he was."

John Jacob Thommen was a peace-loving man, although at the close of the Napoleonic Wars his native Switzerland was anything but peaceful. When he saw circulars describing Texas as a new Eden, he and Verna made a decision: Compared to what they had to endure in Switzerland, they believed that frontier hardships would seem like blessings. They sailed to New Orleans, then traveled overland to Galveston. From there John Jacob walked 225 miles to Corpus Christi. His family followed in a sailboat, and they settled first on San José Island. He served in the quartermaster's corps of Gen. Zachary Taylor's army during the Mexican War, then moved his family moved to Salt Creek in 1850. Thommen changed his last name to Thomas during the war.

The Indians who captured Sarah made a stop at Goliad, where she recognized a woman who had been to her home several weeks before—a blue-eyed, fair-skinned squaw. The Thommens had helped that woman, as had other families—the Perrys, Welders, and O'Connors. The captive members of each family realized the blue-eyed squaw spy had given the Comanches information for their raids. At San Saba, Sarah and the others survived principally on horsemeat and nuts.

The year after Sarah's release, Eve Thommen married Henry Ludwig Kroeger. Sarah married neighbor Anton Strauch sometime before 1861.

One version of the abduction story held that Cópanes, not Comanches, captured the Thommen girls. This seems unlikely, since Cópanes were so diminished in number, as early as the 1830s, that they had merged with other Karánkawa tribes and were no longer identifiable as a particular group.

Another tale of the Thommen abduction placed the home on Saus Creek, north of El Cópano. However, since both girls married men from Salt Creek/Lamar and Vincey McRae told a version of the story, the Salt Creek location seems more likely. Vincey related her tale in somewhat more dramatic fashion than others: "An old squaw could not make Eva stay on a horse, so they scalped her, filled her with arrows, and left her on the prairie to die."

Sarah's middle name was Salina (Salome), encouraging at least one historical writer to refer to her by that more colorful appellation.

The Karánkawas of this period were a pitiful remnant of the old clans. No Cópanes remained; the Caoques, Cocos, Cujanes, and Coopites had blended into one. Throughout the 1840s, they roamed Power country singly or in pairs, committing petty thefts and begging for food.

Mary's last name has been variously recorded as Amaro, Amarso, and Amaroo. Her first name is sometimes given as Maria. Some sources say that her father, brother, and son were all named Thomas; others give the name Domingo to one generation or another.

No reports remain to tell us how her parents died. They had Christian names (Thomas and Cassilda), and so may have lived in or near the mission. It could have been disease in the mission that killed them, rather than some wild raid. Col. John H. Wood administered a small estate for Mary and her brother, so again, it seems that their parents were accustomed to the ways of white settlers.

Mary's married name, Pathoff, is often recorded as Pothoff, which we consider a phonetic misspelling.

The expulsion of Karánkawas from Power country may have occurred in 1851 or 1852. However, some reports indicated that several Karánkawas remained in the county as servants or retainers to white families.

Several years later a Karánkawa man and his wife came from Mexico to search for gold from the wrecked Spanish vessel on Barkentine Creek.

SMITH V. POWER

At Copano, Power built a new wharf and organized a freight transport business. He encouraged new immigrants to utilize his port, and three-masted schooners hauled tallow and hides from his docks to eastern markets. Since fresh water was still a problem at Copano, mule teams hauled people for a weekly clothes washing day on Melon Creek, several miles away. A Ben Goodwin article in the *Corpus Christi Caller-Times* added color to our information about the town.

Land ownership suits and petitions went on for years. One filed by James B. Wells, M. H. Jones, W. R. Roberts, and Jonas A. Casterline serves as an example. The four men owned or had leased properties from James Byrne, where they had "erected houses and made other improvements." They were dismayed to find the land "now unexpectedly and against all former decisions . . . decided to be the property of the State." They petitioned the "honorable body" to issue grants or quitclaims to them for the amounts of land, including their homesteads.

POWER'S PASSING

Some of the phrases commemorating James Power's life came from Lucille Fagan Snider's *Refugio County History.*

In 1873 someone broke into James Power's grave. Judge John Hynes had the sad duty of reporting the atrocity to Power's son, James: "Only think of the thing! Yesterday I was forced to take into my house the bones of one of my best friends who has been nearly twenty-one years buried. . . . The hair on my head felt like each and every particle was the size of a fence rail and standing erect. . . . I am truly sorry to think that there be living in this nineteenth century and enlightened age such demands [demons?] in human form."

Citizens of Refugio moved the remains of James Power, Sr., to their Mount Calvary Cemetery, where now an appropriate marker honors the *empresario's* life.

Nothing remains of any Power town. As the buildings at Aransas City gradually crumbled, they were replaced by an oil field camp and then by vacation homes; Saluria washed away in a storm.

Copano was deserted by the 1880s. Now on private property and accessible only from the water by shallow-draft boat, its ruins fall more and more into the bay; a marker placed there some years ago is no longer visible and presumed sunk.

Only two walls of the old Mexican cistern, some partial walls of houses, and good imagination attest that a bustling town ever existed there.

THE LIGHT

Cyrus Egery, a noted Indian fighter, settled on an island near the mouth of the Aransas River, a spot that had been used as a landing place from earliest times. When Smith started his town of Black Point there, he reserved an entire bayfront block for personal use and built a fine multi-story shellcrete home on the site.

During the Texas Revolution, John Howland Wood was a member of the New York Battalion, and his company followed the Mexican retreat. When they reached Goliad, Wood wrote later, he and his comrades had the sad duty of laying to rest "the charred and partly-consumed bones of the heroes who gave up their lives for Texas."

Families had to have cows for milk. When the cistern water gave out for watering cows, people hauled water from Saus Creek, which entered Mission Bay nine miles from Saint Mary's. Russell wrote: "It is the only case I have ever read of where people hauled water with horse teams nine miles to water cows . . . and it looked as if an old cow could empty a fifty-gallon whisky barrel filled with water before she would stop for breath."

Despite such problems at St. Mary's, optimists platted Court House Square and established a public school. Stores and churches went up as well. Today the town lies half-hidden beneath the sleepy town of Bayside. North of there, just off Farm-to-Market Road 136, the St. Mary's cemetery slumbers among live oaks.

Prospectors, lured by gold in California, moved through Aransas, seeking shorter routes to the West Coast. Former Provisional Governor Henry Smith followed them and there he died, leaving no will.

Corpus Christi, Henry Kinney's town, became the county seat of a reorganized San Patricio County and then of new Nueces County that reached all the way to the Mexican border. That county boasted 2,845 residents. White males made up forty-three percent of the population and thirty-four percent were white females. Blacks of both sexes made up the rest.

South of Aransas, in Mexico, other changes were underway. At the town of Puebla, between Mexico City and Veracruz, Gen. Ignacio Zaragoza led an outnumbered force that repelled a French invasion on the fifth day of May in 1846. His heroic victory gave Mexico its great national patriotic anniversary, *Cinco de Mayo*. The date is celebrated as sincerely by many South Texas populations and most especially at Goliad. Zaragoza was born there in 1829, just outside the walls of the presidio that figured so grandly and so painfully in Aransas history.

Bare beach gives no hint of the grand town that once was Indianola. Inland, between bayous and on a slight rise, a cemetery holds grave markers written in German.

Three books on the lighthouse provided information and inspiration: *The*

Aransas Pass Light Station: A History, F. R. Holland, Jr; *Lighthouses of Texas*, T. Lindsay Baker, with paintings by Rockport Center for the Arts member Harold Phoenix; and *Aransas Pass, Texas*, published by that town's Chamber of Commerce.

The 1859 *Light List* informed ship captains: "The light, when bearing NW1/2W, will be seen between the two points of the pass; but the bar shifts so often that no direction can be given for crossing without a pilot."

Aransas Pass Light Station was decommissioned in 1852.

CIVIL WAR

Texas in the Confederacy by Bill Winsor proved helpful, and a 1940 *Webster's New International Dictionary of the English Language* provided definitions for words not included in the newer dictionary we generally depend upon.

ALL SORTS AND CONDITIONS OF MEN

Caroline Ennels Duke had a beautiful garden each year, milked the cows, churned the butter, and helped doctor the cattle. She often walked seven miles into town on Sunday morning with some of her grandchildren. She enjoyed sitting on her front porch telling them slavery stories, some funny and others sad.

One report stated that Caroline Duke was a former slave of the McRae family of Lamar. That same report said that Hannah Williams was also a McRae slave. Mack Williams, who related the story of his grandfather Thornton, wrote: "There are some things I will not tell, how they got here, and who brought them." Mack does mention that his forebears "are buried in the O'Connor Cemetery on the San Antonio River Ranch."

Mack worked at the Aransas National Wildlife Refuge for years, and he was a favorite with visitors. He was fluent in Spanish, helpful with tourists from south of the border.

THE SIXTH FLAG

Capt. Edward Upton's Lamar Home Guards included 1st Lt. Richard Jordan, 2d Lt. Samuel Upton, Sgt. John Thomas, and these privates:

Lugenio Ballou	Francisco Garza	Jas. Patterson, Jr.
Lyman Brightman	J. de Leon Garza	A. M. Peaks
James W. Byrne	August Graf	E. Ramirez
John Cisneros	Joel Heard	V. Swartz
Charles Dean	Eloco Lambardo	Antoine Strauch
W. H. Dulaney	Manuel Ledesma	John Teal
Cornelius Duffy	Juan A. Ledesma	J. J. Thomas
P. Finnegan	G. R. Little	R. A. Upton
José Maria Garcia	Murdoch McRae	W. H. Upton
Paulino Garcia	John Miers	Ricardo Virizell
Lionisio Garcia	J. S. Patterson	

Capt. Edwin Hobby married Edna Adeline Pettus, daughter of Dr. John Pettus, one of Stephen F. Austin's first 300 colonists. In the 1850s, Pettus settled near the Bee County town that now bears his name. Edwin and Edna Hobby's son, William Pettus Hobby, became governor of Texas and president of the *Houston Post* newspaper. Members of the Hobby family continue to serve the state.

Shell Bank Island now appears as only a slender oyster reef marking the north side of a passage to California Hole, a favorite fishing spot.

The lens of the Aransas Light was never found. Most likely, it lies hidden somewhere in the marshes that surround the tower. The Pass Cavallo Light, preserved and on display at the Port Lavaca museum, is a good example of the lens type also used at Aransas.

As Brigadier General Bee retreated in December 1863, he established a camp on the west side of the lower San Antonio River, at Larco Creek. Familiarly, it was called "Camp Fagan."

According to one account, Mary Amaro Pathoff's brother Domingo gave his life on the battlefield. Another story held that an irate officer ran a sword through him when he refused to work. Yet, a third related that Amaro "served honorably" the four years of the struggle, then returned to St. Mary's and made his home with his sister.

WAR IN THE GULF

Fort Semmes was named for Adm. Raphael Semmes. As a Confederate naval officer, he ravaged the Union's merchant marine on every body of water from the West Indies to Singapore.

According to the *Handbook of Texas,* edited by Walter Prescott Webb, Robert Mercer settled on San José Island in 1850, but he started grazing cattle on Mustang Island. Five years later he built a cabin on Mustang and moved there. An 1862 map indicated his San José wharf.

A Columbiad was a heavy, long-chambered, muzzle-loading gun, very thick behind the pivots and designed for throwing shells and shot at high angles of elevation.

Capt. Benjamin F. Neal had been Chief Justice of Aransas/Refugio County during the Republic. He was an ardent Secessionist before the Civil War and during it resigned his command to become district judge of the Refugio-Corpus Christi district.

Blind Bayou, where Kittridge's launches ran aground, is likely the Blind Pass now popular with fishermen on the bay side of San José Island.

HOMEFRONT

Copperas, crystalized ferrous sulphate, is a by-product of the process of obtaining copper by precipitation or of pickling iron. It should have been reasonably available because of wartime production.

The road from Matamoros to Bagdad is still well-marked, but signs refer to it only as a *playa*, a beach. And that is what it is. Floods, hurricanes, and military attacks have taken their toll. Absolutely nothing remains of a town that was larger than Rockport grew to be by 1997.

The letter from Aransas Prescott, and several others he penned, were contributed by Rockport resident Ann Guynes. Prescott, her grandfather, was born on San José Island in 1846. His English father and Scots mother had come to El Cópano for land and moved to San Antonio in 1850. They were living there when Prescott wrote his war letters.

BATTLES IN THE BAYS
Hannah Brundrett lost an adopted son, Henry Matt, in the Battle of Corpus Christi. Joseph A. Lemore died in the Yankee prison.

CAMELS
William Duke's great-uncle Dan, an Arab, and great-aunt Abbey, an African, were among the handler group that accompanied the imported camels.

THE END
Henrietta Gregory Little was John Little's wife and Jane O'Connor's sister.
James Wells, broken in health and spirit, lived on until 1880. He was seventy-two when he died and was buried at Lamar.

AFTERMATH
"June Teenth," the day news of emancipation reached Texas slaves, continues to be a day of celebration and recollection of heritage for black citizens across the state.
Hally Little's full name was William Halliburton Little. His father, George Little, was a resident of Copano and a county judge. George also ran a Lamar store from 1840 to 1850.
Capt. Charlie Johnson married Bertha Harris (Herrer), Capt. Peter Johnson's step-daughter.
In the Snider-edited *Refugio County History*, Lottie Pearl Hensley McNew wrote: "In the early 1920s, my grandmother, Kate Jane Tucker Huff, was living with our family. One morning a knock came on our back door, and I was sent to answer. I was frightened stiff when a small but sturdy black man with white hair asked if he could see Miss Kate. My grandmother, a frail Southern lady, came to the door and started crying and laughing at the same time and hugging and patting

this man. I remember he was nicely dressed in a dark suit and held a derby hat in his hand. They talked and talked and hugged and cried some more. It seems that they had been children together and he and his family had been slaves of her father, Lemuel Tarleton Tucker. . . . My grandmother explained to me that they had cared for their slaves like members of their own family, but when the war was over the released slaves did not want to move with them to Brady, Texas, where the Tuckers and Huffs were starting over, so they were deeded bits of land and stayed where their roots were."

Solis/Bryan Researchers listed the following Confederate veterans in Aransas County at the time of the 1910 census. We give their ages as of 1861, the year Texas seceded from the Union:

NAME	BIRTHPLACE	AGE	WIFE	AGE
George Ansley	Ireland	16	Mary E.	0
Osborn F. Bailey	Connecticut	36		
James H. Benham	Kentucky	28	Elizabeth	26
Edward Bets	New York			
Bernard Bludworth	Louisiana	21	Mary	20
William Brown	Tennessee	15		
George A. Brundrett	Michigan	25	F.C.	13
John M. Brundrett	Michigan	21	Lula M.	0
William H. Cabell	Virginia	16	Jennie M.	0
James W. Collins	Mississippi	17	T.H.	5
Charles L. [Dron]	Denmark	26	Mattie	11
William Evans	England	38		
Napolean B. Gentry	Kentucky	29		
James O. Goffing	[Texas]	21	Kate	0
Richard M. Hanks	Mississippi		Alice E.	5
Andrew J. Harryman	Missouri	27	Louisa J.	11
M[ote] J. [Henry]	N. Carolina	22	Sarah M.	15
William Hunt	Georgia	31		
[Swan] A. Hutchins	Georgia	15	Lucind C.	15
Theodore Johnson	Denmark	25		
John H. Kennedy	Georgia	16	W. J.	15
George [T] Lee	Virginia	12		
Janes H. Madden	Louisiana	14		
Zachariah McElfred	Virginia	20		
James M. Mills	Georgia	14	Pratha C.	9
Louis [Peden], Sr.	Louisiana	19	Susanna	15
[Seabury] Phillips	Illinois	19	Louisa V.	6
Richard Ratcliffe	Georgia	29	Maude M.	0
John S. Roberts	Georgia	13	Lillie Lu	0
Benjamin Robertson	Texas	20		
John Simpson	Scotland	27	Katrina	16

James H. Sparks	Texas	16	Mary A.	13
Robert J. Tedford	Tennessee	34		
William A. Terrell	Kentucky	17		
John H. Traylor	Virginia	22	Pauline	17
Samuel C. Upton	Virginia	22		
George E. Waterwall	Louisiana	13	Mary E.	18
Frank Wendell	Louisiana	17		
Joseph H. Wilson	Alabama	14	Nancy	13

James W. Sneed, who enlisted at age sixteen and served with Hood's Texas Brigade, was twice wounded in the war. He moved to Aransas in 1914 and, therefore, was not included in the 1910 census.

Caroline Williams, Richard Taylor Byrne's great-granddaughter, said Richard was so eager to join the battle that he took his hunting gun to Arkansas and enlisted with the Regulars there. She suggests that this action may have followed his involvement with Capt. Edward Upton's Lamar Home Guard.

Other Aransans who served in the war included:

Capt. Charles F. Bailey, 8th Regiment, Texas Infantry
Walter C. Gay, 142 and 36th Texas Infantry
Robert A. Cole, Alabama
James Vernon, Nevada

BUILDING BLOCKS
THE ROCKY POINT

In modern times, anglers may be among the most likely to recognize Samuel Allyn's name; a favorite fishing spot on the west shore of San José Island is called "Allyn's Bight."

Although part of the rocky point was blasted away to build Rockport Harbor in 1928, the location of the old wharves is still easy to find. They stood, appropriately enough, at the end of Wharf Street.

The Old Beach Road by Winifred E. Lowther, provided a clear picture of the Rocky Point. Alpha Kennedy Wood's *Texas Coastal Bend* also furnished information, as did the Aransas County Historical Commission's exhaustive research for historical markers. These sources continued to be rich in information for subsequent sections of this history.

Information on the Bracht family's move from Mexico to Rockport came from a *Rockport Pilot* news story in the Historical Society archives and from one author's conversation with a member of the family.

The National Registry Assessment of the *SS Mary* provided helpful information regarding the Morgan Steamship Line.

By 1872, the following had purchased lots in Rockport:

D. Ackroy
L. Alexander
Roger W. Archer
Martha E. Andrews
Sarah Andrews
J. J. Armstrong
E. Atkinson
J. H. Atkinson
U. N. Atkinson
W. N. Atkinson
John Aviegonat
William August
Charles F. Bailey
F. A. Bailey
J. B. Bain
Seth T. Ballou
Williford C. Ballou
Lugenio Ballou
Baptist Church
T. W. Baxter
John W. Baylor
J. Z. J. Beatley
L. Beatley
S. Beatley
M. A. Belcher
James H. Benham
William Benson
L. Bessones
M. K. Box
Viktor Bracht
Martha E. Brent
Mrs. C. H. Brown
C. L. Brown
J. F. Burnett
J. S. Burton
Frank H. Bushick
Bridget Byrne
Charles R. Byrne
Nellie Byrne
Sarah B. Byrne
Frances M. Carroll
J. E. Carroll
John E. C. Carroll
Henry Clark
J. W. Cleaseman

John Collins
Tim Conlan
L. W. Corkodale
A. F. Coxvan
Amelia V. Cox
J. E. Curry
Charles Dean
Thomas M. Dennis
A. V. Doak
William Dorethy
James M. Doughty
Edmond M. Downs
Jeremiah O. Driscoll
Robert Driscoll
Calvary Droddy
Rev. C. M. Dubois
W. W. Dunlap
Jerome Clark Dwyer
Jacob Euper
S. P. Farwell
J. M. Friday
Michael Friday
Joseph Friend
J. M. Gaffney
James O. Gaffney
M. T. Gaffney
J. W. B. Gary
I. B. Geary
John Gentry
H. K. Gibbs
John Gibney
August Graff
Elizabeth Graff
Mary W. Grant
Oscar F. Grant
Louis Greenough
Charles Griner
_____ Hadfield
J. N. Hancock
Luke Hart
Robert A. Hasbrook
Leonhard Henkey
Mollie Henry
James T. Herring
S. A. Hightower

Ophelia Hodges
John N. Hoffman
A. J. Hogan
John W. Hollman
J. T. James
W. T. Johns
A. Johnson
Annie Johnson
David I. Johnson
Richard Jordan
Charles J. Kerk
Richard King
J. L. Kingsbury
W. G. Kingsbury
Henry Kroger
Sam Laconey
P. F. Latting
S. L. Lewis
J. B. Lenoir
T. J. Lewis
C. Liles
E. M. Liles
W. C. Livingston
J. Lucy
Elizabeth Lynch
Martha A. McBride
T. M. McDonald
J. A. McFaddin
Patrick McGloin
William P. McGrew
_____ McIntosh
James McLeon
Jennie McNeal
T. P. McNeal
Michael Mahanney
F. J. Malone
James. M. Manning
Isaac Martin
John N. Martin
John N. Mathis
J. M. Mathis
Roxy A. Maynard
George W. Meriwether
William Miller
P. Mills

P. R. Mitchell

Enoch Moffat

Jos. B. Moffat

J. Williamson Moses

Thomas Myers

James E. Nagle

Carrie P. Nations

Mrs. C. E. Neel

Porter M. Neel

John Nelson

Henry B. Newberry

R. F. Nicholson

Mary North

Rufus A. Nott

John H. O'Connor

William Oertling

Malinda Oertling

Charles H. Packard

Louisa Packard

Augusta M. Parks

Stephen Peters

Mary A. Pettil

N. C. Phillips

Paul Power

David E. Pruett

S. D. Rabb

S. P. Rabb

L. Rabeth [or Rabbit]

Florence Reed

Oliver P. Reed

Edward W. Richards

Ophelia C. Rogers

Benjamin Rozell

Mrs. P. J. Rozell

D. D. Scrivner

Daniel M. Seward

E. D. Sidbury

William Silberson

Margaret Sills

E. A. Skidmore

M. A. Skidmore

S. C. Skidmore

Joseph F. Smith

Sam H. Smith

Thomas Speake

O. H. Stapp

Thomas R. Stewart

Thomas Stokes

J. W. Stockley

E. L. Stout

O. E. Stout

Catherine Sullivan

L. R. Sullivan

J. R. Talley

Moseley J. Terry

Rudolf F. Theurer

J. H. Thomas

Alfred S. Thurmond

William R. Unitz

Mary C. Upton

Frank Waer

H. F. Waer

William Walker

Sarah L. Wallace

G. Wallingford

Frantz Walters

John Welder

John Wilett

J. Williams

Minnie L. Williamson

Thomas T. Williamson

James B. Wood

John H. Wood

Maria G. Wood

Richard H. Wood

W. H. Woodward

Terrill M. Bledsoe was the historian of Rockport Lodge No. 323, A.F. & A.M. He presented his information in a document on the lodge letterhead, now held in the county archives.

In time, other fraternal and beneficial organizations became active in Aransas as well. The Rotary Club was organized in Rockport in March 1948, followed by the Woman's Club of Aransas County in June, and the Lions, at Fulton, in October.

Clara Driscoll was active and financially generous in civic and political affairs as early as 1903, when she provided funds to prevent a hotel from buying the Alamo Long Barracks in San Antonio. Before her death in 1945, she set up the Driscoll Foundation to provide a hospital and free clinic for sick and crippled children in Corpus Christi. A marker north of Bayside marks the site of the old Driscoll home.

The report regarding Clara Driscoll's childish remarks came from Lyman Russell, who wrote that "business managers and owners of the packeries in Fulton . . . petted her and taught her to give that answer."

The Williamson Moses home still stands at 409 Broadway in Rockport, and is generally known as the Bruhl-Gibson home. Moses was a justice of Refugio County and first Chief Justice of Aransas County. He was also the Rockport postmaster for a short time. The house was bought by James Fulton, and then by his son-in-law Albert Bruhl, whose daughter married Charlie Gibson. Their son still owns the house.

Dr. John W. Baylor's home remains at 617 South Water Street. He was a wealthy cattleman and one of the incorporators of the Texas and Mexican Railroad.

John Mathis deeded the Church Street mansion to his cousin, Thomas Henry Mathis.

The Lowe house developed an interesting history. After John C. Herring married Laura Olivia Clark, they bought the house and their daughter Lola was born there. Later it became the Baptist parsonage. As the bluff north of Fulton began to develop in the 1940s, the house was moved to the 1800 block of Fulton Beach Road. It was named "Casanda," meaning "the house that moved." The home's cypress floors were lovingly restored around 1990. Since then, another owner has altered the old house considerably.

The Scrivner home was located northwest of the intersection of Austin and the present business route of Highway 35.

Charles Bailey's house, no longer owned by the family, still stands at 717 South Church.

Richard Wood, son of pioneer John Howland Wood, built a fine Rockport home on Magnolia Street. William Welder Wood was born there in 1871, and John Howland Wood died there in 1904.

THE FULTON FAMILY

On July 4, 1870, George Fulton's oldest son, Henry Smith Fulton, died when he was thirty years old. He was buried in the Fulton Cemetery, high on the ridge at Myrtle and Fifth streets in Fulton.

The original of the railroad letter from Doughty to Fulton is in the Fulton Mansion files.

The Fulton Mansion Docent Manual noted that when George Fulton organized the Fulton Town Company, he already had commitments from investors, suggesting that he planned the project before leaving Kentucky.

Charles Carroll Fulton, the brother of George Ware Fulton, was the owner and editor of *The Baltimore American* newspaper.

COWBOYS

According to T. R. Fehrenbach, Hernán Cortés was the first man to use brands applied to live flesh with a hot iron. He branded not cattle, however, but Aztec slaves. The letter *G* burned into an Aztec cheek signified *guerra*, a prisoner of war. Since many of these men were put to work herding cattle, the transfer of the brand from man to beast came about quite naturally. "The brand," Fehrenbach wrote, "took on both legal and symbolic connotations. It became sacred."

Our description of branding operations came from an article written by C. C. Fulton on February 27, 1874, now in the archives of Texas A&M/Corpus Christi.

Among the first brands recorded in Aransas/Refugio was that of Col. James Power, who later sold the mark to John White Bower. The early record has been lost. Brands used in Aransas included:

1807	James Power	**1852**	Richard Wood
1840	J. M. Byrne & Sam Hewes		Tobias Wood
1845	Fredrick Welder		Thomas Welder
1847	J. W. Byrne	**1853**	Patrick Byrne
	William R. Pay	**1854**	James Power
	Moses Simpson	**1856**	Anson Barber
1848	Thomas O'Connor	**1857**	Richard T. Byrne
1849	Thomas K. Byrne		Delmas Dubois
	Jonas A. Casterline		Justillian Dubois
	John Wood	**1858**	Felix Dubois
1850	John Hynes		Lucas Dubois Jr.
	Henry Kroeger		John Thomas
1851	Martin S. Byrne	**1859**	Richard T. Byrne

Peter Fagan

Antoine Strauch

1860 Lizzie Doughty

P. J. Doughty

1864 Thomas Brundrett

1866 B. F. Doughty

Jefferson A. Dubois

1867 John Simpson

1869 C. B. Byrne

John D. Fagan

W. Traylor & Pat Hughes

1870 Summerville Dubois

Felix Dubois

Philip Power

1871 C. R. Byrne

Lucas Dubois Jr.

1872 A. H. Barber

A. L. Barber

George A. Brundrett

George A. Brundrett

George A. Brundrett

George A. Brundrett

Hannah Brundrett

John H. S. Brundrett

William A. E. Brundrett

1873 Felix Dubois

Mrs. Ellen Fagan

ℐ

1874   Neiville Dubois

D⌄D

1875   Lucas Dubois

S

Lucas Dubois Sr.

S X

Moner M. Dubois

D–D

1876   John E. Barber

Z ⅄

The following Aransas and area ranchers were among those who rode the great cattle trails sometime between 1867 and 1885: John C. Herring, Charles E. Johnson, Peter A. Johnson, Cyrus B. Lucas, Charles E. Simpson, Moses Findlay Simpson, Tobias Wood.

PACKERIES

On Fulton's Chaparral Street, just west of Fulton Beach Road, a historical marker stands beside a weed-covered, nondescript pile of rubble. It is all that remains of a rendering vat that was part of the Merriam Packing Company. The Texas Maritime Museum now displays a painting of this packery, created by John Grant Tobias in 1920 and originally owned by Arthur Bracht. Bracht stated that Tobias worked from an 1875 photograph and talked with old-timers who remembered the plant when it was in operation. However, the painting includes some inaccuracies—such as deep-water near shore and palm trees which were not brought to Aransas until later.

Between 1868 and 1882, packeries in addition to those mentioned in the text included: Lyman Meat Packing and Canning; Coleman, Mathis and Fulton; The American Meat Company; J. W. Baylor and Company; McNeill, Nash, and Company; D. L. and E. G. Holden; The American Beef Packery; Boston Packing Company; West and Weiser; Butler and Company; J. M. Doughty, and A. W. Clarke.

A small brochure, "A History of the Meat Packing Industry at Fulton, Texas, Before the Trail Drives," was published by Bracht's Food Store at some later date. It indicated that Cushman's Packery was located first on the island now known as Key Allegro, and later in Fulton. Doughty and Clark's packeries were south of Rockport.

The Fulton Mansion staff provided an original letter by James C. Fulton, George Fulton's son, detailing early packery failures: "In 1867, The American Packing Company put up the first packing plant that was built at Fulton. They were a northern company, undertook to cure meat by the ordinary brine method, but could do it only during real cold weather.

"Then a man named Cushman took over the same plant, but he made a failure.

"Another party took charge by the name of Dr. Spears. He was an embalmer during the Civil War, and tried to use something of the same process for curing beef. They would tie beeves up by their heels, cut their jugular veins, insert a tube and force brine into the carcasses until all the blood was displaced by it." The idea had no chance of success; too little salt permeated the meat to preserve it.

Professor Lyman and his son were next on the scene. They canned *roast* meat with a "perfect process" that James Fulton thought surely should have been a success. Perhaps the Lymans were ahead of their time.

Another early packery in Fulton belonged to William S. Hall. He operated there for eight years, slaughtering more than 40,000 head of cattle—over 11,000 of them in one year—but he, too, could pack beef only when the weather was cool.

The J. Frank Dobie quote about Rockport packeries came from an interview by writer/historian Shirley Ratisseau. Additional information on packeries came from "Texas Industry," written by Vera Lea Dugas and published in *The Southwestern Historical Quarterly*, October 1955.

A. H. McHugh, from the Blackjacks ranching family, provided a description of packery operations published in *The Progressive Farmer*. As young boy, McHugh worked with his father in the packery and remembered the cattle horns as enormously long, some measuring eight to nine feet from tip to tip. Mary Ellen McHugh's "Eating House" stood on Fulton Beach Road, closer to Cactus Street than Broadway. Her family still owns the property, but the original building was lost in a storm.

The Mercer log reported on June 11, 1870, that "the steamer *Fire Fly* arrived from Rockport with refrigerated beef on board."

THE LAMAR COMMUNITY

In 1869 Murdoch McRae and his partner Richard Byrne went to Galveston and purchased the *Neptune*, a two-masted schooner, for $300. They had the ship hauled into the deep bayou between Goose Island and the mainland, but never got around to repairing or launching her. They had intended to use the ship for coastal trade, but for years she lay in the bayou, slowly rotting away. In time, wind blew sand over the schooner, forming a little mound that everyone referred to as "Neptune Knoll." That knoll is no more; a canal community, Neptune Harbor, marks the spot where Murdoch's schooner lay.

James and Lydia Ann Wells' daughter Hannah married James McOscary Brundrett, son of Hannah Hillingsworth and George Brundrett. Hannah Wells Brundrett's younger sister, nicknamed Joe, was also sometimes called Zoe, a shortened form of her Christian name, Zobedia. Susie's full name was Susan E. F. Wells.

Martha Wellington's letter was included in "Letters by Lamplight: A Woman's View of Everyday Life in South Texas, 1873-1883," by Lois E. Myers.

The New County Seat

Various petitions favoring Rockport as county seat was signed by these citizens of Rockport, Fulton and Lamar:

F. I. Adams
George Adams
Willie Adams
W. G. Addams
A. F. Alfred
Alonso Allen
Thomas Allen
W. E. Allen
J. A. Andrews
Andrews
R. J. Andrews
R. W. Archer
U. N. Atkinson
J. Aviegonat
C. F. Bailey
A. H. Baker
Lugenio Ballou
Moses Ballou
Seth T. Ballou
Wilford C. Ballou
J. A. Barnefelt
J. Ogden Barclay
John Bartelt
Barth
T. J. Baylor
C. Bazen
Fredrich Bedeker
S. Z. J. Beetley
Leon Bendix
John D. Benham
J. W. Benson
P. Bickford
E. Bouch
William Brightman
C. L. Brown
James W. Brown
Louis Brown
John Brundrett
J. F. Burnett
C. R. Byrne
R. T. Byrne

T. K. Byrne
Orlando Cable
Frank Campbell
Rafael Cardenas
Francis M. Carroll
P. E. Carroll
Charles Carter
S. Gay Carter
Caruthers, Fulton & Co.
William Casterline
James Claherty
Joseph Cline
T. S. Coates
John T. Coates
J. H. Coons
A. Coustois
Peter Coyne
Frank Crowder
Anthony Culkin
John Cunningham
Elijah Decros
T. M. Dennis
M. H. Dickens
R. I. Dickey
W. C. Dickey
W. L. Dickson
Joseph Diebrell
Charles Diez
A. V. Doak
Donoghue
W. Dorethy
Joseph Doughty
E. G. Douglass
Charles Duke
S. A. Duke
Willis Duke
George Duran
L. J. Durmont
Jerome C. Dwyer
L. Eckhardt
R. T. Fabian

John Farrell
John Feldman
Henry Finegan
Nelson Flato
H. W. Fly
M. Friday
G. W. Fulton, Jr.
James G. Fulton
Don A. Fumes
M. T. Gaffney
Arthur Gamble
Ynocencio Garcia
Antonio Garza
B. K. George
T. B. Glenn
Lew Glover
C. A. Gorman
James Gourley
Jacob Graf
William D. Gregory
J. Greenough
William S. Hall
S. W. Hancock
Charles J. Harrison
James Harrison
E. D. Hastings
John Hauck
J. W. Hayes
Patrick Haynes
John Charles Herring
Charles M. Holden
D. L. Holden
E. G. Holden
John C. Howard
Harry Howard
George Howell
M. Jacobs
Andrew Johnson
D. I. Johnson
Peter Johnson
Theodore Johnson

C. H. Jones
Amos Jordan
James Kain
Henry Kaysing
Samuel King
Thomas S. King
Henry Kroeger
B. Kuykendall
T. H. Kuykendall
R. Labardie
Samuel Laconey
E. T. Lamford
P. Larkin
C. A. Leibrook
John Lewis
P. J. Lewis
C. Lily
R. A. Little
A. J. Logan
John E. Lozano
Ernest Luttjorhorn
J. E. Malone
J. Marsh
R. Martin
T. H. Mathis
Dennis McClure
Peter McGentry
James McLeod
McNeill, Nash & Co.
Burl McGrew
J. H. McGrew
William McGrew
William P. McGrew
J. A. McRae
M. W. McRae
W. S. McWhorter
Henry Miller
R. Miller
William Miller
E. Moffett
J. B. Moffett
J. Mohr
J. M. Moorhead

J. Williamson Moses
William Moritz
P. M. Neel
J. E. Newton
J. C. Nolan
John Obryon
William Oertling
Benjamin J. Overman
Charles Packard
John H. Paschal
Thomas Paulson
E. A. Perrenot
H. C. Phillips
Victor Eude Poillen
Charles S. Ponder
W. Powell
Jno. R. Pulliam
D. C. Rachal
O. P. Reid
P. L. Reid
U. Reinle
Mick Reinle
James Reynolds
E. W. Richards
W. W. Ricks
J. H. Roark
C. Roberts
H. A. Robertson
P. H. Robertson
J. C. Rooke
D. Ruice
E. Scheeberg
Augustus Shannon
Clark Shaefer
J. W. Shaw
J. Shirley
I. H. Shortridge
Adolf Shull
Joseph Simons
E. A. Skidmore
E. O. Skidmore
S. C. Skidmore
H. Slocumb

H. S. Smith
T. R. Smith
W. H. Snow
Stefani Sorokosh
R. H. Stafford
Thomas R. Stewart
Anton Strauch
Val Swartz
Matthew Talbot
J. R. Tally
Charles H. Teal
D. Teas
Louis Thaler
J. J. Thomas
John Thomas
W. T. Townsend
L. T. Tucker
D. McN. Turner
J. W. Twyman
E. P. Upton
F. P. Upton
S. E. Upton
Santos Valdez
R. D. Walsh
H. F. Waer
B. N. Wanters
Harrey Warren
James B. Wells
James B. Wells, Jr.
M. White
Albert Wiegard
Charles F. Williams
J. D. Williams
W. A. Williamson
Willis B. Willon
E. S. Winsor
R. H. Wood
Thomas Woods
W. H. Woodward
James Wright
L. H. Wyatt
Frank Yager

BARONS

PARTNERS

The Taft Ranch: A Texas Principality by Alva Ray Stevens, provided helpful information, as did research summaries and original documents in the files of the Fulton Mansion. One of the latter was a long letter from W. Richardson in Galveston. He seemed surprised when George Fulton wrote to him, avid to learn the whereabouts of members of the Smith family. "Indeed a generation has passed since we saw each other," Richardson responded, then supplied Fulton with much information that was helpful to him.

George Fulton was president of the proposed "Rockport, Fulton, Laredo and Mexican Pacific Railroad." James M. Doughty, John Mathis, and J. H. Hynes completed the executive board.

Andrew Sorenson subsequently went back to the sea as captain of the racing boat *Alice*, owned by Capt. S. B. Allyn. Sorenson made regular runs, giving bay rides to tourists, or making trips to the town of Tarpon on Mustang Island. In 1888 he married Sallie Hawes of the Matagorda ranching family and took a job captaining the boat that worked between Rockport and Quarantine Island, where Dr. W. E. Pugh was the physician in charge.

George William Fulton married Lee Caruthers, the daughter of his father's beef-packery partner. By 1878, she had borne him a daughter.

Northern markets wanted more than Texas beef. Milliners in Boston and New York avidly sought the feathers of Aransas birds to decorate their designs. In particular, they advertised for "heron plumes, egret plumes . . . seabirds of all species." Hides, too, were of value: "alligator skins . . . silver gray heron skins with plumes, white pelican and swan skins."

Aransas provided enough birds to satisfy the clothiers' needs, the interests of game hunters, and the appetite of egg hunters. One weekend foray brought in thousands of bird eggs, according to a news report. No one thought about species survival; the birds, fish, and animals had always been there, so everyone believed they would remain.

The last quarter of the nineteenth century was a time for attention to balance sheets, rather than a balance with nature. Aransas, and all of America, focused on its growth. Any cost to the environment seemed inconsequential.

By 1894, the whooping crane population stood at just 1,000.

ISLAND FORTRESS

Franz Josef Frandolig was named for the emperor of Austria. He named his son Napoleon Alexander Bonaparte Frandolig, honoring the emperor of France. Napoleon Frandolig's grandson James Stephen cleared up these confusions in an interview in 1991 and supplied other information to the authors in 1996. He still lived in Rockport.

Duval County honors John C. Duval, who escaped the Goliad massacre in

1836 and was the last survivor of Fannin's army to die. South Texans pronounce the name "*DOO-vahl.*"

According to James Frandolig, his grandfather sold Frandolig Point for $3,500. James considered that "a sizeable fortune" for the time, noting that "people were working for as little as fifteen dollars a month in this area."

The south end of Frandolig Point is designated as Nine Mile Point, although for years that term was incorrectly used for Live Oak Point.

MANSIONS

A 1910 promotional brochure clearly marked the location of William S. Hall's home on the bayfront, just north of Traylor Street.

The Fulton Mansion contains enough lumber to build twelve small tract homes.

Harriet Fulton sometimes had as many as seven servants, but fewer than half of them helped her with household chores; the rest worked on the Oakhurst grounds. Most were day-laborers, earning from seventy-five cents to double that each day.

For wealthy families like the Fultons, life offered opportunities to enjoy the "back to nature" move inspired by Thoreau, Emerson, and Rousseau. Harriet, like many before and after her, saw the broad sweep of Aransas as a source of perfect and inspirational beauty. But in keeping with the character of her times, she idealized nature and stayed a little distant from the wilderness. Harriet had a conservatory just off the mansion vestibule; there she could experience the excitement of exotic life through a safe profusion of greenery.

"Society" at Aransas was a rare thing; even Harriet's closest friends lived too far away simply to drop by for tea. The Mathises, only a few miles south, generally stayed for a full day at least and often overnight. Harriet entertained them with croquet on the lawn, or perhaps a swim from the wharf in front of her home. It had room at the end for a portable gazebo-shaped bath house.

If the weather was poor, visitors might enjoy the Ouija board, or the piano. Women sometimes joined Harriet for handicrafts. She particularly enjoyed making Battenburg lace, and her daughter Annie liked to paint china. Examples of Harriet's lace—Battenburg, bobbin, and knitted—were for a time on display at the Witte Museum in San Antonio. They were transferred to the mansion in 1994.

Only one child was born at the mansion—Annie and Eldridge Holden's daughter, Linda May. Harriet had to adjust to the way her daughters raised their children. When she was rearing those girls, and her sons, Harriet had followed strict Victorian standards: Children were miniature adults, to be seen and not heard; frolicking was definitely frowned upon. But Annie and Hattie, as mothers, encouraged the play of innocent, "natural children."

RIVALRY

The description of the Coleman home was included in the *Rockport Pilot's* centennial edition. After Charles Phelps Taft took over cattle company management, the ranch came to be known by his name. David Sinton was memorialized by the Texas town that bears his name.

HARSH REALITY

Losses

Rockport's first burial ground, in use 1868-1869, was located behind the shell ridge along Water Street. According to Winifred Lowther, the burials there included Confederate veterans Uncle Mote, Uncle Pick, and Mr. Ansley. In 1872 J. M. Doughty and J. W. Baylor deeded to Samuel H. Smith six and a half acres for a new cemetery north of Rockport. It is accessible from Picton or Tule streets. In time the remains from at least seven graves were relocated to the new site. Lowther wrote that some graves were never moved, but other accounts differ.

Some information regarding the wreck of the *Mary* came from *Sixty Years in the Nueces Valley* by South Texas pioneer Mrs. S. G. Miller. Lillian Benson, daughter of the *Mary's* captain, married Jed Brundrett in 1873.

Lydia Ann Wells' grave is marked simply: L. A. D. Wells. The unidentified news report of her funeral was quoted in Ruttiger's book regarding the Lamar cemetery.

John Fagan, Nicholas' son, is buried with his daughter Mary in the Lamar cemetery. John, his wife Ellen, and their children had lived at Lamar at one time, but then inherited San Antonio River land from bachelor John Williams. John Fagan had taken sixteen-year-old Mary back to Lamar to shop in May 1860. There, according to Lucile Fagan Snider, they caught cholera and died.

The Blackjacks and the Island

Hannah Wells Brundrett, second child of James and Lydia Ann Wells, was the wife of John McOscary Brundrett. John's sister, Mary, was married to Bernard Leonard Bludworth.

Helpful information came from the ranch family files of the Aransas National Wildlife Refuge and from a December 9, 1956, article in the *Corpus Christi Caller-Times*, written by Mrs. S. F. Jackson.

Bill Mott Bayou (Bilmott, Belle Mott, or Del Mott) was also known as Casterline Bayou.

Brundrett family descendant William Radeker provided an alternative version of the fire that took Hannah Brundrett's life: She was cooking a pot of beans which suddenly boiled over, causing sparks that caught her dress afire. Hannah ran outdoors to protect six-month-old John McOscary—and to prevent the house from burning down—but high winds fanned the flames that engulfed her dress. On her deathbed, Hannah asked her mother-in-law, doughty old Hannah Brundrett Thompson Gaston, to raise the baby. Lydia Ann Brundrett later joined the Catholic church and took the name Genevieve.

Linda Frome, *Rockport Pilot* reporter, was working on a long article about the Seward/Picarazzi families at the time of her death. We found her notes invaluable.

LAST OF A BREED

Josie McRae Bennet's diary revealed that she, her mother Mary Ann, and her surviving sisters held a three-day reunion in 1908, "camping out at the old home."

The shop built by Archibald McRae, and used by his son Murdoch, collapsed in the next storm. Josie reported that half of it blew into Mrs. Hawes' yard, "but Ella carried it all back, piece by piece. It is sacred to her." Mary Ann Heard McRae died where she had lived her last years—in Cuero with her daughter, Ruth. She is buried in the Rockport cemetery beside her daughter, Marie Herring.

Ella McRae Clay lived in the old house until her death. She had no children and heirs sold the property to their relative, Jim Heard of Refugio. Not long after, the house began to crumble and had to be torn down. The great oak, undisputed monument to early pioneer Archibald McRae, his wife Vincey, and his son Murdoch, is equally a memorial to Mary Ann and to a family tree of daughters who carried McRae blood, though not the name.

A school opened in Sparks Colony in 1893, serving about twenty-five students. But some years there just weren't enough pupils to hold classes, so the few were sent to Rockport. Captain Evans' daughter Mary taught at Sparks Colony and later Leopold Bracht's daughter Lola did too.

WEATHER

In 1870 the U.S. Weather Bureau made its first meteorological observations based on reports gathered by telegraph from twenty-four locations. A year later, the Bureau began keeping official weather records.

Some storm information came from *Indianola: The Mother of Western Texas* by Brownson Malsch.

Capt. Marion Seward was caught at sea during the 1875 storm. As he fought his way home to San José, he remembered his wife's frequently voiced fear that a great storm would come and blow them off their fragile isle. When he found his family safe, Captain Seward moved them inland.

The 1886 Indianola storm ended St. Mary's, as well as Indianola. It tore down homes and washed away all the valuable lumber that could have rebuilt them. At Lamar, that hurricane took the Presbyterian Church. Bert Ballou bought the lumber for $6, loaded it on Ham Smith's barge, and took it to Rockport for the Presbyterian church there.

In 1898 another sort of storm shook America as a whole: The United States government demanded that Spain withdraw from Cuba, and Spain responded by declaring war. On July 1 Teddy Roosevelt made a victorious assault on San Juan Hill, Cuba, and two days later, the United States Navy defeated the Spanish fleet in Santiago Harbor.

THE CITY OF ROCKPORT
HOMES AND BUSINESSES

Here and in subsequent sections, we borrowed text from *Rockport Artists' Sketchbook* by Sue Taylor.

Local professional historian Bruce Taylor-Hille provided this helpful analogy concerning conveyances. A surrey was the "soccer mom car" of its day, a coach was the equivalent of a standard sedan, and a carriage was like a luxury car.

James Fulton bought the home that had belonged to Williamson and Victoriana Moses; he and his wife Fannie Dunlap made the improvements on it. After pharmacist Albert Bruhl married the Fulton's daughter Hattie, he bought the house for her.

The Kennedy girls, as heirs of their grandfather Joseph F. Smith, owned sixteen lots along Austin Street south of the present Highway 35 business route. They used eight of the lots to build their house and outbuildings.

James M. Hoopes was married to Annie Gibbs. He served in the Union army during the Civil War and built his house on the corner of Broadway and the present Business Route of Highway 35 in the 1880s. Hoopes turned the place into a hotel in the early 1890s.

Leopold Bracht's wife was Clara Freitag. Mrs. Roland Bracht was the former Zoe Prophet. Judge John Hynes married Ellen (possibly Mary Ellen) Cody. W. M. Moore's wife may have been Myrtle Hays.

Leopold Bracht's home was built in the Oklahoma community—a little south of Rockport—in 1881 and moved to 902 Cornwall, in Rockport, eight years later. It still stands, as does Adolph Bracht's home near the southwest corner of Highway 35 and Magnolia.

John Hynes had San Antonio architect Viggo Kohler design his home built in 1874. Hynes' son Thomas married Frances Brundrett, granddaughter of George Brundrett and James Wells, interweaving several Aransas dynasties.

Hynes gave his Austin Street house to his daughter Clara as a wedding gift. Her husband, Sam H. Smith, had only been in Rockport since 1867. Before that, he was a Texan soldier and the first sheriff of Montgomery County. By the time of the Civil War, Sam Smith had moved to Bee County and served in the army as one of its citizens.

Albert Bruhl's home, bounded by the bay and Patton, Sabinal, Cedar, and Lady Clare streets, had several owners before the O'Connor family bought it and added more rooms.

The Baylor, Hanks, and John Sorenson homes still stand on Water Street. Baylor sold his to cattleman T. P. McCampbell, who rented and then sold it to the Norvells. Much later, John Lee Herring, son of Marie McRae and James Clark Herring, bought and restored the house, then sold it to his sister, Mary Pearl Herring Patrick. Regrettably, Irene's lattice was removed in a more recent renovation.

L. O. Terry built a four-room cedar house in 1867. Although it has been altered a little over the years, it still stands on its original site, 618 North Magnolia, and is generally considered the oldest wood structure still in use in the area. In later years, residents knew it as the Joe Johnson home. Across the street, at 617 North Magnolia, stands the Mathis/Sneed home, dating from about 1906.

The Sorenson Place condominiums now occupy Simon Sorenson's homesite at Water and Bay streets. The house was moved to 802 N. Live Oak in 1984. Sorenson's ship chandlery, which remained as a family grocery business until the 1970s, now houses the Estelle Stair Art Gallery. An original canopy remains in front of a neighboring shop at 504 South Austin.

The original Methodist church was located at the corner of Bay and Live Oak streets. The tin-roofed parsonage remains just behind that site, at the corner of Bay and Church. Local lore holds that it was a "kit" house from Sears and Roebuck, although no records remain to prove it.

The Baptists built on South Church Street in 1873, a year after the Methodists. James M. Doughty, Dr. John W. Baylor, and Mr. and Mrs. D. D. Scrivner were among the charter members.

The Presbyterian congregation met at the Baptist Church before building their own in 1906-7, when T. H. Mathis donated land at the corner of Market and South Magnolia.

The first Aransas County Court House (following use of Mehle Hall on the west side of Austin Street north of Market) stood, as the modern one does, on a block bounded by Concho, Live Oak, Mimosa, and Magnolia streets.

Rockport's First National Bank was organized July 29, 1890. The Board of Directors—J. E. Elgin, R. H. Ellers, G. W. Fulton, Jr., James C. Fulton, J. M. Hoopes, John R. Hoxie, Victor Kohler, L. B. Randall, J. P. Smith, John H. Traylor, and R. H. Wood—elected Wood as president and Hoopes as secretary and first cashier.

Simon B. Sorenson purchased Traylor's Del Mar Hotel in 1910, but as values became depressed, the building deteriorated.

Other notable older homes in Rockport include the 1904 "old Jameson place" at 811 N. Live Oak and the 1915 Ferris home at 601 North Magnolia. The Piercy home at 614 North Magnolia was moved there from Little Bay Shores, where it was constructed in 1906.

The Oklahoma community was about one and one half miles south of Market Street, near and west of the intersection of Highway 35 and Loop 70 (Church Street).

Bates McFarland built a prestigious bayfront home that still stands, greatly altered, between Orleans and Sabinal, then not far from the water's edge. The fine structure featured a square turret to the third floor, wraparound covered porches on both the first and second floors, white Doric columns, and low banisters. McFarland installed two fireplaces and he, or a subsequent owner, hung an amethyst crystal chandelier that remains in the house.

In March 1894 Bates McFarland deeded his various land acquisitions, including his homestead, to his wife. She wrote a will naming G. R. Scott, her husband's law partner, as guardian of her four small children and executor of her $38,000 estate. When she died within the year, Bates must have been shocked by

Paragraph Eight of that will: "I have not forgotten my husband, Bates McFarland, but no part of my estate shall go to him for life nor in fee."

The McFarland home was purchased by bank president Charles G. Johnson, son of Capt. Peter Johnson. Charles served as mayor of Rockport from 1910 to 1914. His daughter Carrie married Charles Thomas Picton, son of jetties engineer David Means Picton. In 1927 Carrie gave birth to a son, Harold Hynes Picton, an influential citizen of Rockport through the 1990s. In the early 1930s, the Picton family remodeled their home in Federal style and covered it with brick veneer.

The Estes school was built in 1906 and served thirty to forty students until it was destroyed by the 1919 storm.

James Stephen Frandolig stated that the oldest cemetery in Aransas lies near Estes. It has recently been "found" and is enjoying some restoration, although the gravestones now legible are relatively new. Most bear Spanish surnames, as perhaps the earliest ones did as well.

THE RAILROAD AND THE TOURISTS

During the summer of 1888, Goliad citizen Elisha Norvell attended a political convention in Corpus Christi, and he took his wife Irene along. They heard all the talk about Rockport and the probability of its becoming a great port.

Some of the conventioneers engaged passage on the *Nellie Swinney*, a small sailboat bound for Rockport. Irene reported on the experience for the *Goliad Guard*.

Later, in a memoir, Irene Norvell wrote that her husband Elisha caught "Rockport fever" and wanted to get in on the ground floor of the town's development. It seems clear, though, that she caught the fever too.

Elisha Norvell spent the rest of the summer in Rockport and secured a job as extension agent for the railroad. In August 1888 he moved his wife and his in-laws into one of the first homes built in the budding town—the old Baylor place on Water Street.

As soon as the family got settled, Irene Barton Norvell went to San Antonio and bought a piano. She put an advertisement in the *Beacon,* soliciting music pupils for herself and boys for her father's classical school. Her first application came from Lola Herring, closely followed by two Bludworth girls and many others.

Irene's students gave recitals for invited guests—but only in her home for the first three years. There was no suitable public place until the Bailey Pavilion opened.

May Mathis was Irene's first art pupil. She was only nine years old, but "very original in her opinions and had one ready for every subject."

Professor Barton hardly had his school opened when the public school began and its trustees asked him to be superintendent. He was ready to accept, but then the trustees, in a move that seemed ahead of their time, told the professor he could not read scripture or pray in the school. As a compromise, the trustees finally agreed that Professor Barton might repeat the Lord's Prayer and read the Bible so long as he made no comment on it.

Este means "east" in Spanish. Anecdotal information suggests that Este Flats—East Flats—became Anglicized as Estes.

Aransas Pass, Texas, published by that town's Chamber of Commerce, provided helpful information, as did the Aransas County Historical Society's historical marker application regarding the SAAP. Sid Freeborn's oral history provided interesting highlights.

Anecdotal information and some family papers indicate that Charles Henry McLester was engineer (or maybe conductor) on the first SAAP train to arrive in Rockport. No one has been able to obtain proof, since the Southern Pacific will not open old records.

The old Merchant's Square is now honored by a historical marker.

Much information on the Bludworth family was provided by the Aransas National Wildlife Refuge. Tom Bludworth gave the Refuge newspaper articles and his handwritten memoir.

The first Rockport school was founded in 1881, on a plot of land bordered by Live Oak, Laurel, Pearl, and Orleans streets. It was made public in about 1884, with Miss Nold as principal, supervising teachers Ella Evans and Ida Clark. On September 24, 1888, a city election approved free schools for Rockport, with J. C. Fulton, G. F. Perrenot, John C. Herring, Sam H. Smith, T. H. Mathis, C. H. Butts, and C. L. Dean as trustees.

Bessie Johnson's handwritten memoir, in the Historical Commission archives, was also helpful, as was a Rockport Chamber of Commerce report, "Aransas County—One Hundred Years."

Rick Benjamin, director of the Paragon Ragtime Orchestra, New York City, provided information on that genre.

SOCIETY PAGES

The King's Daughters, founded in 1886 for development of interdominational spiritual life, was a part of the Chautauqua movement. It is still active.

HEADLINES

A 1956 *Corpus Christi Caller-Times* article and another by Mrs. E. H. Norvell, published in Goliad's newspaper the *Guard*, helped our description of the Shell Hotel. The fires of which Mrs. Norvell wrote followed the collapse of the building boom in 1891.

The *Beacon* newspaper gave its address as the corner of St. Mary and Magnolia streets. The word *buncomb*, or correctly *buncombe*, is a variant of *bumkum*, defined as empty or meaningless talk, especially by a politician. The term arose from a remark made around 1820, referring to Bumcombe County, North Carolina.

The fire department motorized in 1912 with a 1911 Model T Ford to hold the chemical tank.

THE *NOVICE*

Some information came from Bludworth records at the Texas State Maritime Museum. The earliest recorded boat built in Rockport was the Bludworth's *Cannie,* christened in 1880 in honor of Alcanza Howard Wood.

On September 4, 1894, *Novice* beat *Wasp* by almost eight minutes and the newspaper proclaimed, "The boat that beats the *Novice* is yet to be made." She came to an ignominious end, wrecked half a mile from Seadrift at the mouth of San Antonio Bay.

A *Corpus Christi Caller-Times* article, undated and pasted in an old scrapbook, reported that Karánkawas had used mahogany drift for dugout canoes. Capt. John Mercer's 1874 log included this: "Captain Hall wanted to see the mahogany logs that are on the beach. He wants to take them to Sabine and have them sawed into planks." In 1882 the *Galveston News* reported: "We learn that quite a business is being introduced on a section of the Gulf Coast by collecting mahogany. Lumber scattered along the beach on Padre Island and elsewhere is being shipped to northern markets." The *Caller-Times* concluded by observing that "mahogany is still being found on the beach," and listed Corpus homes that feature mahogany driftwood decor.

In 1997 John (Jay) Bludworth lived in Rockport, but the rest of the family had moved on. Jay explained that his father, the oldest of the Bludworth boys, had the opportunity to open a new shipyard in Galveston. Most of the family followed him. The shipyard, named for the family, was among many that would eventually dot the eastern Texas coast: John Bludworth Marine in Galveston, Bludworth Bond in Texas City, and Bludworth Shipyard Inc. in Houston. All the shipyards are in operation today and are still run by the family.

THE TOWN OF FULTON

TURTLES

We found helpful information in *The Coast Fisheries of Texas,* an 1890 report by the Commissioner of Fish and Fisheries. "While the supply of fish may be decreasing," the report stated, "yet there does not appear to be an urgent necessity for very great restriction." Reasons for the conclusion were economic—throwing men out of work, removing revenue from towns, eliminating a "cheap and wholesome article of food."

Modern anglers might be surprised at the list of fish caught in the bays; many are considered offshore species today. According to Karen Meador, at the Parks and Wildlife Marine Lab, jackfish, bluefish, pompano, and robalo (snook) are still seen in the bays. Spanish mackerel are sometimes caught in Lydia Ann Channel. Hogfish, sawfish, and jewfish are certainly considered offshore species.

Turtle canneries other than those mentioned were located at Turtle Cove south of Port Aransas and at Packery Channel on North Padre Island, now within the city limits of Corpus Christi.

Henry Bailey recounted his turtle story for publication in the *Rockport Pilot.*

Other information came from a Historical Society interview with Marion Johnson, and our conversations and correspondence with Shirley Ratisseau.

GOLD AND ASHES

The work Theodore Roosevelt referred to in his letter to Colonel Fulton was his book, *Winning of the West.*

WOMEN ALONE

The Simpson house was probably built in St. Mary's in 1867. Simpson acquired two Fulton lots, at the corner of Broadway and Second streets, during the winter of 1898-99. He got a barge to move his thirty-year-old house from St. Mary's to Fulton and the house was on the lots by 1900. It still stands.

Captain Joel Stinson served in the War of 1812 and arrived in Texas about 1841. It is likely that he and his family came to Aransas in 1881-82. Ropesville would later be known as Tarpon and then as Port Aransas.

Kathrine Isabella Simpson subsequently married William Burke Johnson.

IN THE NAME OF PROGRESS
THE JETTIES

Information on Corpus Christi's efforts in 1859 came from "First Annual Report of the Directors of the Corpus Christi Ship Channel Company for the year 1859," a document recently acquired by the Mary and Jeff Bell Library, Texas A&M University, Corpus Christi.

It's interesting to note that on April 25, 1859, ground was broken for another channel—the Suez Canal.

Portions of Rockport's 1868 dike on San José are sometimes visible, sometimes obscured by shifting sands. Granite boulders lie just north of the lighthouse, some yards east of the opposite shore.

Bailey's 1870 editorial was reprinted in the *Rockport Pilot* on July 2, 1959.

The man who designed the Mansfield jetty, Brig. Gen. Samuel M. Mansfield, was responsible for much engineering work along the entire coast during this period.

Alice Craig, granddaughter of David Means Picton, stated that her grandfather owned a quarry near San Antonio from which came much of the sandstone used in his work. She added that most of the granite used in jetty construction came from Granite Mountain near Austin.

It was the Galveston Wharf Company that earned the epithet "Octopus of the Gulf" because of its grasping policies. We have broadened the characterization, as we feel Aransas citizens must have done in 1889.

The March 17, 1892, issue of *The Aransas Harbor Herald* carried a long article by George Fulton, who took great pains to establish, once again, James Power's neglect and the validity of the claim to Aransas made by Fulton, Henry Smith, and others.

New sources providing helpful information were Dorothy Nims' thesis, "A History of the Village of Rockport" and *Rails Across the Bay* by F. A. Schmidt.

Some timbers and much flint roadbed of the rail terminal to the old Corpus Christi channel remain on oyster reefs in Redfish Bay.

A Sportsman's Paradise

Aransas' rich reserve of wildlife proved both an asset and a liabiliity. To protect such reserves, the State of Texas banned commercial hunting in 1903, but had few wardens to enforce the law.

In 1907 Governor T. M. Campbell undertook a more extensive revision of the laws regulating wildlife, addressing sports issues as well as commercial ones. Since Campbell had enjoyed both hunting and fishing on Richard Wood's San José ranch, he commissioned his friend to draft a comprehensive conservation plan. When it was adopted as law, Campbell appointed Wood the first Game, Fish and Oyster Commissioner of Texas.

Andrew Sorenson's first site was on Swan Lake and it is still operated as a hunting center. Sorenson purchased his second property in 1910, calling it the Sorenson Club. One of the two buildings he moved there is still in use. The dining room was torn down in 1994 and replaced by another on the same site.

Through the years, Andrew entertained many notable individuals including Governor Peek of Wisconsin, Tris Speaker, Connie Mack, W. L. Moody, Jr., George V. Maverick, Col. C. M. Hobby, and a long list of doctors, lawyers, bankers, and other Texas leaders.

Andrew Sorenson served as manager of his club until 1918. He was followed by Arthur Curry, George Harrell, Milton Harrell (his son), and Dave "Bubba" Davis. Davis preferred not to divulge the names of famous members. "Whenever they got here they were just another duck hunter," he said. "Nobody was treated like a big shot, but nobody acted like one either." The current club manager is Robert Atkins.

Various records give I. C. Thurmond's home as San Antonio, Amarillo, and elsewhere. It is likely that he had business in all these places.

Fish Houses

Information came from a 1939 newspaper interview with David Rockport Scrivner, the interview with Marion Johnson, the family history written by Bruce Davis and the Aransas County Centennial booklet.

The *Corpus Christi Caller-Times*, 1958, reported that the first ice shipped to Texas came by schooner from the lakes of Maine and New York. The article cited Andrew Sorenson as explaining that the ice was cut in slabs four feet square and packed in sawdust.

THE OIL BUSINESS

Hamill's description of the Spindletop gusher came from his oral history in The University of Texas Archives. Wildcatters obtained Aransas oil and gas leases and followed one dream after another. J. T. Corrigan, F. Gordon Gibson, James H. Sorenson, Sr., Frank Sparks, and the Texas Coastal Oil Syndicate were among those associated with these early tests. The County archives includes interesting promotional materials from the period.

POPULATIONS

WEBER'S STORE

The Weber grocery in Fulton, previously owned by the Caruthers family, stood on Fulton Beach Road north of Cactus. Marion Johnson gave the description of his grandfather Weber's store in an interview for the Historical Society. Delphine Weber subsequently married Marvin Davis and also provided a helpful interview to the Historical Society.

The original Fulton school building is now the Town Hall, just north of Broadway on Eighth Street. The first school bell hangs at the modern Fulton Elementary School. Each year on the last day of school, fourth graders are "rung out" of elementary school by the historic bell.

PROMOTERS

In 1909 three San Antonians—E. O. Burton, H. H. Danforth, and W. Nelson—chartered the Aransas Pass Channel and Dock Company. Their plan was to construct and maintain a deep water channel from Harbor Island to Aransas Pass and to operate docks there. They also started work on a new railroad from Aransas Pass to Harbor Island.

Still people in Rockport and Fulton were more concerned about competition from Corpus Christi, with a population over 8,000, than Aransas Pass, with only 1,197 citizens. Rockport had a population of 1,382, ahead of Aransas Pass, but woefully behind Corpus Christi. When Rockport promoters added in eight households in the Blackjacks (fifty more people), nine homes in Lamar (another fifty), twenty-five in eight farms near around Salt and Copano Creeks, and the few remaining in Fulton, they arrived at a grand total of over 1,500 people.

The Gulf Coast Immigration Company had offices in the telephone bulding that fronted on Water Street, right next door to the First National Bank. GCIC's thirty-two-page brochure is a treasure of photographs and information. It included photographs of farm houses, city residences, lush farms, and open lands on Live Oak and Blackjack peninsulas. There were pictures of bathers, yachtsmen, duck hunters, and fishermen.

The brochure noted that Rockport "is the first safe Port north of the Panama Canal and the last one south of Galveston, and is just the right distance between the Great Mexican Harbor of Tampico and the Galveston, Texas, harbor."

The promoters included their sketch of a proposed Sportsmen's Club; they displayed photos of a pleasure pier and dancing pavilion, a "beautiful shell drive along the beach," and an "automobile speedway." They pointed out that the beautiful oleander-lined bayfront at Market Street was a "favorite trysting place for lovers."

We find the brochure's last page ironic. The president of this immigration effort was named A. D. Powers.

As newcomers responded to the publicity, the Shell Hotel became the Oak Shore Club. Later Andrew Sorenson renamed it Oak Shore Inn and made it a tourist resort well remembered for large parties during duck hunting season.

Andrew Sorenson spent over forty years as a Commissioner of the Texas Game, Fish and Oyster Commission.

IMMIGRANTS

In his oral history for the Historical Society, Frank Covarúbbias said that the first Covarúbbias family in Rockport was that of his grandfather. The man had arrived here from Port Isabel, but was originally from Sota la Marina, Mexico. We are intrigued by another possibility, however. Hobart Huson listed a "Cobarrubias" among the original Power colonists. Perhaps forgotten pioneers moved south when Texas gained her independence and their decendants slowly returned.

THE YOUTH OF ROCKPORT

Mary Pearl Herring's schoolmates included Bessie Johnson, Pattie Bailey, John Lee Herring, Gladys Bruhl, Dudley Bracht, Joe Sneed, Eddie Picton, and Velma Picton.

Two years after President Taft's visit to Rockport, Harriet Fulton died. When the will was probated, her estate's total value was listed at little more than Harriet and Colonel Fulton had paid for the mansion's rugs thirty-five years before.

In 1912 the worldwide population of whooping cranes stood at just 200. But birds were not the concern of most people in those days.

Ed Moore opened a transport company in 1914, achieving a number of "firsts" for the town. His was a new type of business for the area; he was the first man ever to drive a motor vehicle over the streets of Rockport; and he was the first person to operate a motor truck from Corpus Christi to Rockport. Optimistic about motor transportation, Ed Moore became the wholesale distributor for all Magnolia Oil Company products. When he started a motor bus line that made four daily trips to Corpus Christi, he became the first man to take a mail contract from the railroad. And he made better mail service a reality.

Judge Baldwin's wife organized the Twentieth Century Club, which flourished for many years. Mrs. Norvell was among the ladies of Aransas who met on Saturday afternoons. She wrote: "We confined our studies almost entirely to Shakespeare, only one year each to Mythology and Texas History."

In the 1930s, and possibly much earlier, Prophet's Confectionary had a black marble counter. Small round tables had tops to match it. The table legs, and the chairs, were of white metal.

LARGE CAUSES, LOCAL EFFECTS
THE WAR TO END WAR

Even though a ship launching was a great event, several months of finish work on each boat remained.

James and Mattie Lou Lathrop built their home at 1229 South Church. Their daughter Lucille later married Ted Little and her audio tape supplied information on the family.

Hammon George Smith's first job in Aransas County was at Hall's Packing Company in Fulton. From there he moved to the Blackjacks, where he managed a small truck farm and used his sailing scow, the *Bugaboo*, to haul produce to market. He also transported groceries, supplies, and lumber to various towns and settlements on Aransas, San Antonio, and Copano Bays. After eight years in the Blackjacks, Ham's wife and six children were weary of isolation, and Ham decided to move them to Fulton.

He was making his final trip of the family move on a cold, rainy day, carrying hogs and chickens, when the boat's gasoline engine exploded. Ham threw the flaming stove overboard, then jumped into the bay himself, his clothing on fire. It took him a year and a half to recover from the burns. Ham then moved to Rockport and continued his freight business with a two-masted sailing ship, the *Jerome Kern*.

PROHIBITION

Bartee Haile's newspaper series, "This Week in Texas History," provided a helpful article about Carry Nation. It included the facts that she moved to Texas a decade after the Civil War, that she farmed near the San Bernard River, operated a hotel at Columbia, and purchased another hotel in Rosenberg. One must wonder if she could have been the same Carrie P. Nations listed as owning a Rockport lot by 1872.

The Prohibition party formed in 1869 and the Woman's Christian Temperance Union in 1874.

Irene Norvell told Ella Evans, Winifred Lowther's sister, of Mrs. Hanks' remarks regarding neighborliness.

Harry Traylor told Shirley Ratisseau the story of smuggled liquor found in the shallows off Nine Mile Point. She added that during a hurricane some twenty-five years later one full bottle, covered with barnacles, drifted onto Fulton beach. Shirley said it caused a real sensation.

"THE WORST HURRICANE IN HISTORY"

Few Rockport newspaper reports of the 1919 hurricane exist. Most of the old papers were washed away in the 1934 storm. We are fortunate to have many eyewitness accounts of the hurricane, however. Among these are the written memoirs of Irene Norvell and the oral histories of Gladys Bruhl Gibson, Paul Clark Sorenson, Lola Bracht Woellert, and Norvell Jackson. Alpha Kennedy Wood published her recollections of the storm in *Texas Coastal Bend: People and Places*. The Rouquette (and related families) history provided additional information.

In Fulton, Frank Casterline let 150 hogs out of his pen, thinking to save them from the hurricane. At feeding time the hogs came back and all but one of them drowned. Frank's wife Florence was afraid the wind would take the breath right out of her baby boy, Leslie Eugene. But he survived until the summer of 1997.

Lawrence and Robert Dietrich, decendants of Mary Ann McHugh, carried their Grandma Jane from the old house to a skiff. Other family members were already in the small boat, waiting. They rowed or drifted toward the school and stayed in the Phillips house nearby. Robert went back home then, to put some furniture up on blocks. He found bread in the oven and took it with him when he drifted back inland. Everyone in the Phillips house had coffee and fresh-baked bread as they awaited the dawn.

Rick Pratt, current lighthouse keeper, wrote "Working with Ghosts" for the Texas Maritime Museum newsletter. We are grateful for the information it supplied regarding the 1916 storm and subsequent sections of this book.

We also found useful information in the Associated Press "Facts on File", F. R. Holland Jr.'s *Aransas Pass Light Station* and Bobby Jackson's thesis, along with other sources previously cited.

In the very early days of telephones in Aransas County, William Britz and J. D. Cravens, Southwestern Bell employees, temporarily strung the lines along barbed wire fences, according to Shirley Ratisseau's recollection of her father's conversation with Britz.

While Alpha Kennedy Wood stated that 6,400 cattle were on San José Island, the San Antonio *Express* newspaper reported only 3,000 there before the storm.

The upper story of the Simon Sorenson house was so badly damaged that it had to be torn down, and the family never replaced it.

Roy Court, the son of county judge Paul P. Court, spent fourteen years with the Texas Quarantine Service and five years with the U.S. Government Quarantine Service.

Rockport Cemetery records listed the following storm victims: H. Frank, Minnie (wife), Olive, Ida; David Little, and David Little, Jr.

The huge fan and most of the works from the Fulton windmill remain in the tree and are visible from the Mansion's back parking lot.

The Rockport high school was replaced by a one-story building. Later, when a new high school was built, the old building became Rockport Elementary and then the Early Childhood Center—kindergarten and first grade. It still served in 1997.

David Rockport Scrivner and his wife lived at 509 S. Live Oak for many years. The house is still standing.

The Heldenfels warehouse and office burned in 1931.

The argument as to whether the 1900 storm struck Galveston at the end of one century, or the beginning of another, is an issue that recurs as Aransas prepares for the turn of the millenium. The question resolves easiest by considering that a child born in 1990 is one year old in 1991, completes ten years in 2000, and begins a second decade in 2001.

AFTER THE STORM
COPING

Ted Atwood married Frances Johanna (Fannie) Schleider. Their son Johnny received a B.S. in Petroleum and Gas Engineering from Texas A&I University and married Gayle Bigelow of Aransas Pass. For most of Johnny's working career, he and Gayle lived in Houston. When the oil crisis was at its worst, Johnny said, "I just quit; I came home."

The 1890 report, *Coast Fisheries of Texas*, described a live barge as "roughly constructed, usually of slats in the form of and about the same size as a skiff; in fact, some of the fishermen use an old skiff, cutting or boring holes in it and covering it with an open slat-work top. The live-fish cars . . . have capacity for four hundred to two thousand pounds of fish, according to their size and the temperature of the water." According to the report, such barges were necessary in part because "the sailboats never have 'wells' in which the fish may be kept alive."

Clara Bracht's beach cottage still stands at 210 Business 35 North, but she would not recognize its modern stone finish.

Fred and Inez Bracht built a stone house on Omohundro, positioned so that residents still look straight down Maple Street and see the bay.

Lucas' ownership in San José Island was described as "all of St. Joseph's Island in Aransas County, Texas (except the parts thereof conveyed to the Aransas Pass Harbor Company and the United States of America prior to June 19, 1914), and comprising approximately 30,688.5 acres, and including all of the Power Hewetson Grant, and all of Blocks Two, Four, Six, Eight and Ten on the South end of said Island." Blocks One, Three, Five, Seven, Nine, and "A" comprised a fifty-two-acre U.S. government right-of-way along the pass. Perry Bass, early an avid yachtsman at Aransas, subsequently acquired the ranch from his uncle Sid Richardson. He and his wife Nancy Lee continue to enjoy their island retreat.

Readers outside cattle country may not know that cow chips, or cow patties, are dried excremental deposits left by bovines. Rich in grass roughage, they make excellent tinder.

Denman's European boars bred with domestic hogs gone wild in the Blackjacks, producing a hybrid feral hog. This animal is in many ways distinct from the native javelina. None of the other exotics that Denman brought in still survive.

The Ku Klux Klan had its beginnings on Christmas Eve in 1865, when a group of Confederate veterans in Pulaski, Tennessee, formed a social club.

Jimmy Silberisen told the Henry Ballou story to Glenn DeForest, who in turn related it to David Herring. David wrote it down and supplied background information on guiding.

Tom DeForest had a concrete-block drugstore (no pharmacy, just patent medicines), soda fountain, and short-order cafe at Broadway and the beach road. James M. Furlong bought it in 1953 and built a driftwood lean-to shack on the north side. There he opened a Fulton restaurant: "Peg Leg Cap'n Jim's." It was a true name, Furlong said, because he was an amputee and a deep-sea captain. For almost twenty years, people enjoyed the beachcomber atmosphere and weekend pig roasts. Tourists on the highway followed the aroma into town—and sometimes they followed the sound of a jazz band playing there.

By 1997, J. F. Bullard's pines towered above businesses along Highway 35, with scattered groves almost to the tip of Live Oak Peninsula and on Lamar. "I won't sell one of the trees," he said in an interview some years earlier, "but I should have enough seed for everyone who wants to try and raise pines." It is obvious that many did so successfully.

PESCADORES AND COLORED COOKS

Hillis Dominguez remembered the Mexican-American community as a six-block area bounded by Ann, Young, Bay, and Hackberry streets. He said that the Mexican section of the movie theater was "on the left hand side up front."

The first two black graduates of Aransas schools were Betty Jean Mack and Howard Predon, in 1960.

Avelina Falcón Piña was elected to the Rockport City Council in 1985 and served a two-year term. In 1997 her family's restaurant—on Highway 35 north of FM 188—offered popular, authentic Mexican food. Information regarding LULAC came from the *Corpus Christi Caller-Times* centennial edition.

The blacks' one-room school was destroyed in the 1919 storm and was never replaced. Later the community Baptist church was set up as an elementary school for the "coloreds."

According to John and Baby Ruth Dunman, the black families of Aransas lived close together on Young Street west of Market. They carried these family names: Brown, Dickey, Dunman, Givens, Huff, Richardson, Stafford, Williams. All their early homes were damaged by Hurricane Celia and then torn down.

GIFTS FROM THE SEA

Ruby Hart described Jim Tuttle as a huge man and "quite a character."

Some information on shrimp and shrimping came from a pamphlet produced by the Texas Parks and Wildlife Department and from an article in *Aransas Pass, Texas.* According to Johnny Atwood, commercial varieties of shrimp include white, brown, Brazilian pink, rock, and hopper shrimp. Shrimp now ranks as the nation's most popular seafood. Texas produces more than 70 million pounds of them each year.

When Zeph Rouquette the younger died, Bunker Wendell bought out his share of their joint business and renamed it Wendell Industries.

HUGGING THE COAST

In 1997 a Rockport realtor priced a front foot of waterfront land at $500 to $1,000.

The SAAP sold its franchise to the Southern Pacific in 1925. The Aransas County Navigation District was established that same year.

Ham Smith's filling station was located on the northeast corner of the Highway 35-Market Street intersection.

Some information on Mills Wharf came from an interview with Marion Johnson, articles in the *Victoria Advocate,* and an unidentified newspaper. Parts of Mills Wharf have been incorporated into the Sea-Gun Resort.

A severe cold wave in January 1940 brought some snow and even ice to the beach line of Copano Bay. When ten-year-old Shirley Ratisseau went out to marvel at it, she found, trapped in the shallows and almost frozen, great numbers of large trout, redfish, and drum. And she may have found the largest octopus ever seen or recorded in Copano Bay. When Harry Mills heard about the creature, he offered Shirley $1.50 for it. She took the money, but insisted also on "lifelong visiting rights" to see her octopus on display with the other oddities at Mills Wharf.

Skeet McHugh's sandwich shop remains as the entry section of a bakery at the same location.

The Cap Davis Drive-in burned, and Charlie replaced it with a new building on the same site. After Charlie was killed in a wreck, Molly leased the drive-in to others. It was called Theodore's Cafe for a while, and then Brocato's. When "Shorty" Kline bought the restaurant, he gave it his own name. So it remains, although drive-in service has been discontinued.

Dave Davis has retired as the manager of the Port Bay Hunting Club. He began working as a seasonal guide for the St. Charles Hunting Club in 1945 and was the Port Bay Club manager for twenty years. The club has changed its name to Port Bay Hunting *and Fishing* Club. Members' wives and children are included in activities, but membership remains by invitation only. In 1997 James Sorenson, Jr., Andrew's grandson, owned the old I. C. Thurmond lodge at the club.

Information on carbon black and the Aransas plant came from *Texas Oil and Gas Since 1543* by C. A. Warner and from a 1988 *Herald* newspaper interview with Loland Grisso.

Shirley Denise Rattiseau added this note to the end of her manta ray narrative: "The manta ray or devilfish is the largest ray found in the warm waters of the Gulf of Mexico and, sometimes, Texas bays. Despite its great size, it is not a dangerous fish."

COTTAGES

In moving to Aransas, George Ratisseau returned to his roots. His great-grandmother Anna Catherine Braun Gunderman was one of the first settlers at Lamar. Anna Catherine's daughter, Rosa Augusta, married P. A. Ratisseau. Their son Louis was George's father.

At George and Thelma Ratisseau's Jolly Roger hunting and fishing camp, cottages rented for $1.75 per day and skiffs for $.75. Fishermen could buy three pounds of bait shrimp for $.60.

Willard and Lillie Whicker of Freer, Texas, were so eager to stay at Palm Courts that they stumbled around carpenters to occupy the first completed unit. Their granddaughter, one of the authors of this history, has never missed a summer in Rockport since. Palm Courts was renamed Palm Village and then, in the 1960s, the cottages were torn down. They were replaced by the Allegro North Condominiums.

MARINERS

During the 1940s, Travis Bailey sailed the *Circe*, a beautiful thirty-six-foot boat.

COMBAT AND INDUSTRY
WORLD WAR II

Staff Sgt. Garnett E. Saint, Jr., was killed in action over the North Sea, August 25, 1944. Johnny Hattenbach, of the 82d Airborne, was killed in Holland on September 25, 1944. Kenneth Bowland, USMC, was killed in action at Okinawa in the spring of 1945. Bryant "Cotton" Sanders, U.S. Navy, was lost in the Pacific when his ship went down. Everett Brundrett, Jr., also gave his life in battle. We regret that these names, and those in the main text, may not comprise a complete list of Aransans who served, were injured, or died in the war.

The Southwest Underwater Archaeology Society provided helpful information.

The *Baddacock* sank on the very day that radio station WTAW, College Station, Texas, broadcast the first play-by-play description of a football game. Texas A&M University played on its home field that day, against The University of Texas.

The *Rockport Pilot*, January 28, 1942, listed these wardens:

Lamar	Otis Yeats
Oak Shore Apartments	M. F. Drunzer
Forest Park Cottages	James Sorenson
Bean's Cottages	Walter Bean
Humble Station	Charlie Garrett
Morrison's Boat House	Hugh Morrison
Westergard Boat Works	C. C. Hayden
Wm. B. Priddy's office	Wm. B. Priddy

Hunt's Court	Fred Hunt
Triple Oaks	D. R. Simmons
Townsend Filling Station	G. M. Townsend
Smith's Filling Station	Francis Smith
High School Supt.'s Office	R. E. Black
Natural Gasoline Corp.	Leonard R. Garrett
Carbon Black Plant	(to be named)
Port Bay Club	R. S. Johnson
residence, Spark's Colony	John Keller
residence	Charlie Roe
Central Power & Light Co.	Herbie Caraway

As if the war wasn't enough to keep a person worried, a renter in the old Bracht house swore she saw a ghost. As she stood at an upstairs window, she heard the front door open and close. No one had come in and no one went out. After that, the woman sometimes heard ghostly groans and a sort of creaking sound. A legend started; people said Leopold Bracht's shade still roamed his old house.

After Clouis Fisher bought the Bracht house, he scoffed at superstitious stories. Most old houses, he said, make odd noises. But one night a cold breeze woke Clouis from a sound sleep. He sat straight up in bed and saw a glow that moved across the room and down the stairs. That made a believer out of Clouis.

His wife and children, who have heard sharp footsteps, believe in the ghost too. They think that Leopold may be upset by renovations to his house. When work is underway, the family hears loud crashes, though nothing is broken or missing. They try to cajole the ghost by explaining that the changes will make his life better. But Clouis senses, persistently, that Leopold is watching. Leopold Bracht's descendants run the hardware store where Clouis buys his building supplies.

Part of the hurricane account came from a newspaper article written years later by Shirley Ratisseau. The award-winning account was first published in the San Antonio *Express-News*, Sunday, October 4, 1964. It is entitled "Hurricanes Along Gulf Have Dogged Her Life."

A Long Island, New York, businessman was the first owner of the *Adroit*. He was one of many who used deluxe boats, built narrow for speed, to commute from their homes on Long Island to the 79th Street Bridge in the city; from there they went to their offices.

The saga of Francis Smith family tragedies at sea actually began when the first Francis M. Smith was twelve years old. He ran away from home (Schenectady, New York) and was aboard a ship that sank in a Gulf of Mexico storm. Francis literally washed up on San José and was discovered, as much dead as alive, by rancher James Stephenson. The Stephensons nursed Francis back to health, and he eventually married their daughter, Arminda.

Francis and Arminda's son Hammon George Smith married Nina Olivia Canevaro, daughter of a Geonese seaman. By odd coincidence, he was also on a ship that sank in a storm. He swam to shore near Port Aransas, liked the area, and decided to stay.

An unidentified magazine article, presumably from a Mooney Airplane owners' publication, provided information regarding ace pilot Buck Bailey. He supplied us with the article, as well as other information concerning his family. After the war, Buck followed a family tradition of sailboat racing and amassed significant trophies.

THE RETURN

John Henry Kroeger, Jr., left a wife and young son. At this writing, John Henry Kroeger III lived in Corpus Christi where he was a major distributor of magazines and books to retail outlets in several states. He also retained title to the Kroeger Ranch on Salt Creek.

A *San Antonio Express* newspaper story by Clarence LaRoche, April 6, 1952, provided a succinct history of the Lamar cemetery restoration. Among the graves that have never been found are those of James and Harriet Odin Byrne; their son William; Marceline, a Mexican who worked for George Little; and Moses Ballou, Seth Ballou's freed slave. Samuel Colt was in Lamar the year he died and may have been buried there as well.

L. E. Casterline was the descendant of Frank Casterline and Katherine Simpson, mentioned in the "Women Alone" section.

Shirley Ratisseau recounted that Corky Agler moved and drove roughly at the speed of light. Once, when a strong wind kicked up over plowed fields and whirled dry dust and dirt high in the air, people on the sidewalk in front of her restaurant saw the huge, dark swirl. "What's that?" one said. Another answered: "It's probably just Corky, driving into town." Divorced and remarried to William Berry, Corky retired in the early 1990s. The restaurant has been brightly repainted and continues under another name.

Glenn DeForest (who accents his last name on the first syllable) provided information on the Fulton Harbor. Members of his family have been in Aransas since the 1860s. Today DeForest Loop runs between the Paws and Taws Building and the harbor. It was named for Glenn's brother, Bernie, who worked for the Navigation District twenty-seven years and was harbormaster for most of that time. He made all the decisions and had all the responsibility, twenty-four hours a day, according to Glenn.

There were few recreational sailboats through the late 1930s and early 1940s; the early emphasis of the Rockport Sailing Club was racing. Later "Cap" Henkel and others stimulated the club's interest in cruising.

The Natalie Apartments, a boarding house, occupied the old Greuy house, identified in an early photograph.

When Europeans first came to Aransas and began controlling the natural wildfires, brush started to choke everything. That is what hid the Hall Mansion and the Lamar cemetery. That's why visitors today see mesquite where Vincey

McRae saw open prairie. Whatever benefits wildfire might provide, communities just can't afford them. The Live Oak Point landowner intended to use fire the way nature did, but what he started got far out of hand.

Lloyd Lassiter was fire chief at the time, and Tommy Blackwell, Roy Lassiter, and David Herring were among the boys pressed into service by the Aransas County Emergency Corps.

The old Weber house, servants' quarters, and one unit of Oak Shore Apartments were destroyed, and one cottage at Forest Park were among the fire's victims. Elbert Mundine knew about the wildlife victims; he enjoyed hunting wildcats and "wolves" (coyotes) in the thickets, using horses and a pack of dogs.

The Aransas National Wildlife Refuge initiates controlled fires as a standard part of its management program.

MAKING A BUCK

The W. W. "Willie" Wendell children, in order, were: Lorraine, Bill, Ralph, Evonne, John, Jerry, and Lynn.

Zeph Rouquette served on the Aransas County school board. One of his grandsons, perhaps responding unconsciously to the combined effects of many bloodlines, is an employee of Halliburton Energy. For a while, he worked the North Sea and most recently has been in charge of testing operations in Algeria.

Jason O. Blackwell bought the *Rockport Pilot* in 1928. He was one of South Texas' better-known country newspaper men and his descendants still live in Rockport.

Dr. A. Ray Stevens, under auspices of the North Texas State University Oral History Collection, conducted two interviews that were most helpful—one with Emory M. Spencer and the other with James Sorenson, Jr. Copies of these interviews are in the Aransas County Historical Society archives.

The "marble tables" Stumberg installed were much like pinball machines. Marvin Davis' first coffee shop was in the building recently noted for the antique sawfish mural on its wall.

Rob Roy and Winnie Rice moved their home to the north side of King Street, just east of Highway 35, where it still stands.

Rob Roy was, as newspaperwoman Juliet Wenger wrote, an "unstoppable entrepreneur" who helped develop the line of homes on the high bluff north of Fulton. Winnie Rice was known as an authority on shells and shelling. After Rob Roy was too infirm to sail his *Rusty*, he sent it to Florida, and there the fine boat burned.

David Pilgrim provided a brochure outlining activities of his Production Services Group.

Our paragraphs on the 1979 oil spill off the Yucatán include some sentiments of Steven C. Wilson and Karen C. Hayden who wrote of the event for *National Geographic*, February 1981.

The idea that revolver-maker Colt actually lived and worked at Lamar has been refuted, and the shop foundation is lost. The Hall home has been torn down.

The Canals of Key Allegro

Raulie Irwin, Jr. provided information on the early canal subdivisions. He also stated that in 1963 George Strickhausen bought Ernest Silberisen's old fishing and hunting camp—twenty acres—to start City by the Sea. The subdivision's original name was—and its legal name still is—Gulf Gate.

Some information came from Nancy Melcher's interview with Carl Krueger. Krueger's "Porpoise Period" piece was published in a Key Allegro newsletter and condensed here.

MODERN TIMES

Boundaries

By the late 1940s and early 1950s, oilmen had found the original Copano Causeway too narrow to accommodate their typical in-shore drilling barges. They managed with specially constructed drilling rigs, and at one time, approximately 300 wells dotted Copano Bay. Some pumping units dominated small islands built for them.

John D. Wendell was the son of William Warren Wendell and Virginia Rouquette. She was the second child of François Zephirin Rouquette and Mary Elizabeth Simpson. John Wendell's interviews with Dr. A. Ray Stephens, and with Katherine Winkelman and Genevieve Hunt, provided information for this chapter. The Fulton Cemetery includes a plot for Confederate soldier Frank Wendell.

Rights

Texas Women: A Pictorial History by Ruthe Winegarten, provided the information on GOP chair Shirley Ratisseau. John Knaggs' *Two Party Texas* was also helpful.

Walter Dickey, John and Baby Ruth Dunman, and L. C. and Elsie Huff provided interviews to the Aransas County Historical Society. The Dunmans and Huffs also talked with one of the writers.

Refugees

Information on the Vietnamese immigration came from Kathryn Winkelman's Aransas County Historical Society interview with Hue Nguyen and from a *Caller-Times* article about the family.

Activists

Librarian Eunice Hammon retired in 1994, after twenty-two years on the job.

THE GIFT

Population figures came from the *Texas Almanac*. Condo manager Barry Schmidt was quoted in a *Corpus Christi Caller-Times* article December 30, 1996.

NATURE AND HERITAGE
ECOLOGY

The United States purchased 47,215 acres from the family of Leroy G. Denman, Sr. and others, for the wildlife sanctuary and paid less than half a million dollars for it. The Denmans leased their mineral rights to Continental Oil Company.

Beverly Fletcher, ranger at the Aransas National Wildlife Refuge, provided us with the paper she wrote on the Aransas Camp of the Civilian Conservation Corps.

Albert Collier married John Sorenson's daughter, Judy, and later served as Rockport's mayor. One of his rather interesting ideas was to place oysters in a revolving drum, make them dizzy and thus easier to shuck. Locals scoffed, believing that the process would make the oysters taste bad.

Local sealife in the Rockport Marine Laboratory aquarium fascinated and instructed tourists for years, but the tanks have been drained and removed. Hedgpeth and Gunter did their earliest studies of marine life at the Rockport Laboratory and were later among the first scientists hired to organize The University of Texas Marine Science Institute at Port Aransas.

The Rockport-Fulton Area Chamber of Commerce has published an extensive *Birder's Guide*. This abbreviated list gives only a summary of birds in Aransas, migratory, seasonal, or full-time. Pluralized names indicate multiple varieties:

Anhinga	Cowbirds	Gallinule	Kingfishers
Ani	Cranes	Gnatcatcher	Kinglets
Avocet	Creeper	Godwits	Kiskadee
Bitterns	Crows	Geese	Kites
Blackbirds	Cuckoos	Grackles	Kittiwake
Bluebirds	Curlew	Grebes	Knot
Bobolink	Dickcissel	Grosbeak	Lark
Bobwhite	Doves	Gulls	Longspurs
Buntings	Dowitchers	Hawks	Loon
Caracara	Ducks	Herons	Martin
Cardinal	Dunlin	Hummingbirds	Meadowlarks
Catbird	Eagles	Ibises	Mockingbird
Chat	Egrets	Jabiru	Moorhen
Chicadee	Falcons	Jacana	Nighthawks
Chuck-Will's-	Finches	Jays	Orioles
Widow	Flicker	Junco	Ovenbird
Coot	Flycatchers	Kildeer	Owls
Cormorant	Frigatebird	Kingbirds	Oystercatcher

Pauraque	Sanderling	Swallows	Vultures
Pelicans	Sandpipers	Swan	Warblers
Pewee	Sapsucker	Swift	Waterthrushes
Phalaropes	Siskin	Tanagers	Waxwing
Phoebe	Shrike	Terns	Whimbrel
Pipits	Skimmer	Thrashers	Whip-poor-will
Plovers	Snipe	Thrushes	Willet
Poorwill	Sora	Titmouse	Woodcock
Prairie Chicken	Sparrows	Towees	Woodpeckers
Pyrrhuloxia	Spoonbill	Turkey	Wrens
Rails	Starling	Turnstone	Yellowlegs
Redstart	Stilt	Veery	Yellowthroat
Roadrunner	Stork	Verdin	
Robin	Storm Petrel	Vireos	

Information regarding the tree ordinances came from City Manager M. H. "Pete" Gildon, Public Works Director Billy Dick, and "Tree Official" Chris Johnson.

ANTHROPOLOGY
Information on the Kent-Crane Shell Midden came from a *Herald* newspaper article February 8, 1990, and from one writer's personal conversations with Dr. Herman Smith.

ENDANGERED SPECIES
Information on the Hawes family dilemma at Matagorda came from an Associated Press release carried by Austin and San Antonio newspapers. Lloyd Hawes, who ran the ranch in 1943, was the son of William Hawes and Alice Bludworth. In 1911 he married Gustava Claire Johnson of Lamar. Roy Lassiter, a current resident of Key Allegro, is the grandson of Libby Power, descendant of James Power. She married Will Hawes, a cousin to Joe and Lloyd, and also a Matagorda rancher.

ORNITHOLOGIST CONNIE HAGAR
Kay McCracken's book, *Connie Hagar: The Life History of a Texas Birdwatcher*, included a complete story of Connie Hagar's persistence in proving her observations to foreign experts. The costs of maintaining whoopers come from "The Revealed Demand for the Public Good: Evidence from Endangered and Threatened Species."

Betty Baker provided the background of the Hummer/Bird Celebration in an article for a special section of the *Rockport Pilot*.

NO NEW THING UNDER THE SUN

The sportswriter quoted was Buddy Gough, writing in the *Corpus Christi Caller-Times*, January 12, 1997.

The description of Schoenstatt came from its brochure.

By the time the old courthouse was torn down, Jim Furlong was president of the Jaycees, a Rockport organization that he had founded.

Miguél Garza said that a scow sloop like the ones his family built had cost between $600 and $700 and could last for twenty-five or thirty years.

Theirs was one of as many as 100 boats working day and night. Miguél said: "In the night time, when we were gonna close, we got some matches and just light three matches." Then the other boat would do the same. "We had lamps, but the matches worked better for us," he added.

Then the state outlawed gill-netting. "One hundred percent in my home town were doing this fishing," Miguél said. When they heard rumors of the new law, no one could believe it. "But no," Miguél said, "they close it—no nets at all. So we had to sell these boats to Mexico." Most men took up shrimping and oystering, or went to work in boatyards.

Additional information on *La Tortuga* came from a Historical Society-taped interview with Miguél Garza and from a memoir written by participant and yachtsman Chris Wenger. These volunteers helped to build the scow sloop:

Ed Armstrong	Danny Hale	Sallye Perry
Ernie Bacon	Andy Hall	Pat Pogue
Hal Blethrod	Dwight Howard	Rick Pratt
Jack Bogle	Roger Harlow	Rich Souchek
Susan Bogle	James Ingram	Ray Tibbits
Charlie Dietz	Wally Ingram	Bill Tilden
Diane Dupnik	Wally Keil	John Uhr
John Eckols	Louis Larrey	Ralph VandDerNaillen
Larry Estes	Tom Marks	Brandon Warren
Miguél Garza, Sr.	Jerry Moore	Chris Wenger
Miguél Garza, Jr.	Harry O'Haver	Al Weslowsky
Michael Gian	Don Perry	

Bill Mann is a retired executive of the General Electric Company. At ninety-six years of age in 1997, he remained an active and popular member of the community.

The replicas of Columbus' ships are on display in Corpus Christi.

The following citizens served as mayor of Rockport:

1870	John M. Mathis	1875	P. H. Terry
1871	Major A. J. Hogan	1875	W. P. McGrew
1871	Dr. E. P. Carpenter	1877	M. J. Terry
1872	S. H. Smith	1878	E. A. Perrenot
1872	W. P. McGrew	1880	R. H. Wood

1882	P. H. Terry	1934	J. Ed Moore
1883	William Curtis	1942	Travis Johnson
1884	Sam H. Smith	1944	Jack Blackwell
1887	John A. Clark	1945	Albert Collier
1889	R. H. Wood	1946	A. L. Bruhl
1893	John A. Clarke	1948	Jack Collins
1894	B. M. Shelton	1948	Travis Bailey
1898	J. W. Hoopes	1952	J. W. Higgins
1900	J. B. Farley	1953	Seth H. Steele
1904	W. S. Brown	1956	Chester Johnson
1906	A. L. Bruhl	1958	Hollis E. Collum
1908	Harry Traylor	1960	Herman C. Johnson
1910	Charles G. Johnson	1964	Hollis E. Collum
1914	J. H. Bell	1966	Delmar R. Hiller
1918	A. R. A. Brice	1972	Walter S. Falk, Jr.
1922	S. F. Jackson	1982	C. H. "Burt" Mills, Jr.
1926	J. Ed Moore	1988	Daniel R. Adams
1930	William Mayer	1990	George L. Martin
1932	S. F. Jackson	1994	Ray J. O'Brien
1932	A. J. Adolphus	1996	Glenda J. Burdick
1932	A. L. Bruhl		

These men and women have served as Aransas County Sheriff:

1872	R. A. Upton	1940	Hattie Brundrett
1874	Samuel Z. J. Beetley	1941	Alice Thomerson
1881	P. P. Court	1943	A. R. Curry
1888	W. M. McWhorter	1951	Arley Cruse Shivers
1890	Samuel Z. J. Beetley	1962	Virginia Shivers
1899	W. T. Bailey	1965	Joe Earl Hunt
1903	John H. Smith	1968	Robert O. Hewes*
1903	H. T. Bailey	1993	David Petrusaitis
1914	J. A. Brundrett		

* Bob Hewes of Fulton, retired, is chaplain of the Sheriffs' Association of Texas.

The Arts: In Varied Forms

Mrs. Joe H. (Dollie) Slocum was president of the Woman's Club when the library was formed; Mrs. Everal (Julia) West headed the committee. Mrs. Atchley was succeeded by Mrs. Donald M. Davis and Val Jean Eaton. Significant donations were made by Mrs. H. E. Butt and the Allied Live Oak Bank (in 1997 Pacific Southwest). Eunice Hammon took over as librarian in 1972, assisted by twenty volunteers, including Gladys Bruhl Gibson. Hammon retired in 1994.

The Fulton Volunteer Fire Department purchased Paws and Taws from the square dancers, then sold it, in 1994, to the town of Fulton.

THE ARTS: SIMON MICHAEL

Dorothy Kucera's book, *Simon Michael: The Man, The Artist, The Teacher,* provided information for our too-brief description of a fascinating man. In 1997 Michael had achieved his ninety-second year and was still painting and teaching.

THE ARTS: ESTELLE STAIR AND THE ART ASSOCIATION

Some information regarding Estelle Stair, and her quotes, came from an article by Larry Hodge in the November 1987 edition of *Texas Highways* magazine. Mrs. Stair died late that year. Her niece Lisa Baer, who now runs the gallery, shared reminiscences.

Thompson's Spa, a popular restaurant in the 1940s, was one of few in the area recommended by Duncan Hines. The family-style seafood dinners, and Mrs. Thompson's pies, were so good that diners put up with her strict rules: No one could smoke or drink alcohol. Men had to wear coats and ties. Young girls in sundresses were frowned upon. The Spa was located on the west side of Austin Street at its intersection with Highway 35. The old building is now part of a private home on Broadway, just south of the Harbor Oaks bridge.

In 1997 a large motel, part of a nationwide chain, went up on the site of the Bruhl/O'Connor beachfront home.

Perhaps because of inspirations like Steve Russell—who as a junior high student at Aransas was first struck by art in the lobby of a local motel—activists at the Art Center have instituted an annual public school competition and have raised funds for art teachers in two elementary schools.

CELEBRATION

The Art Festival followed on the heels of Seafair and is joined by almost a celebration a month in Aransas. Notable among them are *Fiesta en la Playa* (Festival on the Beach) sponsored by the Mexican-American community.

According to Jerry Wendell, the fireworks display began simply as beach entertainment for visiting friends. When a few people at the Key Allegro Marina wanted to become involved, the Wendells began launching from a vacant lot on Frandolig's old island. As the celebration continued to grow and moved again to the beach, members of the fireworks crew—Wendells and others—earned pyrotechnician certificates and purchased more elegant rockets. The City of Rockport assumed responsibility for the event and Carl Krueger, Key Allegro developer, solicited funds. People gave what they could; one elderly woman donated a few simple Roman candles. The elaborate fireworks display belongs to everyone now, but still the Wendells do the work, and they deserve the credit.

THE PAST AND PRESENT MEET

One exciting aspect of the excavation of *La Belle* is that archaeologists plan DNA testing on the intact skeleton found inside, which appears to contain brain matter. They hope to reconstruct the face of the man—apparently in his late thirties or forties—and to locate his family, possibly named Baranger. It is a name not unlike that of the first European to discover the pass at Aransas.

West of that pass lie the bays, the heart of Aransas. They remain, in most respects, unchanged.

Whooping cranes

Acknowledgments

This history has been a joint project of the
ARANSAS COUNTY HISTORICAL SOCIETY
and the
ROCKPORT CENTER FOR THE ARTS

We express our deep appreciation to
THE EXECUTIVE COMMITTEE
OF THE ARANSAS COUNTY HISTORY PROJECT
Glenn Guillory, David Herring, Genevieve Hunt,
Raulie Irwin, John Jackson, Gordon Stanley, Sue Taylor

THEIR SUBCOMMITTEES
Phil Albin, Gayle Atwood, Verne Benson,
Chris Blum, Thom Evans, Fulton Mansion Staff, Mary Hoekstra,
Pam McRae Heard, Diana Kirby, Leta Layman, Sandra Taylor

and also to:

THOSE WHO ENTRUSTED US WITH
THEIR PRIZED BOOKS, MEMOIRS, AND CLIPPINGS:
The Fulton Mansion State Historic Park,
Gayle Atwood, Bobby Jackson, John Jackson,
Raulie Irwin, Mary Pearl Herring Patrick, Gordon Stanley,
Bruce and Kandy Taylor-Hille, Pat Walzel,
Chris Wenger, Caroline Williams, Winston Woellert

THOSE WHO SHARED PREVIOUS RESEARCH,
SOUGHT MORE INFORMATION,
POINTED OUT SIGNIFICANT LOCALES,
OR PROVIDED SPECIAL SERVICES:
The Office of the County Attorney,
Barbara Armstrong, Joe Harold Brown, Bubba Casterline,
David Herring, *Pisces* Capt. John Howell, Daniel Mello,
Virginia Meynard, Harold Picton, Shirley Ratisseau, Doris Ruttiger,
Jerry Shaw, Lucile Fagan Snider, Juliet Wenger

AND
the many generous souls
who have allowed us to reproduce their family photographs.

Index

About the Authors

WILLIAM ALLEN is the author of five books, including the Pulitzer-nominated *Fire in the Birdbath and Other Disturbances* (W. W. Norton) and *Walking Distance: An Ohio Odyssey* (Black Oak Books). His work has been anthologized in over fifteen college textbooks, and he has written for numerous magazines and periodicals, including *Atlantic Monthly, Esquire, New York Times, Saturday Review,* and *Reader's Digest.* He is considered one of the country's leading essayists.

Allen is professor emeritus at Ohio State University, where he teaches literary nonfiction writing each summer. He is the founding editor of OSU's literary magazine, *The Journal,* and also initiated the school's Master of Fine Arts program in creative writing.

Born and raised in the Dallas area, William Allen is a member of the Texas Institute of Letters and taught at the Cedar Hill (TX) Writer's Workshop and the Dallas Institute of Art and Culture. He has been a regular winter visitor to the Rockport area since 1985 and co-founded the Rockport Writing Series. Allen now makes his home at Ft. Davis, TX.

SUE HASTINGS TAYLOR is the leading authority on the history of Aransas County. Her recent two years of comprehensive research for this book has capped a lifetime of collecting anecdotal information on the area. Taylor is the author of *Rockport Artists' Sketchbook* and articles for various Texas magazines.

Born and educated in San Antonio, Texas, Taylor was imbued with a lasting love for local history. After spending her childhood and adult summers in Rockport, she became a permanent resident of Rockport eleven years ago.

Sue Taylor has served as docent of the Fulton mansion, executive board member of the Rockport Art Association, and member of the Aransas County Historical Association. Taylor co-founded the Rockport Writing Series and is currently consulting with the Texas Maritime Museum in Rockport to integrate local history into its current mission. She is a popular speaker at local gatherings and is currently at work on "Aransas: The Novel."

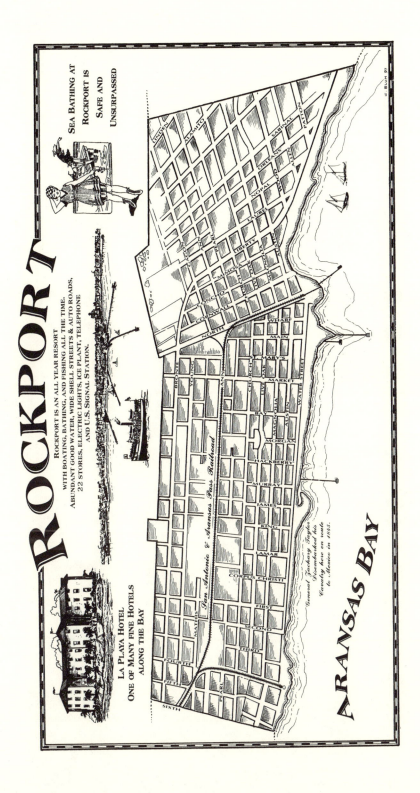

ROCKPORT

ROCKPORT IS AN ALL YEAR RESORT
WITH BOATING, BATHING, AND FISHING ALL THE TIME.
ABUNDANT GOOD WATER, WIDE SHELL STREETS & AUTO ROADS.
22 STORES, ELECTRIC LIGHTS, ICE PLANT, TELEPHONE
AND U.S. SIGNAL STATION.

**SEA BATHING AT
ROCKPORT IS
SAFE AND
UNSURPASSED**

**LA PLAYA HOTEL
ONE OF MANY FINE HOTELS
ALONG THE BAY**

San Antonio & Aransas Pass Railroad

*General Zachary Taylor
Disembarked his
Cavalry here en route
to Mexico in 1845.*

ARANSAS BAY

C. Blum 37